Movement and Action in Learning and Development: Clinical Implications for Pervasive Developmental Disorders

Movement and Action in Learning and Development: Clinical Implications for Pervasive Developmental Disorders

Ida J. Stockman, PhD

ELSEVIER
ACADEMIC
PRESS

Amsterdam   Boston   Heidelberg   London   New York   Oxford
Paris   San Diego   San Francisco   Singapore   Sydney   Tokyo

Elsevier Academic Press
525 B Street, Suite 1900, San Diego, California 92101-4495, USA
84 Theobald's Road, London WCIX 8RR, UK

This book is printed on acid-free paper. ∞

Library of Congress Cataloging-in-Publication Data
Application submitted

British Library Cataloguing in Publication Data
A catalogue record for this book is available from the British Library

ISBN: 0-12-671860-1

For all information on all Academic Press publications
visit our Web site at www.academicpress.com

Printed in the United States of America
04   05   06   07   08   09   9   8   7   6   5   4   3   2   1

To
Hamilton, my Godson, who might have chosen to read this book if only
we knew more about learning disabilities.
and to
Hamilton's family, and all the other families living with learning
disabilities, who empower themselves by seeking alternative interventions
in their search for answers

CONTENTS

Acknowledgments

The seeds for this book were planted in a year-long public symposium series, *Movement and Action: Links to Intelligent Behavior*, which I organized at Michigan State University across the 1995–96 school year. Most of the contributors to this book were invited symposium speakers. This lecture series was simultaneously coordinated with a year-long course on clinical praxis with pervasive developmental disorders for an invited group of 21 participants. These participants included parents of children with pervasive developmental disorders and experienced professionals who represented the major disciplines that frequently work with this population in schools, clinics and homes, namely clinical psychologists, special education teachers, and physical, occupational, and speech-language therapists. I am indebted to the Michigan State University community for its financial support of this year-long project via grants from the Office of the Vice Provost for University Outreach and contributions from individual academic units that spanned 12 different colleges, departments, and programs. Special acknowledgment is given to my former co-worker, Jacqueline Graham, and to former graduate student Nikki Calleen who helped me with the daily operations that were required to undertake such an ambitious project.

However, this book is more than a record of what was learned during that lecture series and course on movement and action themes in development. It represents the culmination of a professional lifetime of searching for answers to questions about pervasive developmental disorders, questions that I began asking as a graduate student at the University of Iowa more than 30 years ago. They were questions that would later send me to study for the doctoral degree at Pennsylvania State University, only to discover that my professors did not have the answers either. They were asking the same questions.

Fortunately, since the 1960s, we have witnessed a tremendous growth in our knowledge about the children who learn differently and children who do not respond readily to our visual and auditory messages about what to do to help them. I have been fortunate to have a lot of help along the way in learning about these children. I am indebted to Félicie Affolter, who invited me to work with her clinical research team in St. Gallen, Switzerland, more than 25 years ago, and to Walter and Helen Bischofberger, Peter Bucher, Doris Clausen, Rosita Helg, Renate Lotz, Hans Sonderegger, Anne Seltz, Esther Stoffel, Emmy Zubüerbhler, and the rest of this Swiss clinical team for teaching me over coffee, dinner, or hiking in the Swiss mountains, even teaching me information that did not necessarily surface in our research reports and conference papers.

I am grateful for all that I have learned from working with those children who challenge our usual way of doing clinical business, and their parents who took a chance on my kind of knowing and brought them to the Oyer Clinic at Michigan State University in the United States. I am equally grateful to the students who have challenged my thinking about clinical issues over the years and applaud those who sought answers to questions by doing their own research.

I am indebted to my longtime friend, Patsy Krug Grady, a veteran clinician, whose many informal conversations here kept me tuned to the daily realities of trying to make a difference in a child's life, and to my husband, George C. Stockman, who did more than his fair share of cooking and listening across the years of this project.

Finally, I thank my former editor, Mark Zadrozny at Academic Press, who believed in this book project enough to help me to keep it alive across the years, and my current editor, Mara Conner at Elsevier, who has been helpful in bringing this book to fruition.

CONTRIBUTORS

Deborah Hayden, M.A., CCC-SLP, holds clinical certifications in speech-language pathology and neurodevelopmental treatment. She is director and founder of the PROMPT Institute in Santa Fe, New Mexico. Ms. Hayden brings more than 20 years of clinical skill and experience to the pioneering development of a tactile cueing system for treating severe speech production disorders. Most recently, she has developed a nationally normed test for assessing children with abnormal speech who are suspected to have developmental apraxia/dysarthria of speech.

Esther Thelen, Ph.D., is professor of psychology at Indiana University. She is a Fellow of the American Association for the Advancement of Science and past president of the International Society for Infant Studies. Dr. Thelen is a leading scholar in motor and cognitive development. She is the current president of the Society for Research in Child Development.

Felicie Affolter, Ph.D., is a developmental psychologist with additional professional training in audiology, deaf education, speech-language pathology, and teacher education. In the 1950's, she studied psychology at the University of Geneva with Jean Piaget. She has been a visiting scholar at the University of Minnesota's Cognitive Science Center for more than 20 years. In 1976, she founded the School and Clinical Center for Perceptual Disorders in St. Gallen, Switzerland. She is credited with pioneering the Guided Interaction Treatment for children with pervasive developmental disorders and adults with severe brain injury. Her seminal book, *Perception, Interaction and Language*, is now published in five languages, and the original German version is now in its 11th printing.

Herbert L. Pick Jr., Ph.D., is a professor in the Institute of Child Development at the University of Minnesota. He is a member of the Cognitive Science Center of the university and served a term as director of the predecessor organization, the Center of Research in Human Learning. He is also a Fellow of the American Psychological Association and was a Fellow at the Center for Advanced Study in the Behavioral Sciences. His research interests have been in the area of perceptual and perceptual motor development.

Ida J. Stockman, Ph.D., is a professor in the Department of Audiology & Speech Sciences at Michigan State Univeristy. She is a certified speech-language pathologist and Fellow of the American Speech-Language-Hearing Association. She has been affiliated with the Affolter clinical research team since the early 1970s. The Michigan State University Symposium on Movement and

Action in 1995–96 were among the professional service contributions that led to distinguished faculty awards from Michigan State University and the Michigan Association for Governing Boards of Institutions of Higher Learning.

Jon Kaas, Ph.D., is a neuroscientist and the Centennial Professor of Psychology at Vanderbilt University in Nashville, Tennessee. He has done pioneering research on neural plasticity. A Fellow of the American Association for the Advancement of Science, Dr. Kaas was a recipient of the Distinguished Scientific Contribution Award from the American Psychological Association.

Jonas Langer, Ph.D., a developmental cognitive psychologist, is the Director of the Institute of Human Development and a professor of psychology at the University of California–Berkeley. He has been a James McKeen Cattell Fellow and a USPHS Special Fellow at the Institut des Sciences de l'Education at the University of Geneva in Switzerland. Dr. Langer is a well-recognized and respected Piagetian scholar and is a member of the Jean Piaget Society's Board of Directors.

Katherine Nelson, Ph.D., is â developmental cognitive psychologist and Distinguished Professor of Psychology Emerita at the City University of New York. She is a Fellow of the American Psychological Association and the American Psychological Society. Dr. Nelson is widely acclaimed for her theoretical work in both cognitive and linguistic development and is a 1999 recipient of the Award for Distinguished Research Contributions from the Society for Research in Child Development.

Lois Bloom, Ph.D. is the Edward Lee Thorndike Professor Emeritus of Psychology and Education at Teachers College, Columbia University. She has received the Honors from the American Speech-Language-Hearing Association; the Distinguished Scientific Contributions Award from the Society for Research in Child Development; and the G. Stanley Hall Medal from the Division of Developmental Psychology, the American Psychological Association. Dr. Bloom, a widely acclaimed scholar of first language acquisition and early infant development, is recognized world wide for her theoretical and applied contributions. Her book, *The Transition from Infancy to Language, Acquiring the Power of Expression* (1993, Cambridge University Press), received the APA Division 7 Eleanor E. Maccoby Book Award.

Walter Bischofberger, Ph.D., is a developmental psychologist . He has been affiliated with the Affolter clinical and research team in Switzerland since 1970. An expert on Guided Interaction Treatment, he was co-founder of the Center for Perceptual Disorders in St. Gallen and served as it director for several years. He also co-founded and served as the president of the Swiss organization for perceptual disorders. Currently, Dr. Bischofberger is Co-Director of the Association of Perception, Learning and Communication in Switzerland, and is a visiting scholar at the Cognitive Science Center at the University of Minnesota. His book on perceptual development in the blind *Aspekte der Entwicklung taktil-kinasthethischer Wahrnehmung, is* now in its second printing.

1

INTRODUCTION: THE CLINICAL PROBLEM

IDA J. STOCKMAN, PHD

This book presents a cross-disciplinary perspective on action in child development. Although the word "action" can be used broadly to refer to any kind of activity (e.g., thinking, talking, listening, looking, touching), this book is not concerned with any type of action. The coupling of the words *action* and *movement* in the book's title is intended to focus attention on action as **cognitively grounded**, perceptual-motor activity embedded in daily problem-solving events. Therefore, this book cannot be concerned with any kind of movement, either. It is focused specifically on **purposeful** movement, which feeds perceptual-cognitive activity and learning in its typical and atypical forms. According to Anzalone and Williamson (2001), action ". . . is the ability to engage in adaptive goal-directed behavior. Motor abilities are involved in action, but action is more complex than just motor function. Action also involves perceptual and cognitive contributions to purposeful behavior" (p. 146).

Movement and action themes are not new to developmental psychology but are rooted in the theories of prominent 20th century scholars, including Jean Piaget (1952). A well-known aspect of Piaget's theory is that sensorimotor processes are foundational for cognitive development. However, Piaget's theory of cognitive development has been challenged by contemporary scholars on multiple fronts (e.g., Karmiloff-Smith 1992; Thelen and Smith 1994; Karmiloff-Smith 1994; Laurenco and Machado 1996). Yet, practitioners do apply movement-oriented interventions to their work with children who are at the floor of development, namely, those with global or pervasive developmental disorders. Such clinical approaches, although not necessarily inspired by Piaget's theory, offer at least a practical reason to understand if and how movement-action themes contribute to learning and developing.

This book gives voice to two streams of thinking about movement and action in development. One stream of thinking relates to abnormal or atypical learners, and the other relates to theories of normal or typical development, which can inform clinical work. Clinical work with atypical learners always has been guided by what is known about typical learners. However, a useful theory about learning and developing needs to be broad enough to explain learning that does and does not occur at the margins of development. Abnormal learners, as nature's selective experiments, expose the range of human variability and adaptation. Learning disorders are surely a strong test of the robustness of human experience in development.

In the following discussion, I identify the clinical population that motivated this book and the challenges it presents for clinical intervention. Then, given what we know about the disorders, I identify four criteria that a workable theoretical framework should meet to support clinical intervention. Finally, I provide an overview of the book's content.

THE CLINICAL MOTIVATION FOR THE BOOK

Clinical populations historically have been test beds for exploring the parameters of human learning and developing. Such examples are the pioneering studies of language acquisition and cognition in children with deafness (Furth 1966; Bellugi 1988; and Bellugi and Studdert-Kennedy 1980); blindness (Landau and Gleitman 1985); Down's syndrome (Chapman 1997); and, more recently, Williams syndrome (Bellugi et al 1994). See Bishop and Mogford (1993) and Tager-Flusberg (1994) for thoughtful reviews of some of this work. The present book is motivated by a broadly defined clinical population that presents none of the well-known reasons why children may develop differently. This clinical population may demonstrate normal physical appearance and exceptional ability to learn, hear, see, and move the body at will. Yet, most domains of human function are adversely affected. Such children may be diagnosed with pervasive developmental disability (PDD).[1] The incidence of PDD is estimated to be at least 1 in 1000 births and can range from 4 or 5 per 10,000 births to 21 in 10,000 depending on how the disorder is defined (Olley and Gutentag 1999).[2]

For practitioners, the PDD diagnosis was used initially to single out children who did not quite fit the profile of classic autism despite multiskill-multisystem deficits. In particular, such children seemed more normal in their social behavior (e.g., affect and attachment) than children with the classic

---

[1] PDD will be used throughout the book to refer to autism spectrum disorders.

[2] These prevalence figures are based on the diagnosis of autism which is included among several syndromes in the autism spectrum. Therefore, the prevalence of PDD as a global diagnostic category is expected to be higher than what is cited here.

autism diagnosis. Alternatively, the term, "multisystem developmental disorder" (MDD) was used by the Zero to Three/National Center for Clinical Infant Programs (1994). The MDD diagnosis identified children with serious nonverbal and verbal deficits who fail to meet all criteria for autism. It is noteworthy that the MDD diagnosis requires significant dysfunction in the processing of visual-spatial, tactual, proprioceptive, and vestibular sensory input. Currently, the PDD diagnosis is an "umbrella" term for multiple clinical sequelae, which has come to be viewed as the autism spectrum disorders by the American Psychiatric Association (1994). The PDD diagnosis refers then to a heterogeneous group of children with multisystem-multiskill deficits. It can apply to children with the classic Kanner-type autism as well as to the less severe group of children diagnosed with PDD–not otherwise specified (PDD-NOS). See Cohen and Volkmar (1997a) for a comprehensive overview of autism and PDD.

Regardless of how children with PDD are described, they are clearly distinguished in research and clinical practices from children who have more limited deficits in other diagnostic groups; specifically, children with the diagnosis of specific language impairment (SLI) or learning disability (LD) (Leonard 1998). SLI presumably affects just spoken language, and LD affects written language and other school-related academic skills. For children with the PDD diagnosis, deficits in language (if language exists at all) often coexist with obvious nonverbal deficits (Fay 1993; Sigman 1994; Olley and Gutentag 1999; Romanczyk et al 1999; Lord and Risi 2000). These children may not engage in play or routine social interaction. They may not even regard or recognize caregivers. Some have obvious sensorimotor deficits, and most fail to solve daily problems at the expected ages. What seems clear is that children with PDD have global deficits that affect their participation in even the most routine events of daily living related to self-care, eating, dressing, bathing routines, and so on.

The atypical development in children with PDD is puzzling. Their behavioral inconsistencies defy casting them simply as delayed in development, which is often how mentally retarded children (e.g., Down's syndrome) are described. They may learn some things quickly; yet, the same task may be performed adequately at one time but not another. Skills that emerge relatively late in normal children may be present much earlier in children with PDD (e.g., visual discrimination of complex patterns, perspective drawing) (Frith and Baron-Cohen 1987; Affolter and Bischofberger 2000). Conversely, some skills acquired early in normal development (e.g., direct imitation) may emerge late in children with PDD (Affolter and Bischofberger 2000). Such islets of normal to superior performances in narrow domains of function (e.g., rote memory) do show ability to learn, despite asynchronous developmental profiles. Still, most of these children never catch up with their same-age peers. The persistence of learning difficulty into adulthood requires long-term commitment of community resources to their care.

CAUSAL EXPLANATIONS FOR PPD

The reason for the atypical development in children with PDD remains a puzzle. This is because the disability cannot be blamed on the well-known reasons why children fail to develop. They are not deaf, blind, or physically handicapped. They look normal and can move their bodies at will. Neurological testing does not consistently show aberrant brain structures. The developmental lag cannot be blamed on reduced environmental stimulation or deprivation. We now know that no social or racial group is immune. PDD is observed in children all around the world (Cohen and Volkmar, 1997b).

A literature survey is likely to reveal no agreed-on causal explanation for PDD. The gamut of explanations offered has ranged from the earliest hypothesis about maternal influences (Bettelheim 1967) to the current emphasis on neurobiological factors (Waterhouse 1994; Singh et al 1998; Tsai 1999; Tager-Flusberg 2000). The fact that abnormal behavior can be observed quite early in life for some children raises the question of an innate or inborn cause. We can assume that innate mechanisms play some role. In the face of early global deficits, something has gone fundamentally wrong with the biological underpinnings of development, due to pathological gene expression and/or prenatal insult to the nervous system. A biological basis for PDD most likely exists even though aberrant brain structures do not consistently turn up in brain scans, inclusive of neuroimaging.

More recent explanations have focused on the secondary, functional aspects of behavior. The view that PDD and other clinical syndromes are caused by information processing deficits is intuitively appealing (Lincoln et al 1992; Reed 1994). This view takes into account the fact that children with PDD grow up in the same social and physical environments in which their unaffected siblings grow up. Therefore, there must be something inherent in how a child with PDD accesses and/or stores the information from these same environments that causes maladaptive behavior. However, the information-processing perspective needs broader definition before it can serve as a useful explanatory framework (Stockman 2000). Whenever the term *information* is used, what readily comes to mind are the external sense impressions of objects and events, as experienced aurally or visually. This perspective is narrow because it implicitly privileges auditory and visual information in considering what kind of sensory input matters in developing cognitive representations. The critical explanation for the perceptual and learning difficulties of children with PDD cannot be vested in auditory and visual processing alone. Neither deafness nor blindness alone prevents adaptive learning and behaving. In contrast, children with PDD can see and hear but still do not develop normally. We should wonder why their good ability to see and hear does not help them to develop more adequately. Information processing needs to be conceptualized more broadly to include all the senses, particularly, the tactile-kinesthetic senses that are vested in body movement and physical interaction with the environment.

CLINICAL INTERVENTION FRAMEWORKS FOR PDD

Although there is no consensus about what causes PDD, professionals still must deliver interventions services to children with PDD. Perhaps it is because some children do not respond to conventional therapies that has forced an undercurrent of nonconventional clinical practices. Such interventions have many faces in contemporary clinical practices. In the United States, one can point to sensory integration (Ayres 1972; Fisher et al 1991; Kranowitz 1998); Doman-Delacato Neurological Patterning (Delacato 1963); coactive movement (Sternberg et al 1985); and, more recently, holding therapy (Welch 1989). Other approaches include the neurodevelopmental approach inspired by Bobath's work with cerebral palsy in England (Bobath 1980); Conductive Education (CE) developed in Budapest, Hungary (Kozma 1995); the Feldenkrais Method developed in Israel (Feldenkrais 1994) and applied to autism in the United States (Donnellan and Ray-Reese 2002); Facilitated Communication developed in Australia (Biklen 1990; Biklen and Cardinal 1997); daily life therapy system developed in Japan (Kitahara 1983a, 1983b, 1984); and guided interaction therapy developed in Switzerland (Affolter 1991; Affolter and Bischofberger 2000).

While these various forms of intervention for PDD-autism are guided by different principles and practices, they differ from more conventional treatment models in the respect that they make focal use of some kind of movement and action experience to stimulate behavioral change and learning. By focusing on movement, such treatments inevitably stimulate sensory input from the **near senses**, namely, tactile-kinesthetic senses. This perceptual input is inherent in movement activity, whether or not it is in the foreground of the intervention philosophy.

Among the near senses, Lederman (1997) distinguishes three types of sensory systems, namely, the tactile, kinesthetic, and haptic systems. The **tactile** sense, or touch, refers to cutaneous input. This complex sensory modality enables sensory awareness that one's body touches or contacts the material world. In addition, taction enables the body to experience a range of other stimulations that include pain, pressure, weight, temperature and the texture, hardness, and gross size and shape of objects.

The **kinesthetic** sense refers to the sensory input arising from the stimulation of receptors in the muscles, tendons, and joints during movement. Lederman (1997) does not single out proprioception as a separate sensory system. But in the present book, however, proprioception is regarded as that part of the kinesthetic sensory input dedicated to the sense of body balance and spatial position.

Haptic perception, or active touch, combines cutaneous or tactile cutaneous and kinesthetic inputs (Lederman 1997). Combined tactual-kinesthetic input "refers to touch and movement, respectively" (Davies 1994, p. 2). Active touch incorportes primal experience with **force** and **resistance**, which are important in gaining knowledge about causes and effects in the world. According to Affolter (1991), infants in the first days of life learn that something else exists in the world besides themselves when they encounter objects that resist or halt their own bodily movements (e.g., the caregiver's body). Their dynamic exploration of object qualities later on leads to more precise representation of the environment than does static touch or touch without movement. Irrespective of the descriptive terms used, the tactile-kinesthetic senses allow the organism to know where its body and limbs are in relation to one another and to other things in space. Although tactile-kinesthetic sensory experiences are singled out in this chapter, it is assumed that complex adaptive behavior is supported by coordinated multisensory experiences. Such experiences include tactual-kinesthetic input plus auditory and visual input, among others.

Some movement-oriented interventions (e.g., sensory integration) are driven precisely by the assumption that movement is connected to perception. On this premise, adaptive movements are expected to be facilitated by modifying sensory input. It is not surprising then, that the professional disciplines concerned with treating movement disorders, namely, occupational and physical therapy, have been in the forefront of developing some of the intervention approaches. Such approaches, which capitalize on the movement senses for learning, stand in the shadows of conventional therapies that rely mainly on auditory and visual input.

A focus on the movement senses seems well motivated. Clinical services for PDD typically include occupational and physical therapy along with speech-language therapy. This is because motor deficits are among the mix of symptoms of PDD (Anzalone and Williamson, 2001; Donnellan and Leary 1995). Stockman (2000) cited more than two dozen studies that implicated sensorimotor deficits among children with PDD and those in other clinical populations with less debilitating developmental deficits, namely those with the diagnosis of SLI and LD.

A broad range of sensorimotor difficulties has been observed on tasks requiring observations of passive touch (e.g., two-point discrimination and dichhaptic stimulation; rate and accuracy of executing fine and gross motor skills such as hopping and balancing; haptic tasks that combine tactual input with input from joint receptors during movement; and motoric execution of routine daily life activities such as dressing and eating (Stockman 2000). Reduced sensitivity to tactual stimulation and slow, clumsy, and uncoordinated movement patterns have been reported. Poor haptic recognition has been observed in addition to bizarre stereotypic motor patterns, such as aimless flapping and rocking of the body and/or the lack of motor planning in daily life activities. Depressed motor performance amounts to more than a slow rate of executing rapid movements, as described by Stark and Tallal (1988) for children with SLI. A motor skill such as static balance can be deficient (Powell and Bishop 1992). Hill's (2001) literature review on motor delays in children with SLI was used to argue that specific language impairment is not so specific after all.

Admittedly, a causal interpretation is not justified by observing a correlation between developmental deficits and depressed sensorimotor skills. It is not surprising, therefore, that motor delays often are viewed as coexisting deficits in the broader mix of those exhibited and not as the cause of the problem. Consequently, the less conventional therapies, which have exploited movement experiences, can be dismissed, often with the sense that their creators have perpetrated a hoax on the public. However, the less conventional therapies may exist precisely because the current clinical approaches to the PDD populations are still too diffuse to adequately prescribe what to do in intervention. We have been so accustomed to leaving out the tactile-kinesthetic system that clear terminology is lacking for describing children with such problems. Practitioners may refer to them as persons with "sensory issues," even though vision and audition also are sensory systems. In the same vein, intervention is referred to as "sensory therapy" when it includes attention to tactile-kinesthetic deficits, whereas therapy involving auditory and visual sensory input is not labeled in the same way.

The goal here is not to debate the merits of using unconventional clinical approaches. Their very existence, hoax or not, raises the broader question of what kind of alternative therapy frameworks are needed to address the type of severe clinical population described here. In other words, it is helpful to ask what kind of frameworks about learning and developing are the most useful for creating an appropriate therapeutic regimen that goes beyond skinnerian-driven behaviorist models such as that advocated by Lovaas (1977, 1981; and 1987). See critiques by Greenspan and Wieder (2001) and Howlin (1989). It is useful to ask further how movement and action fit into this broader view, if at all. In the discussion that follows, I identify four criteria that a useful framework should meet. Then I discuss why a constructivist embodiment theory of development is a suitable framework for guiding clinical work with PDD.

CRITERIA FOR A SUITABLE THEORETICAL FRAMEWORK OF DEVELOPMENT

In this book it is argued that clinical intervention for children with PPD should be guided by a theoretical framework of development that meets four general criteria, as identified in Table 1.

TABLE 1   Four Criteria for a Suitable Theoretical Framework

1. It must orient us toward learning from daily life experiences.
2. It must orient us toward the learning process.
3. It must orient us toward perceptual processes embedded in action/interaction experience.
4. It must orient us to a homologous basis for development.

BEYOND SIMPLISTIC NATIVISM: THE NEED FOR AN EXPERIENTIAL INTERACTIONIST VIEW OF LEARNING AND DEVELOPING

The present book is written at a time when nativist explanations are being propelled by remarkable gains in genetic mapping and gene manipulation. At the same time, methods for eliciting learned responses to experimental tasks (e.g., the preferential looking method) have led to an unprecedented era of research on infant cognition (e.g., Meltzoff 1999; Baillargeon 2002).

Rochat and Striano (1998) observed "in the frenzy of emerging new experimental techniques and paradigms for the study of infants, we have developed a formidable appetite for demonstrations of discrete sophistication in specific domains at the youngest age possible" (p. 112).

Infants' preferential looking responses to experimental tasks reveal that they seem to know and learn a lot more than was thought possible. Such findings can have the effect of minimizing the role of experience in accounting for development. A strong form of nativism (cf. representational nativism as opposed to architectural or chronotopic nativism, after Elman et al [1999]) has been pitted against experience as the determinant of behavior in some discussions (cf. Mandler 1998; Müller and Overton 1998).

For clinical work though, it is not enough to propose simply that a problem is innate. Global developmental deficits make clear that something has gone fundamentally wrong with the biological underpinnings of development. More than that, simply knowing a biological cause of abnormal development does not tell practitioners what to do to enhance learning from intervention. This is the case unless biomedical intervention (e.g., genetic engineering or brain surgery) can reverse the damage to the central nervous system so that a person learns to function without special help. Otherwise, professionals still must rely on some kind of experience to guide their attempts to modify behavior. Framing the clinical problem in terms of an abstract, innate mechanism such as a missing "theory of mind" (Frith and Happe 1994; Baron-Cohen 1995) will not help either. If a theory of mind is not innate, then this knowledge also must be constructed from experience. Thus, practitioners are forced to take the position that experience matters in addition to biological makeup. Otherwise there is no reason to believe that any treatment based on experience can enhance development.

The issue is not simply whether experience matters. It is equally important to consider what kind of experience matters to development. We need to appeal to experiential models that tell us something about how knowledge gets constructed from **ordinary daily life experiences** as opposed to just laboratory controlled events. Natural daily life experience, however, has not been the venue for investigating learning in psychology. Perhaps it is the nature of everyday experience that prevents it from being regarded as a desirable context for exploring learning experimentally. Its dynamic, transient, and unpredictable characteristics convey the sense of a "messy" venue for exploring learning in any controlled way. Still, the adaptive behavior of typically developing children shows that they do negotiate such experiential contexts. They do so without intervention that goes beyond the ordinary scaffolding from caregivers in a given culture. Even when clinical intervention isolates learning from the natural contexts of daily life, clinicians still must be concerned about whether a child can carry over or integrate what was learned into the stream of everyday life. The point is that clinical work does not escape the need to be concerned with adaptive behavior in ordinary daily experience.

At the same time, children's biological limitations early on in life cannot be ignored either. Bates (1999) reminds us that "all reasonable scholars today agree that genes and environment interact to determine complex cognitive outcomes. . ." (p. 195). Such an **interactionist** perspective of development acknowledges that behavioral outcomes, adaptive or not, are the product of experience and innate genetic tendencies. We already know that even the best intervention efforts cannot always normalize development enough. For this reason, clinical fields increasingly refer to achieving functional outcomes. A *functional outcome* refers here to the practical utility of the behavior learned or relearned in therapy. Functional constraints on intervention outcomes suggest implicitly that biological factors may limit how much intervention experience alone can impact development. It does **not preclude the facilitating effects of experience on development**.

A suitable framework for clinical intervention then should view development as the end product of the **interaction** between biology and experience in its **mentally constructed** form. We need frameworks that maximize the learning from experience within the limits of whatever biological limitations or brain architecture there is to work with.

FROM LEARNING PRODUCT TO LEARNING PROCESS IN EXPERIENTIAL CONTEXTS

A useful theory to guide clinical work must be committed to more than the assumption that development is influenced by daily life experience. It is equally important that it tells us something about the **process** by which daily experiences are negotiated and translated into the memories and categories of representation that are the evidence of learned behavior. However, it has been easier to document the developmental milestones that are reached at different ages. Such normative data are useful for figuring out whether intervention is needed. Clinicians may be less confident about how to eradicate the deficits once they are identified. This is because developmental frameworks have focused less often on the **learning process** than on the competence or product of the learning process.

It is the knowing about the **learning process** that ultimately will inform practitioners about how to change behavior. Intervention must be guided by frameworks that say something about knowledge acquisition, for example, how children create plans of action, memories, and perceptual and conceptual categories from the dynamic web of ordinary daily experiences in the real world.

Numerous learning opportunities are presented as a natural part of solving the problems of daily living. While just getting through an ordinary day, children learn to solve many problems outside of a clinician's watchful eyes and ears in the 30 to 60 minutes of directed therapy. At home, children learn to solve problems outside of the moments of nurtured learning with even the most zealous caregivers: How do I get my shoe off? How do I lift this heavy rock? How do I open this door? Problems arise when a child has a goal to achieve but is not sure about how to achieve that goal (Holyoak 1990). Problem-solving activity involves a "search" for some solution or end state. This search converges the multiple perceptual and cognitive subsystems that are required for generating and testing hypotheses, and, therefore, reasoning; mental planning; rule inferencing or induction; and so on. Solving problems of daily life creates the possibility for elaborating knowledge about how the world works.

Understandably, it is difficult to observe the actual on-line events involved in problem-solving activity (Stockman 2000). The usual point-and-push button response methods used in experimental research do not offer much overt behavior to observe. Participants look and listen. They respond to the distant auditory and visual effects created by the researchers' own interactions with the environment. Consequently, the problem-solving process must be inferred from covert rather than overt activity. In contrast, nonverbal problem solving in real situations does not involve such passive-receptive activity. From the earliest stages of development, children's nonverbal problem-solving activity is reflected in their overt physical interactions with the environment. Intervention should be guided by developmental frameworks that are informed by observations of children's social and physical engagement of the environment during natural problem-solving events in daily life.

MOVEMENT AND ACTION/INTERACTION IN LEARNING AND DEVELOPING: BEYOND THE EYES AND EARS IN DESCRIBING PERCEPTUAL INPUT

In focusing attention on the **process** of constructing memories and mental representations from everyday experiences, it is necessary to consider if and how movement experiences (i.e., motor behavior) are relevant. For one thing, the reality of everyday events (even ordinary ones) has an inescapable dynamic physical quality because of movement and the changes it creates in the environment. The learner moves. Other people move. Inanimate objects are moved too by natural forces such as the wind and by the people who touch them. The environment and its relationship to the learner are constantly transformed by the movements that lead to touching or contact between people and their physical environments, an environment which also includes other people as physical and social agents. It is difficult, therefore, to imagine a world of ordinary experiences in which nothing ever moves. Nevertheless, scholars have preferred to focus on the residue of such experiences, that is, the stable and abstract mental representation of knowledge that is sorted out from the messy contexts of ordinary daily experience.

But clinicians cannot afford this luxury if they want to understand why children with PDD fail to develop normally and how to help them.

However, a suitable theoretical framework that includes movement and action in ways that inform us about atypical learning must not be focused narrowly on just the physical act of moving, namely the displacement of body mass in space due to muscle contraction. We already know that **some** children appear to develop normal cognition even when their muscles contract abnormally because of early neurological insult, as in the case of cerebral palsy (Lewis 1987). They also may develop normally when congenitally missing body limbs preclude some muscle contractions altogether, as in the case of children with congenital limb malformation caused by thalidomide exposure in utero (Decarie 1969). In contrast, children with PDD typically can move their bodies at will, sometimes with great agility; but, they may not look normal when they move to execute the tasks of daily living. Consider the following clinical descriptions of two children with a PDD diagnosis:

> R. (6 yrs old) has no receptive or expressive language nor does he engage in social interaction with anyone, including his mother. He also does not participate in the routine daily events of self-care, dressing, and is just learning to eat with a spoon. R. can move quickly and with agility; he runs and is not afraid to jump into a swimming pool. Although R. touches objects in the environment, he rarely grasps or lifts them from their support. He makes nonverbal sounds but does not communicate intentionally with significant others in his social environment . . ..

> D. (6 yrs old) also has no language. But he has just started to use conventional gestures such as pointing to signal communicative intent in a given situation. He moves, but how? He goes to the bathroom himself although the self-care routines are accomplished slowly, awkwardly, and sometimes without all the steps needed to accomplish the goal. D. touches and grasps objects, but how? Sometimes facial grimaces (i.e., collateral movements) can be seen while he moves a simple toy across the table. His mouth opens as if he is concentrating very hard on moving an object. D. walks and can even go up and down a slide on the playground with help, but D. is afraid to go into the water for swimming. He plays in stereotypical patterns by placing toy objects side by side on the floor so that each object touches the other in a line . . .

Neither child has language or participates in the daily routines at home or classroom like typically developing children their age. Nevertheless, both children are capable of moving their bodies at will, one skillfully and the other with great timidity and caution. What makes these two children appear so abnormal is not just the pervasiveness of their developmental deficits, but the fact that their movements either are not purposeful and/or they are characterized by stereotypical and monotonous patterns. In sum, the perceptual-cognitive development of neither child is normal despite the ability to move at will.

Consequently, a useful framework of learning and development must have something to say about how our physical movements become goal-directed action-interaction experience in the service of learning and developing. Doing so requires that frameworks for perception be expanded to include the movement senses. In the context of perception, motor activity is more than an **output** response. Motor activity also is **sensory input** to the nervous system along with other perceptual experiences that mediate cognitive growth (Thelan 1995). Movement provides input to the nervous system via sensory modalities that are not in the foreground of clinical work aimed at enhancing perceptual development, namely, the tactile-kinesthetic system. For example, clinicians may concede that purposeful actions are guided by a motor plan, but they may not consider where motor plans come from or the possibility that they come from some kind of perceptual map that is not based on just visual information. Even when clinicians embrace the importance of participatory learning, for example, having the child actively participate by doing something in an event, they may not consider that the stored perceptual input from such experiences involves more than looking and listening.

Such narrow clinical perspectives have been encouraged by the view of the tactual-kinesthetic system as a secondary rather than a primary player in perceptual-cognitive development (Klatzky et al 1985; Lederman and Klatsky 1987). So the distance senses, vision and audition, have been privileged in framing developmental learning theory and intervention paradigms. It is not surprising, therefore, that the aberrant movement patterns observed in children with PDD are viewed as a separate "output" problem, which has little or no relationship to perception, cognition, or language.

A useful framework, though, should sensitize us to the view that what looks like a motor problem may be a perceptual problem — one that can have as much to do with the aberrant tactual-kinesthetic input as with its coordinated visual and/or auditory input. The acquisition of complex human skills, language included, is undoubtedly a multisensory task involving collaboration of all the senses. Otherwise we could not account for why persons with only deafness or blindness still can develop and reach a normal level of functioning after a delay, or for that matter, why the story of Helen Keller, who lost access to both sight and sound early in life, could be told. The kind of children who motivated this book, however, can see and hear but still do not develop language or many nonverbal cognitive skills easily, if at all. Such observations, on their face, raise questions about whether the critical input to learning can be simply visual and/or auditory sensory-perceptual experience. Tactual-kinesthethic sensory-perceptual input is embedded in the concrete reality of everyday real-world experiences. Making things happen in even the most mundane or monotonous daily life events requires goal-directed movement, action-interaction activity, plus the perceptions entailed in knowing that we change the reality of the world in reaching action-interaction goals. The essential point here is that normal learning results from the collaboration of sensory input, which includes not only the distance senses (i.e., audition and vision) but also the tactile-kinesthetic senses. In this view, any theoretical framework that is useful for clinical work should not leave out the movement senses when considering what kind of input enhances learning and developing.

FROM MODULAR TO HOMOLOGOUS MODELS OF DEVELOPMENT

We need theoretical frameworks that embrace not only a process-oriented approach to learning in the real-world contexts of purposeful moving and acting, but we also need a homologous framework. The term *homologous* comes from the Greek/Latin root words, *homos* or *homo* meaning "same" and *logos* meaning "relations" combined to mean "a similarity often attributable to a common origin" (Webster's Third New International Dictionary 1988). As used in this book, a homologous model aims to predict how multiple skills in seemingly different domains of human behavior develop from a single causal mechanism. The implication is that we should not search for separate causal mechanisms underlying each of the many deficits (e.g., affective, language, social, perceptual, cognition, and so on) observed in children with PDD. In principle, a homologous model presumes that the multiple deficits are all related to one another in the sense that they are traceable to a common root source. This view of a homologous relationship fits the "shared origins" model described by Bates et al (1979). It assumes that ". . . any experience which enhances the underlying base should spill over into any domain that depends on that base" (p. 9). Indeed, Bates et al (1979) reported that this type of homologous relationship fit best with their own research findings. It also fit best with the research observations reported by Affolter and Bischofberger (2000), described later in this book.

Such a model brings parsimony or efficiency to theoretical explanation, which is helpful to clinical work with PDD. This kind of clinical problem is associated with system-wide deficits that cross verbal and nonverbal domains of function. How long should therapy last if clinicians must work on so many skill deficits, and each one at a time?

Homologous modeling of skill learning has the expectation that clinical work on an underlying root cause can affect skills system-wide, even though clinicians do not work directly on each one. This is not a far-fetched proposal. Children have been observed to improve in areas not targeted in intervention, even when clinicians do not necessarily expect this phenomenon, or can explain it.

Whatever form a homologous systems approach takes, it must be broad enough to account for **self-initiated learning experience** in addition to directed learning in therapy or at home. Self-initiated learning experience means learning from one's own actions and mental reflections. There is an important reason to embrace self-initiated learning. Adult-guided learning does not take place in every waking hour of a child's day, however scaffolded the learning may need to take place so that behavior comes to match the cultural group. For example, the 30 minutes or so of directed therapy in a week cannot compete with the countless opportunities for learning in the waking hours of a child's daily experiences outside of therapy. Opportunities for learning in the natural environment of playing, eating, bathing, and socializing also go beyond the moments of scaffolded learning with even the most zealous caregiver.

Thus, self-initiated learning becomes important then because we cannot teach a child everything he or she can come to know over the course of a lifetime. There simply are not enough resources (i.e., time, skill, or money) to teach a child every skill. How long should therapy last if it is to be devoted to teaching every skill, and teaching them in isolation of one another at that? Because the skills we need do change across the life span, how long must therapy go on to help someone with so many deficits? Therapy is very costly in time, money, and manpower supply, particularly if one has to have a different professional for speech, occupational, and physical therapy in addition to special education services for reading, math, and so on. We should not be surprised then that even those professionals who subscribe to a specific skills orientation to intervention implicitly hope or expect that children will bootstrap themselves enough to continue learning and developing after intervention ends. In this respect, even the traditional approaches to intervention, which focus on a few isolated skills at a time, may be implicitly homologous in their long-range expected outcomes.

Still, the specific skills chosen for the intervention focus are not necessarily guided by theoretical assumptions about which skills can cause system-wide change. More often than not, the specific skills focused on in intervention are guided by which ones seem to be missing in the system relative to the expected age (a deficit orientation), and might be modified within some practical time limit set by a service delivery agency. For example, speech-language pathologists might have a goal as specific as the child will learn to use a given set of grammatical inflections or answer "wh" questions.

At the same time, theories about learning also may be narrowly framed around a particular domain of behavior. Theories of language learning can be framed in isolation of what is required to learn nonverbal skills. Theories of social development can be framed in isolation of what is required for cognitive development, and so on. Local domain theories may not help clinicians to deal with multisystem problems. Theories governing isolated domains of function contrast sharply with any homologous theory that presupposes relationships among them all.

Fortunately, there are some hints in the literature that show how a homologous model might work for clinically intervening with multiple deficits within a single domain of functioning. In the field of language, distinctive feature theory (Jakobson et al 1952; McReynolds and Bennett 1972) is a good example of the courtship with this kind of outlook. Distinctive feature theory provided a parsimonious framework for representing speech-sound relationships. The 40 or more distinctive speech sounds, or phonemes, of English were described in terms of the combinatorial relationships among 13 to 15 articulatory and perceptual speech sound properties. It is, therefore, possible to describe some articulation errors on multiple phonemes in terms of a few missing distinctive features. Therapy tries to build in psychological representation of a missing feature contrast (e.g., continuancy as characteristic of sounds like /s/ in *soap* or /sh/ in *shoe* or /f/ in *fox*). The expectation is that the whole phonological system (at least performance on the class of speech sounds affected by the continuancy feature) gets reorganized by working on a few sounds with that feature. A homologous perspective also appears to drive the Whole Language intervention movement (Norris and Hoffman 1990, 1993) as well as Milieu therapy (Kaiser and Hester 1994, which focus on language deficits at a broader level than just the phonological system.

The broader question is whether there are more global homologies, which are not so domain specific, and can apply across the verbal and nonverbal domains of function. In reviewing the research on children with language disorders, Judith Johnston (1988) stated that we need to consider the possibility that a more global aberrant mechanism may underlie both depressed verbal and nonverbal performances.

After examining the temporal relationships between the emergence of selected verbal and nonverbal skills, Bates et al (1979) concluded that a homologous model must be viewed in local rather than broad terms. A local homologous model follows from narrowly rather than broadly correlated verbal and nonverbal skills. For example, some aspects of children's nonverbal conceptual knowledge (e.g., object permanence) precedes their verbal skills (e.g., the use of disappearance words such as *all gone*) but not the emergence of first word use. However, local homologous models may not be adequate to account for the broad range of skill deficits observed in children with PDD.

PURPOSE AND SCOPE OF THE BOOK

Although atypical learners are in the foreground in this book, it is recognized that clinical intervention frameworks should be guided by what is known about learning in general. To do so, the theoretical landscape must be broad enough to account for behaviors at the margins of development as well as those that represent the central tendencies. As pointed out earlier, a theory of development that can well serve clinical intervention frameworks for children with PDD should have at least four characteristics. It should (1) respect experience as the basis for learning and developing, and in particular, the experiences encountered in everyday problem-solving events; (2) address the learning process, for example, how everyday experience gets translated into the categories of representation and memories that define learned behaviors; (3) specify how action-interaction experiences inform developing and learning; and (4) favor homologous as opposed to modular explanatory models.

A main goal of this book is to reveal how these four guidelines are met in some measure by the work of contemporary scholars in developmental psychology, particularly those whose work is broadly representative of an embodiment constructivist view of development. A second goal of this book is to illustrate how these same principles translate into clinical practice. This is done by describing two clinical intervention frameworks that now are being used with a variety of clinical populations, including children with PDD. Therefore, the structure of the book is anchored by its focus on normal and abnormal development.

Accordingly, the chapters are organized into two main parts to reflect this dual focus. In Part I, the eight chapters focus on the theoretical frameworks of development that have evolved mainly from studying normal or typical learners. In Part II, the three chapters emphasize the application of theoretical principles described in Part I to clinical assessment and intervention and to the evaluation of clinical efficacy. Introductory commentary to each of these two sections is intended to connect the flow of argument across the content of the different chapters and perspectives. In the final chapter, Part III, I reflect on how the theoretical frameworks described in this book may challenge current intervention practices and research issues.

The invited contributors bring a rich and well-seasoned history of research scholarship and/or clinical practice to its 12 chapters. It is irrelevant that their respective views have been aired separately elsewhere. The goal of this book is to present a collective perspective that is clinically relevant to intervention for children with the diagnosis of PDD.

Introductory commentary to each of the book's three sections is intended to connect the flow of argument across the content of its different chapters and perspectives.

REFERENCES

Affolter, F. 1991. *Perception, Interaction, and Language.* New York: Springer (original work published in 1967).

Affolter, F., and Bischofberger, W. 2000. *Nonverbal Perceptual and Cognitive Processes in Children with Language Disorders: Toward a New Framework for Clinical Intervention.* Mahwah, NJ: Erlbaum.

American Psychiatric Association. 1994. *Diagnosis and Statistical Manual of Mental Disorders* (4th ed.). Washington, DC: Author.

Anzalone, M.E., and Williamson, G.G. 2001. Sensory Processing and Motor Performance in Autism Spectrum Disorders. In A.M. Wetherby, and B.M. Prizant (Editors), *Autism Spectrum Disorders: A Transactional Perspective* (pp. 143–166). Baltimore, MD: Brookes.

Ayres, J. 1972. Types of Sensory integrative dysfunction among disabled learners. *Am J of Occup Ther* 26:13–18.

Baillargeon, R. (2002). The acquisition of physical knowledge in infancy: A summary in eight lessons. In U. Goswami (Editor), *Handbook of Childhood Cognitive Development* (pp. 47–83). Oxford, England: Blackwell.

Baron-Cohen, S. 1995. *Mindblindness: An Essay on Autism and Theory of Mind.* Cambridge, MA: MIT Press.

Bates, E., Benigni, L., Betherton, I., Camaioni, L., and Volterra, V. 1979. *The Emergence of Symbols: Cognition and Communication in Infancy.* New York: Academic Press.

Bates, E. 1999. Language and the Infant Brain. *Journal of Communication Disorders* 32:195–205.

Bellugi, U., and Studdert-Kennedy, M. 1980. *Signed and Spoken Language: Biological Constraints on Linguistic Form.* Verlag Chemie: Weinheim.

Bellugi, U. 1988. The acquisition of a spatial language. In F. Kessell (Editor), *The Development of Language and Language researchers: Essays in Honor of Roger Brown* (pp. 153–185). Hillsdale, NJ: Erlbaum.

Bellugi, U., Wang, P., and Jernigan, T. 1994. Williams syndrome: An unusual neuropsychological profile. In S. Broman and J. Grafman (Editors), *Atypical Cognitive Deficits in Developmental Disorders: Implications for Brain Function* (pp. 23–56). Hillsdale, NJ: Lawrence Erlbaum.

Bettelheim, B. 1967. *The Empty Fortress: Infantile Autism and the Birth of Self.* New York: The Free Press.

Biklen, D. 1990. Communication abound: Autism and praxis. *Harvard Educational Review* 60:291–314.

Biklen, D., and Cardinal, D.N. 1997. *Contested Words, Contested Science: Unraveling the Facilitated Communication Controversy.* New York: Teachers College Press.

Bishop, D., and Mogford, K. 1993. *Language Development in Exceptional Circumstances.* Hillsdale, NJ: Erlbaum.

Bobath, K. 1980. *A Neurophysiological Basis for the Treatment of Cerebral Palsy* (2nd ed.). Philadelphia, PA: J.B. Lippincott.

Chapman, R. 1997. Language development in children and adolescents with Down syndrome. *Men Retard Dev Disabil Res Rev* 3:307–312.

Cohen, D.J., and Volkmar, F.R. 1997a. *Handbook of Autism and Pervasive Developmental Disorders.* New York: John Wiley & Sons.

Cohen, D.J., and Volkmar, F.R. 1997b. Conceptualization of autism and intervention practices: International perspectives. In D.J. Cohen and F.R. Volkmar (Editors), *Handbook of Autism and Pervasive Developmental Disorders* (pp. 947–1003). New York: John Wiley & Sons.

Decarie, T.G. 1969. A study of the mental and emotional development of the Thalidomide child. In Foss, B.M., (Editor), *Determinants of Infant Behavior* (Vol. IV, pp. 167–187). London: Methuen.

Davies, P.M. 1994. *Starting Again: Early Rehabilitation After Traumatic Brain Injury or Other Severe Brain Lesion.* Berlin, Germany: Springer Verlag.

Delacato, C.H. 1963. *The Diagnosis and Treatment of Speech and Reading Problems.* Springfield, IL: Charles C. Thomas.

Donnellan, A.M., and Leary, M.R. 1995. *Movement Differences and Diversity in Autism/Mental Retardation: Appreciating and Accommodating People with Communication Challenges.* Madison, WI: DRI Press.

Donnellan, A.M., and Ray-Reese, D. 2002. *Understanding Autism as a Movement Disorder: Applying the Feldenkrais Method.* A course presented at the Reese Movement Institute, Oceanside, CA.

Elman, J.L., Bates, E.A., Johnson, M., Karmiloff-Smith, A., Parisi, D., and Plunkett, K. 1999. *Rethinking Innateness: A Connectionist Perspective on Development.* Cambridge, MA: MIT Press.

Fay, W.H. 1993. Infantile autism. In Bishop, D., and Mogford K., (Editors), *Language Development in Exceptional Circumstances* (pp. 190–202). Hillsdale, NJ: Erlbaum.

Feldenkrais, M. 1994. *Body Awareness as Healing Therapy: A case of Nora.* Berkeley, CA: Frog Press (Original publication in 1977).

Fisher, A., Murray, E., and Bundy, A. 1991. *Sensory Integration: Theory and Practice.* Philadelphia, PA: F.A. Davis.

Frith, U., and Baron-Cohen, S. 1987. Perception in autistic children. In Cohen, D.J., and Donnellan, A.M., (Editors), *Handbook of Autism and Pervasive Developmental Disorders* (pp. 85–102). Silver Spring, MD: V.H. Winston.

Frith, U., and Happe, F. 1994. Autism: Beyond "theory of mind." *Cognition,* 50, 115–132.

Furth, H.G. 1966. *Thinking without Language: Psychological Implications of Deafness.* New York: Basic Books.

Greenspan, S.I., and Wieder, S. 2001. A developmental approach to difficulties in relating and communicating in autism spectrum disorders and related syndromes. In A. Wetherby, and B.M. Prizant (Editors), *Autism Spectrum Disorders: A Transactional Developmental Perspective* (pp. 279–306). Baltimore, MD: Brookes.

Hill, E.L. 2001. Non-specific nature of specific language impairment: A review of the literature with regard to concomitant motor impairments. *International Journal of Communication Disorders* 36:149–171.

Holyoak, K.J. 1990. Problem-solving. In Osherson, D.N., and Smith, E.E., (Editors), *Thinking: An Invitation to Cognitive Science* (pp. 117–147). Cambridge, MA: MIT Press.

Howlin, P. 1989. Changing approaches to communication training with autistic children. *Br J Disord Commun* 24:151–168.

Jakobson, R., Fant, G., and Halle, M. 1952. *Preliminaries to Speech Analysis: The Distinctive Features and Their Correlates*. Cambridge, MA: MIT Press.

Johnston, J. 1988. Specific language disorders in the child. In Lass, N., McReynolds, L., Northern, J., and Yoder, D., (Editors), *Handbook of Speech-Language Pathology & Audiology* (pp. 685–715). Philadelphia, PA: B.C. Decker.

Kaiser, A., and Hester, P. 1994. Generalized effects of enhanced milieu teaching. *J Speech Hear Res* 37:1320–1340.

Karmiloff-Smith, A. 1992. Taking development seriously. In Karmiloff-Smith A., (Editor), *Beyond Modularity: A Developmental Perspective on Cognitive Science* (pp. 1–29). Cambridge, MA: MIT Press.

Karmiloff-Smith, A. 1994. Precis of beyond modularity: A developmental perspective on cognitive science. *Behav Brain Sci* 17:693–745.

Kitahara, K. 1983a. *Daily Life Therapy: A Method of Educating Autistic Children* (Volume 1). Boston, MA: The Nemrod Press (English Translation).

Kitahara, K. 1983b. *Daily Life Therapy: A Method of Educating Autistic Children* (Volume 2). Boston, MA: The Nemrod Press (English Translation).

Kitahara, K. 1984. *Daily Life Therapy: A Method of Educating Autistic Children* (Volume 3). Boston, MA: The Nemrod Press (English Translation).

Klatzky, R., Lederman, S.J., and Metzer, V.A. 1985. Identifying objects by touch: An "expert system." *Perception Psychophys* 37(4):299–302.

Kozma, I. 1995. The basic principles and present practice of conductive education. *European J Spec Needs Educ* 10(2):111–123.

Kranowitz, C.S. 1998. *The Out-of-Sync Child: Recognizing and Coping with Sensory Integration Dysfunction*. New York, NY: Berkeley Publishing Group.

Landau, B., and Gleitman, L. 1985. *Language and Experience: Evidence from the Blind Child*. London, England: Harvard University Press.

Lederman, S.J. 1997. Skin and touch. *Encyclopedia of Human Biology* (2nd ed.): 8 (pp. 49–61) New York: Academic Press.

Lederman, S.J., and Klatsky, R.L. 1987. Hand movements: A window into haptic object recognition. *Cogn Psychology* 19:342–368.

Leonard, L. 1998. *Specific Language Impairment*. Cambridge, MA: MIT Press.

Lewis, V. 1987. How do children with motor handicaps develop? In Lewis V., (Editor), *Development and Handicap* (pp. 82–103). Cambridge, England: Blackwell.

Lincoln, A.J., Dickstein, P., Courchesne, E., Elmasian, R., and Tallal, P. 1992. Auditory processing abilities in non-retarded adolescents and young adults with developmental receptive language disorder and autism. *Brain and Language* 43:613–622.

Lord, C., and Risi, S. 2000. Diagnosis of autism spectrum disorders in young children. In A.M. Wetherby, and B.M. Prizant, (Editors), *Autism Spectrum Disorders: A Transactional Developmental Perspective* (pp. 11–30). Baltimore, MD: Brookes.

Lourenco, O., and Machado, A. 1996. In defense of Piaget's theory: A reply to 10 common criticisms. *Psych Rev* 103(1):143–164.

Lovaas, O.I. 1977. *The Autistic Child: Language Development through Behavior Modification*. New York: Irvington Press.

Lovaas, O.I. 1981. *Teaching Developmentally Disabled Children: The ME Book*. Baltimore, MD: University Park Press.

Lovaas, O.I. 1987. Behavioral treatment and normal educational and intellectual functioning in young autistic children. *Journal of Consulting and Clinical Psychology,* 55: 3–9.

Mandler, J.M. 1998. Babies think before they speak. *Hum Dev* 41:116–126.

McReynolds, L.V., and Bennett, S. 1972. Distinctive feature generalization in articulation training. *J Speech Hearing Disord* 46:197–204.

Meltzoff, A.N. 1999. Origins of theory of mind, cognition and communication. *Journal of Communication Disorders* 32:251–269.

Mogford, K., and Bishop, D.V.M. 1993. *Language Development in Exceptional Circumstances* (pp. 239–260). Hillsdale, NJ: Erlbaum.

Müller, U., and Overton, W.F. 1998a. How to grow a baby: A reevaluation of image-schema and Piagetian action approaches to representation. *Hum Dev* 41:71–111.

Müller, U., and Overton, W. 1998b. Action theory of mind and representational theory of mind: Is dialogue possible? A reply to Mandler, and Rochat and Striano. *Human Development* 41:127–133.

Norris, J., and Hoffman, P. 1990. Language intervention within naturalistic environments. *Language Speech Hearing Serv Schools* 21:72–84.

Norris, J., and Hoffman, P. 1993. *Whole Language Intervention for School-Age Children*. San Diego: Singular Publishing Group.

Olley J.G., and Gutentag, S.S. 1999. Autism: Historical overview, definition and characteristics. In Zager, D.B., (Editor), *Autism: Intervention, Education, and Treatment* (pp. 3–23). Mahwah, NJ: Erlbaum.

Piaget, J. 1952. *The Origins of Intelligence in Children*. New York: International Universities Press. (Original work published in 1936).

Powell, R.P., and Bishop, D.V.M. 1992. Clumsiness and perceptual problems in children with specific language impairment. *Dev Med Child Neurol* 34:755–765.

Reed, T. 1994. Performance of autistic and control subjects on three cognitive perspective taking tasks. *J Autism Dev Disord* 24:53–66.

Rochat, P., and Striano, T. 1998. Primacy of action in early ontogeny. *Human Development* 41:112–115.

Romanczyk, R.G., Weiner, T., Lockshin, S., and Ekdanl, M. 1999. Research in autism: Myths, controversies, and perspectives. In Zager, D.B., (Editor), *Autism: Identification, Education and Treatment* (2nd ed.) (pp. 23–62). Mahwah, NJ: Erlbaum.

Sigman, M. 1994. What are the core deficits in autism. In Broman, S., and Grafman, J., (Editors), *Atypical Cognitive Deficits in Developmental Disorders: Implications for Brain Function* (pp. 139–158). Hillsdale, NJ: Erlbaum.

Singh, V.K., Lin, S.X., and Yang, V.C. 1998. Serological association of measles virus and human herpesvirus-6 with brain autoantibodies in autism. *Clin Immunol Immunopathol* 89:105–108.

Stark, R., and Tallal, P. 1988. *Language, Speech and Reading Disorders in Children: Neuropsychological Studies*. Boston, MA: Little, Brown.

Sternberg, L., McNerney, C., and Pegnatore, L. 1985. Developing co-active imitative behaviors with profoundly mentally handicapped children. *Educ Train Mental Retard* 20:260–267.

Stockman, I. 2000. Introduction: From product to process in investigating problem solving in children with language disorders. In F. Affolter and Walter Bischofberger, (Editors), *Nonverbal Perceptual and Cognitive Processes in Children with Language Disorders: Toward a New Framework for Clinical Intervention* (pp. xi–xxv). Mahwah, NJ: Erlbaum.

Tager-Flusberg, H. 1994. *Constraints on Language Acquisition: Studies of Atypical Children*. Hillsdale, NJ: Erlbaum.

Tager-Flusberg, H. 2000. *Neuro Developmental Disorders*. M.I.T. Press: Cambridge, MA.

Thelen, E. 1995. Motor Development: A new synthesis. *Am Psychol* 50(2):79–95.

Thelen, E. and Smith, L.B. 1994. *A Dynamic Systems Approach to the Development of Cognition and Action*. Cambridge, MA: The MIT Press.

Tsai, L.Y. 1999. Recent neurobiological research in autism. In Zager, D.B., (Editor), *Autism: Identification, Education, and Treatment* (pp. 63–96). Mahwah, NJ: Erlbaum.

Waterhouse, L. 1994. Severity of impairment in autism. In Broman, S., and Grafman, J., (Editors), *Atypical Cognitive Deficits in Developmental Disorders: Implications for Brain Function* (pp. 159–180). Hillsdale, NJ: Erlbaum.

Welch, M.G. 1989. *Holding Time*. New York: Simon and Schuster.

Zero to Three/National Center for Clinical Infants Programs. 1994. *Disorders of Relating and Communication* (pp. 40–45). Arlington, VA.

I

INTRODUCTORY COMMENTARY

A THEORETICAL FRAMEWORK FOR CLINICAL INTERVENTION WITH PERVASIVE DEVELOPMENTAL DISORDERS

IDA J. STOCKMAN, PHD

MEETING THE CRITERIA FOR A CLINICAL INTERVENTION FRAMEWORK

The authors of the eight chapters in Part I are concerned with knowledge acquisition. It is fitting that their theorizing is justified with observations of infants and young children, given this book's emphasis on pervasive developmental disorders, which often place children at the floor of development. The chapters emphasize different aspects of development, but the authors commonly recognize **ordinary daily life experience** as the raw material from which children begin to structure their knowledge of the world. Theory tries to explain how children develop from experience in which **action** plays some role in harvesting knowledge. These chapters also are attuned to the underlying **process** by which children come to know about the world, so that what children come to know has less prominence than how they come to know it. In putting a measurable face on experience, the authors more often than not appeal to some kind of homologous explanation for development. While such proposals are scaled at different levels of specificity, they try to account for learning across the nonverbal and verbal domains of human learning or, if just one of these domains is emphasized, they consider how its learning is influenced by the other one.

Thus the content of the chapters to follow is oriented to meet the four guidelines for framing a suitable clinical intervention framework for PDD, as sketched in Chapter 1; namely, they focus on (1) the emergence of cognition from everyday real-world experience; (2) the process as opposed to just the mental representation of experience; (3) the inclusion of movement and action-interaction experience in the learning process and knowledge outcomes; and (4) the homologous modeling of learning and developing at some level.

ALIGNING WITH EMBODIMENT CONSTRUCTIVIST THEORY

In meeting the guidelines for a clinical intervention framework, the content themes in this book are broadly allied with a neopiagetian view (Overton and Palermo 1994), or what is refered to as an embodiment constructivist view of mind (Lakoff 1987; Johnson 1987) or enactive cognition (Varela et al 1991). See further discussion of embodied cognition in Thelen and Smith (1994, pp. 321–324) and Overton (1994). This view also shows up in frameworks of memory (Glenberg 1997) and language development (MacWhinney 1999; Glenberg and Robertson 2000; Glenberg and Kaschak 2002)

Embodiment constructivist theory aims to explain how children develop their memories and concepts from experience in which their own bodily **actions** play a role in harvesting knowledge. According to Overton (1994), embodiment theory views the mind as rooted in systems of action and as the emergent product of the brain. Contrary to the historical tendency to separate the body from the mind, the brain is viewed as a living, self-organizing system that is not separate from the rest of the body. Brain and body are intricately linked in creating the intelligent behavior that results from physical and social interactions in daily experience. Such an organismic view is not new to developmental psychology. Piaget's theory of development is similarly grounded.

However, unlike classic Piagetian theory, contemporary scholars like those who contributed to this book are not solely concerned with revealing mental knowledge as developmental end points (i.e., what knowledge is acquired). They are particularly vested in the **process** of constructing knowledge in real time and space. They try to explain how children cope with the dynamic, complex, and messy contexts of ordinary day-to-day experience in developing memories, concepts, and behaviors that are relevant to their social, cultural, and physical environments. Their competence (i.e., what they know) is not viewed in isolation of the variable contexts of real performance. Such context variability was historically dismissed as irrelevant to a theory of mental development. Mental knowledge was not pursued or crudely represented in Skinnerian — inspired learning theory — or it was represented as more or less stable end points or products of activity in other frameworks such as Piaget's. But scholars working within neopiagetian constructivist view of learning confront context variability head on. Competence is viewed as context dependent. For example, see Thelen and Smith (1994) and Wozniak and Fischer (1993).

The collective view of the scholars who contributed to this book, and others with like-minded views, contrast with simplistic nativist and mechanistic views that marginalize experience. A radical nativist view, for example, assumes that development is the gradual expansion of explicit **representational knowledge** that already exists at birth (cf. Müeller and Overton 1998 a/b and Mandler 1998). The new cognitive science, spurred on by computer technology, is driven by machine modeling of intelligent systems and innately endowed brains for processing information in isolated domains of experience. It should be pointed out, though, that more organismic approaches to machine intelligence are now being pursued. They include ongoing pioneering work on the autonomous mental development of robots (Almassy et al 1998; Weng et al 2001; Weng and Stockman 2002).

The theoretical perspective presented in this book brings human experience to center stage along with speculations about how cognition as knowledge acquisition process may take into account the experiences of moving, acting, and interacting in real-world contexts.

CONNECTING THE CHAPTER THEMES

The following chapter overviews show that the relationship of action to perception and cognition has historical presence (Herbert L. Pick, Jr., Chapter 2). It is also revealed that a dynamic systems perspective is useful for explaining how development emerges from the multiple domains and contexts of experience that also includes action as perceptual-motor activity (Esther Thelen, Chapter 3).

Yet in daily life, we experience a multitude of events. We obviously do not pay conscious attention to all of the stimuli that impact the nervous system in experiencing the world during our waking hours (and maybe sleeping ones too). Given that ordinary daily experiences do vary across learners and contexts of action, is it reasonable to ask how experiences are selectively tuned so that children develop just the ones that get them judged as typical of their social groups? To answer this question, it is necessary to consider not only the underlying mechanisms that may drive learning; but, we also must consider the ways in which the developing system may be constrained or biased so that children end up with enough similarity to be judged as normal in their respective social groups at any one point along the developmental continuum.

Several types of constraints can be inferred from reading the remaining chapters in Part I of this book. They include neurobiological temporal constraints or chronotopic innateness (Elman et al 1999), as observed within the same species across age (Jon H. Kaas, Chapter 4) and across different species at the same age (Jonas Langer, Chapter 5). From Katherine Nelson (Chapter 6), we can infer social biases that govern the types of event structures represented in experiences. In Chapter 7, Lois Bloom's focus on language calls attention to constraints on how much information can be processed at one time in the context of language learning. In Chapter 8, the information processing bias is extended to include the actual sensory modality of input in Félicie Affolter's argument for biases in the perceptual organization of experiences, a bias that favors the primacy of tactual-kinesthetic experience over visual and auditory experiences in developing nonverbal and verbal cognition.

So each chapter by itself does not tell the whole story. As the following overviews reveal, it is the eight chapters combined that offer a glimpse of the multifaceted nature of experience that drives the development of complex behavior.

SUMMARIZING CHAPTER CONTENT

CHAPTER 2: INTERRELATION OF ACTION, PERCEPTION, AND COGNITION IN DEVELOPMENT: AN HISTORICAL PERSPECTIVE

Motor behavior is inherently overt and accessible to observation. So it is not surprising that action as goal-directed perceptual-motor activity has been narrowly viewed as just response output. Motor behavior has been viewed less often as a system for perceiving and elaborating mental knowledge. This is the case even though we can readily demonstrate the dependency of motor responses on perceptual input. For example, movement patterns can be changed by simply blindfolding a sighted person or having a sighted person walk in the dark. Conversely, the perceptual feeling of the body (psychological and emotional security, too) can be changed when a normal person walks on an unstable surface.

Nevertheless, there are empirical hints at the relationship among action, perception and cognition as sketched by **Herbert L. Pick, Jr.**, in Chapter 2. He traces the evidence for pairwise relationships among action, perception, and cognition across more than a century of research. One should leave the chapter with the sense that action as perceptual motor activity is not outside of cognition. It is not movement in and of itself that is important, but rather the perceptual-cognitive consequences of motor acts that reveal something about the inner workings of the mind.

CHAPTER 3: THE CENTRAL ROLE OF ACTION IN TYPICAL AND ATYPICAL DEVELOPMENT: A DYNAMIC SYSTEMS PERSPECTIVE

In contrast to the tenuous historical status of action as a perceptual-cognitive system in developmental psychology, contemporary theorizing attributes a more central role to action in ways that go beyond even Piaget's theory of cognitive development. In Chapter 3, **Esther Thelen** summarizes some basic principles of dynamic systems theory. It offers a fresh, theoretical platform from which to argue that motor acts cannot be isolated from the rest of development, including cognition, as traditionally viewed. Motor acts are among the fluid assembly of multiple physical, mental, and biomechanical factors that are flexibly assembled to meet the variable context demands of learning and performing in real situations. Behavioral outcomes of a dynamic system depend on the prior history and the current conditions for acting in a specific situation. This principle is supported by empirical studies of babies' looking and reaching responses to the classic Piagetian-inspired task for demonstrating the A-not-B error. The observation that the error was made under some manipulated context conditions but not others counters the notion that knowing something is stably tucked away in the brain. One should leave the chapter with the sense that the variable and fluid contexts of experience make whatever we come to know provisional and context dependent.

CHAPTER 4: PLASTICITY OF SOMATOSENSORY AND MOTOR SYSTEMS IN DEVELOPING AND MATURE PRIMATE BRAINS

A dynamic systems approach to movement and action-interaction as described by Esther Thelen in Chapter 3 must be served by a brain that can respond flexibly to the changing context demands on behavior. But such an assumption contrasts with the long-held view that brain function and organization become fixed early in life and remain relatively unchanged across the lifespan. **Jon H. Kaas** counters this view in Chapter 4. He summarizes research evidence for plasticity even in the mature brain of nonhuman primates. While plasticity effects have been shown throughout the brain, this chapter focuses on the plasticity of its somatosensory and motor systems, which neurally mediate sensorimotor experience. The somatosensory cortex is dedicated to tactual input from localized body surfaces. Scientists can isolate neural responses to the stimulation of specific body parts (e.g., the fingers of each hand) well enough to establish a reliable baseline against which to measure the effects of an experimental manipulation. Focal experience is shown to enlarge the size of cortical representation dedicated to an input or motor act. When peripheral input is denied to a given brain area, the healthy neurons that served that area do not become dormant or inactive. They can acquire new receptive fields. For example, the neurons once responsive to a limb may subsequently respond to input from another body part, for example, the face. Kaas' evidence for neuroplasticity shows that the brain is responsive to variability in experience, even though the way it organizes itself may be irreversibly affected by the age at which neurological insult occurs.

CHAPTER 5: CONSTRUCTIVE MANIPULATORY ACTION AND THE ORIGIN OF COGNITION IN HUMAN AND NONHUMAN PRIMATES

The preceding chapters consider action as a perceptual-motor system and its corresponding neuroplasticity to be important in the mix of what makes learning and development happen. Yet, physical movement as action experience is characteristic of all animals, not just human ones. In fact, the movement of nonhuman primates on which much of the neuroplasticity research is based rivals that of humans in quantity, agility, and quickness. Their activity, like that of humans, is oriented toward solving problems of daily life as played out in the search for food, shelter, mating partners, and so on. So, movement must be purposeful or goal oriented. Some nonhuman species even have more keen hearing and sight than humans; still, they do not develop language or other forms of intellect that create the kind of civilizations that only humans can describe. Such observations can on their face suggest that the key to human development cannot be simply movement experience, however goal oriented or planned it might be. The question can be, about what kind of basic mechanisms may explain the phylogenetic differences in expressions of intelligent behavior?

In Chapter 5, **Jonas Langer** answers this question by considering how the early cognition of human and nonhuman primates is similar and different in the acquisition of logical classifying, often regarded as a quintessential feature of intelligent behavior. He argues that logical classifying originates in the constructive sensorimotor activity of human and nonhuman primates. His "originalist" hypothesis is defended by comparing the human and nonhuman infants. His research team observed how the infants construct sets of relationships in their spontaneous manipulations of a standard set of objects. The observed difference between human and nonhuman primates is explained in terms of the temporal organization of experience, specifically developmental processes that favor greater temporal overlap of cross-domain experiences in human than in nonhuman primates. The operation of biological, **hetereochronic** processes are argued to change the phylogenetic course of development.

CHAPTER 6: THE EVENT BASIS OF CONCEPTUAL AND LANGUAGE DEVELOPMENT

Whereas Chapter 5 emphasizes the role of childrens' interaction experiences with the physical environment in developing cognition, **Katherine Nelson** puts a social face on experience in Chapter 6. A central point made in this chapter is that acquiring knowledge about the world is based on much richer experiences than the action-object relationships explored independently by the child. We are reminded that childrens' action experiences in a real-world environment are structured by the social and cultural habits of their caregivers. The sociocultural context has the effect of biasing the contexts of experiences in an obvious way. For example, it even determines what objects at what time and in what space children get to explore the environment in a physically interactive way! Given the variability and complexity of daily life experience, the question is, how can the context of development be captured in ways that resist specific cultural forms and therefore is general enough to be applied across cultural groups?

Nelson argues that the mental representation of early daily event structure provides the homologous basis for nonverbal and verbal cognition. The socially mediated daily events of **eating, dressing, bathing, going to the store,** and so on include not only the child's actions but also the actions of others, along with affect, social rules for interacting, and language.

CHAPTER 7: THE INTEGRATION OF EXPRESSION INTO THE STREAM OF EVERYDAY ACTIVITY

The preceding six chapters attune the reader to the complexity of real-world contexts for learning and developing language. The complexity of language learning contexts is created by the fact that daily events simultaneously embed nonverbal and verbal acts plus emotional feelings about them. So a child's physical interaction with objects is just one of several behavioral domains that competes for attention in daily events.

In proposing how children develop intentional acts of expression in the face of such complexity, **Lois Bloom** argues in Chapter 7 that their attention is mediated by their own self-**engagement** or motivation to establish contact with another person and the effort or amount of work required to do so. Tradeoffs between the two forces are modulated by how relevant, discrepant, or elaborate the linguistic content is relative to past experience and the requirements for performing in a given situation.

This means that performance will **not** just reflect a child's stored knowledge about linguistic rules, but it also will reflect performance constraints that are created when multiple factors in the contexts for using language compete for essentially limited mental resources. To support this claim, Bloom and her colleagues have studied the temporal sequencing of childrens' expressive language in relation to other domains of activity in an event, namely, their spontaneous non-verbal play with objects, their affective expression, and their mothers' talk as addressed to them. This chapter systematically describes the results of these experimental manipulations. It exposes how performance is differentially influenced by the multiple factors that contribute to the attentional demands on learning and using language spontaneously in real events. It can be inferred that language learning reflects a child's own intentional effort and interest in learning language in addition to the external input from the environment.

CHAPTER 8: FROM ACTION TO INTERACTION AS PRIMARY ROOT FOR DEVELOPMENT

In this final chapter of Part I, **Félicie Affolter** describes a developmental perspective that affirms some of the ideas in the preceding chapters but expands or departs from others. Like the preceding chapters, Affolter's view is compatible with the notion that young children construct their knowledge from participatory experiences in daily events, a process informed by their actions in it. Unlike earlier chapters, **action** is more explicitly distinguished from **interaction** in framing what the learning process entails. In arguing for the primacy of nonverbal interaction in development, Affolter orients readers to the need (1) to consider the reciprocal relationship between action and the environment, and (2) to expand the usual view of perception so that it includes the movement senses (i.e., tactile-kinesthetic information) in addition to the visual and auditory senses so frequently catered to. The argument for the primacy of tactual information in the organization of perceptual-cognitive activity is supported by studies of typically developing children and of atypically developing children with PDD. Thus, Chapter 8 provides a bridge between normal and abnormal learning by describing a homologous theory of development that draws on observations of both populations.

First, the differences between action and interaction are pointed out. Then the remainder of the chapter focuses on the cognitive consequences of nonverbal interaction and the research findings that led her and her colleagues to propose nonverbal problem solving in daily interaction events as the homologous root of verbal and nonverbal development.

REFERENCES

Almassy, N., Edelman, G.M., and Sporns, O. 1998. Behavioral constraints in the development of neural properties: A cortical model embedded in a real world device. *Cereb Cortex* 8:346–361.

Elman, J.L., Bates, E.A., Johnson, M., Karmiloff-Smith, A., Parisi, D., and Plunkett, K. 1999. *Rethinking Innateness: A Connectionist Perspective on Development.* Cambridge, MA: MIT Press.

Glenberg, A. 1997. What is memory for? *Behav Brain Sci* 20:1–55.

Glenburg, A.M., and Kaschak, M.P. 2002. Grounding language in action. *Psychon Bull Rev* 9:558–565.

Glenberg, A.M., and Robertson, D.A. 2000. Symbol grounding and meaning: a comparison of high dimensional and embodied theories of meaning. *J Mem Lang* 43:379–401.

Johnson, M. 1987. *The Body in the Mind: The Bodily Basis of Meaning, Imagination, and Reason.* Chicago, IL: University of Chicago Press.

Lakoff, G. 1987. *Women, Fire and Dangerous Things: What Categories Reveal About the Mind.* Chicago: University of Chicago Press.

MacWhinney, B. 1999. The Emergence of Language from Embodiment. In MacWhinney, B. (Editor), *The Emergence of Language* pp. 213–256. Mahwah, NJ: Erlbaum.

Mandler, J.M. 1998a. Babies think before they speak. *Hum Dev* 41:116–126.

Müeller, U., and Overton, W.F. 1998a. How to grow a baby: A reevaluation of image-schema and Piagetian action approaches to representation. *Hum Dev* 41:71–111.

Müeller, U., and Overton, W. 1998b. Action theory of mind and representational theory of mind: Is dialogue possible? A reply to Mandler, and Rochat and Striano. *Hum Dev* 41:127–133.

Overton, W.F. 1994. Contexts of meaning: The computational and the embodied mind. In W.F. Overton, and D.S. Palermo (Editors), *The Nature and Ontogenesis of Meaning* pp.1–18. Hillsdale, NJ: Erlbaum.

Overton, W.F., and Palermo, D.S. (Editors), 1994. *The Nature and Ontogenesis of Meaning.* Hillsdale, NJ: Erlbaum.

Thelen, E., and Smith, L. 1994. *A Dynamic Systems Approach to the Development of Cognition and Action.* Cambridge, MA: MIT Press.

Varela, F., Thompson, E., and Rosch, E. 1991. *The Embodied Mind.* Cambridge, MA: MIT Press.

Weng, J., McClelland, J., Pentland, A., Sporns, O., Stockman, I., Sur, M., and Thelen, E. 2001. Autonomous mental development by robots and animals. *Science* 291:5504 599–600.

Weng, J., and Stockman, I. 2002. Autonomous mental development: Workshop on Development and Learning WDL. *Artif Intell Mag* 23:95–98.

Wozniak, R.H., and Fischer, K. 1993. *Development in Context: Acting and Thinking in Specific Environments.* Hillsdale, NJ: Erlbaum.

2

INTERRELATION OF ACTION, PERCEPTION, AND COGNITION IN DEVELOPMENT: AN HISTORICAL PERSPECTIVE

HERBERT L. PICK, JR., PHD

As an academic psychologist, I often hear knowledgeable lay people and students complaining that I do not deal with the whole child. They point out that in my teaching and discussions, I always focus on the narrow area of perception and perceptual development. In recent years, this narrow focus has been brought home to me when wrestling with practical problems faced by children. One example posed to two colleagues (Jodie Plumert and Martha Arterberry) and me concerned a question as to what age children could safely operate all terrain vehicles (ATVs). From the perspective of my academic specialty my initial response was to regard this as a perceptual-motor problem. I asked such questions as: What sensory information did a child have to detect in order to operate an ATV? What reaction time was required? How precisely did the vehicle need to be steered? How much motor strength was needed to operate the various controls?

However, we realized that such a natural, practical problem involved a heavy cognitive aspect. What did the child understand about the vehicle operation? Could the child understand training materials, either written or spoken and demonstrated? Could the child understand the risks involved in operating the vehicle and how these changed depending on the context?

Finally, there seemed to be a social aspect. Children often operate ATVs in a social setting with other children. To what extent are there social pressures to engage in risky behaviors? To what extent is the social context distracting from the demanding task of vehicle operation?

Even disregarding the social component, the performance of such complex skills demands the integration of several of the isolated domains with which we academic psychologists often deal. Thus, for operation of ATVs, perception is integrated with action and cognition. The tenor of many chapters in this book leans toward linking action to perception and cognition. However, this kind of connection between action as motor activity and perception and cognition has not been a strong tradition in the history of psychology, although there have been some hints here and there of such relationships. In the following pages, I step back and summarize some of the ways issues of the interrelations of perception, cognition, and action have been dealt with during the history of psychology. I first discuss some origins of concerns with these interrelations, then indicate that more recent researchers have, in fact, integrated these three components in the following pairwise fashion: perception and action, cognition and perception, and cognition and action.

EARLY CONCERNS WITH PERCEPTION/ACTION/COGNITION RELATIONSHIPS

Of course, an initial question is how far to step back. It is appropriate to mention that ideas about some of these relations are rooted in the empiricist philosophy of the 17th and 18th centuries. However, the emphasis in this book on action and interaction in the perception and cognition of the developing child is in contrast with the ambivalence of traditional psychology about the role of action. The ideas of Bishop Berkeley, in his 1709 work, *An Essay Towards a New Theory of Vision*, provided one of the sharpest early examples in which action was implicated in understanding the process of perception. Berkeley, among other philosophers, pointed out the difficulty of accounting for our veridical perception of the world (especially distance and size of objects) through visual sensory perception alone. He noted that the visual direction of a point source of light from an object (and hence its shape) could be specified by its retinal projection. However, the distance of a source was not so specified. Distance was ambiguous because sources at different distances in the same direction would project onto the same retinal location. For an observer to apprehend the distance of an object, some additional information was required. One kind of additional information suggested by Berkeley was the difference in sense of strain of the eye muscles when the eyes converged on a very near object as opposed to a distant one. Thus, here was an early proposal that object perception is based on the integration of sensory information from different sources, in this case the sensory information based on action of the eye muscles.

Berkeley went on to note that perception of size would be ambiguous from visual information alone. Any given size of retinal image could arise from smaller, closer objects and larger, more distant objects. One way that observers could disambiguate their perception, at least for recognized objects, was to rely on their previous tactual exploration of these objects. Berkeley's ideas about muscle strain and tactual exploration as supplementary information for veridical perception introduced psychology to the possibility that "touch teaches vision" and that current ongoing perception is based on prior experience.

Although considerable progress has been made in our knowledge since then, the relative primacy of touch and vision and how prior experience influences perception are issues that have persisted through the years and are reflected in contemporary psychology. Berkeley's ideas about the role of muscle strain and tactual exploration raise the general question of the relation between action and perception. His suggestion that prior (tactual) experience affects perception implies that memory has a role in perception and also raises the general issue of the relation between cognition and perception.

Subsequent empiricist philosophers of the 18th and 19th centuries elaborated these issues in various forms. A notable impetus for continuing the focus on the relation of cognition and perception was provided by Helmholtz (1925), a physicist, physiologist, and psychologist. He observed that a number of perceptual phenomena depended on the combined input of two or more sources of sensory stimulation. By studying vision, Helmholtz hypothesized that any experience of color could be generated by stimulation in the correct proportion of a small set of color receptor types, each type sensitive to a specific wavelength of light. Similarly for audition, he hypothesized that any experience of sound could be generated by combined stimulation in the correct proportion of a relatively small set of receptors sensitive to specific frequencies of sound. For Helmholtz, even very basic but complex processes of perception were made up of the combination or integration of very elemental sensations. This seemed so automatic, apparently based on repeated experience of such integration, that he described them as unconscious inferences.

A striking feature of the thinking and observations up to the mid-19th century was that these early philosophers and psychologists considered the role of earlier experience in the perception and cognition of adults, but there had been no concern about, or observations of, actual development in children. This lack of attention to development itself began to change in the latter half of the 19th century. The signal events were Wilhelm Preyer's 1887, The *Mind of the Child*, and G. Stanley Hall's 1883, *Contents of Children's Minds*. The impetus to study early development also came from embryologists and ethologically oriented animal researchers, including Spalding (1873), Preyer (1887), and others.

A strong theme in the work of these early developmental researchers was the distinction between instinct and habit or learning. The possibility that psychological development (even of development of motor action) was based on learning, at the very least an associative process, carries the implication of a cognitive component. This theme was reflected in the developmental research of the first 30 years of the 20th century. It is exemplified most notably by the work of Gesell and others (Gesell and Thompson 1929; Gesell 1933; see also Thelen and

Adolph 1992) and McGraw and others (McGraw 1935; see also Bergenn et al 1992) and their use of co-twin control studies. As is well known about these studies, one of a pair of twins (sometimes labeled T) was given special training, usually in particular motor skills, while the other twin (C) was allowed to develop normally. The question was whether the special training imparts any long-lasting advantage to twin T. Their results and several analogous studies with animals were interpreted as support for the nature over the nurture, or learning perspective. Although twin T showed some initial advantage from the training, twin C often caught up very quickly, either spontaneously, or, after later training. The conclusion that the development of some motor skill was due to physiological maturation seemed to imply that it did not involve any cognitive component. (The possible role of perception in the performance of the skill was not typically considered.)

To summarize, the ideas of the philosopher predecessors of psychology and even of Helmholtz were oriented towards the goal of understanding the origins of our knowledge. To explain how knowledge was veridical, they integrated perception, cognition, and action. However, as psychology evolved in the late 19th and 20th centuries, there has been a strong tendency to look at each of these domains in isolation. Thus in perception, the psychophysical tradition has emphasized the study of "pure" sensation and perception. The study of cognition evolved to a point where perception was largely ignored except for recognizing that the information had to get into the system somehow in the first place. In general, the cognitivists and perceptionists ignored action. At the same time, a field of motor behavior evolved that did not pay much attention to cognition and paid little to perception. However, these trends have been opposed by tendencies to consider at least pairwise relations among perception, cognition, and action, for example, the relation between action and cognition, action and perception, and perception and action. In the remainder of this chapter, I review some of the research for each of these pairwise relations. Taken together, these pairwise trends suggest that motor activity as goal-directed action has not been completely isolated from its reciprocal relationships to perception and cognition.

ACTION AND PERCEPTION

ACTION INFLUENCES PERCEPTION

Berkeley's idea that touch teaches vision implied an intimate connection between action and perception. This particular connection between action and perception is directional: perception is dependent on action and not the converse. As noted earlier, Berkeley proposed that it was prior tactual experience that played the important role in some cases. However, at various times in the history of psychology, action in the form of various types of movements was considered to play a very immediate role in perception. The possibility of movements being the basis of perception seems most obvious in the tactual perception of objects. When exploring an object tactually, an observer's arm and hand movements necessarily trace out the shape of an object. Some theorists have suggested that similarly the visual perception of shape is based on eye movements that trace out the form of an object. This position was worked out most thoroughly by Soviet-Russian psychologists between 1955 and 1965 (Zaporozhets 1957; Zinchenko et al 1962).

There was a similar element in American learning theory in the concept of acquired distinctiveness of cues. The concept was applied to observers learning to discriminate between a pair of similar objects. It was argued that if observers could learn to make a distinctive movement or response to each of the two stimuli, they would be better able to differentiate between them. The two different stimuli plus the distinctive movements would be more discriminable than just the stimuli by themselves. There was even a motor theory of speech perception (Liberman and Cooper 1967). Its basic tenet was that the perceptual decoding of speech signals is based on motor units.

In a more direct and obvious way, our perception generally depends on and improves with a variety of exploratory actions. We apprehend the three-dimensional shape of an object by moving around it and viewing it from a variety of perspectives. We perceive the layout of a space by moving through it. An intriguing aspect of such exploratory action is that we often are unaware of the action or movements we are making but are very aware of the perceptual information that the action provides. A graphic example of this phenomenon occurs in active tactual exploration. Suppose an observer tactually explores an unfamiliar object so as to be able to identify it, while a researcher records the hand and finger movements. The movements are many and varied as the fingers and hands move over the object in complex temporal and spatial patterns. The observer, if asked, has a great deal of difficulty describing his or her exploratory movements, but the object can be identified or described with relative ease. In short, the complexity of the movements is transparent to the object of exploration (Gibson 1966).

PERCEPTION INFLUENCES ACTION

The relation between perception and action can also go in the opposite direction. Researchers have often pointed out that action is based on perception. At one time reflexes (e.g., conditioned reflexes) were proposed as the building blocks of complex behavior. Unconditioned and conditioned reflexes were initiated by the occurrence of a stimulus. So in this simplistic way, action was dependent on perception, at least with respect to the detection of an eliciting stimulus. Then, as researchers began to study the details of complex behavior, it became apparent that much behavior was really not stereotyped reflexive behavior, but behavior that was finely tuned to the environmental situation. It was recognized that complex action was often guided by how well the motor performance matched the intended action, in short by perceptual feedback.

The theoretical concept of an **efferent copy** was one elaboration of the feedback concept. Researchers such as von Holst (1954) and Held (1963) suggested that when a motor command was formulated in the brain and transmitted to the muscles for execution, an "efferent copy" was maintained in the brain for comparison with the perceived result.

In a different vein, Gibson and his students also have demonstrated that action detects (and in some cases even generates) information for its own guidance. A prototypic example is the optical flow stimulation, which is a consequence of a person's own locomotion (Gibson 1979). If a person approaches a surface (or object), there is a regular optical expansion of the retinal image. The rate of expansion in relation to the size of the image specifies when he or she will make contact with the object (Lee 1978).

Gibson was very fond of a saying that captures both directions of the perception-action relationship: we perceive in order to act and we act in order to perceive. The intimate "bi-directional" connection between perception and action is emphasized in this book by Esther Thelen (Chapter 3) when she stresses that perception is not only the detection of external stimuli but also "most importantly the sense of movement and body awareness perceived continuously as we move." It is also apparent in Katherine Nelson's claim (Chapter 6) that children's representations of events do not arise from passive observation of world events but from their active participation in those events. Active participation has a lot of consequences that certainly include sensitizing the child to new information generated by its own actions. In neurophysiological terms, Jon H. Kaas (Chapter 4) reported that prolonged stimulation of a particular type could change the sensory mapping in the brain. He pointed out that this biased sensory stimulation can be generated by an organism's own action, such as monkeys holding their finger tips against a rotating disk or the tactual stimulation obtained by a mother rat nursing her offspring.

COGNITION AND PERCEPTION

Having discussed the pairwise relations between perception and action, let us consider the relations between cognition and perception. Cognition is usually considered to include higher mental processes such as memory, thinking, problem solving, etc.

COGNITION INFLUENCES PERCEPTION

An initial example can again be taken from Berkeley's analysis of prior experience influencing perception. In this case, the reference is to perception of distance on the basis of what is now sometimes called *aerial perspective*. This is the fact that very distant objects often appear faint and blurred while the same objects close by appear sharp and clear. Berkeley suggested that our prior experience with such differences of appearance enables us to infer the distance of new objects without direct knowledge of their distance. The implication is that the cognitive processes of memory and inference guide our perception of distance. As with the relation of perception and action, the relation between cognition and perception is bi-directional. We can ask what the role of cognition in perception is and what the role of perception in cognition is. The aforementioned example from Berkeley concerns how cognition affects perception.

Following Berkeley in regard to size perception, Helmholtz (1925) suggested that the visual perception of object size depends on the perception of its distance. Information about object size based on the size of the retinal image had to be adjusted for perceived distance. However, introspectively our perception of size is immediate; we do not seem to calculate subjectively to correct the image size based on our conscious awareness of distance. Such observations led Helmholtz to the concept of "unconscious inference" by which he meant that perception is an inference. Making inferences can be considered another cognitive process, in this case correcting or combining one sensory input with information from another.

The general impact of this kind of reasoning on psychology was the sharp distinction created between sensation and perception. Perception came to be considered by many as the end result of an inferential or cognitive process, often, as in this case, involving more than detection of sensory stimulation. Thus, one important and persisting view of the relation between perception and cognition is that they are tightly coupled. The implication is that perception is essentially a cognitive process, based on an integration of sensation with memory, thinking, problem solving, and so on. There are some relatively modern vestiges of this conceptualization, for example, in research on size constancy (Leibowitz 1961) and on susceptibility to illusions (Segall et al 1966). In particular, many interpretations in the cross-cultural study of susceptibility to illusions exemplify this legacy.

Consider the Ponzo (railroad track) illusion. In this illusion, two converging lines displayed on a sheet of paper can be perceived as a representation of railroad lines or sides of a road or path going off into the distance. A line segment is placed across these lines where they have converged and are close together. A second parallel line segment of equal size is placed between the lines where they are still far apart. This second line segment is often perceived incorrectly as smaller (shorter) than the first. One explanation for this illusion is that the converging lines are seen as parallel lines going off into the distance. If a bar (line segment) extends across the lines at some far distance and a parallel bar does not extend across the lines at some other near distance, then that second bar must be shorter because the converging lines are perceived as being a representation of parallel lines (Figure 2.1).

This explanation suggests that susceptibility to this illusion depends on perceiving converging lines as parallel lines extending into the distance. Why would a person perceive converging lines this way? One suggestion is that he or she had

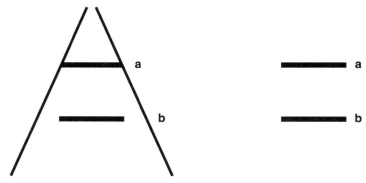

FIGURE 2.1   Ponzo illusion. Line segment *a* is usually perceived as longer than line segment *b* in left panel but not in the right panel.

experience looking down parallel railroad tracks or roads that extend into the distance. The retinal image of such real stimuli takes the form of converging lines. Thus, when a person is shown converging lines on a sheet of paper or artist's canvas, he or she makes the inference (has the perception) of them as parallel lines extending in distance or depth. A person who has grown up in environments in which there are not such features as roads and railroad tracks extending into the distance should be less susceptible to this illusion. Such reasoning led to cross-cultural studies comparing susceptibility among people from different environments. The general idea is that a person's experience with parallel lines that extend in the distance creating linear perspective will influence perception of graphic representations. In other words, memory and inference influence perception. This is an example of how researchers have taken a cognitive perspective on understanding perception; but, in fact, the results of such cross-cultural research did not turn out to support this view (Pick and Pick 1979).

Suppose cognition does strongly influence perception or even that perception is basically a cognitive process. One inference that has been made from time to time is that good perceivers should be smart people and vice versa. Some of the early psychologists were interested in individual differences in intelligence, and perceptual tests were developed as a method of mental measurement (e.g., Galton 1883; Cattell 1890). However, these perceptual tests proved unsatisfactory as measures of intelligence, for adults and even for school-aged children. They were replaced by tests that tapped more transparent cognitive processes, such as those tests in the psychometric tradition of Alfred Binet.

As intelligence tests began to be developed for children in the early part of the 20th century, research on children's cognitive abilities greatly increased. This interest in the early development of intelligence was exemplified by the work of Bayley (1933). Among her many interests was the mental development of very young children. Subsequent results indicated that performance in the first year or two of life showed very little relation with later intelligence measures. However, the measures of intelligence for the very early ages were heavily weighted with sensory-motor items. Bayley (1933) noted these sensory-motor skills may tap very different processes from later mental activities (see also Rosenblith 1992).

Only very recently has there been any success in showing that later intelligence can be predicted by early perceptual functioning. The success comes from studies of infant habituation and dishabituation. Some researchers have found that measures of speed of habituation and subsequent dishabituation show remarkable correlations with later performance on intelligence tests and school performance (e.g., Bornstein 1989; McCall and Carriger 1993).

One other more modern type of research in the information processing tradition may be interpreted as a powerful effect of cognition on perception. This is in the domain of selective attention and/or levels of processing. It is exemplified by the Stroop effect. One of the many ways to test this effect is to ask persons to report the color of the print of words that are displayed on a screen. This is typically a relatively easy task and can be performed quickly (i.e., with a very short reaction time). However, if the printed word itself is a color name of a different color, reaction time increases dramatically as there is great interference in naming the print color. Suppose, for example, the word "green" is printed in red letters. One's reaction time for reporting the color of the letters is considerably slowed. The perceiver in this case seems unable to overcome a level of cognitive processing in reading that is engaged automatically by the printed word. This may be related to Lois Bloom's (Chapter 7) intentionality model of language acquisition. The meaning of the word in a sense takes on a powerful communicating life of its own that interferes with a primitive level of simple sensory processing.

PERCEPTION INFLUENCES COGNITION

Let us consider the other direction in the relation between perception and cognition: the role of perception in cognition. The empirical philosophers (e.g. James Mill, John Stuart Mill, David Hume) who followed Berkeley developed an associationist doctrine of knowledge in which the initial elements were sensations from external stimulation. Vivid or repeated sensations were thought to leave traces of themselves, which were sometimes referred to as **ideas**. Sensations that occurred in frequent temporal contiguity were thought to become associated so that one sensation could arouse the **ideas** of others. Similarly, one idea could arouse other ideas that had frequently occurred with it. Very complex concepts of objects such as houses were considered to be based on the elaborate association of sensations and simple ideas. In essence, this was a doctrine that placed perception at the base of our knowledge and cognition. Early structuralist psychologists like Titchener (1926) adopted this general perspective.

In the developmental arena, Piaget (1952) was the strongest proponent of the view that perception plays a role in cognition. He proposed that cognitive development started with an initial sensory-motor stage. Piaget, along with other astute observers of young infants, was impressed with their sensitivity to stimulation as indicated by their orientation to visual, tactual, and other sensory stimulation. This sensitivity was manifest by movements of the receptor organs, limbs, and body. At first, such movements seemed to be reflexive but quickly became instrumental with primary and secondary circular reactions. Piaget was unique among these researchers in showing how such sensory motor behavior could be the foundation of more abstract cognitive development. A milestone in that direction, which is related to the development of object permanence, was the occurrence and then the resolution of the A-not-B problem. Piaget noted that infants approximately 8 months of age would continue to reach in one location for a hidden object that they had retrieved a number of times from that location, even though they watched the object being hidden in another location. He interpreted this error as evidence that, for infants, the existence of an out-of-sight object was defined at least partially by their interaction with it. Thelen (Chapter 3) presents compelling evidence for an alternative explanation of this error. Nevertheless, for Piaget the error was evidence of a sensory-motor component of cognitive development.

A possibly more radical suggestion for the role of perception in cognition comes from the work of James and Eleanor Gibson. James Gibson (1979) elaborated an ecological approach to visual perception. One aspect of this approach was to identify stimulus information that might underlie our awareness of very complex and possibly abstract aspects of our environment. As an example of this aspect of the approach, Gibson suggested that there might be perceptual information for the continued existence of an object when it was out of sight, for example, for object permanence. He noted that objects go out of sight in various ways. They go so far away that they disappear, other objects occlude them, they evaporate, they explode, and so on. Some of these ways of disappearing are congruent with continued existence and some are not. Gibson suggested that there are distinctive optical transformations that specify, for example, something as disappearing by virtue of being occluded rather than disappearing by going out of existence, such as in an explosion. If a child were sensitive to the information carried by this optical transformation, one would not have to impute a high-level abstract symbolic process. The Gibsons extended and generalized this notion to the concept of **affordance** mentioned previously. The underlying notion is that many complex, meaningful, and functional properties of the world are specified by their stimulus properties. Appreciation of these properties may involve detecting this stimulus information rather than enriching impoverished stimulation by complex cognitive processes (Gibson 1982).

As suggested earlier, one traditional view in psychology was that perception is a cognitive process, that is, sensations are mentally processed and give rise to meaningful perception. The Gibsonian view, that there is stimulus information that specifies complex perception, turns this traditional view upside down. That is, at least some aspects of what we think of as cognition are really perception. With tongue-in-cheek I describe this aspect of the Gibsonian view (to which I subscribe) as one of "perceptual imperialism."

An example of the optical information for an affordance is the optical texture for specifying a surface. But an affordance requires more than just the texture information. Information for the orientation of the texture is also essential. If a horizontal surface is specified there is the possible affordance of support, as with a floor, but if a vertical surface is specified the affordance may be of an obstruction or an enclosure, as with a wall. Surfaces of support and surfaces of enclosure also are specified by tactual and proprioceptive information. Gibson has reported how children just beginning to walk tactually explore surfaces that provide ambiguous optical information for support. Proprioception and active tactual perception almost by definition implicate action. This brings to mind Affolter's description of the sensitivity of some of her children with developmental delays to nearby surfaces. Her analysis emphasizes the relevance of tactual and proprioceptive stimulation to children's action on and interaction with nearby surfaces.

The concept of affordance also provides an avenue for connecting perception with Nelson's (Chapter 6) analysis of event representation. While Nelson emphasizes the role of action in attaining event representation, the affordance concept carries the implication that there is important higher-order perceptual information for events and their structure. The perceptual information from this perspective also involves specification of one's own movements or action. So, let us turn to the pairwise relation between cognition and action.

COGNITION AND ACTION

As with the other pair comparisons in this discussion, cognition and action have a reciprocal relation. What role does action play in cognition, and conversely how is cognition involved in action? Some of the historical perspective has already been addressed. Research concerned with sensory-motor involvement in cognition has as much to do with action and cognition as it does with perception and cognition because much research emphasized motor performance as perceptual sensitivity. Thus, the work of Galton (1883), Cattell (1890), Bayley (1933), and Piaget (1952) would all be relevant here.

ACTION INFLUENCES COGNITION

The general approach of **behaviorism** may be added to this list, although perhaps more on the action side. One way to characterize a behaviorist perspective is that it equates cognition with action (admittedly an oversimplification). That is, the actions are what must be explained, and explanations can be given without the need to infer complex **unobservable** mental processes. If behaviorism is characterized instead as the relation between stimulus and response, then cognition might be whatever that relation is, a sort of modern associationism. (My own view is that behaviorism in the form of stimulus-response (S-R) psychology focused on the association and rarely carried out a deep analysis of the stimulus or the response.)

In the present volume, Jonas Langer's chapter seems most relevant to issues of action and cognition (i.e., cognition broadly viewed as the abstract mental representation of knowledge rather than the processes leading to such representation). His observations and analysis point to how quite abstract cognitive processes can be identified in the way nonverbal organisms, young human children, and nonhuman primates act on objects. In his words, such action may be ". . . going beyond the information given in the environment to transformative operations constructing knowledge." He finds that the manipulatory behavior of human children advances from classifying on the basis of concrete properties to classifying on the basis of the equivalence relations that they have established. Langer's analysis in a sense suggests how action of a sensory motor type manifests and generates abstract cognitive processes. He has carried Piaget's sensory-motor stage to the next level.

COGNITION INFLUENCES ACTION

How is cognition implicated in action? The empiricist philosophers like John Locke, Berkeley, Hume, and others were interested in the origin of knowledge; hence, they focused on the relation between cognition and perception. They did not pay much attention to action. A concern about motor development probably originates in biology and physiology. In terms of physiology, an early discovery was that sensory and motor nerves are separated. Then a further distinction among sensory nerves was captured in the doctrine of "specific nerve energies." On the biology side, following Darwin there was a major interest in animal behavior that led to embryological and ethological approaches. All of this was going on in the latter half of the 19th century and early in the 20th century. This period was followed, as noted previously, by research interest in early motor development in humans in the tradition of Gesell (1933), Halverson (1931), Shirley (1931), McGraw (1935), and others. Much of that work was descriptive in nature and resulted in many age norms.

During the early 20th century, the strong interest in reflexive behavior culminated in Pavlov's discovery and investigation of conditioned reflexes. American behaviorism arose at the same time and evolved into traditional S-R instrumental learning theory. Theorists of the Pavlovian and S-R approaches thought that much complex behavior could be explained by the chaining together of very simple S-R associations. Although association might be considered a minimal form of cognition, it hardly suggests an important place of cognition in action. Moreover, there were at least two telling counterarguments against explanations of complex behavior in terms of chains of simple associations. One was offered by Bernshtein (1947; see also Bernstein 1996), a Russian physiologist. He argued against Pavlovian conditioned reflexes as the basis of complex behavior. His thesis was that complex skillful behavior was characterized by the same resultant behavior being realized in very variable contexts. Thus, a ball throw can occur from all sorts of different arm and body postures, or a step can occur from all sorts of different leg and body postures. However, an invariant reflex movement would have very different consequences depending on the initial conditions of position and the state of the participating limbs.

Lashley (1951) offered another counterargument against conditioned reflexes as the basis for complex behavior. His thesis was that skilled rapid movements such as those of a musician playing a rapid melody (or even the rapid articulation of a fast speaker) could not be a chain of associations because each movement occurred too soon to be a response to the stimulus of the previous movement, that is, it was much faster than any humanly possible reaction time.

As a solution to Lashley's objection, some motor theorists hypothesized the existence of a neural motor program or score. It comprised a series of movements that could be executed in sequence without each individual movement having to be triggered by the previous one. Such an idea has the connotation of a plan that has a much stronger cognitive flavor than an association.

Bernshtein also proposed a theoretical perspective that provided a framework for overcoming his own criticism of associationist theory. His perspective was that motor control was organized in a hierarchical system of levels. The lowest level was that of muscle tone, which provided a substratum for any movement. The next was the joint-muscle level, which essentially set the interrelation of body parts during the execution of any movement. The next level was a spatial level that had to do with the positioning of the body or body parts. Above that was the level of action that had to do with the performance of a **goal-directed** or **functional act**. In the motor performance of a goal-directed act, the actor sets a goal and a general way of accomplishing that goal, which might require a particular spatial configuration of the body. The joint-muscle level would automatically achieve that configuration because of synergetic organization of the joint muscles. Bernshtein's perspective, especially his space and action levels, have a distinctly cognitive flavor.

More recently, cognitive psychology was infused with the information processing perspective, due partially to the advent of the computer age. The brain, like a computer, was considered to have its own hardware structure, but it received input (information) from the environment. That input went through several stages before it was operated on, and then information was stored and used to initiate and control action. Implicit in this simplified characterization is the idea that action is a cognitive (decision-making and problem-solving) process. An analysis and experimental study by Rosenbaum (1980) illustrates the approach. In many natural situations, we may want to pick up an object and move it somewhere. Rosenbaum created an experimental situation that captured some of the properties of this kind of situation. Subjects had to reach for and press one of a set of buttons. The set of buttons was laid out in an arrangement that required subjects on each trial to move either their left or right arm, a shorter or longer distance, in a direction either toward or away from his or her body.

Rosenbaum's experimental data supported an analysis that these components of the movement involved independent decisions. The decisions were made serially with choice of arm requiring the longest time followed in turn by the choice of movement direction, while extent of movement required the least time.

A cognitive role was attributed to action as the information processing approach was applied in developmental research. A traditional task in the study of motor control is that of pursuit tracking in which an observer tries to hold a stylus or cursor on a target that moves in a more or less unpredictable trajectory. Pew and Rupp (1971) investigated developmental changes in performing this kind of task. The children ranged in age from 4th to 10th graders. Improvement with age occurred independently in how quickly the response was made to the target's changing position and in how well a measure reflected the strategies used to track the movement of the stylus. The reaction time changes were attributed to a basic physiological maturation while the strategy changes were interpreted as a manifestation of cognitive development.

Still another developmental example of the information processing approach to the role of cognition in action comes from Gachoud et al's (1983) research on the action of children and adults in lifting small weights by hand. The actual movement patterns did not differ between the children and adults. However, electromyographic recordings from the muscles indicated that children used agonist and antagonist muscles in accomplishing the movements, thus actively producing forces to start and stop the movements. Adults, on the other hand, actively initiated the movements but relied much more on inertial and viscoelastic forces to stop the movement. The interpretation of the results was that the children still did not have a good internal representation of these passive forces that could be exploited for movement control.

CONCLUSION

In sum, historical analysis and research on relations among action, perception, and cognition have been treated in pairwise fashion in psychology. However, there seems to be a more recent shift toward recognizing that these three domains are tightly coupled and need to be treated more integrally. This is evident in the dynamical systems perspective (e.g., Thelen, Chapter 3) in which significant changes in development are considered to result from changes in many components, including motor, perceptual, cognitive, and motoric components.

Why is this shift occurring? To some extent it may be because the pairwise approach is reaching a point of diminishing returns. That is, there is a desire to make our theoretical analyses and experimental research more consistent with the complexities of the real world. In natural situations, action is inextricably bound with perception and cognition, and isolating them is likely to introduce distortions. The social domain is one context in which the complexity of the real world is obvious. Language and communication are central in the social domain.

Thus, the research of Katherine Nelson and Lois Bloom (Chapters 6 and 7) make obvious the need to integrate action, perception, and cognition.

Furthermore, the complexity of the real world becomes particularly obvious when we try to intervene to change behavior in clinical populations. So, the application of research to clinical patients as is done by Félicie Affolter, Walter Bischofberger, and Deborah Hayden (Chapters 8, 9, and 10) makes even more apparent that it is not possible to isolate one or another component of the action/perception/cognition triad.

This is not to say that we understand all about the pairwise relations either. In fact, as mentioned earlier, Affolter's concept of children interacting with (as opposed to simply acting on) physical surfaces has not been deeply explored. Similarly, Jonas Langer's analysis of action promoting cognition and the research described by Kaas of action altering the physiological basis of perception show that there is much to be learned from careful analysis and observation of the pair relations.

Nevertheless, the empirical evidence for the reciprocal relationships revealed by the pairwise comparisons in this chapter imply that perception and cognition are tightly coupled, and action is tightly coupled with perception and cognition. So there is the potential to model the interrelations among all three components. Optimistically, the contribution of the previous and future research on the pairwise relations is likely to contribute to achieving such integration.

REFERENCES

Bayley, N. 1933. Mental growth during the first three years: A developmental study of sixty-one children by repeated tests. *Gene Psychol Monogr* 14:1–92.

Bergenn, V.W., Dalton, T.C., and Lipsitt, L.P. 1992. Myrtle B. McGraw: A growth scientist. *Dev Psychol* 28:381–389.

Berkeley, G. 1709. *An Essay Towards a New Theory of Vision* (2nd ed.). Dublin, Ireland: A. Rhames.

Bernshtein, N.A. 1947. O postroienii dvizhenii (On the structure of movements). Moscow: Medgiz.

Bernstein, N.A. 1996. On Dexterity and its Development. In Latash, M.L., and Turvey, M.T. (Editors), *Dexterity and its Development* (pp. 1–244). Hillsdale, NJ: Erlbaum.

Bornstein, M.H. 1989. Stability in early mental development: From attention and information processing in infancy to language and cognition in childhood. In Bornstein, M.H., and Krasnegor, N.A., (Editors), *Stability and Continuity in Mental Development: Behavioral and Biological Perspectives* (pp. 147–170). Hillsdale, NJ: Erlbaum.

Cattell, J.M. 1890. Mental tests and measurements. *Mind* 15:373–381.

Galton, F. 1883. *Inquiries into Human Faculty and its Development*. London, England: Macmillan.

Gesell, A. 1933. Maturation and the patterning of behavior. In Murchison, C. (Editor), *Handbook of Child Psychology* pp. 209–235. Worcester, MA: Clark University Press.

Gesell, A. and Thompson, H. 1929. Learning and growth in identical infant twins: An experimental study by the method of co-twin control. *Gene Psychol Monogr* 6:1–124.

Gibson, J.J. 1966. *The Senses Considered as Perceptual Systems*. New York: Houghton Mifflin.

Gibson, J.J. 1979. *The Ecological Approach to Visual Perception*. Boston: Houghton-Mifflin.

Gibson, E.J. 1982. The concept of affordances in development: The renascence of functionalism. In Collins, W.A. (Editor), *The Concept of Development: The minnesota symposium on child psychology*, Vol. 15. Hillsdale, NJ: Erlbaum.

Hall, G.S. 1893. *The Contents of Children's Minds on Entering School.* New York: E.L. Kellogg & Co.

Halverson, H.M. 1931. An experimental study of prehension in human infants by means of systematic cinema records. *Gene Psychol Monogr* 10:107–283.

Held, R. 1963. Plasticity in human sensori-motor control. *Science* 142:455–462.

Helmholtz, H.V. 1925. *Handbook of Physiological Optics,* Volume III. (Translated by J.P.C. Southall). New York: Optical Society of America.

Lashley, K.S. 1951. The problem of serial order in behavior. In Jeffress, L.A., (Editor), *Cerebral mechanisms in behavior* (pp. 112–146). New York: John Wiley and Sons.

Lee, D.N. 1978. The functions of vision. In Pick Jr., H.L. and Saltzman, E., (Editors), *Modes of Perceiving and Processing Information.* Hillsdale, NJ: Erlbaum.

Leibowitz, H. 1961. Apparent visual size as a function of distance for mentally deficient subjects. *Am J Psychol* 74:98–100.

Liberman, A.M., Cooper, F.S., Shankweiler, D.P., and Studdert-Kennedy, M. 1967. Perception of the speech code. *Psychol Rev* 74:431–461.

McCall, R.B., and Carriger, M.S. 1993. A metaanalysis of infant habituation and recognition memory performance as predictors of later IQ. *Child Dev* 64:57–79.

McGraw, M.B. 1935. *Growth: A Study of Johnny and Jimmy.* New York: Appleton-Century.

Gachoud, J.P., Mounoud, P., Hauert, C.A., and Viviani, P. 1983. Motor strategies in lifting movements: A comparison of adult and child performance. *J Motor Behav* 15:202–216.

Pew, R.W. and Rupp, G.L. 1971. Two quantitative measures of skill development *J Exp Psychol* 90:1–7.

Piaget, J. 1952. *The Origins of Intelligence in Children.* New York: International Universities Press.

Pick, A.D., and Pick, H.L., Jr. 1979. Cross cultural studies of perception. In Carterette, E.C., and Friedman, M.P., (Editors), *Handbook of Perception,* Vol. IX. New York: Academic Press.

Preyer, W.T. 1887. *L'ame de L'enfant: Observations sur le D'eveloppement.* Paris, France: Ancienne Librarie Germer Bailliere et Cie.

Rosenblith, J.F. 1992. A singular career: Nancy Bayley. *Dev Psychol* 28:747–758.

Rosenbaum, D.A. 1980. Human movement initiation: Specification of arm, direction, and extent. *J Exp Psychol: Gen* 109:444–474.

Segall, M.H., Campbell, D.T., and Herskovitz, M.J. 1966. *The Influence of Culture on Visual Perception.* Indianapolis, IN: Bobbs-Merrill Co.

Shirley, M. 1931. The sequential method for the study of maturing behavior patterns. *Psychol Rev* 38:507–528.

Spalding, D.A. 1873. Instinct: With original observations on young animals. *MacMillan's Magazine* 27:282–293. Reprinted in *Br J Anim Behav* 1954, 2:1–11.

Thelen, E. and Adolph, K. 1992. Arnold L. Gesell: The paradox of nature and nurture. *Dev Psycny* 28:368–380.

Titchener, E.B. 1926. *A Textbook of Psychology.* New York: Macmillan Co.

Von Holst, E.V. 1954. Relations between the central nervous system and the peripheral organs. *British J Anim Behav* 2:89–94.

Zaporozhets, A.V. 1957. The development of voluntary movements. In Simon, B., (Editor), *Psychology in the Soviet Union* (pp. 108–114). Stanford, CA: Stanford University Press.

Zinchenko, V.P., Chzhi-tsin, V., and Tarakanov, V.V. 1962. Stanovlenie i razvitie pertsivnykh deistvii. [Formation and development of perceptive behavior.] *Voprosii Psikologii* 8:1–14.

3

THE CENTRAL ROLE OF ACTION IN TYPICAL AND ATYPICAL DEVELOPMENT: A DYNAMIC SYSTEMS PERSPECTIVE

ESTHER THELEN, PHD

Every year, tens of thousands of children are diagnosed with a developmental disorder. Most will receive some sort of therapeutic intervention in the form of speech, physical, or occupational therapy; counseling; behavioral treatments; or drugs. What sorts of interventions are appropriate for which children? One organizing theme of this book is that clinical interventions should be informed by good science and undertaken with a strong theoretical and empirical basis: atypical development can best be understood by considering the nature of development in general. In this chapter, I argue that a dynamic systems approach to development provides such a theoretical and empirical foundation. More specifically, the dynamic view considers bodily movement as a central mechanism in development, co-equal with the processes of perception and cognition and indeed inseparable from them. This means that the foundations of complex human thought and behavior have their origins in action and are always embedded in a history of acting. Thus, I also suggest that many of the problems associated with developmental delays or disorders may have common origins in deficits of basic perceptual-motor processes that distort childrens' interactions with the world around them, and that these deficits can cascade into serious problems in functioning.

I support this view by the detailed consideration of perseverative reaching, a single, intriguing phenomenon seen in 8- to 10-month-old infants. Although at first glance the behavior seems amusing or even trivial, my colleagues and I have used it as a window to view the mechanisms by which behavior emerges, becomes stable, and changes. We believe that by a full understanding of the complex dynamics of this task, we can more completely understand how normal development happens, and thus, how developmental processes also can go awry.

THE NATURE OF DEVELOPMENT

Developmental psychologists are still working on an age-old problem that has intrigued philosophers and scientists for thousands of years. How can children and adults develop such rich mental lives from such simple beginnings? Consider what newborn infants can do. They can suck, look, sleep, cry, and thrash around. However, their visual worlds are limited, and they have virtually no control of their limbs or head. Although a baby looks nothing like a poet, a warrior, or a scientist, everyone knows that each poet, warrior, and scientist began as this seemingly simple creature.

We owe to the Swiss developmental psychologist and philosopher, Jean Piaget, our understanding of the continuity between the early so-called "sensorimotor activities" of infants and later skilled, intentional action and thought. Piaget (1952; 1954) believed that the everyday activities of infants and young children were incorporated into the structures of mind. Through their actions on the environment, some of them initiated by chance, infants gradually absorbed the logical structure and cause-and-effect nature of the world around them. These activities, Piaget claimed, changed the structure of the child's mind in profound ways. At first, infants only know the world through their actions on it. They live in the here and now and cannot plan, think abstractly, or represent what they cannot perceive. At approximately 18 months, according to Piaget, there is a qualitative change that allows symbolic representation and a kind of logical reasoning. At ages 5 or 6, children reach another plateau in mental complexity in which they are no longer deceived by their senses and can make higher-level logical inferences. Only at the time of adolescence are children able to reason in a formally logical and abstract manner. At all points in this gradual process, according to Piaget, children are assimilating the structure of the environment and using it to reorganize the operations of their minds.

We cannot underestimate Piaget's legacy, in my view. Two of his insights have been particularly influential for our understanding of the nature of development. First, there is his belief in the continuity of development that even the most abstract human abilities had to evolve from precursors in a very systematic way. The second, was Piaget's emphasis on the importance of the child's own activity in this process. Piaget's formulation of child-environment interaction was much deeper than simple acknowledgement that both organism and environment interact. Rather, he showed in great detail how children used their perception and actions in the world to construct mental life, and how, in turn, these new structures changed children's subsequent actions. In this chapter, I also focus on the child's activity (the actual movement) as part and parcel of cognitive development.

Despite Piaget's monumental achievements as a developmental theorist, his theory has been strongly criticized. The heart of the criticism is that Piaget underestimated the mental capacities of infants. For example, Piaget (1952) claimed that before 8 or 10 months, children do not understand that objects still exist when they are hidden from sight: they cannot think abstractly about an "object concept" in the absence of the object itself. But others have claimed that by testing infants with different tasks, they can show that infants do have a concept of objects many months earlier and that Piaget's gradualist account is not correct (e.g., Baillargeon and DeVos 1991). Indeed, some of these contemporary theorists believe that human mental life and language are so complex that they could not have developed in each individual from perception and action. Rather, they believe that infants are born with particular core principles about the nature of the world and about the structure of language, mathematics, and logic (e.g., Spelke et al 1992; Pinker 1994). Such innate modules may be enriched by experience, but they are not created by it. Thus, there is a real, ongoing, and deep division among those who study development as to its fundamental nature.

WHY THEORY MATTERS

Are these theoretical issues relevant? This version of the perennial "nature vs. nurture" debate does have implications for how we understand atypical development and thus how we intervene to change or modify it. A good example is how developmental psychologists view children with autism. As is well known, these children have profound difficulties with normal social relationships. They are often unable to participate in the verbal and nonverbal aspects of normal social dialogue; they seem obsessively self-absorbed or focused on inanimate objects and display socially inappropriate behavior. Forty years ago, it was widely believed that their mothers' cold and rejecting behavior was the source of childrens' autism (Bettelheim 1972). Implicit in this view was that the early emotional environment was so critical that it could produce permanent damage. Today, one well-accepted theory about children with autism is that they are born lacking a particular module in their brains, the part responsible for developing a "theory of mind" (Baron-Cohen 1995). A "theory of mind" is that ability to understand how another person thinks, and a "theory of mind" module is a dedicated brain structure used for this purpose. The theoretical assumption here is that social behavior has a strong innate component and that the environment is not as critical.

When mothers were deemed at fault, therapists removed children from their homes. Alternatively, if a therapist believes that the core problem is a missing brain module, he or she might choose an intervention focused only on that aspect of the child's behavior or may decide that such a brain lesion means that no intervention is possible. Parents and friends may likewise decide that the person with autism is so deficient in social understanding that he or she cannot benefit from normal discourse. In short, how one views the etiology of a disorder—and one's implicit or explicit theories of development—can profoundly alter how one treats a child.

A DYNAMIC SYSTEMS THEORY

What is an appropriate and useful theory, given that our explicit and implicit theories of development matter in everyday interactions with typically developing children and with children with developmental problems?

Development is first and foremost about change. Change can happen over many different timescales. When we think about development, we usually imagine changes over months and years. We are, however, equally interested in a shorter timescale of change, such as when a child repeats an interesting action, or when, over the course of the day, a baby takes his or her first halting steps. Most important, we are concerned with how these different timescales of change interact. That is, how do everyday second-by-second activities create and influence changes over a longer time span? How these activities do so impacts directly on intervention. Any intervention is based on the premise that activities in the here and now will affect long-term change. Thus, a useful developmental theory must account for the final outcome of development and for the mechanisms that enable change.

Likewise, a good developmental theory must encompass all outcomes, individual and atypical, as well as those that are universal and typical. The basic principles of development apply in every case, although the initial conditions may be different and environments may vary greatly. For example, I show in this chapter that there are circumstances in which behavioral options are limited and circumstances in which children seem free to explore new options. A dynamic systems theory addresses these issues of mechanism and outcome.

A METAPHOR

All theories are metaphoric. Metaphors help us make the bridge from the phenomenon to the theory. Piaget, for instance, gave children certain kinds of problems to solve and then described mental structures in terms of logical formalisms. His metaphor for the human mind was a system of Western logical thought. When other theorists speak of "language modules" or "mathematics modules," their implicit metaphor is one of machines composed of interchangeable parts, like a computer.

The metaphor behind development as a dynamic system is different. It must encompass notions of continuous change and flow. I like to picture a mountain stream. Why is this a good metaphor for human development? First, a mountain stream is dynamic; it is moving all the time. Development is itself continuous—whatever happened in the past influences what happens in the future. However, the stream also has patterns. We can see whirlpools, eddies, and waterfalls as well as places where the water is moving rapidly and places where it is still. Like the stream, development also has recognizable patterns, including milestones and plateaus and ages and stages where behavior is predictable. In the mountain stream, there are no programs or instructions constructing those patterns. There is just water. The patterns arise from the water and natural parts of the stream and the environment, such as the stream bed, the rocks, the flow of the water, the current temperature, and the wind. These patterns reflect the immediate conditions of the stream and the history of the whole system, including the snowfall on the mountain last winter, the conditions on the mountain last summer, and the entire geological history of the region, which determined the incline of the stream and its path through the mountain.

Development also has these system properties. How a child behaves depends not only on the immediate current situation but also on his or her continuous short-term and long-term history of acting, the social situation, and the biological constraints he or she was born with. Every action has within it the traces of previous behavior. Two questions to ask, therefore, are these: how dominant and strong are the old patterns and how do they interact with the new situation?

There is another way in which development is like a mountain stream. Depending on the conditions of the stream, a similar action may have different results. Thus, if I throw a rock into a deep pool, the pool may be disturbed by ripples for a short time, but it will remain largely unchanged. The same rock tossed into a shallow part may divert the stream completely, with consequences further down stream. Developmental patterns also show this kind of nonlinearity. Therefore it is difficult, and maybe impossible, to predict the outcome of the process for any child in any particular situation. Sometimes chance events have large consequences; at other times, they have little impact. The same event in the family or the school may have vastly different effects on different children. Some children are resilient to what seem to be very damaging environments, while others grow up with problems despite a privileged background. A theory must be able to handle both the predictable aspects of development and those aspects that surprise us.

TWO PRINCIPLES OF DYNAMIC SYSTEMS THEORY

A dynamic approach to development is based on more general theories governing pattern formation in complex physical and biological systems (Thelen and Ulrich 1991; Smith and Thelen 1993; Thelen and Smith 1994; Kelso 1995; Port and van Gelder 1995). The science of these complex systems has gained popularity under the name *chaos theory*. Chaos theory is based on the notion that, under certain thermodynamic conditions, collections of many, often heterogeneous, parts appear to self-organize to produce ordered patterns without any particular part having a code or recipe for the pattern. Common examples range from clouds and fluid-flow systems to communities of one-celled organisms through elaborate ecosystems and social systems. Nothing gives directions, yet the whole system has an order over time. New systems of mathematics have been developed to describe the behavior of such complex systems. They are nonlinear in the sense that, depending on the conditions, large changes in the system may be generated by small differences, and they are dynamic in the sense that they are continuous in time.

Complexity

The first useful principle from the science of complex systems is the notion of complexity. Human behavior, whether mental activity or overt movement, is the product of many interacting parts, which, under particular task and social and environmental constraints, work together to produce a coherent pattern. Every behavior is the condensation of these heterogeneous components. For instance, when I walk across the room, you could describe my behavior rather well with only a few variables, like the relationships of phasing of my legs and arms. Yet, those relatively few variables contain within them highly complex physiological, mental, and metabolic processes interacting with the surface of the floor, the ambient light, and so on. All of the components are co-equal in producing the behavior. Just as my gait may change if I develop arthritis in my knee, it must also change if the floor is highly polished and slippery.

This idea that "everything counts" in producing behavior has profound implications for how we conceptualize developmental causality. In particular, we must reconsider any single-cause explanation, be it organic or environment. Instead, we must focus on interactions and entertain the possibility that the interactions are nonlinear. This means that it may not be easy to find a clear causal chain from previous conditions to a later outcome and that the contributions to that outcome may be unexpected.

I am particularly interested in the contributions of movement and perception in the production and development of behavior. By perception I mean the detection of external stimuli as in vision or audition and, most importantly, the senses of movement and body awareness perceived continually as we move. These include kinesthetic senses generated by muscle, joint, and tendon receptors as well as those from skin deformations or tactual input.

People perceive and move continually during every waking minute. Yet, in most psychological accounts, the roles of perception and especially movement are considered secondary to mental activities. I propose here, based on principles of dynamics, that mental activities are not only founded in perception and action but are part of the causal web of behavior throughout life. Moreover, I suggest that even small difficulties with these processes early in life can have life-long consequences.

Dynamic Stability

The second principle of dynamic systems important for development is the concept of dynamic stability. When complex systems organize into patterns, the patterns may have different degrees of stability and flexibility. Some human behavior is so stable and reliable, we are tempted to say it is programmed in. For example, all human children who are not seriously damaged learn to walk and to speak a language. Some have argued that because of their universality, walking and language are genetically or developmentally programmed. From a dynamic systems point of view, the question does not lie with whether a behavior is wired-in or learned, it lies with understanding a behavior's stability. Walking and speaking are so constrained by human structure and social system, they are highly stable behavior patterns.

But stability does not mean immutability. Even in highly practiced actions, stability is dynamic. Patterns are assembled and maintained "softly," on line and in response to the context (Kugler and Turvey 1987). Because these patterns are the confluence of many components, they also can be flexible, able to shift and rearrange as befits the situation. For example, I can walk across the room wearing high-heeled shoes or with a brace on my leg while carrying on a conversation. Walking is resistant to many perturbations in me or in my environment. On the other hand, I could also tap-dance across the room, but it would not be a very stable behavior. To tap dance, I would have to concentrate, and I could not do it with a brace or while talking. I would need to practice every day to maintain the steps, and if I were to hear the fire alarm while shuffling, I would quickly revert to my more stable form of locomotion. The old, practiced behavior would be rapidly assembled, and walking would dominate the novel pattern.

I see development as this process of assembling patterns of behavior to meet the demands of the task within the biological possibilities of the child at that time. Sometimes the behaviors are stable for a time, that is, they are easily elicited and frequently performed. Then, other behaviors emerge and the old ones become less available or preferred. In this sense, children are always problem-solving, using what they have to perform some action that is intrinsically rewarding or pleasurable for them. Development is thus the product of the child's daily and continual efforts to make things happen in the world.

Consider the behavior of crawling on hands and knees. In the classic views of motor development, crawling is seen as an important developmental stage in the progression to upright locomotion, a stage which reflects the maturation of the voluntary centers of the brain over the spinal and subcortical areas (McGraw 1945). (Some have even imagined crawling as an ontogenetic throwback to our quadrupedal ancestors.) In a dynamic view, crawling is an on-line solution that babies individually discover when they want to get to something that they cannot reach but when they lack the balance control and strength needed for upright walking. It is an opportunistic assembly of the components, resulting in a temporarily stable and useful pattern. For many months, it becomes infants' preferred mode of self-transport. Infants often begin crawling using a variety of patterns of limb coordination, but they soon settle on their own mode, which is usually an alternating pattern among the four limbs. But some infants find and use a "combat crawl," using hands, feet, and the belly, while others maintain an idiosyncratic asymmetric gait. As infants gain experience in the balance of standing alone and shifting their weight, they venture to step forward, and the preferred mode of transport shifts to walking. However, when infants are new walkers, it is common to see them revert back to crawling when the surface is unfamiliar or when they want to move quickly to get a desired toy. The crawling pattern does not disappear; for example, adults may choose to crawl under certain circumstances, but crawling is supplanted by the more efficient upright mode.

If infants have physical or mental limitations, they may not have the balance control to assume an upright posture. If crawling works, then infants with physical or mental limitations may continue to crawl. Failure to walk is not a "delay" in the sense that the whole system is stalled in the progression to upright locomotion. Rather, crawling is like a default option; it is a choice to keep using a pattern that fits the task and is available.

There are other atypical behavior patterns that also can be viewed as adaptive solutions that use the child's available resources. For example, some have suggested that the spasticity associated with cerebral palsy is a learned response to poor motor control (O'Dwyer and Ada 1996). If a brain lesion interrupts the normal motor pathways, muscle agonist-antagonist balance is disrupted, and movements are impossible to predict and control. In such a situation, a reasonable adaptive response is to stiffen all the muscles to provide stability in, for instance, position of the head or movements of the arm. Indeed, people without physical problems use this solution when learning a new task (e.g., a good way to keep from falling over when learning to ice-skate is to stiffen the muscles around the leg and ankle). (Of course all this muscle effort is very tiring, and, after a while, your legs begin to ache.) But some control, however inefficient, is better than none. Likewise, if a child with autism begins life with serious perceptual deficiencies and distortions, as many have suggested, one way to adaptively deal with a world that is intrusively unpatterned is to avoid the input altogether. This may lead to social withdrawal or repetitive or self-stimulatory behavior, which replaces the chaotic perceptual world with a predictable one.

The hallmark of typical development is that the patterns which coalesce to meet tasks are so fluid and flexible that they can be replaced when new solutions are possible. Walking replaces crawling. Complex sentences emerge after simple ones. Cooperative play increases as parallel play decreases. But one important feature of all atypical development is that children do not have such flexibility. Patterns that are initially adaptive may become so habitual that the child cannot shift into new ones. Thus, a child who has spent his or her waking hours contracting muscles to provide some stability for posture and movement may learn stiff muscles so completely that other options are unavailable. A child with distorted and disturbing visual and auditory perception may learn to avoid troublesome social interactions so well that this behavior persists even when the perceptual issues may not be relevant.

In dynamic terms, the patterns of behavior act like attractors with varying degrees of stability. When a pattern is stable, easily performed, not very variable, and not easily perturbed, the degrees of freedom in the system form a deep attractor. Attractors are so named because such patterns tend to pull into them or attract other patterns. For example, a 180-degree alternation of the legs is such a deep, stable attractor that any tendency to walk at say, 160 degrees, will be damped out. We might be able to walk at 160 degrees with years of practice. One way for attractors to become very stable is through repetition (Zanone and Kelso 1991). Children with difficulties may find a solution and repeat it so often and under so many circumstances that the attractors become very deep. When new circumstances arise, they cannot assemble a new pattern. Interventions must then compete with old habits, which may be very stable indeed. We need to ask, therefore, what led to the old habits, how stable they are, and how we can use the current circumstances to increase adaptive flexibility.

I have outlined how two concepts from a dynamic theory of development—complexity and dynamic stability—can help explain typical and atypical patterns of development. In the remainder of the chapter, I support these ideas with descriptive and experimental studies. I show at a micro-level how development can lead to either flexibility or "stuckness," depending on the long-term and immediate history of the child as well as the context of the behavior.

A NEW LOOK AT AN OLD TASK

To illustrate this developmental story, I use a classic task in developmental psychology, probably one of the most widely studied tasks in infancy. The task was discovered by Piaget in his observations of his own children's reactions to objects in the world (Piaget 1952). As is well known, young infants act as though they do not know that an object exists when it is out of sight. Thus, 6- or 7-month-old infants will reach eagerly for a toy, but if the parent hides the toy behind a pillow, as did Piaget, the babies lose interest completely and do not search for the toy. A month or so later, infants will lift the pillow and recover the hidden toy.

It is the next stage in Piaget's series of the development of the object concept that has intrigued so many researchers. At approximately 8 months of age, infants will uncover the toy when it is hidden at one location, called A, but if the hiding event is then switched to a second nearby location, called B, infants will resolutely search at the first place where they recovered the toy. Even as they watch the toy being hidden at B, they switch back to A. Piaget called this the "A-not-B error" and ever since, this name has been used to describe this perseverative behavior. Piaget's explanation for the A-not-B error was that infants in this transition stage only understood that objects existed in places where they had just acted upon them. That is, the concept of object was so fragile that it was associated with the visual percept of the location of the action.

Since Piaget's original observations, researchers have conducted dozens and dozens of experiments exploring the A-not-B error (see reviews by Acredolo

1985; Bremner 1985; Wellman et al 1986; Harris 1987; Diamond 1990; Munakata 1998; Marcovitch and Zelazo 1999; Smith et al 1999; and Thelen et al 2001). The general conclusion is that the error is entirely robust and reproducible when experiments are conducted in a certain way, but infants do not make the A-not-B error when the conditions are altered. In the canonical task, an infant faces two identical covers or hiding wells, placed several inches apart. The investigator attracts the infant's interest in a small toy and then trains the baby to uncover the toy by first presenting the toy near the hiding place, partially covered, and then fully hidden. When the infant can do this, the investigator then hides the toy at location "A" several times and encourages the infant to recover it. Then the investigator switches the hiding to the "B" location, making sure that the infant sees the toy as it hidden. After the toy is hidden, the investigator imposes a delay of a few seconds, sometimes distracting the infant's attention from the hiding place. The infant is then allowed to reach. Under these conditions, approximately 80% of infants from 8 to 10 months reach back to the A location, hence the term *perseverative reaching*.

What has made this simple infant task so intriguing, however, is not just the puzzling perseveration but also the fragility of the response when the situation of the experiment changes. Infants will not make the location error, that is, they will reach correctly or at least randomly when the two hiding places are quite distinct from one another when there is no delay between the hiding and reaching, when there are only a few trials at the A location, or even when an especially appealing object, such as a cookie, is hidden at the B location. If infants' performance on this task were simply a matter of their knowledge about the permanence of objects, then these contextual changes should not be so critical. Indeed, in the last two decades, researchers have sometimes recast the A-not-B error as a problem in spatial localization or memory as well as in the classic Piagetian framework of object representation.

A DYNAMIC SYSTEMS APPROACH

When my colleague Linda Smith and I were writing our 1994 book, *A Dynamic Systems Approach to the Development of Cognition and Action*, we wanted to apply the principles of dynamic systems to a new task, one that had a more cognitive component than the motor tasks we had previously described. Piaget's A-not-B error seemed a likely candidate because it had been so thoroughly studied but remained essentially unexplained. We set forth a conceptual model in the book and since then have implemented and expanded it with experiments and a mathematical model. We have even shown that the model works on a robot!

As I describe the model and experiments in considerable detail, keep in mind that my colleagues and I intended a careful dissection of this simple task to show the power of a dynamic systems approach (Smith et al 1999; Thelen et al 2001). We believe that the task is a window on more general developmental processes and that a similar type of explanation can be applied to any behavioral task; the principles are the same. Moreover, my colleagues and I are convinced that one useful way to understand development is to know the dynamics of a given task, a behavior that happens in a short time and can be experimentally manipulated. This gave us a way to probe the mechanisms of change in a dynamic system. What elements of this simple task are stable and which ones undergo developmental change? In a similar manner, the understanding of these basic mechanisms may give us insight into atypical development. What are the components that may be derailed? How can changes in one aspect of the task impact on performance at a later time?

The A-not-B is About Reaching

A grounding assumption of this model is that the puzzling perseverative behavior seen in 8- to 12-month-old infants emerges from the same processes that produce reaching for objects in general (Smith et al 1999; Thelen et al 2001). In other words, we want to situate this "error" as part of normal perceptual, motor, and cognitive development. This is similar to Piaget's interpretation that the A-not-B error emerged as a normal stage in infants' object representation. But unlike Piaget, my colleagues and I show that there is no single "cause" for perseverative reaching. Whether infants reach perseveratively or not results from a confluence of the child's own organic status, level of skill, the task conditions, and the child's history of acting in the particular situation and in similar situations in the past. These elements interact dynamically; that is, over time, and in nonlinear ways. Nonetheless, we can model these dynamics precisely and predict the outcomes of novel experiments. Moreover, my colleagues and I show that the task is deeply "embodied" and influenced not just by the visual perceptual scene, but also by the child's movement and movement sense. In this chapter, I argue that if A-not-B is so embodied, then it is likely that all other tasks that involve such interactions with the world must also be embodied.

A Task Analysis

The A-not-B error can be conceptualized as a behavior that arises from the confluence of the ordinary processes of looking, deciding, reaching, and remembering. First, infants look at the task layout. In the typical case, this consists of two identical target places, usually cloths or lids to hiding wells, placed 6 to 8 inches apart. This task layout provides a more or less continuous input to the infant, indicating the two choices, reach to A or reach to B. In a similar manner, there is always a rather consistent visual environment within which we all make action choices. Shall I reach for the almost-cold cup of coffee sitting on my desk? In the A-not-B, experiment, the investigator then provides additional visual and auditory cues to the child as to the desirability of the toy and about the place where the toy will be hidden. This is a transient cue that the infant sees for only a few seconds. Then the investigator sometimes imposes a time delay. In everyday behavior, these cues may be **external** (The doorbell rings. Do I answer it or pretend I am not at home?) or **internal** (I crave coffee. Do I reach for it even though it is cold?). In many cases, these cues also may be rather fleeting, especially in relation to the saliency of the other aspects of the perceptual world.

If there is a delay between a cue to act and the action itself, the cue must be remembered. Sometimes it is not. (Something in the environment or my intentions compelled me to walk to the kitchen. I am in the kitchen. Why am I here?) In the time between the cue and the action itself, the person must make an action decision. Do I reach to A or to B? Do I reach to the coffee cup or to the computer mouse? This decision is not only a function of the cue (interesting toy? thirsty? guilty?) but also of my past history. Both the baby and I come into our situations with a set of expectations built from past experiences. The baby has enjoyed mouthing toys in the past. I have savored the taste of coffee. Thus, for any task, daily life or experimental condition, an action decision is the condensation of multiple factors that have influence over multiple timescales.

Equally important is that once the action decision is executed (i.e., the infant reaches to A or to B, or I do drink that cold coffee), that action is remembered and, in turn, influences subsequent decisions. Thus, my immediate past history contributes to the next action, and so on. Some actions have a strong memory trace and others do not. Again, the decision is a function of the varying strengths of the inputs, including those contained in the systems from past experiences. In this way, everyday actions cascade to form a rich and complex internal context that includes not only the consequences of the action but also its execution in movement and perception.

By this account, then, infants produce the A-not-B error because they face a task context that is somewhat novel and confusing to them since they are faced with two identical targets. They are enticed to choose one target to reach to by the investigator's attention-getting activities at that target. This pulls their decision to the A side, and they set the appropriate muscle synergies in motion. When they have reached once to A, however, the memory of the A reach lingers long enough to exert influence on the next decision. One reach to the A side gives a slight bias to the A decision. This memory bias grows as the investigator continually cues the A side. After a number of A side reaches, the target is switched. Now the infant gets a transient cue to the B side. Because of the child's internal dynamics, the memory of the B cue fades, but the memory of the A reaches does not. Over a short delay, therefore, the A memory competes with the B cue and it wins out. Infants reach back to A. This mechanism is illustrated in Figure 3.1.

This account is dynamic because the processes that lead to the reach decision are continuous in time and continuously meshed together. The ultimate behavior is a function of these time dynamics and the relative strengths of the components that interact. Note that this is a cognitive act because it requires memory and decision making, but it is also a perceptual-motor one. In the next section, I describe a series of experiments that support this claim.

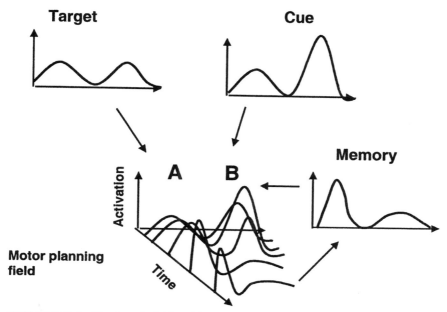

FIGURE 3.1   The dynamic field model of the A-not-B error. The motor planning field is conceptualized as a continuous space of activation sites representing the abstract parameters needed to plan a reach to the A location or to the B location. The field receives various inputs and then integrates them to form a single decision. This requires that the visual inputs from the task (upper left, representing two identical targets at A and B), the cue (upper right, a cue to B), and the memory of the previous reaches (many reaches to A) be in the same parameter space. This figure shows what happens when, after many reaches to A, which have built up a strong memory to the A location, the infant receives the cue to B. In the field, the B cue is transient and fades, while over the short delay, the A-side memory dominates. The infant reaches back to A.

An Embodied A-not-B

I have claimed that the A-not-B error arises from the multiple processes that produce the act of reaching for objects and not from the purely cognitive aspect of the object concept, the mental representation of the hidden toy. In Smith et al (1999), we reported a critical experiment. We eliminated the hidden toy altogether. Instead, we repeated the same sequences of events using only the always-visible "lid" to the hiding well as the targets. Here, the investigator simply waved the lid to catch the infant's attention, placed it on the table, and allowed the infant to reach. After the infant reached several times to the A side, the investigator cued the B lid. Infants reached as eagerly for the always-visible lid as for the toy when it was hidden in the well, and they perseverated (reached to A when B was cued) at the same rates as when a toy was actually hidden. Indeed, in many subsequent experiments in which we and others compared performance, infants' behavior without the hidden toy was no different than when the toy was hidden.

Why do infants perseverate in this reaching task? We proposed that this behavior was dynamically emergent from a confluence of the multiple factors that produce reaching in general. We have been systematically testing these factors. The picture that emerges is of a deeply embodied behavior.

Remembering

The dynamic perspective states that behavior is created within the special circumstances of the task itself. In other words, perseveration is not an inevitable response of infants at a particular age. Rather, it emerges as a result of the interaction of the structure of the task and the developmental status of the infants.

In particular, the structure of a typical A-not-B task involves repetition, as infants are always cued more than once to the A side. This repetition is critical because it is the memory of the A reaches that sets up the conditions for perseveration. Specifically, we proposed that repeated reaching to the A side creates a kind of habit. Each reach to A is remembered, and that memory biases the infant's next action. A straightforward prediction of this assumption is that the more reaches to the A target, the more likely infants would perseverate when tested at the B target. In Smith et al (1999), my colleagues and I tested this prediction directly. Infants who reached one or three times to A did not reliably perseverate, while infants who reached five times did. In other experiments, we also showed that individual infants who consistently reached to A on the A trials continued to reach to A on the B trials. Those who, for whatever reason, reached to B on the A trials were more likely to stay at B on the B trials.

The A-not-B task is thus a good window on how such habits are formed. What are the factors that lead to repeating an old behavior, even in the face of new information? Why does a behavior become stable, and what conditions disrupt that stability? This question is critical because clinical interventions for atypically developing children involve as much disrupting of old habits as encouraging new behavior.

Looking

One factor that contributes to perseveration is looking. Babies (and adults) reach where they look. In a series of experiments, we asked how *what* the infants looked at and *where* they looked influenced whether they reached to target A or to target B.

First, in one set of experiments, my colleagues and I manipulated the saliency of the visual targets to the A or B locations (Diedrich et al 2001). In everyday life, certain distinct or novel objects or events capture our attention. This is also true of infants. But infants also are not usually faced with two identical targets. We hypothesized that one reason that infants made the A-not-B error was their confusion when facing the novel two-target task. Previous experiments by others and our model predicted that if the two hiding places or visible targets were very different from one another, infants were less likely to perseverate. We tested infants without hidden objects but with visible "lids." The A side lid was always red, as was the background. But four groups of infants had four different B lids, either red, orange, yellow, or a lid painted with colorful stripes and a smiley face. Thus, when they faced the targets, the B target was either exactly the same as the A target, or differed by varying amounts.

We found that the infants in the red-red and red-orange condition reached for A when B was cued (perseverated) to the same degree as infants in our typical experiments (approximately 80% of the time). They were equally confused by red or orange. Conversely, the infants in the red-striped condition did not perseverate. Rather, they correctly reached for the B cue approximately 80% of the time. The infants in the red-yellow condition reached randomly to A or B at the B cue. Thus, when one target was salient and distinct, infants behaved differently. The perseverative behavior was thus a function of the visual environment.

We also tested another aspect of the visual scene. Here we proposed that infants' reaching would be influenced by how strong the cue is to either side (Clearfield et al 2001b). Recall that in the classic A-not-B task, infants must remember the hiding place of the toy over a short delay of a few seconds. We reasoned that if this cue was strong enough (or the delay were short enough) then infants would not revert back to the memory of the old reaches, but rather would reach to B when B was cued. We used the typical hidden toy task for one group of infants. For three other groups, we did not hide a toy. Rather, we varied the visual interest of the lids. One set was plain brown. The second set was painted with stripes and a smiley face, and the third set had colored flashing lights. Thus, when the investigator waved the lid (or hid the toy) to indicate the target, infants saw objects that were either plain or visually interesting. Since we changed only the bottom of the lids, after the waving or hiding, all the infants saw two similar plain brown lids.

The results of this experiment confirmed our model's predictions. Infants who saw the cue with the flashing lights did not perseverate, rather they more often reached correctly to the cued B target. The brown lids and the hidden toy both produced consistent perseveration, and the painted lid was in-between. In other words, when we increased the strength of the event that had to be remembered, this cue overwhelmed the memory of previous reaches. Moreover, reducing the delay had the same effect. Another four groups of infants saw the same stimulus events, but now we did not use a time delay between cue and allowing the infant to reach. Under these conditions, only the babies in the hidden toy condition perseverated. The others reached correctly or in a random way. As the delay allows the event memory to fade, reducing the delay produced much less perseveration.

Looking was also important in another way. In Smith et al (1999), we showed that **where** infants were looking during the experiment also had an effect. In this study, we gave infants the usual training and hidden-toy trials at A. But before the B trials, we distracted them by pointing to a small object placed on the table to the investigator's far right or left side. The investigator merely touched the object and called the infants' attention to it. Babies responded by turning their heads and eyes and looking. If the visual distraction was directed toward the A side, infants strongly perseverated on the B trials. That is, they reached back to A where they had also just looked. But if the distraction was directed toward the new, B side, infants were very likely to reach to B; that is, they did not commit the error. We concluded from this experiment that looking was indeed coupled to reaching in such a way that the decision could be influenced by where the head and eyes were directed. Simply making infants momentarily move their eyes changed where they subsequently reached.

Another way to demonstrate the close connections between looking and reaching is to watch where the infants actually look during the task. In Figure 3.2, I show a record of an infant's gaze direction during the B test trial. The infant looks at the investigator waving the B lid during the first part of the trial. At the solid line, the investigator stops waving the lid and starts a 3-second delay. Note how, during the delay, the infants gaze drifts back to the A side, even though there is no additional cue there. At the first dotted line, the investigator pushes the box containing the targets closer to the infant and allows him to reach. Again, note that the infant looks briefly to the cued side but again is pulled back to A and reaches to A. Even before the reach to A, the infant looks back to it. Looking and reaching are mutually coupled.

These and the other experiments illustrate an important point. Infants' behavior in this task is not something that they have or know as a permanent trait, but it is entirely emergent in the particular current situation and in light of particular previous experiences. If we can show this is true for one task, I claim it must be true for all tasks and for all children, whether typically or atypically developing. Moreover, from a dynamic view, as every task is constituted from all of the multiple, interacting components, behavior also involves perception and action in

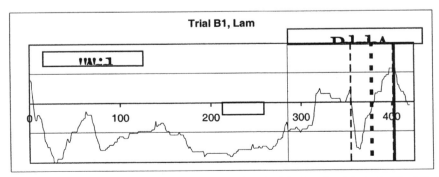

FIGURE 3.2 Perseveration in looking at the first B trial after six trials to A. The infant watches the investigator cue the B side, shown as a trace of the nose. At the first solid vertical line, the cue stops and the delay begins. During the delay, the infant's eyes drift back to the A side. Then the box containing the lids is pushed forward (first dotted vertical line). The infant glances back to B, but returns to A just before reaching to A (second dotted line).

a deep and lifelong way. This becomes even more clear as I continue to describe the A-not-B experiments.

Reaching

In traditional cognitive and information-processing views, movement itself is the end result of a series of mental events. In the computer metaphor, the brain provides the central processing unit, which then feeds instructions to an output device, the body. With computers, it does not affect the central processing if the output is sent to a screen, to a printer, or to the internet. But human behavior is different. Movement cannot be separated from perception and cognition; these processes are continually and dynamically interacting. The acts of perceiving and planning are always in reference to eventual movement, and movement is part of what is remembered. Over a lifetime, I believe, these interactions with the world construct our cognition and maintain it. Some examples from the A-not-B task illustrate my points.

I have proposed that the A-not-B error emerges from the ordinary processes that produce reaching for an object. Let us examine how posture and movement were involved. If the A-not-B error were about reaching and not just about representations or memory, then experimental manipulations that involve movement might produce interesting changes in infants' behavior.

In Smith et al (1999), my colleagues and I included two simple movement-related experiments. The first, described earlier, showed that the movement of looking changed whether or not infants made the A-not-B error. In the second experiment, we again gave infants the usual number of A trials. But now, before the B trials, we asked parents to stand the infant up in their laps. For a control, we talked to infants for the same amount of time it took to stand them up. Infants in the stand-up group were overwhelmingly correct on the B trials. By this bodily intervention, we nearly eliminated perseveration. Of the 20 reaches produced by 10 infants in 2 B test trials, only 3 reaches were back to A. The control group perseverated at the usual rate.

We concluded that infants must have incorporated the "feel" of the body and an embodied memory of the visual scene. When they repeated the reaches to the A side, they remembered more than the location and nature of the target. These memories influenced their subsequent actions. When the habit memory was disrupted, infants no longer perseverated.

Memory of Movement is Part of Memory of Events

These first experiments raised the question of just what is remembered when a person moves in order to attain some goal. How does a behavior then become habitual?

Habits develop when a person repeats the same activity many times. We know we have developed a habit because, like the infants, the behavior becomes very stable and sometimes persists even when the circumstances change. This is why people do not often rearrange their kitchen cabinets! At the neuronal level, networks that have been repeatedly strengthened by use tend to be activated more easily. One condition for habit formation, therefore, is that behavior be stable enough to be repeated in the same form over again.

The A-not-B task allowed us to actually see infants form such habits over the course of the experiment (Diedrich et al 2000). We presented infants with the typical task involving no hidden objects. As they performed the task, we monitored the infants' hand movements while they reached, using special computer-assisted cameras. This gave us a detailed picture of the actual trajectories of their hands.

At 8 to 10 months of age, infants can reach well, but their movements are not fully skilled. This can be seen only in the fine details of the movement trajectories. When adults reach for objects, their hands trace a smooth path in space, gradually speeding up and then slowing down as they approach the target. Infants, in contrast, show bumpy hand paths reflecting somewhat jerky movements and less than perfect control. Normally, each reach shows its own pattern of such speed changes.

But when infants repeated their reaches under the special conditions of the A-not-B task, we found a remarkable result. As the number of reaches to the same place increased, the trajectories of infants' hands became more and more alike. This is shown in Figure 3.3. Note that the individual and idiosyncratic patterns

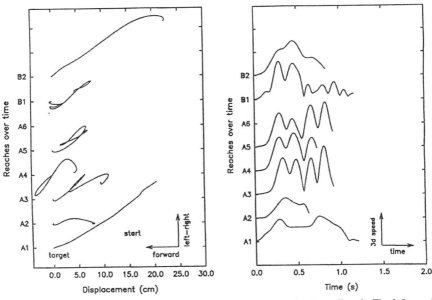

FIGURE 3.3 The build-up of memory of trajectory over in the A-not-B task. The left panel shows the overhead view of the path of the hand from the start of the movement on the right to the target as a function of the A and B trials. The right panel shows the corresponding velocity changes. Note that infant reaches are not very straight toward the target and show multiple speed bumps, which become more alike as the trials progress.

persisted as the task progressed. When infants of the same age reached for a single target, each reach path was distinct.

These results show that infants retained a memory of the time-space details of the reach itself and that this memory persisted to influence the next reach. Here we saw the actual build-up of a memory from repeating an action. We assume that the memory included not only the location of the goal but also the **feel** of the movements that infants used to attain their goals. Why did infants show this habit in an A-not-B task, but not when reaching for a single object? We speculated that the particular difficulty and novelty of this task (since babies almost always reach for single well-defined objects) required infants to pay attention to the movements and to aim for the right target. This constrained the movement such that infants were more likely to do the same reach over again. Once a pattern is repeated, it becomes progressively easier to repeat it again. Eventually, the movement becomes such a deep attractor that the new location cue cannot compete with it.

We demonstrated in these experiments that, with repetition, infants' reaches became more alike, and the memory trace became stronger. For this to occur, infants must be able to control their movements sufficiently well to repeat the same action over again in the same situation. This is a testable hypothesis because young infants do not have good control over their arms. Therefore, we reasoned that perseveration in the A-not-B task would emerge only as reaching skill was well enough developed to allow infants to control the trajectory.

Developmental Changes

We tested this hypothesis in a longitudinal study that began when infants were 5 months old (Clearfield et al 2001a). At this age, infants can reach for objects, but their arm movements are jerky and variable. Previous researchers had not looked at such young infants in the A-not-B task because they assumed the task was about hidden objects, and infants younger than approximately 7 months cannot be trained to uncover a hidden object. However, when we eliminated the hidden object and just used the always-visible "lids," even some 5-month-old infants could do the task.

This study pitted two competing hypotheses. In traditional views, younger infants should perseverate more than older ones. Their concepts of objects should be more fragile, their memories for the cuing event should be shorter, and their abilities to inhibit their responses should be less. However, from the dynamic perspective, which includes the movement as part of the response, we predicted less perseveration in younger infants because their reaching skill did not allow for stable and repeatable responses.

Our study (Clearfield et al 2001a) supported the dynamic account. At 5 months, only 7 of the 14 infants would reach at all when given the two-target task, although they eagerly reached for a single target. This supports our assumption that the task is novel and confusing at all ages. However, in those infants who did reach and complete the A trials, five of them were correct and reached for B at the first B test trial. Correct responding decreased with age, such that at 6 and 7 months infants were reaching randomly for A or B on the B trials. But by 8 months, 85% of the same infants who were correct when younger perseverated on the B trials. Infants were given the same 3-second delay at all ages. So the task did not change, but perseveration did. Can we attribute the onset of perseveration to changes in reaching?

Our data are only correlational, but there is further evidence that this relationship between reaching skill and perseveration is important. In a separate study of 10 infants (Clearfield et al 2001a) whom we tracked very frequently over the first year, we saw dramatic stabilization in the control of reaching around 7 months of age. This supports the dynamic view that movement itself is an important component to the developmental story of perseverative reaching. Note that the special circumstances of the A-not-B task all act together: the emerging control of the arm within a somewhat novel and confusing task where repetition is critical.

We reasoned further that if this movement-based explanation were correct, then disrupting the feel of the arm should decrease perseveration by breaking the habit. Alternatively, increasing attention and the feel of the arm should etch in a stronger habit and make perseveration easier. These predictions were borne out in two additional sets of experiments.

Breaking the Habit

In the first set of experiments, we gave three groups of infants the usual two-target A-not-B task, but without hidden toys. The first group completed the A trials as usual. But just before the B trials, we added small weights to the infants' arms. These were sufficient for infants to notice but not enough to prevent them from reaching. For the second group, we added the weights at the beginning of the trials so that the A trials were with weighted arms, but we removed the weights for the B trials. The third group completed the experiment as usual and was the control condition. As expected, 75% of the infants in the control group made the A-not-B error. However, in the weights-added group, only 50% made the error, and in the weights-removed group only 56% did so. The experimental groups were thus at chance levels of reaching to A or B. Therefore, disrupting the feel of the arms by making them heavier or lighter disrupted the tendency to perseverate. We concluded that the habit that developed included the feel of the arms. The second set of experiments tested the alternative prediction that we could increase perseveration by increasing factors that make the habit stronger. We already knew that repetition was one way to increase the memory for an action. But if our assumption was correct, that perseveration resulted from strengthened neural pathways, then stronger input to those pathways should make infants perseverate with fewer repetitions. We gave one group of infants a situation in which their visual attention was heightened. We fashioned two "sleeves" made of gold lamé, which the infants seemed to notice. We gave a second group a situation in which their movement perception was heightened by having them lift a quite heavy "lid." One control group wore sleeves made of pastel flannel, which was not interesting to the infants, and the second wore a gold lamé bib, which was not part of the arm that was reaching. For each group, we reduced the number of A trials from the usual six, which produces robust perseveration under typical conditions, to four, which does not (Smith et al 1999).

Indeed, we discovered conditions that would make habits stronger. Seventy-five percent of the infants who wore the glittery sleeves perseverated on the B test after only four trials, and 80% of those who lifted the heavy lids also made the A-not-B error. Perseveration rates for the two control groups were 50% and 40%, respectively. This is random responding, which we would expect after only four trials reaching to stimulus A. By paying attention—increasing the saliency of response conditions—infants retained a stronger memory of the action. Notably, this strengthening of the habit could be achieved by modifying either the saliency of the visual input or the movement sense, that is, the perceived kinesthetic sense of the arms.

What Develops?

I have argued that the perseverative behavior seen in 8- to 10-month-old infants is emergent from the ordinary processes that produce reaching and the basic mechanisms needed to acquire skill, such as visual attention, decision making, and memory. Given that perseverative behavior is a normal product of reaching, it does not go away as people get older, but the conditions for eliciting it change. For instance, Spencer et al (2001) found that 2-year-olds made A-not-B errors when they reached for toys hidden in a sandbox. Here the targets were not specified once the toys were hidden, making the task more difficult. In fact, adults also make A-not-B errors in the laboratory when the conditions are appropriate (fast cues, long delays, many repetitions to A) (Ghilardi et al 1995). But adults also make A-not-B errors frequently in everyday life! For instance, we used to hang our telephone on the wall, but then changed the location to the countertop. For many weeks, when the phone rang, I reached up toward the old wall location, despite the phone being clearly visible on the counter.

Our careful task analysis showed that in infants, many factors contributed to performance. Likewise, developmental change may involve any or all of them. We saw that reaching skill itself was critical, but we might also expect changes across ages in infants' abilities to distinguish between two similar locations, to hold the cue or the target locations in memory longer, or to suppress the memory of the previous reaches more efficiently. We feel confident, however, that no single factor works in isolation and that at whatever age, behavior involves a similar dynamic interplay of perception, cognition, and movement.

CONCLUSIONS AND CLINICAL IMPLICATIONS

Taken together, these experiments provide compelling support for a dynamic account. First, my colleagues and I demonstrated that this "error" was a result of normal mechanisms that produce reaching to a target, which are, at the same time, perceptual, motor, and cognitive. Our experiments illustrated a cornerstone of dynamic theory: behavior and its development are multiply determined. No one structure or process is the single cause of an outcome. Rather, component processes dynamically interact in a delicate and changing way in each environmental situation.

Second, we showed that perseveration is truly emergent at a particular age because of the developmental status of the component processes. We illustrated with "real-time" experiments some ways in which behavior may become stable and sometimes so stable that the baby could not make a switch when the conditions changed. These experiments tap a critical mechanism in development. Infants must learn what works from multiple interactions with the world, and then they must form categories of movements that fit categories of situations. Thus, behavior must be sufficiently controllable so that when an action is successful and useful, it can be repeated, and when it is repeated it must be remembered. Infants err because these processes are working correctly! We have created a situation with the A-not-B task that makes the processes clearly observable. Finally, because many processes are involved, we could change behavior in many different ways. We could disrupt stability by changing the visual environment, the memory and feel of the body, the direction of gaze, and so on.

I believe there are important implications from our detailed study of this one task in typically developing infants to understanding and intervening with children whose developmental course is not typical. For instance, children who are diagnosed with pervasive developmental delay, autism, or specific language impairment often show a spectrum of deficits in many areas of daily-life functioning. These deficits include clumsiness, poor language, and inappropriate social behavior. Although for the purposes of diagnosis and treatment assignment, clinicians may focus on one problem or another, it may be that all developmental problems have multiple manifestations.

A dynamic approach can help us understand how such a constellation can arise from even small disturbances in the most basic components of behavior: perceiving, deciding, remembering, and moving. An infant whose vision and hearing do not provide continuous, rapid, and accurate inputs will get a confusing and distorted view of the world right from the start. This is especially critical for processing language and other social behavior, which is itself subtle, rapid, and highly contingent. Children without a sensitive sense of their own movements and body positions cannot monitor them and will lack any sort of predictive control. Without reliable input from the external and internal worlds, it is not possible to form stable and reliable categories. If a child's perception of sounds is distorted, speech and language are very difficult to acquire. If the verbal and visual signals from the infant's social partners are unmanageable and uninterpretable, the child may adapt by withdrawing. If body sense is poor, sequencing behavior is difficult, and social interactions are unpredictable, then normal skills are very difficult to acquire. Each of these difficulties can lead to frustration, emotional withdrawal, or aggressive and inappropriate behavior. In this way, even small distortions in basic processes can cascade over development and lead to multiple, overlapping problems. By the time a child is diagnosed, however, the original source of the delays may be entirely masked by the emergent and compensating behavior. What looks like a problem of theory of mind may have more general developmental roots.

I have earlier characterized development as a series of problem-solving situations, where the child will opportunistically discover a solution, use it while it works, and then abandon it as new solutions emerge. Children with disordered processes also seek to solve problems. One way to cope with an uncontrollable world is to seize upon the best solution at that time. Thus, if perception and movement are disordered, it may be adaptive to withdraw and engage in predictable self-stimulatory behavior. If movements are uncontrollable, it is adaptive to co-contract and stiffen the limbs. If speech is difficult to produce and is unintelligible, it may be a good idea to stop speaking and find alternative means of communication.

The problem for children whose development is atypical is that they may get "stuck" in these ad hoc solutions. They have repeated them so often that the habits are strong, and the attractors are deep. It is like an infant reaching to the A side not just six times but hundreds of times. When the B cue comes along, the old pattern is so persistent, it cannot compete. Children with developmental problems often find it difficult to adjust their behavior to new situations.

A dynamic view suggests that you have to disrupt the old habits with new and more salient input. If this is true, then the other lesson from the dynamic systems approach is that there may be multiple ways to get these children "unstuck." These ways may not have a direct relationship to the presenting problem. If aggressive and inappropriate behaviors are reactions to an uncontrollable world, it may be that trying to provide order in basic perceptual-motor mechanisms can lead to improvements of behavior that is further "downstream." As I illustrated with the A-not-B example, movement and its perception are a part of every action and are a part of the behavioral "habit." This suggests that one potent way to move children out of fixed patterns is through novel and interesting movement.

What are the directions for future research? Conventionally, research in atypical development has focused on describing the ways typical and atypical children differ. But it may be equally fruitful to understand how they are alike. In either case, we want to know how behavior is learned, how it becomes stable, and how children develop adaptive flexibility. When we begin to understand how day-by-day actions lead to long-term developmental changes, we can identify those transitions that may lead to getting "stuck" instead of progressing. As we continue to learn about how small differences early in life can lead to problems, we may better be able to intervene with appropriate and humane treatments.

REFERENCES

Acredolo, L.P. 1985. Coordinating perspectives on infant spatial orientation. In Cohen, R. (Editor), *The Development of Spatial Cognition* (pp. 114–140). Hillsdale, NJ: Erlbaum.

Baillargeon, R., and DeVos, J. 1991. Object permanence in young infants: Further evidence. *Child Dev* 62:1227–1246.

Baron-Cohen, S. 1995. *Mindblindness: An Essay on Autism and "Theory of Mind."* Cambridge, MA: MIT Press.

Bettelheim, B. 1972. *The Empty Fortress: Infantile Autism and the Birth of the Self.* New York: Free Press.

Bremner, J.G. 1985. Object tracking and search in infancy: A review of the data and a theoretical evaluation. *Dev Rev* 5:371–396.

Clearfield, M.W., Diedrich, F.J., Thelen, E., and Smith, L.B. 2001a. Reaching really matters: The development of infant perseverative reaching. Manuscript submitted for publication.

Clearfield, M.W., Thelen, E., Smith, L.B., and Scheier, C. 2001b. Cue salience and memory in infant perseverative reaching: Tests of a dynamic field model. Manuscript submitted for publication.

Diamond, A. 1990. Development and neural bases of AB and DR. In Diamond, A. (Editor), *The Development and Neural Bases of Higher Cognitive Functions* (pp. 267–317). New York: New York Academy of Sciences.

Diedrich, F.J., Highlands, T., Thelen, E, and Smith, L.B. 2001. The role of target distinctiveness in infant perseverative reaching errors. *J Exp Child Psychol* 78:263–290.

Diedrich, F.J., Thelen, E., Smith, L.B., and Corbetta, D. 2000. Motor memory is a factor in infant perseverative errors. *Developmental Science* 3:479–494.

Ghilardi, M.F., Gordon, J., and Ghez, C. 1995. Learning a visuomotor transformation in a local area of work space produces directional biases in other areas. *J Neurophysiol* 73:2535–2539.

Harris, P.L. 1987. The development of search. In Salapatek, P., and Cohen, L.B. (Editors), *Handbook of Infant Perception,* (Vol. 2, pp. 48–62). New York: Academic Press.

Kelso, J.A.S. 1995. *Dynamic Patterns: The Self-Organization of Brain and Behavior.* Cambridge, MA: MIT Press.

Kugler, P., and Turvey, M.T. 1987. *Information, Natural Law, and the Self-Assembly of Rhythmic Movement.* Hillsdale NJ: Erlbaum.

Marcovitch, S., and Zelazo, P.D. 1999. The A-not-B error: Results from a logistic meta-analysis. *Child Dev* 70:1297–1313.

McGraw, M. 1945. *The Neuromuscular Maturation of the Human Infant.* New York: Columbia University Press.

Munakata, Y. 1998. Infant perseveration and implications for object permanence theories: A PDP model of the AB task. *Developmental Science* 1:161–184.

O'Dwyer, N.J., and Ada, L. 1996. Reflex hyperexcitability and muscle contracture in relation to spastic hypertonia. *Current Opinion in Neurology* 9:451–455.

Piaget, J. 1952. *The Origins of Intelligence in Children.* International Universities Press.

Piaget, J. 1954. *The Construction of Reality in the Child.* Basic Books.

Pinker, S. 1994. *The Language Instinct.* New York: Harper.

Port, R., and van Gelder, R. 1995, (Editors), *Mind as Motion: Explorations in the Dynamics of Cognition.* Cambridge MA: MIT Press.

Smith, L.B., and Thelen, E. 1993. *Dynamic Sytems in Development: Applications.* Cambridge, MA: MIT Press.

Smith, L.B., Thelen, E., Titzer, R., and McLin, D. 1999. Knowing in the context of action: The task dynamics of the A-not-B error. *Psychological Review* 106:235–260.

Spelke, E.S., Breinlinger, K., Macomber, J., and Jacobson, K. 1992. Origins of knowledge. *Psychol Rev* 99:605–632.

Spencer, J.P., Smith, L.B., and Thelen, E. 2001. Tests of a dynamic systems account of the A-not-B error: The influence of prior experience on the spatial memory abilities of 2-year-olds. *Child Dev* 72:1327–1346.

Thelen, E., and Smith, L.B. 1994. *A Dynamic Systems Approach to the Development of Perception and Action.* Cambridge, MA: MIT Press.

Thelen, E., and Ulrich, B.D. 1991. Hidden skills: A dynamical systems analysis of treadmill stepping during the first year. *Monog Soc Res Child Dev* Vol. 56, No. 223.

Thelen, E., Schoner, G., Scheier, C., and Smith, L.B. 2001. The dynamics of embodiment: A field theory of infant perseverative reaching. *Behav Brain Sci* 24:1–34.

Wellman, H.M., Cross, D., and Bartsch, K. 1986. Infant search and object permanence: A meta-analysis of the A-not-B error. *Monog Soc Res Child Dev* Vol. 54, No. 214.

Zanone, P.G., and Kelso, J.A.S. 1991. Experimental studies of behavioral attractractors and their evolution with learning. In Requin, J. and Stelmach, G.E., (Editors), *Tutorials in Motor Neuroscience* (pp. 121–133). Dordrecht, Netherlands: Kluwer.

4

PLASTICITY OF SOMATOSENSORY AND MOTOR SYSTEMS IN DEVELOPING AND MATURE PRIMATE BRAINS

JON H. KAAS, PHD

INTRODUCTION

Neuroscientists have long known that developing sensory systems can be altered by perturbations of the sensory environment, especially sensory deprivation (see Casagrande and Weincken-Barger 2001). Thus, the detailed organization of sensory systems is not completely prespecified by information inherited in the genetic code. As a notable example, the visual system normally processes information from the two eyes in a balanced fashion. However, in mammals reared with one eye covered (called *monocular deprivation*), the visual system develops to maximize the impact of the nondeprived eye, so that inputs from the deprived eye have little effect. The neural circuitry devoted to the eyes shifts dramatically, and the territories occupied by the nondeprived eye become much larger than normal while those related to the deprived eye are reduced considerably. Similar outcomes have been seen in other sensory systems and in the motor system after early developmental perturbations.

For many years, such remarkable potential for change, called *plasticity*, was viewed as a unique feature of the developing brain. Periods of visual deprivation in adults produced only limited shifts in functional and structural organization in the brain. Because of such observations, mature sensory systems have long been considered to be fixed in basic organization. However, we now know from experimental results that have accumulated over the last 20 years that even the mature brain is capable of functional and structural reorganization. The potential for change is not as dramatic in adult brains as during development, but the mature brain is capable of marked reorganization.

In this chapter, I focus on changes in the organization of somatosensory and motor systems that follow the loss of sensory inputs or motor targets (also see Kaas and Florence 2001). Alterations in these systems also occur as individuals learn new motor skills and acquire new perceptual abilities; however, changes of this nature are relatively small and not easily demonstrated (Ebner et al 1997; Nicolelis 1997; see Buonomano and Merzenich 1998). In contrast, deprivation leads to modifications that are robust. Thus, I concentrate on studies that describe changes after sensory or motor loss; however, much of what is learned from such experiments probably applies to changes in brain organization produced by other triggers (e.g., learning). I discuss how neural changes emerge as well as the functional consequences of the reorganization. For the most part, the discussion is directed to the data on adult plasticity; however, the patterns of changes that are produced after sensory loss early in life are contrasted with the evidence from adults.

THE NORMAL ORGANIZATION OF SENSORY AND MOTOR SYSTEMS

NEURAL MAPS

Research on the plasticity of the central nervous system is possible because of the orderly organization of neural maps that normally develop in response to experience. That is, the functions of the sensory and motor systems of humans and other primates depend on highly specific and orderly patterns of connections between cells in the brain that monitor and respond to our world. The brain cells are situated in multiple areas of the brain, from the spinal cord to the highest level of processing in the brain, the cerebral cortex (see Kaas 1993; Wu et al 2000). Cells in each of the areas are interconnected in stereotypic patterns that seem to be essential for processing sensory information and for generating well-controlled movements. For the sensory and motor systems, the typical pattern is a remarkably detailed representation (or map) of the body surface. In the somatosensory system, the arrays of sensory receptors in the skin and deeper tissues serve as the blueprints for orderly sequences of neural connections. Similarly, in the motor system, connections mirror the pattern of movements in a progression from head to toe. In cortex, sequence of organization for the sensory and motor systems is in register. For example, in primates, the primary somatosensory area, termed *S1* or *area 3b*, and the primary motor area, termed *M1* or *area 4*, represent tactile receptors or body movements from foot to trunk to hand to face in a sequence from medial to lateral across strips of cortex in the contralateral cerebral hemisphere. Such representations are basically isomorphs (same structure) of the body, and they are referred to as topographic maps of sensory surfaces or muscle arrangements.

Topographic maps seem to be an advantageous form of organization in sensory and motor systems, as this type of organization simplifies the problem of connecting individual neurons into circuits of neurons that perform similar computations (Kaas 1997). For proper function, the connections of neurons in sensory and motor systems need to be highly specific and orderly. In sensory systems, such organization is important for preserving as much information as possible about peripheral sensory events. In the motor system, such connectional precision is needed to activate muscles in extremely precise patterns to produce fine, practiced movements. Even though these processes would seem to be remarkable achievements, the necessary circuits emerge reliably. Moreover, across individuals of the same species, the patterns of organization are surprisingly consistent. Yet, the detailed patterns of connections across individuals typically are not identical. The most notable examples are individuals with exceptional motor skills or sensory-perceptual abilities (e.g., athletes or musicians); in such cases, the organizations of the motor and sensory systems are specialized in ways that facilitate highly practiced skills.

Across species, patterns of organization may differ considerably; however, many similarities may persist between closely related species. In some highly divergent species, the basic design of some portions of the brain may be specialized to accommodate abilities unique to that particular species. Notable examples are the somatosensory and motor circuits devoted to the hand in primates that are large and exceptionally well-developed. For this reason, the plasticity studies are often performed on cortex devoted to the hand.

THE EXPERIMENTAL APPROACH

To investigate brain changes, manipulations are needed that affect a readily demarcated portion of the sensory or motor periphery and reliably produce changes that are sufficiently robust to be distinguished from normal variability. For most of my studies, my colleagues and I have investigated the consequences of hand or forelimb denervation on primary somatosensory cortex (area 3b) of monkeys. Primary somatosensory cortex is particularly suitable for these types of studies because the normal organization of this region has been known for some time (Kaas et al 1979). Area 3b can be identified easily by its unique appearance in appropriately stained brain sections. In monkeys and humans, the area constitutes a long, narrow strip of cortex in each cerebral hemisphere that extends from the medial wall at the brain midline to the lateral fissure.

Representation of the body surface in area 3b can be determined by recording neuronal activity from many locations in area 3b with fine-recording microelectrodes. At each of many, closely spaced recording sites, the part of the body where light touch activates nearby neurons is identified. This region is referred to as the receptive field of the recorded neurons. In all primates, including humans, the foot is represented most medially, followed by the trunk, forearm, hand, face, and tongue and teeth. Because the hand is such an important receptor surface for monkeys and humans, the hand forms an especially large portion of the total representation, and digits 1 through 5 (thumb through little finger) are represented in order from lateral to medial in the hand portion of area 3b.

Many of our studies have been with macaque monkeys, Old World monkeys that are commonly used in neuroscience research because their brains more closely resemble human brains than do those of more distantly related species (e.g., New World monkeys). However, in both macaque monkeys and humans, most of area 3b (S1) is buried on the posterior wall of the deep central sulcus where recording must be done without visual guidance (Figure 4.1A). This poses a technical challenge because the shape of the sulcus is variable so that the location of the tip of the electrode is in question. Therefore, studies also have been done on New World owl monkeys and squirrel monkeys in which most of area 3b is exposed on the surface of the brain (Figure 4.1B).

The typical experimental approach has been to use microelectrode recording techniques to determine the normal organization of the hand representation in areas 3b and then examine how the organization changes after some manipulation that alters sensory inputs. A study by Jenkins et al (1990) exemplifies this approach. In an untrained monkey, microelectrode recording reveals a normal pattern of representation of the hand (Figure 4.2) in the monkey. Rows of recordings show the approximate extent of the territories where neurons are activated by touching digits 2, 3, and 4 as well as part of the palm (Figure 4.2B). After weeks of training so that the monkey selectivity stimulated digit 3, recordings revealed that more neurons had receptive fields on digit 3. The summary map, generated by outlining all recorded neurons with receptive fields on the same skin site, showed that the cortical territory for digit 3 was larger than in inexperienced monkeys (Figure 4.2C). Additional changes such as an increase or decrease in average receptive field size also is likely to occur. Similar alterations in cortical organization can even be demonstrated in humans using noninvasive imaging methods. For example, Elbert et al (1995) reported that cortical representations of the fingers used in playing string instruments are larger in skilled musicians than in nonplayers. Apparently, years of extensively stimulating those fingers resulted in larger cortical representations of those fingers.

Another advantage of the hand representation in monkeys is that the subdivisions of the hand representation in area 3b can be visualized in brain sections cut parallel to the brain surface (Figure 4.3). In the development of the hand representation in normal monkeys, inputs from the thalamus apparently segregate into territories for each digit in a manner that is so precise that a narrow septal region free of inputs emerges between the representations of individual digits (Jain et al 1998). These septal borders last for life, even after loss of many of the hand inputs produces considerable cortical reorganization. Thus, changes can be determined accurately by reference to the septal boundaries.

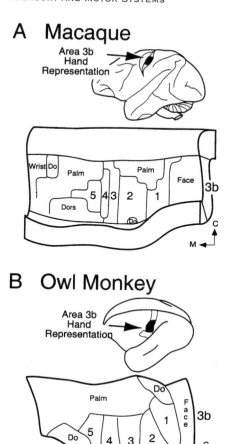

FIGURE 4.1 The representation of the hand in a portion of area 3b (primary somatosensory cortex or S1) in the posterior wall of the central sulcus of a monkey. **A,** (*Top*) A lateral view of the left cerebral hemisphere of a macaque monkey brain with part of the central sulcus opened to show the location of the hand representation in area 3b. (*Bottom*) A face-on view of the hand representation in area 3b of the central sulcus. Territories for each digit (1–5), palm, dorsal hairy surface of the hand and digits (Dors or Do), wrist, and face are indicated. **B,** Lateral brain view (*top*) and hand map (*bottom*) of area 3b in a squirrel monkey.

Finally, it is important to recognize that area 3b is just one stage in an extended processing network that constitutes the somatosensory system (Figure 4.4). Afferents from the hand enter the cervical enlargement of the spinal cord where they branch to contribute to spinal cord circuits and to provide an ascending branch that travels in the dorsal columns to the cuneate nucleus of the dorsal column nuclei of the lower brain stem. Neurons in the cuneate nucleus project to the hand

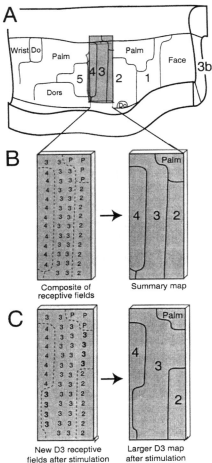

FIGURE 4.2 Summary map of the hand representation is constructed from the results of microelectrode recordings. **A,** Summary map of the normal hand representation in area 3b of a macaque monkey. The box indicates the region shown enlarged below. **B,** At each small number on the left, neurons were found to have a receptive field on the designated digit (2, 3, or 4) or on the palm (P). As shown on the right, boundaries were drawn between receptive fields on different skin locations, and those on the same skin location were grouped. **C,** When extensive sensory stimulation is applied to any given skin surface, such as digit 3 as shown in this cartoon, neurons that formally had receptive fields on nearby skin surfaces may acquire new receptive fields on digit 3 (*left*). Consequently, the reorganized summary map (*right*) displays a larger representation of D3.

subnucleus of the ventroposterior nucleus (VP) on the opposite side of the brain. The information is relayed to neurons in VP, which in turn project to the hand representation of area 3b in cortex. Area 3b is only the first step in the cortical relay of somatosensory information; it has synaptic connections with multiple other

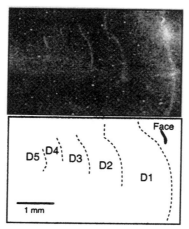

FIGURE 4.3 Evidence for digit territories in area 3b of macaque monkeys. Cortex from the hand region of the cerebral sulcus has been cut parallel to the surface into thin brain sections. A section stained for myelin (a fatty substance around neural axons) shows narrow myelin-poor septa that separate the territories for each digit (as numbered below). These septa do not change with cortical reorganization in adults. Compare with Figure 4.2.

cortical areas that project to progressively higher order cortical regions (see Kaas 1993). Peripheral sensory manipulations, such as deprivation, could initiate changes in the organization of one or more of the somatosensory relays. Moreover, changes at any given level likely would be communicated to the next higher level and so on. Thus, the alterations that are detected in the hand representation of cortical area 3b could reflect synaptic modifications that were initiated in the VP or the cuneate nucleus. An ongoing challenge in plasticity research is to understand where reorganizations are initiated and how change effects each level of the processing circuit.

OBSERVED REORGANIZATIONS AFTER SENSORY LOSS

Most of us have an area of skin on the hand or elsewhere that has been somewhat numb as a result of injury to a peripheral sensory nerve. Some of our first experiments on the somatosensory cortex of monkeys addressed the issue of what happens to the orderly representation of the hand in area 3b when a nerve in the hand is cut. Depending on the size of the skin territory affected, outcomes will differ. However, in general, preserved inputs adjacent to those that are lost expand their representation and take over the deprived zone. For example, cutting a nerve to the finger removes part of the input from that finger, and a small zone of neurons in area 3b is deprived of its normal source of activation.

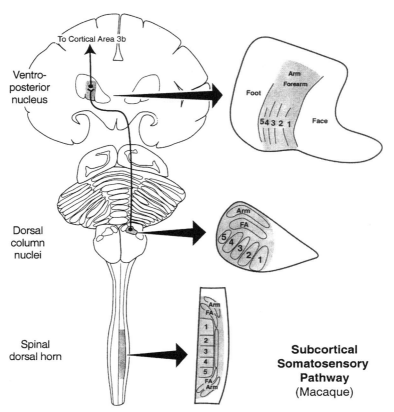

FIGURE 4.4 Early stages of processing somatosensory inputs from the forearm of macaque monkeys. Afferents from the arm enter the cervical enlargement of the spinal cord to branch and terminate in a somatotopic pattern in the neurons of the dorsal horn of the spinal cord and to ascend in the dorsal columns of axons to the cuneate nucleus of the dorsal column nuclei to form a second somatotopic representation. The spinal cord terminations contribute to other circuits and pathways, including the spinothalamic tract, while the dorsal column terminations are on neurons that project to the ventroposterior nucleus of the opposite side of the brain. The ventroposterior nucleus contains another representation of the forelimb and other body parts. Ventroposterior nucleus neurons project to area 3b of somatosensory cortex, forming a fourth map of the tactile receptors of the skin. Territories for each digit are numbered 1–5 (thumb–little finger), and the territories for the forearm (FA) and arm are indicated.

The neurons are not nonresponsive, however. Instead, they become responsive to remaining inputs from that finger. If an injured finger has been amputated so that no inputs from that finger remain, then the deprived region of cortex is activated by inputs from the adjacent, intact fingers and from the palm (Merzenich et al 1984; Florence and Kaas 1995; Manger et al 1996; Jain et al 1998). A more dramatic sensory loss produced by cutting the median nerve at the level of the wrist deprives the glabrous skin of digits 1, 2, and 3 but not the hairy skin of the backs of those digits (Figure 4.5). Over a recovery of several weeks, the neurons throughout the deprived region of cortex acquire new receptive fields on the dorsal skin of the hand (Merzenich et al 1983; Wall et al 1993; Garraghty et al 1994).

Even more substantial reactivations of somatosensory cortex can occur with long recovery times. Accidental limb loss in monkeys or injuries that are sufficiently severe to require therapeutic amputation occur occasionally, because monkeys, like all primates, use their hands for defense and for exploration. A few monkeys have become available for experimental study after a longstanding loss of a forelimb (Florence and Kaas 1995; also see Pons et al 1991). In nearly all cases, the monkeys were acquired for study years after the injury, so plasticity mechanisms in the central nervous system had ample time to affect brain organization. The findings were that the totally deprived hand region of area 3b had regained responsiveness to touch on the stump of the arm or on the face. The scale of the recovery in the brain was many millimeters larger than had ever

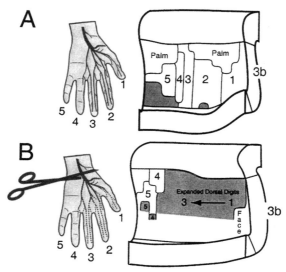

FIGURE 4.5   Change in the hand representation of area 3b of macaque monkeys as a result of median nerve section. **A**, The typical distribution of the median nerve in the hand is shown to the left. The palmar surfaces of digits 1, 2, and 3 are completely innervated by the median nerve (occasionally the medial half of digit 4 is also innervated). The ulnar nerve innervates digits 4 and 5, and the radial nerve innervates the dorsal, hairy surfaces of all digits (not shown). As shown to the right, the median nerve hand representation in area 3b is quite large with only small, patchy representations of the dorsal surfaces of the hand. **B**, If the median nerve is cut (*left*), all sensory innervation to the palmar surfaces of digits 1–3 is lost. The neurons in area 3b no longer respond to stimulation of the median nerve innervated skin; however, they are not silent. Instead, the neurons throughout the deprived zone respond to stimulation of the dorsal hand. (Based on Florence and Kaas, unpublished observations.)

been described. Major cortical reorganization also can be demonstrated in monkeys in which the ascending branches of afferents from the forelimb have been cut, or "sectioned," in the dorsal columns of the spinal cord. Such spinal cord sections leave the spinal cord circuits and spinal cord relays of sensory information intact but totally deactivate the hand portion of area 3b. After a recovery of 6 to 8 months, the hand cortex becomes responsive to touch on the chin and other parts of the face (Jain et al 1997). Comparable changes appear to occur in somatosensory cortex of humans with longstanding amputations or spinal cord injury (see Flor et al 1998).

While dramatic changes in cortical organization have been demonstrated, at least some of these changes seem to be relayed from the VP of the thalamus. After median nerve section (Garraghty and Kaas 1991), loss of an arm (Florence et al 2000), or loss of afferents from an arm (Jones and Pons 1998) in monkeys, the deprived portions of the hand subnucleus of the VP become reactivated by remaining inputs from the hand, stump, or face. Similar results have been obtained from human patients who suffer chronic pain after limb amputations (Davis et al 1998). During surgical procedures to treat the pain, neuronal recordings using microelectrode recording techniques like those used in monkey experiments have revealed that the neurons in the deprived portions of VP have become reactivated by inputs from the stump of the arm. Moreover, when brief electrical pulses are passed through the recording microelectrodes, stimulation of the reactivated neurons produces sensations in the missing hand called *phantom limb sensations* (Davis et al 1998). Thus, the reactivated neurons still participate in signaling the locations of their original receptive fields but are activated, or turned on, by inputs that originate from far distant skin sites. Some of the reorganization following sensory loss that is seen at the level of VP is likely to occur at the level of the cuneate nucleus of the brainstem (Florence and Kaas 1995; Xu and Wall 1997; Jain et al 2000).

OBSERVED MOTOR CORTEX REORGANIZATION

In monkeys, the primary motor cortex, M1 or area 4, is located just anterior to the somatosensory cortex on the anterior wall of the central sulcus and the adjoining surface of the frontal lobe. As for the primary somatosensory cortex, the hindlimb, trunk, forelimb, and face are represented in a mediolateral sequence across M1 (Figure 4.6). This organization can be revealed by passing small (threshold levels) currents through stimulating electrodes to activate motor neurons in the deeper layers of cortex. The neurons that are activated by the stimulation trigger movements of a highly localized part of the body surface. In normal monkeys, threshold stimulations within the large hand and forelimb representation typically result in small movements of individual digits or several digits; less frequently, the stimulation evokes movements in the wrist, forearm, or upper arm.

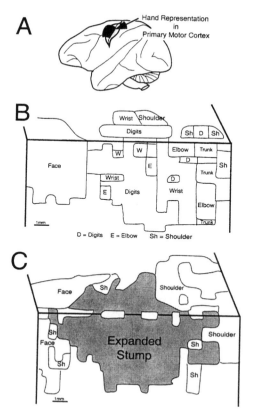

FIGURE 4.6 The reorganization of primary motor cortex (area 4) in a macaque monkey after a therapeutic amputation of an arm. **A,** A lateral view of the brain showing the hand representation in motor cortex. Area 4 forms a strip of cortex in the posterior part of the frontal lobe that includes the dorsolateral surface and the anterior wall of the central sulcus. **B,** A face-on view of the anterior wall of the central sulcus showing the territories where electrical stimulation evoked movements of designated body parts. The representation of the face is followed by a large region devoted to digits, followed by shoulder and trunk. **C,** In a monkey long after a therapeutic amputation of an arm, stimulation of a large region, formerly devoted to digits, wrist, and elbow movements, moves the stump and shoulder.

Conversely, in monkeys with a longstanding amputation of a forelimb, microstimulations throughout the same region of cortex produce movements of the remaining stump of the arm and intact shoulder (see Figure 4.4) (Schieber and Deuel 1997; Wu and Kaas 1999; Qi et al 2000). This indicates that some neurons in the motor cortex may acquire new functional roles after peripheral loss. In humans, a different technique has been used to demonstrate similar reorganizations. The relatively new, noninvasive technique, focal magnetic stimulation produces local activation of neurons in M1. The stimulation evokes limb and hand movements in a pattern not unlike that seen in monkeys. In individuals who had arm amputation, stimulation of the hand region using focal magnetic stimulation evokes stump movements (Cohen et al 1991). Thus, the neurons in M1 of monkeys and humans formerly involved in mediating finger movements become involved in producing stump and shoulder movements.

REORGANIZATIONS AFTER SENSORY LOSS IN DEVELOPING AND MATURE MONKEYS

The consequences of sensory loss in the developing somatosensory system of monkeys have not been studied extensively, as it takes years for developing macaque monkeys to mature. However, results from two studies clearly indicate that the consequences of the same manipulations can differ in developing and mature monkeys. In one study, Florence et al (1996) cut and reconnected the median nerve to the hand (see Figure 4.4B) in fetal or newborn macaque monkeys, and then these monkeys were allowed to mature. In adult monkeys, the reconnected nerve regenerates, but because the alignment of the cut ends is only approximate, the individual axons regenerate to incorrect locations, producing a mixed-up, disorderly map of the first 3 digits of the hand in area 3b of cortex (Paul et al 1972; Wall et al 1986; Florence et al 1994). In the monkeys that experienced nerve cut early in life, nerve repair also resulted in a disorderly regrowth of axons into the hand. However, in area 3b, orderly representations of the skin of the hand were found. Thus, mechanisms of plasticity that are available to the developing somatosensory system, but apparently not present in adults, allowed the topographical disorder contained in the regenerated nerve to be suppressed so that only the sensory inputs that contained accurate information about the peripheral sensory relationships were expressed.

Another example of different outcomes in developing and mature somatosensory systems comes from comparing the effects of dorsal column sections in newborn and mature monkeys. In mature monkeys, a section near the junction of the spinal cord with the brainstem removes all inputs from the hand and most of the forelimb from the cuneate nucleus. As a result, the hand portions of VP and area 3b are totally deprived. After long recoveries, these regions are activated by intact inputs from the face (see earlier discussion). While there are intact spinothalamic connections in these monkeys that relay tactile information from the hand to the thalamus, these inputs do not activate VP or area 3b. In contrast, in lesioned infant monkeys studied as adults, the spinothalamic relay of inputs from the hand become effective, and the hand rather than the face activates the hand region of cortex (Jain et al 2001). The reactivated cortex was not normal, as the map of the hand was less orderly than normal, and neurons had larger than normal receptive fields. Nevertheless, inputs from the hand activated the hand cortex, and the monkeys had nearly normal use of the hand. In contrast, the monkeys with the same lesions as adults had difficulty in manipulating food with the affected fingers, solving a loss of sensory guidance of motor behavior. Again, a more favorable outcome occurred in the developing brain.

HOW DO BRAIN CHANGES OCCUR?

The reorganizations that occur in area 3b and in earlier stages of somatosensory processing seem to use several ways of altering the effectiveness of synaptic connections. First, any input from the hand will activate a population of neurons in the cuneate nucleus that projects, in turn, to a larger population of VP neurons, which project to even more area 3b neurons. A tendency for each relay to spread activity over proportionately more of the hand representation is countered by the existence of inhibitory neurons at each stage. In the cuneate nucleus, VP, and area 3b, the arriving excitatory inputs activate excitatory relay neurons and inhibitory neurons with local connections that dampen the spread of excitation by suppressing the weaker sources of activation. This is generally called *lateral inhibition*. Removing an input from a region of skin immediately removes the source of inhibition on the remaining inputs from adjacent skin, and inhibited "silent" synapses became "unmasked" (Wall 1977) or "disinhibited" (Calford and Tweedale 1988). Thus, neurons with receptive fields in the denervated representation can rapidly acquire new receptive fields on the adjoining innervated skin. However, these immediate changes are limited in extent.

Other cellular mechanisms occur as deprived neurons become inactive. The reduction in activity induces changes in gene expression and molecular responses. As one important example, the production of the major inhibitory neurotransmitter GABA (gamma aminobutyric acid) and the cellular receptors for GABA are down-regulated in deprived neurons within hours of the denervation. The effect is that inhibition is reduced so weak excitatory inputs can be expressed (see Arckens et al 1998 for review). Many other molecular components of inactive neurons also are altered, but the consequences of these changes are less obvious.

In addition, weak synaptic connections can be strengthened by high levels of neural activity (long-term potentiation [LTP] see Brown et al 1988). Stimulus conditions that strongly activate neurons can strengthen weak connections. Inputs that may have been ineffective before the onset of "potentiating" levels of current are able to activate the target neurons at suprathreshold levels after potentiation. Activity-induced alterations in synaptic strength initially were postulated to be a basis for learning by Donald Hebb (1949). Thus, such processes are referred to as *Hebbian mechanisms of plasticity* (see Rauschecker 1991 for review). Changes in the effectiveness of already existing connections can be especially important in cortex where axons spread information horizontally over several millimeters of sensory representations.

Finally, sensory loss and other conditions may cause neurons to grow new connections, even over considerable distances in the brain. This was once thought to be unlikely in the mature brain, but such new growth has now been demonstrated after sensory loss in monkeys in the spinal cord (see Florence et al 1993), in intact afferents in the dorsal column nuclei (Florence and Kaas 1995; Jain et al 2000), and in the horizontal connections in the deprived cortex (Darian-Smith and Gilbert 1994; Florence et al 1998). In the motor system, spinal cord neurons with cut axons as a result of limb amputation may regenerate to hyper-innervate remaining stump muscles (Wu and Kaas 2000). At a more local level, the growth of new connections and the formation of new synapses may be a common occurrence, but such limited growth would be difficult to detect.

WHAT ARE THE FUNCTIONAL CONSEQUENCES OF THE REORGANIZATION OF SENSORY SYSTEMS?

The functional consequences of the types of reorganization described here are somewhat uncertain, but several conclusions seem supportable. First, cortical and subcortical reorganizations associated with sensory experience and improvements in performance may be partly or largely responsible for the improved behavior. As an example, Nudo et al (1996) found that monkeys with partial lesions of the hand representation in primary motor cortex had difficulty manipulating objects with the affected hand. However, the performance of the monkeys improved over time with practice, and this improvement was associated with a reorganization of motor cortex so that more cortex was devoted to the digits. Other examples are reviewed by Buonomano and Merzenich (1998). Thus, the mature nervous system maintains an ability to alter neural circuits so that practice leads to improved performance. However, such improvements may occur at the cost of unpracticed functions or unused portions of the neural circuits. Second, the developing brain appears to have more capacity to reorganize in functionally relevant ways. If topological maps of sensory receptors are functionally better than the nontopographic maps as postulated (Kaas 1997), then the recovery of a topography map of the hand after nerve repair in a developing but not a mature monkey should result in more normal sensory abilities. While this remains to be tested, more normal use of the hand follows the reactivation of the hand cortex by afferents from the hand in monkeys with dorsal-column lesions of the developing somatosensory system. Third, major reorganizations seem to exceed the capacity for mature sensory and motor systems to integrate the altered neurons into functionally meaningful circuits. Instead, the reactivated neurons seem to mediate perceptual and motor errors. In humans with an amputated arm, for example, a touch on the face may be felt on a missing hand (Ramachandran and Hirstein, 1998). Excessive use of motor circuits (e.g., by over-practice) may fix motor responses so that unwanted movements, such as in those in focal dystonias, occur (Byl et al 1996). Other negative outcomes that may result from brain plasticity include phantom pain in missing limbs (Flor et al 1998) and tinnitus (ringing in the ears) after a partial hearing loss. Thus, research on the plasticity of mature and developing sensory and motor systems may have very practical consequences as we learn how to control and guide the mechanisms of brain plasticity. Ultimately, such knowledge may allow clinicians to maximize the potential for achieving beneficial outcomes and avoid harmful outcomes.

ACKNOWLEDGEMENT

Dr. Sherre Florence provided helpful suggestions on the manuscript and the figures. She was an important contributor to much of the research described.

REFERENCES

Arckens, L., Eysel, U.T., Vanderhaeghen, J.J., Orban, G.A., and Vandesande, F. 1998. Effect of sensory deafferentation on the GABAergic circuitry of the adult cat visual system. *Neurosci* 83:381–391.

Brown, T.H., Chapman, P.F., Kairiss, E.W., and Keenan, C.L. 1988. Long-term synaptic potentiation. *Science* 242:724–728.

Buonomano, D.V., and Merzenich, M.M. 1998. Cortical plasticity: From synapses to maps. *Ann Rev of Neurosci* 21:149–186.

Byl, N.N., Merzenich, M.M., and Jenkins, W.M. 1996. A primate genesis model of focal dystonia and repetitive strain injury: I. Learning-induced dedifferentiation of the representation of the hand in the primary somatosensory cortex in adult monkeys. *Neurology* 47:508–520.

Calford, M.B., and Tweedale, R. 1988. Immediate and chronic changes in responses of somatosensory cortex in adult flying-fox after digit amputation. *Nature* 332:446–448.

Casagrande, V.A., and Weincken-Barger, A.E. 2001. Developmental plasticity in the mammalian visual system. In J.H. Kaas, (Editor), *The Mutable Brain* (pp. 1–48). Amsterdam, The Netherlands: Harwood Academic Publishers.

Cohen, L.G., Bandinelli, S., Findley, T.W., and Hallett, M. 1991. Motor reorganization after upper limb amputation in man: A study with focal magnetic stimulation. *Brain* 114:615–627.

Darian-Smith, C., and Gilbert, C.D. 1994. Axonal sprouting accompanies functional reorganization in adult cat striate cortex. *Nature* 368:737–740.

Davis, K.D., Kiss, Z.H., Luo, L., Tasker, R.R., Lozano, A.M., and Dostrovsky, J.O. 1998. Phantom sensations generated by thalamic microstimulation. *Nature* 391:385–387.

Ebner, F.F., Rema, V., Sachdev, R., Symons, F.J. 1997. Activity-dependent plasticity in adult somatic sensory cortex. *Semi Neurosci* 9:47–58.

Elbert, T., Pantev, C., Wienbruch, C., Rockstroh, B., and Taub, E. 1995. Increased cortical representation of the fingers of the left hand in string players. *Science* 270:305–307.

Flor, H., Elbert, T., Muhlnickel, W., Pantev, C., Wienbruch, C., and Taub, E. 1998. Cortical reorganization and phantom phenomena in congenital and traumatic upper-extremity amputees. *Exp Brain Res* 119:205–212.

Florence, S.L., Garraghty, P.E., Carlson, M., and Kaas, J.H. 1993. Sprouting of peripheral nerve axons in the spinal cord of monkeys. *Brain Res* 601:343–348.

Florence, S.L., Garraghty, P.E., Wall, J.T., and Kaas, J.H. 1994. Sensory afferent projections and area 3b somatotopy following median nerve cut and repair in macaque monkeys. *Cereb Cortex* 4:391–407.

Florence, S.L., and Kaas, J.H. 1995. Large-scale reorganization at multiple levels of the somatosensory pathway follows therapeutic amputation of the hand in monkeys. *J Neurosci* 15:8083–8095.

Florence, S.L., Jain, N., Pospichal, M.W., Beck, P.D., Sly, D.L., and Kaas, J.H. 1996. Central reorganization of sensory pathways following peripheral nerve regeneration in fetal monkeys. *Nature* 381:69–71.

Florence, S.L., Taub, H.B., and Kaas, J.H. 1998. Large-scale sprouting of cortical connections after peripheral injury in adult macaque monkeys. *Science* 282:1117–1121.

Florence, S.L., Hackett, T.A., and Strata, F. 2000. Thalamic and cortical contributions to neural plasticity after limb amputation. *J Neurophysiol* 83:3154–3159.

Garraghty, P.E., and Kaas, J.H. 1991. Functional reorganization in adult monkey thalamus after peripheral nerve injury. *Neuroreport* 2:747–750.

Garraghty, P.E., Hanes, D.P., Florence, S.L., and Kaas, J.H. 1994. Pattern of peripheral deafferentation predicts reorganizational limits in adult primate somatosensory cortex. *Somatosen Mot Res* 11:109–117.

Hebb, D.O. 1949. *The Organization of Behavior.* New York: Wiley and Sons.

Jain, N., Catania, K.C., and Kaas, J.H. 1997. Deactivation and reactivation of somatosensory cortex after dorsal spinal cord injury. *Nature* 386:495–598.

Jain, N., Catania, K.C., and Kaas, J.H. 1998. A histologically visible representation of the fingers and palm in primate area 3b and its immutability following long-term deafferentations. *Cereb Cortex* 8:227–236.

Jain, N., Florence, S.L., Qi, H.X., and Kaas, J.H. 2000. Growth of new brainstem connections in adult monkeys with massive sensory loss. *Proc Natl Acad Sci U S A* 97:5546–5550.

Jain, N., Qi, H.X., Collins, C.E., Lyon, D.C., and Kaas, J.H. 2001. Reorganization of somatosensory cortical area 3b following early postnatal dorsal column lesions in macaque monkeys. *Society for Neuroscience Abstracts*; no. 396.1, 27.

Jenkins, W.M., Merzenich, M.M., Ochs, M.T., Allard, T., and Guic-Robles, E. 1990. Functional reorganization of primary somatosensory cortex in adult owl monkeys after behaviorally controlled tactile stimulation. *J Neurophysiol* 63:82–104.

Jones, E.G., and Pons, T.P. 1998. Thalamic and brainstem contributions to large-scale plasticity of primate somatosensory cortex. *Science* 282:1121–1125.

Kaas, J.H. 1993. The functional organization of somatosensory cortex in primates. *Ann Anat* 175:509–518.

Kaas, J.H. 1997. Topographic maps are fundamental to sensory processing. *Brain Res Bull* 44:107–112.

Kaas, J.H., and Florence, S.L. 2001. Reorganization of sensory and motor systems in adult mammals after injury. In Kaas, J.H. (Editor), *The Mutable Brain* (pp. 165–242). Harwood Academic Publishers.

Kaas, J.H., Nelson, R.J., Sur, M., Lin, C.S., and Merzenich, M.M. 1979. Multiple representations of the body within "S-I" of primates. *Science* 204:521–523.

Manger, P.R., Woods, T.M., and Jones, E.G. 1996. Plasticity of the somatosensory cortical map in macaque monkeys after chronic partial amputation of a digit. *Proc R Soc Lon, B* 263:933–939.

Merzenich, M.M., Kaas, J.H., Wall, J.T., Nelson, R.J., Sur, M., and Felleman, D. 1983. Topographic reorganization of somatosensory cortical areas 3b and 1 in adult monkeys following restricted deafferentation. *Neurosci* 8:33–55.

Merzenich, M.M., Nelson, R.J., Stryker, M.P., Cynader, M.S., Schoppmann, A., and Zook, J.M. 1984. Somatosensory cortical map changes following digit amputation in adult monkeys. *J Comp Neurol* 224:591–605.

Nicolelis, M.A. 1997. Dynamic and distributed somatosensory representations as the substrate for cortical and subcortical plasticity. *Semi in Neurosci* 9:24–33.

Nudo, R.J., Wise, B.M., SiFuentes, F., and Milliken, G.W. 1996. Neural substrates for the effects of rehabilitative training on motor recovery after ischemic infarct. *Science* 272:1791–1794.

Paul, R.L., Goodman, H., and Merzenich, M. 1972. Alterations in mechano-receptor input to Brodmann's Areas 1 and 3 of the postcentral hand area of *Macaca mulatto* after nerve section and regeneration. *Brain Res* 39:1–19.

Pons, T.P., Garraghty, P.E., Ommaya, A.K., Kaas, J.H., Taub, E., and Mishkin, M. 1991. Massive cortical reorganization after sensory deafferentation in adult macaques. *Science* 252:1857–1860.

Qi, H.X., Stepniewska, I., and Kaas, J.H. 2000. Reorganization of primary motor cortex in adult macaque monkeys with longstanding amputations. *J Neurophysiol* 84:2133–2147.

Ramachandran, V.S., and Hirstein, W. 1998. The perception of phantom limbs. The D.O. Hebb lecture. *Brain* 121:1603–1630.

Rauschecker, J.P. 1991. Mechanisms of visual plasticity: Hebb synapses, NMDA receptors, and beyond. *Physiol Rev* 71:587–615.

Schieber, M.H., and Deuel, R.K. 1997. Primary motor cortex reorganization in a long-term monkey amputee. *Somatosens Mot Res* 14:157–167.

Wall, J.T., Kaas, J.H., Merzenich, M.M., Sur, M., Nelson, R.J., and Felleman, D.J. 1986. Functional reorganization in somatosensory cortical areas 3b and 1 of adult monkeys after median nerve repair: Possible relationships to sensory recovery in humans. *J Neurosci* 6:218–233.

Wall, J.T., Nepomucceno, V., and Rasey, S.K. 1993. Nerve innervation of the hand and associated nerve dominance aggregates in the somatosensory cortex of a primate (squirrel monkey). *J Comp Neurol* 337:191–207.

Wall, P.D. 1977. The presence of ineffective synapses and the circumstances which unmask them. *Philos Trans Royal Soc Lond B Biol Sci* 278:361–372.

Wu, C.W.H., and Kaas, J.H. 1999. The organization of motor cortex of squirrel monkeys with longstanding therapeutic amputations. *J Neurosci* 19:76–79.

Wu, C.W.H., and Kaas, J.H. 2000. Spinal cord atrophy and reorganization of motor neuron connections following longstanding limb loss in primates. *Neuron* 28:1–20.

Wu, C.W.H., Bichot, N.P., and Kaas, J.H. 2000. Converging evidence from microstimulation, architecture, and connections for multiple motor areas in the frontal and cingulate cortex of prosimian primates. *J Comp Neurol* 423:140–177.

Xu, J., and Wall, J.T. 1997. Rapid changes in brainstem maps of adult primates after peripheral injury. *Brain Res* 774:211–215.

5

CONSTRUCTIVE MANIPULATORY ACTION AND THE ORIGIN OF COGNITION IN HUMAN AND NONHUMAN PRIMATES

JONAS LANGER, PHD

To know is to act, but to act is not necessarily to know. Agnostic acting (i.e., mere moving that does not lead to developing knowledge) is not addressed in this chapter. Only gnostic acting (i.e., acting that leads to developing knowledge) is addressed. Minimally, gnostic acting is receptively perceiving information that is given in the environment and that does not involve any manipulatory behavior. Maximally, gnostic acting goes beyond the information given in the environment by constructing new knowledge through transformative operations. Constructed knowledge is not only new to its constructor, it is new to the environment when it is truly created by transformative operations on it.

In this chapter, I review how this constructivist thesis applies to the origins of cognition about physical phenomena (e.g., causal effects) and logical relations (e.g., hierarchical class inclusion). The central focus is on findings on the comparative origins and development of logical cognition in primates. I conclude by drawing the implications of these comparative findings have for understanding how cognitive development evolved in primates.

THE ORIGINS OF PHYSICAL COGNITION

Transformative operations originate from or in sensorimotor manipulatory interactions with the environment. Newborns, certainly all primate neonates, are endowed with the biopsychological organs and functions necessary to act in their environment and, thereby, potentially to know. Their gnostic acts already comprise repeatable and generalizable patterns of interaction with their environment (e.g., rooting on and looking at) that generate practical, if transient, knowledge about physical space, time, causality, and objects. To illustrate, neonates begin to develop knowledge of object permanence-by-searching (Piaget 1954). That is, by their transformative operation of searching after objects, neonates begin to construct their knowledge about the existence properties of objects. Minimally, object permanence-by-searching is manifest in neonates' receptive nonmanipulatory perceptual behavior, for example, in their visual tracking of objects in their environment. Maximally, it is manifest in neonates' constructive manipulatory sensorimotor behavior, for example, in their rooting on objects in their environment. Werner (1948) aptly labeled this primitive cognitive state of affairs as constructing "thing-of-action" knowledge.

Classical theories of cognitive development (Jerome Bruner, Eleanor Gibson, Kurt Koffka, Jean Piaget, Lev Vygotsky, and Heinz Werner) acknowledge that the sensorimotor manipulatory actions and perceptual nonmanipulatory reactions of human infants and nonhuman primates enable them to develop preverbal (presymbolic) physical cognition. This includes elementary physical knowledge about objects, space, time, and causality. For example, much knowledge about object permanence needs not to be symbolic (i.e., the first five of Piaget's six stages [1954]); all primate species tested so far develop this knowledge (see Parker and McKinney 1999 for a review).

THE ORIGINS OF LOGICAL COGNITION

In contrast, it usually has been assumed (with some notable exceptions, especially Piaget) that even the most elementary logical cognition (e.g., classifying) is representational and that language is the sine qua non of representation. Rudiments of language (the 1- and 2-word stages) develop in childrens' second year (e.g., Brown 1973), while more generally recognizable grammatical development only begins during their third year (e.g., Bickerton 1990; Lieberman 1991). It follows that the onset of logical cognition is a derivative of postinfancy human development that must await at least early childhood.

Given this derivationist view, a variety of different roles has been ascribed to linguistic representation in the development of logical cognition. The minimalist supposition is that language is a necessary but insufficient notational instrument that makes logical operations possible (e.g., Werner and Kaplan 1963). The maximalist supposition is that logic is nothing but a set of syntactic linguistic conventions (e.g., Carnap 1960). Both the minimalists and maximalists agree on the central assumption; namely, that logic is symbolic logic (Cassirer 1953, 1957). This assumption also is shared by symbol-based artificial intelligence perspectives on information processing, including those focused on cognitive development (e.g., Klahr 1989).

Similar but more cautious views have been proposed in historical analyses of the rise of logic from their Sumerian and Babylonian forms onward (e.g., Damerow 1998). These analyses assume that the introduction of special systems of arbitrary symbols to represent objects, quantities, variables, operations, relations, and so on, led to the initial great advances in logic and mathematics (see Kneale and Kneale 1962; Kramer 1970, for reviews). It has not been denied that the rudiments of logic, on which these advances were built, were constructed in ordinary language. Further, the issue of prelinguistic antecedents of logic has not been addressed in historical analyses.

Another classical claim, made particularly by Gestalt theory, is that all cognition, including logical cognition, is initially perceptual (e.g., the immediate visual recognition of similarity between the identical elements of a field). A variety of different roles has been ascribed to this nonmanipulatory perceptual processing of the environment in the origins of logical cognition. In the minimalist Gestalt view, perception is a necessary but insufficient condition for the origins of logical operations (e.g., classifying). To emerge, logical operations require the re-representation of perceptual knowledge in culturally transformed and communicable forms (Koffka 1928). In the maximalist view, logical knowledge (e.g., of class relations) is nothing but the cultural expression of productive thinking about implicit configurational principles (e.g., similarity) prefigured in perception (Wertheimer 1945). Thus, traditional minimalist and maximalist Gestalt views, assume that logical cognition is a derived (secondary), and not an original (primary), form of knowledge. The assumption is that it is a derived form in both ontogeny (i.e., the life history course of development of the individual organism) and phylogeny (i.e., the evolutionary history course of a genetically related group of species such as primates).

THE ORIGINALIST HYPOTHESIS

Linguistic and perceptual hypotheses remain plausible as long as there are no contrary data on the logical development of human infants and nonhuman primates. Our comparative developmental research (Langer 1993, 1994a, 1998, 2000a, 2000b), however, is advancing a third alternative: The originalist hypothesis assumes that logical cognition is a *primary* development in primates and is not secondary to (i.e., derivative in) ontogenetic or phylogenetic developments. It is predicated on the constructivist view that logical cognition itself is an evolutionary and developmental product. Like other natural cognitive phenomena (e.g., physical cognition), the phylogenetic and ontogenetic roots of logic predate the onset of language, even if its unique, systematic formalization in the natural reasoning by human adults requires symbolic representation. Hence, I trace the development of natural logical cognition to its evolutionary and developmental roots in prelinguistic manipulatory action by human infants and nonhuman primates, that is, to their constructive sensorimotor actions on their environment.

Receptive gnostic forms of perception undeniably contribute to the origins of logical cognition. However, I propose that the main source or origin of logical cognition and early development is constructive sensorimotor activity. On this view, manipulatory sensorimotor activity is the original form of transformative operations on their environment with which human infants and nonhuman primates construct logical cognition. **My Originalist Hypothesis is that Sensorimotor Action Generates Elementary Logical Cognition.**

This originalist hypothesis clearly includes the corollary hypothesis that logical cognition originates in prelinguistic developments. Therefore, I do not expect language to be necessary, let alone constitutive. Therefore, too, logical cognition is not expected to be unique to human development. Some aspects of elementary logical cognition should develop in nonhuman primates as well.

I am not claiming that developing logical cognition is unique to the evolution of primate species but that we have not studied nonprimate species. I hasten to add that I am not proposing a theory of cognitive evolution in which a species' ontogenetic stages recapitulate its phylogenetic stages. Instead, research is finding divergent and invariant cognitive development across primate species. Such findings provide the basis for drawing the ("heterochronic") inferences about the evolution of cognitive development, which I consider at the end of the chapter. Since logical classifying is foundational to all cognition and its development in all primate species studied, it serves as the focus of discussion in this chapter.

THE CONSTRUCTIVIST RESEARCH METHOD

This constructivist theory of the phylogenetic and ontogenetic origins of logic led to studying its development in five primate species. The research began by presenting 6- to 60-month-old children with objects like those illustrated in Figure 5.1 (see Langer 1980, Appendix, for details on the research design). The variety of objects presented were highly manipulable: geometric forms such as cylinders, ring shapes, and realistic objects such as cups, spoons, and Fisher-Price dolls. This variety covers much of the range of objects with which infants and young children are likely to interact ordinarily. Some (e.g., those in Figure 5.1), but not all, sets of objects presented to them embodied class structures.

The children were encouraged to play spontaneously with these objects. I did not pose any problems for them to solve. So the response elicitation procedure was nonverbal and nondirective. This procedure has obvious advantages for a comparative study of human and nonhuman primates. The nonhuman primates studied were infant to juvenile monkeys (New World *Cebus apella* ages 16 to 48 months and Old World *Macaca fascicularis* ages 22 to 34 months) and infant to

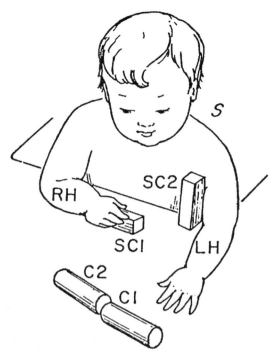

FIGURE 5.1   Infant manipulating cylinders (C1 and C2) and square columns (SC1 and SC2) to construct two categories. *RH*, right hand; *LH*, left hand

adult chimpanzees (common *Pan troglodytes* ages 1 to 21 years and bonobo *Pan paniscus* ages 6 to 11 years).

With the children only, I followed up their spontaneous object manipulations with provoked probes. For example, I presented classificatory grouping errors such as an alignment of three cups and one spoon next to an alignment of three spoons and one cup. At age 21 months, infants began to correct such classifying mistakes by switching the positions of the misplaced objects (Langer 1986). Note that these provoked procedures were also nonverbal. Moreover, they did not require the children to do anything in particular with the objects if they did not want to. They could have just continued playing freely with the objects in any way they wished.

These procedures generated systematic comparative developmental data on constructive logical cognition in sensorimotor action. A good illustration is the just cited manipulatory action which was done to correct logical misclassification by 21-month-old human infants. These procedures also generated parallel data on constructive arithmetic cognition in sensorimotor action. For example, while observed at different ages, all five primate species preserve the initial number of objects in a set that they have constructed by taking away one or two objects from the set followed by putting back an equal number of objects (Langer 1980; Poti and Antinucci 1989; Poti 1997; Poti et al 1999). This substitution operation, then, constructs quantitative equivalence in the transformed set of objects.

Many of the human findings that I now review, including those on the development of logical classifying, have been replicated with impoverished 8- to 21-month-old Indian infants living in the Sierra Madre mountains of Peru (Jacobsen 1984) and with 6- to 30-month-old infants in the San Francisco Bay Area who were exposed in utero to crack-cocaine (Ahl 1993). The cross-cultural replications indicate that our human findings are universal. The replication with infants exposed in utero to crack-cocaine is an optimistic prognosticator for their intellectual development; their early cognitive growth does not seem impaired even though their emotional and social development is disrupted.

THE COMPARATIVE DEVELOPMENT OF LOGICAL CLASSIFYING

Classifying is central to cognition (see Langer 1994b). Without it, for example, animals would not be able to recognize predators or prey. It is therefore expected that all five primate species construct single categories when presented with random arrays of objects embodying two or more classes (e.g., blue and red, triangular and cross rings). They do this by spontaneously composing object sets in space and/or time. That is, all primates eventually and spontaneously construct single sets of identical objects (e.g., two blue triangular rings) and of similar objects (e.g., a red and a blue triangular ring or a blue triangular and a blue cross ring). However, not all primate species develop classifying beyond single categories.

CONSTRUCTING SINGLE CATEGORIES

Constructing Single Categories in Space

The developmental trajectories of constructing single-category classifying in space are similar for young humans (Langer 1980) and common chimpanzees (Spinozzi 1993). They comprise a four-stage sequence in both species (Figure 5.2). Surprisingly, at the first stage, both species consistently group different objects together (e.g., blue triangular with red cross rings). At the second stage, they randomly or inconsistently group objects together (e.g., blue triangular with red cross rings as well as with blue triangular rings). At the third stage, they consistently group identical objects together (e.g., blue triangular with blue triangular rings only). At the fourth stage, they also consistently group similar objects together (e.g., blue triangular with red triangular rings as well).

Other major features of their developmental trajectories diverge (see Figure 5.2). The onset and offset ages of single-category classifying are much later in

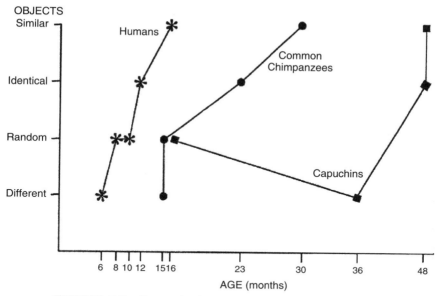

FIGURE 5.2 Comparative development of single-category classifying.

common chimpanzees than in humans, and the rate of their development is slower (see Langer 2000a, 2000b for details). In contrast, classifying is precocious and greatly accelerated in young humans. These differences are not attributable to the assessment methods because essentially the same nonverbal and nondirective procedures were used with all primate species tested.

While the stage sequence is similar in humans and common chimpanzees, it is different in capuchin and macaques monkeys (Spinozzi and Natale 1989). For instance, the developmental trajectory in juvenile capuchins is: (1) mainly random or inconsistent object grouping, (2) consistently grouping different objects together, and (3) consistently grouping identical or similar objects together.

Like common chimpanzees, monkeys' development of classificatory categorizing is also delayed in comparison to young humans (e.g., later onset and offset ages plus slower velocity). But their developmental trajectory differs from common chimpanzees and humans. Still, all primate species tested so far eventually construct at least single categories of identical objects and similar objects. This finding applies to bonobo chimpanzees as well, but we do not yet have the ontogenetic data on their onset and offset ages, velocity, and sequence (Spinozzi et al 1999).

These data are among our findings that disconfirm the theory that cognitive ontogeny simply recapitulates its phylogeny. The origins of classifying across primate species are marked by diverging ontogenetic onset and offset ages, velocity, and even developmental sequence (although not between humans and common chimpanzees). At the same time, our data are confirming the theory that cognitive ontogeny is consistent with its cognitive phylogeny (Langer 2000a, 2000b). All five species spontaneously construct single categories of identical objects and of similar objects.

Constructing Single Categories in Time

The origin of classifying does not hinge on grouping objects together in space. Manipulating objects at the same time is sufficient to construct classes (e.g., holding an object in one hand while pushing another object with the other hand). Classifying objects requires forming some minimal binary relation, but the relation can be spatial or temporal (Langer 1980). The supporting evidence, so far, comes from young humans (Langer et al 1998) and common chimpanzees (Spinozzi et al 1998; Spinozzi and Langer 1999). Both species' ontogenetic trajectories of composing single categories by manipulating objects at the same time but separately parallels their trajectories of composing single categories by grouping objects together in space.

Human infants progress from serial (one at a time) to parallel (more than one at a time) manipulation of objects. At age 6 months, their acts are primarily serial one-at-a-time manipulations of objects. The objects are consistently different when infants manipulate two or more objects at the same time, even when not grouped together. By age 12 months, infants' acts change markedly. They shift to predominantly parallel two-at-a-time manipulations of objects. The objects are consistently identical when infants separately manipulate two or more objects at the same time.

The developmental shift from doing single things in a series to doing two things in parallel reflects the human infants' progressive ability to split their attention (Langer 1980). However, when they begin to split their manipulatory attention by doing two things at a time (e.g., picking up an object with one hand while shoving another object with the other hand), the acts are usually restricted to two different parallel transformations. By age 18 months, about half of their parallel manipulatory transformations become identical or reciprocal (Langer et al 1998).

Transforming objects identically (e.g., from a horizontal to a vertical position) by manipulating them in the same way (e.g., rotating both 90 degrees) allows infants to construct functional equivalence classes even when the objects are different (Piaget 1952). For example, throwing a stick and a toy turns them both into "throwables." Transforming objects by manipulating them in reciprocal ways allows infants to construct functional complementary or dependent classes even when the objects do not belong to the same logical class hierarchy (Langer et al 1998). For example, using a stick to retrieve a toy makes them both complements of event hierarchies such as "getting." Infants' parallel manipulatory transformations allow them to construct functional equivalence and complementary classes beginning around age 18 months.

To compose equivalence and complementary classes, infants assimilate objects to their action schemes while disregarding the objects' actual class properties. In contrast, infants' earlier construction of identity classes by age

12 months required them to accommodate their action schemes to objects' actual class properties while disregarding their functional properties.

Like human infants, young common chimpanzees' manipulations also progress from serial one-at-a-time acts to parallel two-at-a-time acts (Spinozzi and Langer 1999; Spinozzi et al 1998). Their parallel manipulations also develop from predominantly different manipulatory acts to predominantly identical or reciprocal acts. Moreover, their acts also shift from manipulating different objects to manipulating identical or similar objects.

In all these behavioral respects, the development of classificatory cognition converges across primate species. But the ontogeny diverges. The onset age for composing manipulatory identity classes by common chimpanzees is the beginning of their third year, twice the chronological age for humans (and about four times the maturational age if we take into account the life history span of each species as detailed in Langer 2000a). Moreover, at this age, chimpanzees just begin to do two things at the same time (Spinozzi et al 1998; Spinozzi and Langer 1999). Only 20% of their behavior comprises parallel two-at-a-time manipulations. In contrast, when human infants shift to composing manipulatory identity classes at age 12 months, 60% of their acts already comprise parallel manipulations (Langer et al 1998). It is not until their fifth year that half of chimpanzees' acts comprise parallel two-at-a-time manipulations. It is also not until their fifth year that more than half of their manipulations become identical or reciprocal transformations.

The trajectories of human infants' developing spontaneous classifying and their manipulatory behavior that constructs it coincide. Their switch to consistently classifying objects by identity co-occurs with their switch to doing primarily identical or reciprocal parallel manipulations. Classifying objects is produced by relatively complex transformations. For instance, infants begin to combine serial one-at-a-time and parallel two-at-a-time manipulations to form hierarchical routines (Langer 1986). To illustrate, by age 15 months, infants begin to collect all objects belonging to one class by serial one-at-a-time identical transformations (e.g., gathering three forks in one hand in succession) and then combine some with objects belonging to another class by parallel two-at-a-time reciprocal transformations (e.g., uprighting and holding a cup with the second hand while the first hand repeatedly inserts and takes out some of the forks it has gathered).

In comparison to human infants, the development of spontaneous classifying and manipulatory transformations are asynchronous in young common chimpanzees. Serial one-at-a-time manipulations still predominate at age 2 years when they switch to classifying objects by identity and similarity (Spinozzi et al 1998; Spinozzi and Langer 1999). Thus, categorizing objects is initially produced by serial manipulations that are not structurally complex.

The divergence between the development of logical cognition by young chimpanzees and humans cascades as the difference in the complexity ratio of their manipulations increases. Comparative asynchrony, temporal retardation, and structural simplicity of chimpanzees' manipulatory transformations are possible causes of their minimal further development of cognition. Next, we shall see how this plays out for classificatory development by primates.

BEYOND SINGLE-CATEGORY CLASSIFYING

Two Category Classifying

The extent to which logical classifying develops varies immensely in primate phylogeny. Capuchin and macaque monkeys are limited to constructing single categories of no more than three objects up to at least age 4 years, effectively their adolescence (Spinozzi and Natale 1989). In general, they seem to be locked into developing nothing more than very simple, first-order, logical cognition (Poti and Antinucci 1989).

Common chimpanzees do develop elementary **two-category** (that is, second order) classifying, but not until their fifth year (Spinozzi 1993). To illustrate, when presented with a random mix of red and yellow cups, chimpanzees pick up red cups in one hand and yellow cups in the other hand. But humans begin to do so at a much earlier age (by age 1 to 1.5 years) (Riccuiti 1965; Nelson 1973; Starkey 1981; Sugarman 1983; Langer 1986). Thus, the developmental velocity is greatly accelerated in humans (see Langer 2000a, 2000b for details).

The fifth year, when common chimpanzees begin to construct two-category classifying, is also the age when most of their object manipulations begin to be generated in parallel (i.e., two-at-a-time acts) as already noted. At this age, chimpanzees begin to manipulate objects belonging to two classes at the same time (e.g., concurrently pushing two rings and two cups apart). Parallel manipulations seem to promote their elementary second-order cognitive development. The products of these manipulations, including elementary two-category classifying, are similar to those of 1 to 1.5-year-old human infants.

The manipulatory transformations by which common chimpanzees compose two categories, however, are limited in comparison to human infants. Common chimpanzees' object compositions remain largely inseparable from their manipulations. They rarely combine or integrate their manipulations to transform or integrate their second-order compositions (see Spinozzi and Langer 1999 for the exceptions). As long as their coordination of their parallel transformations does not become more structurally complex, common chimpanzees' development of logical classifying remains relatively limited. Thus, their classifying development does not progress with age beyond its elementary second-order level (Spinozzi et al 1999). Even in adolescent bonobo and adult common chimpanzees, classifying does not advance beyond the two-category level they already achieve by their fifth year. The extent of development does not seem to vary by chimpanzee species.

The chronological onset age of spontaneous classifying is later in chimpanzees, the beginning of their second year (Spinozzi 1993), than in humans (Langer 1980; see Langer 2000a, 2000b for details). But their developmental offset age is much earlier, their fifth or sixth year (Spinozzi et al 1999). In humans, classification continues developing through early adolescence at least (e.g., Inhelder and Piaget 1964; Markman 1978; see Langer 1994b for a recent review). This illustrates chimpanzees' extremely brief ontogenetic window of cognitive development relative to humans (see Langer 2000a, 2000b for the relative briefness of their other cognitive developments such as of causal relations). Whereas chimpanzees are confined to constructing no more than two-category classifying, humans already begin to develop three-category classifying during early childhood. When presented with a random mix of different colored cups, for example, humans begin to group them into three separate sets by color.

Three-Category Classifying

Three-category classifying is a vital difference in the cognitive development attainable by chimpanzees and humans. It determines whether hierarchically integrated cognition becomes possible. Three-category classifying opens up the possibility of hierarchization, whereas two-category classifying permits nothing more than linear cognition. Minimally, hierarchical inclusion requires two complementary subordinate classes integrated by one superordinate class. Thus, young human children already open up the possibility of hierarchizing nested classes to form a genealogical tree structure (Langer 1994a). However, even adolescent bonobo and adult common chimpanzees do not. They seem limited to linear cognition of classes because they cannot construct more than two categories at the same time.

IMPLICATIONS OF FINDINGS FOR UNDERSTANDING DEVELOPMENT

THE DEVELOPMENT OF REPRESENTATIONAL COGNITION IN ACTION

Another vital difference in their potential cognitive development is that human infants already begin to map their cognitions onto each other toward the end of their second year, that is, their cognitions become recursive (Langer 1986). Even adolescent bonobo and adult common chimpanzees rarely map their cognitions onto one another; and, when they do, they do so only at a transitional level (Poti et al 1999). This is why I have claimed that only the cognition of human infants becomes recursive among young primates and that recursiveness is a key to changing the rules of cognitive development (Langer 1994a). Recursiveness opens up possibilities for transforming linear into hierarchic cognition in humans.

The elements of cognitive development are almost limited to the contents or properties of actual or particular objects in all nonhuman primates we have studied, including chimpanzees (Poti et al 1999). In comparison, the elements of cognitive development are not limited to the properties of actual or particular sets of objects in humans. By late infancy, the elements expand to include relations (e.g., classifications, correspondences, and exchanges) as well as concrete objects, sets, series, etc. (Langer 1986). Toward the end of their second year, human infants begin to map their cognitive constructions onto each other. For example, infants may compose two sets of objects in spatial and numerical one-to-one correspondence relation. Then they exchange equal numbers of objects between the two sets such that they preserve the correspondence relation between them. These infants map substitutions onto their correspondence mappings. Thereby, they produce equivalence upon equivalence relations. By mapping their cognitions onto each other, they generate the onset of more advanced (representational) cognitions. This outcome lends further empirical support to the hypothesis that human infants develop hierarchical cognition while capuchins, macaques, and chimpanzees develop little more than linear cognitions.

By mapping their cognitions onto each other as well as onto objects, human infants begin to detach their intellectual constructions from their initial interaction with concrete objects. In comparison, the logical cognitions of even adolescent bonobo and adult common chimpanzees remain almost entirely bound to concrete objects. Detaching cognitions from their initial concrete object referents and, instead, mapping them onto other cognitions is pivotal to the formation of representational intelligence.

Representational intelligence, in this constructivist theory, begins with hierarchic mappings upon mappings (Langer 1982, 1986, 1994a). Its conceptual origins in human ontogenesis are 2-year-olds' mappings of cognitions onto cognitions mapped onto objects, as in the above illustration of 2-year-old infants' mapping substitution onto correspondence mapped onto two sets of objects. The referents of the substitution operations are no longer limited to the concrete objects forming the two corresponding sets. The referents can become equivalence **relations**. But relations are more abstract than objects. So the referents become abstract.

In general, with the formation of hierarchical cognition, the referents of human infants' intellectual operations are no longer limited to objects. Cognition is no longer limited to the concrete. Progressively, the referents of infants' cognitions become relations, such as numerical equivalence and causal dependency, that are the products of other intellectual operations mapped onto objects. By mapping cognitions onto relations, infants' intelligence becomes abstract and reflective. Understanding phenomena—how they work as well as what works—can begin to be constructed. However, infants' manipulatory activity is the origin or proximate cause of this development from pragmatic know-how to representational understanding.

THE DEVELOPMENT OF LANGUAGE AND COGNITION

What is the possible role of language in cognitive development? Cognition and language only become associated in human development. But their developmental trajectories are asynchronic, cognition preceding language onset.

Cognition and language are necessarily dissociated in nonhuman primates because they do not develop language. Still, young monkeys and chimpanzees develop first-order cognition (e.g., single-category classifying) without the benefit of any language. Young chimpanzees also develop second-order cognition (e.g., two-category classifying) without the benefit of any language.

In humans, language does not emerge until around the end of the first year with the onset of the one-word stage (Brown 1973). By then, infants are already in transition to second-order cognition (Langer 1980). So, the ontogenetic onset and earliest developmental stages of human cognition precede the onset of language by about a year.

On the other hand, the developmental offset of language forms precedes the offset of human cognitive forms by decades. The offset of cognitive forms is around age 25 to 30 years in humans (Kuhn et al 1977). Extended cognitive forms in humans are consistent with our prolonged brain maturation, including glial cell growth, synaptogenesis, and, especially, dendritic growth in the cortex up to young adulthood (Purves 1988; Gibson 1990, 1991; Paus et al 1999; Sowell et al 1999). The offset of language development is between age 5 years and puberty. (I use this large age spread because there is no consensually agreed on measure for determining the offset age of language development.) As compared with cognitive ontogeny, then, the velocity of language development is accelerated. Thus, the initial lag in linguistic development is overcome rapidly.

In phylogeny and ontogeny, then, cognition originates and develops before and without any language. Conversely, language does not originate before and without cognition. The phylogenetic dissociation proves that language is not a necessary condition for the origins of cognition and its development up to at least second-order cognition. It has long been recognized that language is not necessary for the early development of elementary physical cognition, such as object permanence and causal instrumentality by chimpanzees (e.g., Kohler 1926, Piaget 1954; Vygotsky 1962). Our research is showing that language is also not necessary for the early development of elementary logical cognition by chimpanzees up to at least second-order constructions, such as two-category classifying (Spinozzi 1993; Spinozzi et al 1999).

Since language development lags behind cognitive development during most of human infancy, it cannot inform cognition early on. As language catches up with cognition in early childhood, the influences between cognition and language may become more mutual.

Given that cognition precedes language onset during human infancy at least up to second-order cognition, the predominant potential influence is from cognition to language. I have, therefore, proposed that second-order cognition is a necessary condition for infants to produce and comprehend arbitrary but conventional rules by which symbols stand for and communicate referents in grammatical form (Langer 1986). Second-order cognitions may be necessary to form grammatical units that are progressively combinable and interchangeable, yet meaningful. This is not possible without the second-order operation of substituting elements within and between two compositions (or sets) that begin to develop toward the end of human infants' second year (Langer 1986). The hypothesis is that second-order constructive operations (of composing, decomposing, matching, commuting, substituting, and so on) provide the rewrite rules that make grammatical constructions possible.

A rudimentary signaling system of symbolizing is possible in capuchin and macaque monkeys that develop first-order but not second-order cognition. Capuchins and macaques do not develop the recursive hierarchical cognition necessary for grammatical language that human infants begin to develop in their second or third year (for related discussions, see Bickerton 1990; Lieberman 1991). Their signal systems are very poor sources for generating new cognitive growth. If, as seems to be the case, capuchins and macaques are limited to signaling, then their symbolizing can only play a minor role in expanding their cognitive development. In contrast, when human infants begin to develop advanced language, their symbolizing can play a progressive role in fostering continued cognitive development. With continuing symbolic development, especially of mathematical skills in childhood and adolescence, new and ever more powerful possibilities open up for cognitive development.

I have hypothesized that second-order cognition is a necessary condition for developing grammatical language by humans. I have also hypothesized that it is a necessary condition for learning protogrammatical language by chimpanzees (Langer 1993). While more research is needed, support for this latter learning hypothesis is provided by Savage-Rumbaugh's (1998) findings on the development of symbolic indexing and the acquisition of protogrammatical language by chimpanzees (Greenfield and Savage-Rumbaugh 1990; Savage-Rumbaugh et al 1993) that develop second-order cognition.

Another question we are currently asking is whether language acquisition by chimpanzees in turn affects their cognitive development. This includes the central issue of whether language-trained chimpanzees, unlike non–language-trained chimpanzees, can develop three-category classifying. The results are negative. We are not finding any difference between language (symbol) and non–language-trained chimpanzees including common and bonobo chimpanzees (Spinozzi et al 1999). Neither group develops beyond constructing two-category classifying. Thus, language (symbol) acquisition does not seem to be a sufficient condition for the development of third-order logical classifying, viewed here as essential to the formation of hierarchical cognition that supports the development of grammatical language.

COMPARATIVE PERCEPTUAL AND SENSORIMOTOR DEVELOPMENT

Theories of cognitive development agree that it is caused by organisms' interactions with their environment (Langer 1969). Infants' two main means of interaction are manipulatory sensorimotor acting on and reactive perceptual processing of the environment. Distinguishing between the contributions that infants' manipulatory sensorimotor action on and reactive nonmanipulatory perception of the environment make to the development of their cognition is problematic. Nevertheless, separating them empirically has become a dominant theme of contemporary research on infant cognitive development. Much of the impetus comes from claims of earlier cognitive development (e.g., object permanence) in reactive perception rather than manipulatory sensorimotor action. This has been the main empirical argument used by neonativism against a constructivist theory of cognitive development (e.g., by Wynn 1992; Leslie 1994; Baillargeon 1995; Spelke and Newport 1998).

Constructivist theory, on the other hand, posits that reactive perception of the environment is usually a poorer source of cognitive development than sensorimotor action on the environment (e.g., Piaget 1969; Langer 1998). The reasons are varied, but several are key. First and foremost, the transformations that perception can impose upon the environment with which it interacts are relatively constrained. Perception is constrained temporally to the near present, spatially to selecting and combining objects within its immediate focal span, and causally to attending to dynamic events. Second, the span of perceptual attention is relatively restricted spatiotemporally. Perception can only attend to a minimal number of environmental features within any given fixation. For example, up to age 3 years, infants' perceptual attention (but not their sensorimotor activity) can encompass only three objects at a time (see Langer et al 2003 for a review). Third, perception cannot externalize its cognitions physically in the environment. Instead, it depends on the perceiver's memory capacity, which is quite small in infants.

In contrast, sensorimotor actions on the environment are a much richer source of infants' cognitive development, for the same reasons that reactive perceptual processing of the environment is a limited source. The transformations that sensorimotor actions can impose on the environment with which infants interact are relatively unconstrained. Actions, but not perceptions, physically manipulate the environment (e.g., by hitting one object into another to construct a causal "launching" relation where there was none). Therefore, only sensorimotor actions construct cognitions by transforming the spatial and sometimes causal relations between objects with which infants interact. Moreover, the cognitions constructed by sensorimotor actions (e.g., quantitative equivalence) are to a great extent externalized physically in objects (e.g., by placing objects in one-to-one correspondence). Thus, infants' sensorimotor manipulatory constructions are relatively free from the spatiotemporal and causal phenomenal constraints plus attentional and mnemonic limitations of their nonmanipulatory perceptual reactions. Hence, I have proposed two developmental hypotheses, one on developmental precocity and the other on the extent of developmental progress.

Developmental Precocity

Cognitive development in manipulatory sensorimotor action may be relatively precocious. In contradistinction to neonativism, sensorimotor cognition need not lag developmentally behind perceptual cognition. We have already proved this for the protophysical cognitions of object permanence (Rivera et al 1999) and of causal relations (Schlesinger and Langer 1999) as well as for the protoarithmetic cognition of adding and subtracting one object to or from a set of no more than three objects (Arriaga et al 1999; Wakeley et al 2000a, 2000b).

A good illustration that cognitive development in sensorimotor manipulatory action precedes cognitive development in reactive nonmanipulatory perception comes from our findings on infants' knowledge about causal entraining relations (Schlesinger and Langer 1999). Causal entraining occurs when a moving object (the causal agent or actor) contacts a stationary object (the patient), causing it to move together with the agent object, that is, to be entrained or carried off. We compared 8- and 12-month-olds' developing sensorimotor actions with their developing perceptual processing *of* the same possible and impossible causal entraining relations (a supporting versus a nonsupporting cloth and a surrounding versus a nonsurrounding cane). On both entraining relations, infants' discriminatory causal manipulatory actions developed months before their discriminatory causal perceptual reactions. For example, when tested with a manipulatory procedure, 8-month-old infants already pulled the possible supporting but not the impossible supporting cloth to entrain the goal object. On the other hand, when tested with a violation-of-expectation procedure, only 12-month-olds looked longer at (a trick photographic display of) the impossible nonsupporting cloth entraining the goal object than at the possible supporting object entraining the goal object.

Measuring Perceptual Development

Many of the currently used perceptual measures of infants' cognitive development are of questionable reliability (e.g., Moore et al 1987; Oaker and Cohen 1990; Bogartz et al 1997; Mix et al 1997; Simon 1997; Clearfield and Mix 1999). This research also questions the validity of these perceptual measures as indicators of the innate "reasoning mechanisms" presumed by neonativism. Here I consider just one comparative development to illustrate this point (see Langer et al 2003 for further details on the reliability and validity of these perceptual measures).

Neonativism claims that human infants' reasoning about object continuity is innately representational. The perceptual measure used to support this claim showed that 4-month-old infants dishabituated to (looked longer at) two objects (e.g., the top and bottom pieces of a rod) and not one object (e.g., a rod) after being habituated to (familiarized with) a single moving object (e.g., a rod) whose middle section was occluded by a nearer object (Kellman and Spelke 1983). So, 4-month-old infants seem to experience the habituation displays (with which they were familiarized) as one continuous object even though its middle was not visible because it was occluded. On this basis, Kellman and Spelke claimed that infants are innately endowed with adult-like competence to reason representationally that an object is continuous even when a part is not visible.

Newborns, however, dishabituated to (looked longer at) one but not two objects (Slater et al 1990, 1994, 1996). Thus, newborns seem to experience the partly occluded habituation displays (with which they were familiarized) as two discontinuous objects. By this perceptual habituation measure, then, human infants are born with only presentational (i.e., what they can directly observe) cognition, not representational knowledge of object continuity. At age 2 months, infants are in transition. They still dishabituated to one but not two objects unless the occluder was very narrow and most of the singular object in the habituation display was showing (Johnson and Aslin 1995). This developmental course seems ensured by infants' interactions with their environment during their first 4 months. Their experience includes numerous, varied, and repeated manipulatory sensorimotor and nonmanipulatory perceptual interactions with continuous singular objects that are partly and temporarily hidden (by infants themselves as well as by their environment) only to re-emerge intact.

These perceptual habituation findings parallel those found by sensorimotor action measures. Sensorimotor action measures find that infants' initial cognition about object continuity develops from their stage 1 presentational (i.e., what they can directly observe) knowledge to their stage 3 anticipatory and recognitory knowledge in which they reconstruct an invisible whole object from a visible part (Piaget 1954). Thus, the ontogenetic findings from perceptual and sensorimotor action measures coincide in supporting the hypothesis that infants' initial cognition of objects develops stage-wise from presentational to anticipatory and recognitory knowledge. Neither set of developmental findings supports the hypothesis that infants are endowed with innate representational reasoning about object continuity.

Moreover, while (big-brained) newborn human infants do **not** represent object continuity by the perceptual habituation measure described, (small brained) newborn domestic chicks (*Gallus gallus*) do represent object continuity by a perceptual imprinting measure (Regolin and Vallortigara 1995; Lea et al 1996). Newly hatched chicks were first imprinted to a single moving rod whose top and bottom pieces were visible but whose center was occluded by a nearer object. In post-imprinting test trials, these newborn chicks preferred approaching a single rod over two rod pieces. By this perceptual imprinting measure, then, newborn chicks are innately endowed with a representational concept of object continuity, whereas newborn humans are not by the perceptual habituation measure. Thus, the validity of such perceptual measures for assessing and comparing human and nonhuman cognitive development, including their so-called "innate representational reasoning mechanisms," is questionable.

Developmental Progress

Cognitive development in manipulatory sensorimotor action progresses to more advanced levels than in nonmanipulatory perceptual processing (see Langer et al 2003 for a review of the confirming evidence). For example, by age 2 years, human infants begin to construct equivalences on equivalences by placing two sets of four objects in one-to-one correspondence and then substituting one object between them (Langer 1986). At this age, their nonmanipulatory perceptual protoarithmetic is still limited to no more than one set of three objects (e.g., Starkey and Cooper 1995; see Langer et al 2003 for a review). Moreover, children's nonmanipulatory visual protoarithmetic adding and subtracting one object to or from one set of no more than three objects does not develop until their third or fourth year (Vilette 1996; Houdé 1997; Vilette and Mazouz 1998). Children were tested using a perceptual violation-of-expectation procedure. On one trial, for example, they were shown two dolls on a toy theater stage that were then curtained from view. Then they saw one other doll added to the curtained set. Finally, the curtain was raised revealing either a correct result of three dolls or an incorrect result of two dolls. Not until age 3.5 years did children successfully discriminate between the correct and incorrect addition results, judging one right and the other wrong.

THE EVOLUTION OF COGNITIVE DEVELOPMENT

Nonhuman primates' comparative cognitive development in manipulatory sensorimotor action is less extensive than that of humans (see Langer 2000b for a review). For example, even adult chimpanzees only construct transitional substituting within but not between two corresponding sets of objects that they have composed (Poti et al 1999). Still, one should not underestimate the development of their constructive sensorimotor cognition. Some of their object manipulation and coordination can be quite powerful as we and others (e.g., Byrne and Russon, 1998; Johnson-Pynn et al 1999; Matsuzawa 1991; Whiten et al 1999) have discovered.

Two sequences of coordinated object manipulations that my colleagues and I have found are illustrative. Chimpanzees' sensorimotor manipulatory actions spontaneously construct three sets of two objects in one-to-one correspondence (Poti et al 1999). They also spontaneously construct hierarchically organized routines with objects (Spinozzi and Langer 1999). For example, the 6-year-old common chimpanzee Panzee did the following with cups and sticks:

1. Panzee picks up stick 1 (S1) with one hand while uprights cup 1 (C1) on the floor.
2. Places S1 on S2 to form a stable stack S1/S2.
3. Adds S3 onto S1/S2 held by the other hand on the floor, increasing the stable stack to S3/S1/S2.
4. Adds cup 1 onto S3/S1/S2 which increases the stable stack to C1/S3/S1/S2.
5. Places C1 on the floor apart from the stable stack S3/S1/S2.
6. Adds C2 on C1 to form a tower C2/C1.
7. After a while, adds C3 on C2 which increases the tower to C3/C2/C1.
8. Picks up the three sticks S3, S1, S2 together and places them on C3/C2/C1.
9. Subtracts S3/S1/S2 from C3/C2/C1 and places them on the floor.

Panzee composed two elementary subroutines (two parts in lines 1 through 4 and 5 through 7, respectively) into an integrated (whole in line 8) routine. Then she reversibly decomposed its product into its initial constituents (two parts in line 9).

FROM ASYNCHRONIC TO SYNCHRONIC COGNITIVE DEVELOPMENT

These and the other comparative findings reviewed in this chapter indicate that primate conceptual universals extend to the development of elementary logical as well as physical cognition. This degree of shared cognitive universals does not imply, however, that primates' cognitive ontogeny must recapitulate their phylogeny. The reasons are varied. Central is the fact that there are striking divergences in developmental sequencing between physical and logical cognition in primates. This outcome instead suggests divergent evolution.

Physical and logical cognition develop in parallel in human children (Figure 5.3). The onset age is the same, very early infancy and probably the neonatal period, and they develop in synchrony. For example, first-order classificatory and causal relations are constructed by infants during their first year (Langer 1980); and second-order classificatory and causal relations are constructed in their second year (Langer 1986). Neither classificatory nor causal cognition begins or ends before the other during childhood. Consequently, both forms of cognition are open to similar environmental influences and to each other's influence.

We find the other extreme in capuchins and macaques; namely, almost total asynchrony between their development of physical and logical cognition. Since

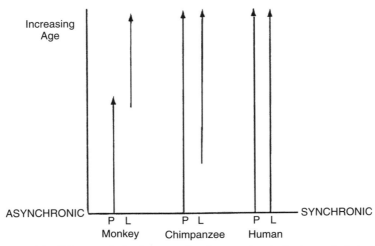

FIGURE 5.3 Primate evolution from asynchronic to synchronic development of physical (P) and logical (L) cognition.

they are out of developmental phase with each other, they are **not** likely to be open to similar environmental influences and to each other's influence. To help grasp the significance this has for the development of cognition, it may help to sketch some representative findings.

Physical cognition (such as causal relations) develops before logical cognition (such as classifying). The development of physical cognition is well underway or completed by the onset of logical cognition. To illustrate, simple first-order causality (e.g., using a support as a tool to get a goal object) develops by age 9 months in capuchins (Spinozzi and Poti 1989). By age 18 to 20 months, capuchins develop more advanced first-order causality (e.g., using a stick as an instrument to get a goal object) (Natale 1989). Thus, capuchins' first-order causality is well developed by the onset of their logical cognition during the middle of their second year.

In chimpanzees' development, physical and logical cognition constitute partially overlapping developmental trajectories (see Figure 5.3). Their development of physical cognition is not completed before the onset of their logical cognition. Physical and logical cognition constitute partially asynchronic developmental trajectories. We can, therefore, expect that these two cognitive domains may eventually begin to be partially open to similar environmental influences and to each other's influence but beginning at a relatively late age compared with humans.

To summarize, the onset age for beginning to develop physical cognition is roughly the same in all primates studied so far, including humans. In capuchin and macaque monkeys, the onset age for logical cognition is retarded such that its development does not overlap with their development of physical cognition. In chimpanzees, the onset age for logical cognition is partially accelerated such that its development partly overlaps with their development of physical cognition. In humans, the onset age for logical cognition is further accelerated such that it becomes contemporaneous with the onset age of their physical cognition.

THE HETEROCHRONY HYPOTHESIS

Evolutionary displacement in the onset or timing of one cognitive developmental trajectory relative to another within the same organism causes a disruption in the repetition of phylogeny in ontogeny. Such heterochronic displacement involves a dislocation of the evolutionary order of succession. It produces a change in the velocity or timing of ancestral processes. The velocity may be accelerated or retarded. But, importantly, as we have seen, the velocity of developing logical cognition is accelerated in humans compared with nonhuman primates.

The comparative data on the organization of and sequencing between cognitive domains are consistent with the hypothesis that heterochrony is a mechanism of the evolution of primate cognition. That is, heterochronic displacement is a mechanism whereby consecutively developing ancestral cognitive domains were transformed in primate evolution into simultaneously developing descendant cognitive domains in humans. Heterochrony produced the reorganization of non-aligned ancestral cognitive development in monkeys into the partly aligned descendant cognitive development in chimpanzees and into the fully aligned descendant cognitive development in human infancy.

This reorganization opened up multiple cascading possibilities for full information flow between logical (e.g., classificatory) and physical (e.g., causal) cognition in human infancy (e.g., making it possible to construct a "logic of experimentation"). But these cognitive domains are predominantly segregated from each other in time and, therefore, in information flow during the early development of monkeys. They are partially segregated from each other in time and, therefore, in information flow in the early development of chimpanzees.

The possibilities opened up for further progress vary accordingly and, I would propose, reciprocally constrain the "direction" of cognitive development in primate evolution. As we have seen, cognitive development is substantial in juvenile monkeys. However, their asynchronic early cognitive development hampers much further progress with age. The partially synchronic and relatively advanced early cognitive development of chimpanzees multiplies the possibilities for substantial, if still limited, further progress with age. Humans' synchronic and still more extensive early cognitive development opens up comparatively unlimited, permanent, unique, and cascading possibilities for further intellectual progress, such as a history of science (see Langer 1969, pages 178–200, for five criteria features of progressive cognitive development).

CONCLUSION

Cognitive evolution, I am suggesting, is an open, cascading developmental system. It begins and grows out of young organisms' constructive manipulatory action. These transformative sensorimotor operations are sufficient and crucial to the origins, development, and evolution of elementary logical as well as physical cognition.

REFERENCES

Ahl, V.A. 1993. Cognitive Development in Infants Prenatally Exposed to Cocaine. Unpublished doctoral dissertation. University of California at Berkeley.

Arriaga, R.I., Joyce, K., Pathmarajah, M., Walthall, A., Treynor, W., and Langer, J. 1999. Do 11-month-olds know more about addition than 5-month-olds? Poster presentation. Irvine, CA: Western Psychological Association.

Baillargeon, R. 1995. A model of physical reasoning in infancy. In Rovee-Collier, C. and Lipsett, L. (Editors), *Advances in Infancy Research*, Vol. 9, pp. 305–371. Norwood, NJ: Ablex.

Bickerton, D. 1990. *Language and Species*. Chicago: University of Chicago Press.

Bogartz, R.S., Shinsky, J.L., and Speaker, C. 1997. Interpreting infant looking: The event set X event set design. *Dev Psychol* 33:408–422.

Brown, R.A. 1973. *A First Language: The Early Stages*. Cambridge: Harvard University Press.

Byrne, R.W. and Russon, A.E. 1998. Learning by imitation: A hierarchical approach. *Behav Brain Sci* 21:667–684.

Carnap, R. 1960. *The Logical Syntax of Language*. Paterson, NJ: Littlefield and Adams.

Cassirer, E. 1953. *Philosophy of Symbolic Forms*, Vol. 1. Language. New Haven, CT: Yale University Press.

Cassirer, E. 1957. *Philosophy of Symbolic Forms*, Vol. 3. Phenomenology of Knowledge. New Haven, CT: Yale University Press.

Clearfield, M.W., and Mix, K.S. 1999. Number versus contour length in infants' discrimination of small visual sets. *Psychol Sci* 10:408–411.

Damerow, P. 1998. Prehistory and cognitive development. In Langer, J. and Killen, M. (Editors), *Piaget, Evolution, and Development*. pp. 247–270. Mahwah, NJ: Erlbaum.

Gibson, K.R. 1990. New perspectives on instincts and intelligence: Brain size and the emergence of hierarchical mental constructional skills. In Parker, S.T., and Gibson, K.R. (Editors), *"Language" and Intelligence in Monkeys and Apes*. pp. 97–128. Cambridge, UK: Cambridge University Press.

Gibson, K.R. 1991. Myelination and behavioral development: A comparative perspective on questions of neoteny, altriciality and intelligence. In Gibson, K.R., and Petersen, A.C. (Editors), *Brain Maturation and Cognitive Development*. pp. 29–63. New York: de Gruyter.

Greenfield, P.M. and Savage-Rumbaugh, E.S. 1990. Grammatical combination in Pan paniscus: Process of learning and invention in the evolution and development of language. In Parker, S.T., and Gibson, K.R. (Editors), *"Language" and Intelligence in Monkeys and Apes: Comparative Developmental Perspectives*. pp. 540–578. Cambridge, UK: Cambridge University Press.

Houdé, O. 1997. Numerical development: From infant to the child. Wynn's 1992 paradigm in 2- and 3-year olds. *Cogn Dev* 12:373–391.

Inhelder, B., and Piaget, J. 1964. *The Early Growth of Logic in the Child*. London, England: Routledge and Kegan Paul.

Jacobsen, T.A. 1984. The Construction and Regulation of Early Structures of Logic. A Cross-Cultural Study of Infant Cognitive Development. Unpublished doctoral dissertation. University of California at Berkeley.

Johnson, S.P., and Aslin, R.N. 1995. Perception of object unity in 2-month-old infants. *Dev Psychol* 315:739–745.

Johnson-Pynn, J., Fragaszy, D.M., Hirsh, E.M., Brakke, K.E., and Greenfield, P.M. 1999. Strategies used to combine seriated cups by chimpanzees Pan troglodytes, bonobos Pan paniscus, and capuchins Cebus apella. *J Comp Psychol* 113:137–148.

Kellman, P.J., and Spelke, E.S. 1983. Perception of partly occluded objects in infancy. *Cogn Psychol* 15:483–524.

Klahr, D. 1989. Information processing approaches to cognitive development. In Vasta, R. (Editor), *Annals of Child Development*, Vol. 6, 133–185.

Kneale, W., and Kneale, M. 1962. *The Development of Logic*. Oxford, England: Oxford University Press.

Koffka, K. 1928. *The Growth of the Mind*. London, England: Routledge and Kegan Paul.

Kohler, W. 1926. *The Mentality of Apes*. New York: Harcourt, Brace.

Kramer, E.E. 1970. *The Nature and Growth of Modern Mathematics*. New York: Hawthorne.

Kuhn, D., Langer, J., Kohlberg, L., and Haan, N. 1977. The development of formal operations in logical and moral judgment. *Genet Psychol Monogr* 95:97–188.

Langer, J. 1969. *Theories of Development*. New York: Holt, Rinehart and Winston.

Langer, J. 1980. *The Origins of Logic: Six to Twelve Months*. New York: Academic Press.

Langer, J. 1982. From prerepresentational to representational cognition. In Forman, G. (Editor), *Action and Thought*. pp. 37–64. New York: Academic Press.

Langer, J. 1986. *The origins of logic: One to two years*. New York: Academic Press.

Langer, J. 1993. Comparative cognitive development. In Gibson, K., and Ingold, T. (Editors), *Tools, Language and Cognition in Human Evolution*. pp. 300–313. New York: Cambridge University Press.

Langer, J. 1994a. From acting to understanding: The comparative development of meaning. In Overton, W.F., and Palermo, D. (Editors), *The Nature and Ontogenesis of Meaning*. pp. 191–213. Norwood, NJ: Erlbaum.

Langer, J. 1994b. Logic. In Ramachandren, V. S., (Editor), *Encyclopedia of Human Behavior*. San Diego: Academic Press.

Langer, J. 1998. Phylogenetic and ontogenetic origins of logic: Classification. In Langer, J., and Killen, M. (Editors), *Piaget, Evolution and Development*. pp. 33–54. Mahwah, NJ: Erlbaum.

Langer, J. 2000a. The heterochronic evolution of primate cognitive development. In Parker, S.T., Langer, J., and McKinney, M.L. (Editors), *Biology, Brains and Behavior: The Evolution of Human Development*. pp. 213–233. Santa Fe, NM: School of American Research Press.

Langer, J. 2000b. The descent of cognitive development. *Dev Sci* 3:361–378.

Langer, J., Rivera, S., Schlesinger, M., and Wakeley, A. 2003. Early cognitive development: Ontogeny and phylogeny. In Valsiner, J., and Connolly, K. (Editors), *Handbook of Developmental Psychology*. pp. 141–171. London, England: Sage.

Langer, J., Schlesinger, M., Spinozzi, G. and Natale, F. 1998. Developing classification in action: I. Human infants. *Hum Evol* 13:107–124.

Lea, S.E.G., Slater, A.M., and Ryan, C.M.E. 1996. Perception of object unity in chicks: A comparison with the human infant. *Infant Behav and Dev* 19:501–504.

Leslie, A.M. 1994. ToMM, To By, and Agency: Core architecture and domain specificity. In Hirschfeld, L., and Gelman, S. (Editors), *Mapping the Mind: Domain Specificity in Cognition and Culture*. pp. 119–148. New York: Cambridge University Press.

Lieberman, P. 1991. *Uniquely Human*. Cambridge, MA: Harvard University Press.

Markman, E.M. 1978. Empirical versus logical solutions to part-whole comparison problems concerning classes and collections. *Child Dev* 49:168–177.

Matsuzawa, T. 1991. Nesting cups and metatools in chimpanzees. *Behav Brain Sci* 14:570–571.

Mix, K.S., Levine, S.C., and Huttenlocher, J. 1997. Numerical abstraction in human infants: Another look. *Dev Psychol* 33:423–428.

Moore, D., Benenson, J., Reznick, J.S., Peterson, M., and Kagan, J. 1987. Effect of auditory numerical information on infants' looking behavior: Contradictory evidence. *Dev Psychol* 23:665–670.

Natale, F. 1989. Causality II: The stick problem. In Antinucci, F. (Editor), *Cognitive Structure and Development in Nonhuman Primates*. pp. 121–133. Hillsdale, NJ: Erlbaum.

Nelson, K. 1973. Some evidence for the primacy of categorization and its functional basis. *Merrill Palmer Q* 19:21–39.

Oakes, L.M., and Cohen, L.B. 1990. Infant perception of a causal event. *Cog Dev* 5:193–207.

Parker, S.T. and McKinney, M.L. 1999. *Origins of Intelligence: The Evolution of Cognitive Development in Monkeys, Apes, and Humans*. Baltimore: Johns Hopkins University Press.

Paus, T., Zijdenbos, A., Worsley, K., Collins, D.L., Blumenthal, J., Giedd, J.N., Rapoport, J.L., and Evans, A.C. 1999. Structural maturation of neural pathways in children and adolescents: In vivo study. *Science* 283:1908–1911.

Piaget, J. 1952. *The Origins of Intelligence in Children*. New York: International Universities Press.

Piaget, J. 1954. *The Construction of Reality in the Child*. New York: Basic Books.

Piaget, J. 1969. *The Mechanisms of Perception*. London, England: Routledge and Kegan Paul.

Poti, P. 1997. Logical structures in young chimpanzees' spontaneous object grouping. *Folia Primatol* 18:33–59.

Poti, P., and Antinucci, F. 1989. Logical operations. In Antinucci, F. (Editor), *Cognitive Structure and Development of Nonhuman Primates*. pp. 189–228. Hillsdale, NJ: Erlbaum.

Poti, P., Langer, J., Savage-Rumbaugh, E.S., and Brakke, K.E. 1999. Spontaneous logicomathematical constructions by chimpanzees Pan troglodytes, Pan paniscus. *Anim Cogn* 2:147–156.

Purves, D. 1988. *Body and Brain: A Trophic Theory of Neural Connections*. Cambridge, MA: Harvard University Press.

Regolin, L., and Vallortigara, G. 1995. Perception of partly occluded objects by young chicks. *Percept Psychophys* 57:971–976.

Riccuiti, H.N. 1965. Object grouping and selective ordering behavior in infants 12 to 24 months. *Merrill Palmer Q* 11:129–148.

Rivera, S.M., Wakeley, A., and Langer, J. 1999. The drawbridge phenomenon: Representational reasoning or perceptual preference? *Dev Psychol* 35:427–435.

Savage-Rumbaugh, E.S. 1998. How science measures the language act. In Langer, J., and Killen, M. (Editors), *Piaget, Evolution and Development*. Hillsdale, NJ: Erlbaum.

Savage-Rumbaugh, E.S., Murphy, J., Sevcik, R.A., Brakke, K.E., Williams, S.L., and Rumbaugh, D.M. 1993. Language comprehension in ape and child. *Monogr Soc Res Child Dev* 58:1–222.

Schlesinger, M., and Langer, J. 1999. Infants' developing expectations of possible and impossible tool-use events between the ages of 8 and 12 months. *Dev Sci* 2:196–206.

Simon, T.J. 1997. Reconceptualizing the origins of number knowledge: A "non-numerical" account. *Cogn Dev* 12:349–372.

Slater, A., Morison, V., Somers, M., Mattock, A., Brown, E., and Taylor, D. 1990. Newborn and older infants' perception of partly occluded objects. *Infant Behav Dev* 13:33–49.

Slater, A., Johnson, S.P., Kellman, P.H., and Spelke, E. 1994. The role of three-dimensional depth cues in infants' perception of partly occluded objects. *Early Dev Parent* 3:187–191.

Slater, A., Johnson, S.P., Brown, E., and Badenoch, M. 1996. Newborn infant's perception of partly occluded objects. *Infant Behav Dev* 191:145–148.

Sowell, E.R., Thompson, P.M., Holmes, C.J., Jernigan, T.L., and Toga, A.W. 1999. In vivo evidence for post-adolescent brain maturation in frontal and striatal regions. *Nat Neurosci* 2:859–861.

Spelke, E.S., and Newport, E.L. 1998. Nativism, empiricism, and the development of knowledge. In Damon, W. (Editor), *Handbook of Child Psychology*, Vol. 1, pp. 275–340. New York: Wiley.

Spinozzi, G. 1993. The development of spontaneous classificatory behavior in chimpanzees Pan troglodytes. *J Comp Psychol* 107:193–200.

Spinozzi, G., and Langer, J. 1999. Spontaneous classification in action by a human-enculturated and language-reared bonobo Pan paniscus and common chimpanzees Pan troglodytes. *J Comp Psychol* 113:286–296.

Spinozzi, G., and Natale, F. 1989. Classification. In Antinucci, F. (Editor), *Cognitive Structure and Development of Nonhuman Primates*. pp. 163–188. Hillsdale, NJ: Erlbaum.

Spinozzi, G., Natale, F., Langer, J., and Brakke, K. 1999. Spontaneous class grouping behavior by bonobos Pan paniscus and common chimpanzees Pan troglodytes. *Anim Cogn* 2:157–170.

Spinozzi, G., Natale, F., Langer, J., and Schlesinger, M. 1998. Developing classification in action: II. Young chimpanzees Pan troglodytes. *Hu Evol* 13:125–139.

Spinozzi, G., and Poti, P. 1989. Causality I: The support problem. In Antinucci, F. (Editor), *Cognitive Structure and Development of Nonhuman Primates*. pp. 113–120. Hillsdale, NJ: Erlbaum.

Starkey, D. 1981. The origins of concept formation: Object sorting and object preference in early infancy. *Child Dev* 52:489–497.

Starkey, P., and Cooper, R.G. 1995. The development of subitizing in young children. *Br J Dev Psychol* 13:399–420.

Sugarman, S. 1983. *Children's Early Thought: Developments in Classification*. New York: Cambridge University Press.

Vilette, B. 1996. De la "proto-arithmétique" aux connaissances additives et soustractives. *Revue de Pychologie de l'éducation* 3:25–43.

Vilette, B., and Mazouz, K. 1998. Les transformations numériques et spatiales entre deux et quatre ans. *Archives de psychologie* 66:35–47.

Vygotsky, L.S. 1962. *Thought and Language*. New York: Wiley and MIT.

Wakeley, A., Rivera, S., and Langer, J. 2000a. Can young infants add and subtract? *Child Dev* 71:1525–1534.

Wakeley, A., Rivera, S., and Langer, J. 2000b. Not proved: Reply to Wynn. *Child Dev* 71:1537–1539.

Werner, H. 1948. *Comparative Psychology of Mental Development*. New York: International Universities Press.

Werner, H. and Kaplan, B. 1963. *Symbol Formation*. New York: Wiley.

Wertheimer, M. 1945. *Productive Thinking*. New York: Harper.

Whiten, A., Goodall, J., McGrew, W.C., Nishida, T., Reynolds, V., Sugiyama, Y., Tutin, C.E.G., Wrangham, R.W., and Boesch, C. 1999. Cultures in chimpanzees. *Nature* 399:682–685.

Wynn, K. 1992. Addition and subtraction in human infants. *Nature* 358:749–750.

6

THE EVENT BASIS OF CONCEPTUAL AND LANGUAGE DEVELOPMENT

KATHERINE NELSON, PHD

In this chapter, I address the issue of event knowledge as the basis of conceptual and language development. My work has focused on action, specifically on sequences of purposeful actions. As the theme of this book attests, the idea of embodied, dynamic, enacted cognition is no longer a proposition beyond the boundaries of mainstream cognitive science, but it still needs considerable clarification.

The focus of this book on "action" raises the question: What is the alternative to action as a link to intelligent behavior? I begin, therefore, with an overview of the alternative to action. I then consider the event knowledge basis of intelligent behavior, both in evolution (phylogenesis) and development (ontogenesis), and its links to symbols in early language. Finally, I outline the extension of this link and its integration into cultural systems through conventional categorical systems established by collaborative construction between children and caregivers.

TRADITIONAL VIEWS OF COGNITION: FOCUS ON OBJECTS

Cognitive psychology inherited its central issues from Western philosophical traditions of epistemology, moving questions of how we know from the arm chair to the laboratory. Beginning with Descartes, the central problem to be solved has been posed as the relationship between thought (in the mind) and things external to the mind, including the body. The move from philosophy to psychology failed to change the basic assumptions of armchair theorists, principally that the problem of knowledge concerns how general concepts may be validly formed on the basis of the perception of objects as they exist in a stable world. These assumptions persist in many ways today. Specifically, they persist in the conceptual models that begin with elemental perceptual units—edges, shadows, spectral rays—and seek to determine how the mind constructs objects therefrom. Philosophers and psychologists seem to share an illusion that isolated people stand in a world surrounded by inexplicable but stable unmoving objects, most of a size to be picked up or bumped into (as MacNamara 1982, put it). In this view, the infant's problem is to analyze the perceptual scene and determine which objects belong to the same categories, how objects in general can be distinguished from their background, how one object may cause another to move, and other problems of this general nature. Solving these problems is such a difficult task that it has occupied psychophysicists, developmental psychologists, and neurocognitive scientists for 150 years.

Piaget (1952), taking a new tack on the problem, linked action to object knowledge, and, thus, ultimately to advanced human intelligence. According to Piaget, the mind constructs object knowledge, but does so through object–action schemas and not solely through perceptual composition. For Piaget, **action** was the key to intelligence. Yet, there are several missing pieces to Piaget's account. The social world in particular is glaringly absent from the infant's environment except in the person of the observer of the infant's behavior. The only action accounted for in his theory is the infant's own action, not the actions of others, and interaction refers only to the interaction of the child with the physical world of concrete objects. In any theory designed to explain the movement from object to concept to symbol, and thus to communicative language, this is a fatal flaw. In contrast, in the present account, **interaction** is conceived as primarily social, and the term refers to the interaction of the child with others in the social world.

To see this point clearly, consider the classic series of object permanence tasks that Piaget used to analyze the infant's growing understanding of the object concept. When we view these classic observations of infant behavior in social interaction rather than object terms, they take on entirely different meanings. Piaget claimed that children must learn that objects are independent of their own actions. To demonstrate this, the experimenter hides objects in different places, culminating in the series of invisible displacements, where the child cannot see whether the experimenter has left the object under the first, second, or third of a series of screens. This series has been exactly replicated in infant tests used today, providing norms that determine when the child is capable of invisible displacements. When the child (between 18 and 24 months) has managed to solve this task, what does it indicate? To Piaget (1952) it indicated that the child had formulated a concept of object permanence, the belief that objects are substantial, persistent through time and space, and independent of the child's own actions.

From a social event perspective, however, what the child learns is not that objects can exist independently, but that people, in particular, adults can dispose of objects in different ways, by hiding them first in one place and then in another. In addition, children must learn that there are search procedures that can successfully uncover the hidden object, regardless of whether they have seen exactly where the adult has hidden it. If the child truly believed that objects moved independently of any person's actions, as Piaget seemed to imply, then there would be no point in playing the game because the object might be any-where once out of sight. Indeed, an important part of the child's acquisition of object knowledge must be the distinction among different types of objects, some of which move independently (e.g., insects), some of which do not; some of which change form (e.g., ice), some of which do not; and some of which are not permanent (e.g., food), and some of which are. In physics and in logic, objects are permanent, but in the infant's experiential world, objects are not necessarily so. And they are not necessarily independent of people's actions on them. These object relations constitute complex social world knowledge that is inadvertently built into the classic series of object permanence.

More recent experiments have shown that infants of only a few months of age are more cognizant of the composition of the object world than Piaget's action theory allows (e.g., Baillargeon 1993). The result is a counterview that has swept the field of infant cognition over the past 20 years, which posits that innate knowledge, the legacy of species evolution, provides the human infant with the concept of objectness. This line of research demonstrating earlier understanding of object relations than Piaget observed disentangles complex social understand-ing from understanding the physical relations involved. The isolation of physical understanding from social complexities could well be the key to the success of these experiments with young infants, although they do not thereby warrant the conclusion that such young infants have a concept of object permanence. In a biological perspective, it seems perfectly reasonable that the perceptual systems are inherently designed to pick out objects from the dynamic array, as Gibson (1986) claimed. All animals that move around in the world need to be able to identify objects of varying sizes, and so on. However, as argued here, this capa-city rests not on the abstractions of physics, innate or constructivist, but on a variegated experiential knowledge base made possible by an array of biological structures and functions.

THE EXPERIENTIALIST ALTERNATIVE

Piaget's view of genetic epistemology was experiential at its base. He noticed what is ruled out by paradigms set in the laboratory where passive infants are seated in infant seats and watch scenes on stages or videotape. Piaget realized that infants in the real world actively explore objects and through action come to know what specific objects can do and the possible relations between themselves and objects. Piaget was not content, as many current investigators are, to study what a child could do at a given age but rather attempted to explain how know-ledge at one point provided the experiential foundation for development of knowledge at the next point. The experiential view stands in contrast to the traditional view based on building up concepts from elemental perceptions, and the neonativist view that object knowledge is innately given.

Piaget argued this contrast repeatedly in his early books. The experientialist view was also the basis of the early American pragmatists, including James Mark Baldwin and John Dewey. The starting point for scientific investigation in this perspective is the analysis of experience in the real world. The experientialist alternative sees the child as making sense of the world he or she lives in, which involves mentally represented everyday experience. This view contrasts dramatically with the perspective of the problem of knowing objects as posed in the standard cognitive development literature. If we change the parameters of the object knowledge problem, which at its base is also the problem of making sense of the world in which we live, we can start with the dynamic world of social events. This perspective is informed by classic theories, beginning with Piaget's insight that the child could only solve the object concept problems by acting on objects rather than just looking at them. Gibson's (1986) insight was that sensory systems were designed to pick up information from the dynamic environment in which they were evolutionarily adapted and, therefore, that some of the thornier problems of objective reality could be bypassed at the outset. Vygotsky (1986) went beyond this point to see that the child would not get very far alone and that having a knowledgeable adult partner around to talk to about the objects and their categories would be helpful. Equally important, as is now recognized, the infant from birth is immediately and necessarily embraced by people and their attentive activities. Unless abandoned by society, the child will become part of the world of social events and, only within that social world, will objects become known and valued.

Experience tends to be highly dynamic; something is always happening, even if it is only talk. Thus, to understand the dynamic world they live in, infants must engage in parsing the events of that world, breaking them apart into comprehensible pieces. Making sense is an activity that relates the infant to the world around her, where the goals and means of the activities are revealed through action, whether in everyday routines, play, or novel events. In this perspective, objects for the infant do not have meaning in and of themselves but only as they relate to the events of which they are a part.

Unlike most older people, young infants do spend time contemplating static objects as well as acting on them, and Jean Mandler (1992) has built a theory of concept development based on this observation. This theory is not inconsistent with others that posit that infants and children attempt to **make sense** of the world around them. Certainly, identifying the shapes and parts of objects visually as well as manually is an important activity, especially in infancy when all objects are novel. The more important point is that "making sense" is an activity that relates the infant to the surrounding world.

This claim leads naturally to the experientialist perspective, which emphasizes both parts of the biocultural embeddedness of human development. The biological is seen as continuous with the cultural, rather than one part as natural and the other as added on (Nelson 1996). Still, most of what the infant and child come to understand about the world is specific to the cultural and historical situation within which each infant exists. Thus, part of the biological given must be the capacity for making sense of these cultural specifics, constructing them from generalizations that fit the world as it is encountered. Event representations are critical to this activity.

EVENT KNOWLEDGE

Events are more complex than objects. Events take place in time through a sequence of actions. They may range in size from a single action extended in time (e.g., walking to school) to a full-scale activity taking place over hours (e.g., a circus). Events combine interest, affect, and utility in a dynamic mix that encompasses people, objects, and actions in one whole configuration. A central claim here is that **participation** in everyday event routines with other people offers to the child a base of secure knowledge as a foundation for the formation of concepts and the acquisition of language.

To make this claim coherent, it is necessary to be specific about the kinds of events that may function for children as a knowledge base. I suggest that there is a natural "mid-size" event that is something like the basic-level object concept (Rosch 1978). It is bounded with a clear beginning and end. Such a mid-size event might be having a bath, changing a diaper, or getting and drinking a bottle of milk. Such events become the basis for the infant's beginning scripts, and there is growing evidence that such scripts have a psychological reality in the young child's representational system. These scripts, or event representations, serve as a foundation for emerging concepts, language, and higher levels of intelligent behavior and thought.

There is a common misconception that event representations are composed through passive uninterpreted observation of ongoing actions in the world, but this is far from the case. The young child's "scripts" are products of participatory interaction with other people; they are social and have causal and social goal meanings. Children form event scripts with the goal of finding the meaning in other people's actions, to make sense and to locate their own place in the world of events. For example, the end point of eating is hardly devoid of either biological or social meaning in the young child's life. It is not surprising then that children build up having lunch scripts, which include their own and the other person's active parts, as well as the possible objects that can occur in the script.

Events are social; they involve social activities in social settings. They are located in particular places; for example, eating lunch may be located in the kitchen. Locations may be part of the context that defines the event for the child, and particular location changes may indicate when one event begins and another ends. Events involve people, actions, and objects that must be tracked across time through the dynamics of temporal and causal relations if they are to be understood. Causal relations are critical to understanding events; they include, but are not limited to, the direct physical causality of one object acting on another. They also include enabling conditions that make a subsequent action possible and effective. For example, getting out the milk enables putting it into the cup, which in turn enables drinking from the cup. Causal relations also include the mental intentions to bring about an action, entailing other actions that preceded or succeeded the central one. These causal relations are understood by children as young as 1 year of age (Tomasello 1992; Bauer et al 1994).

CONCEPTS, OBJECTS, AND WORDS

Where do concepts come from? In an experientialist view, everyday concepts of objects, actions, and persons are the beginning points of cognitive contents. Abstract concepts such as causality, agency, and intentionality (and others that philosophers and psychologists are fond of) are abstractions from mental and behavioral processes that emerge from mature reflection and discourse. They do not emerge from the child's interactions with the physical and social world. However, in the present theory, concepts of objects are assumed to be developmental derivations from events.

This proposal was originally formulated in terms of a Functional Core Concept (Nelson 1974). In that version of the theory, I argued that infants begin to form concepts of objects in terms of the functions they served from the infant's perspective. This perspective involves what interesting and salient things do and what infants can do with them. The functional core concept has since been expanded through the recognition that infants often organize their concepts of objects around the typical events where they are encountered in everyday life. For example, the foods the child eats are encountered at special meal and snack times. Bedtime incorporates particular routines and objects (bedclothes, crib, stuffed toys). The time and place of the event forms part of the knowledge of the object in the life of the child at the same time that the event itself is conceptualized as a whole representation.

This idea can be illustrated through the simple example of an event in a young child's life, the bath event. This is a general event that children come to know, and we can model it in the laboratory by giving Teddy a pretend bath. Two-year-olds, even an 18-month-old, will follow along and imitate the model. A 3-year-old child will tell you if you are carrying out the activity in the wrong way (Rothstein 1991). The bath event changes over the months of the child's life, involving changes in the bathing container (e.g., from a small tub to a big tub), the objects involved, the person who gives the bath, and so on. But much of the bath event remains the same, with a stable sequence of actions that at any particular time, consists of such things as undressing, getting into the tub, splashing with the toy duck, scrubbing, getting out of the tub, toweling down, and dressing. The bath tends to be a prototypical event in the child's life, so much so that an infant younger than 1 year who hears the word, "bath," often responds by looking or crawling toward the bath location. "Bath" is commonly one of the first words in the child's own expressive vocabulary at approximately one year of age. Interestingly, "duck" also is often one of the child's first words and typically refers to the toy duck played with in the bath (Barrett 1985).

The bath example illustrates how the original functional core concept and the event representation knowledge base are theoretically integrated. The toy duck inherits its function from the context of the event in which it plays a part. Martyn Barrett (1985) has provided a nice example of a word that was first embedded in his son's bath event, namely the word, "duck," which was "initially produced by Adam only while he was engaged in the process of hitting one of his toy yellow ducks off the edge of the bathtub, which was where they were normally kept. He was never observed producing this word in any other situation at this initial stage. He never produced it while he was playing with his toy ducks in other situations or while he was looking at or feeding real ducks, although he apparently engaged in these activities. Adam had not yet learned that the word *duck* could be used to refer either to his toy ducks outside the bath context or to real ducks. He had simply identified one particular event in the context in which it was appropriate for him to produce the word. *Duck* was obviously one of the important components of this bath event. This restriction to single event contexts of words, that for adults refers to categories of objects, is precisely what one would expect if the child is interpreting and using words in terms of mental event representations. Soon after the point where *duck* was used only for the bath situation, Barrett's son began extending the term *duck* to other instances of ducks in other contexts. That is, he began to generalize its use from its original referent and restricted context to refer to members of the duck category in general.

Embeddedness of first words in activity contexts is not a new observation but has been documented by many observers, including Piaget and Vygotsky. A nice example from a study of first word uses by Leslie Rescorla (1980) shows how a broad category term may be derived from an event context. One of the children she studied at 16 months used the word *Lardi* to refer to all kinds of fruits and vegetables. *Lardi* was a term used in a specific event context in which a produce man, Mr. Lardi, delivered produce to the child's house twice a week. From the mother's use of the phrases, "Here comes Mr. Lardi," and "Look what Mr. Lardi brought us," the child extracted the word *Lardi* and applied it to objects delivered. From one point of view, this was an incorrect term for a correct generalization to a higher-order category of a type of food. But the child began by using *Lardi* to indicate the whole event, announcing the man's arrival, no doubt in imitation of the mother's use. Like most mothers, this mother did not correct the child's extension of the word from the man to his products but rather interpreted the child's use as being relevant to the context.

Examples like Barrett's *duck* and Rescorla's *Lardi* provide a way of thinking about the relation among events, words, concepts, and event representations. Events in the world are dynamic. The produce delivery by Mr. Lardi includes a complex series of actions and social interactions taking place over time, and the child observes this sequence of interesting events. In the case of the Lardi event, the child is on the periphery and is not a central participant. Nonetheless she forms an event representation that allows her to predict what is going to happen in this situation and to predict what will happen next. But that representation is necessarily also dynamic because it moves through time and incorporates causal relations. Learning and using the word make it possible to refer to the event as a whole, in effect stabilizing and unitizing the dynamic representation. In some cases, the word pulls out a part of the unit, such as "duck," or it may be used to refer to the whole situation or activity. In either case, the word make a stable whole out of what is an ongoing stream of activity. The concept, whether of the whole event, a part of an event, or a category of objects, then becomes stabilized as the word comes to be used to refer to particular aspects of the dynamic whole.

Examples like those given here suggested the importance of function, based on the child's action, as a basis for concepts that underlie the child's first object words (Nelson 1974). This idea led to the broader notion of the derivation of concepts from events in which language use plays an important role. The role of language is crucial because of the dynamics of events and mental event representations. The temporality of events demands a stabilizing force to "make sense" through generalization. This is particularly true for the growing child who constantly experiences a changing environment. By virtue of the very pace of growth, events change while they also remain in some ways the same. The bath may remain the same from one day to the next, but over time it changes substantially, as noted previously. Yet it remains "the bath." To make this point more convincing, I next consider the levels of understanding beyond the event representation and how they may fit into the connection between concepts, words, and events.

LEVELS OF REPRESENTATION

Merlin Donald (1991) proposed the idea of **the hybrid mind** as the conception of the modern adult cognitive system. The "hybrid mind" in this proposal is composed of different types of representations, layered sequentially in human evolution and history. This theory suggests how event knowledge, concepts, and language constitute separate levels of a whole representational system. Donald is not a developmentalist, but the model is relevant to developmental issues. I have proposed (Nelson 1996) a similar model of layers of knowledge representation approached from a developmental perspective. In both versions, event representations take their place as basic representations within the system. (Indeed, both

Donald and I independently proposed that events are "basic building blocks" of knowledge.)

There are four levels involved in Donald's model: event representations, mimetic representation, linguistic representations, and graphemic representations. The idea is that for the adult hybrid mind, these four levels coexist and perform different functions in the cognitive system. It is not that one replaces the other but that they each integrate knowledge in different ways, yet they continue to remain available for particular representational tasks.

The different representational tasks can be seen in terms of three different situational demands common to humans and other animals, but for some of which humans have worked out unique, and uniquely valuable, solutions. These modes are action in the world, action with others, and communication between self and others.

The first mode—action in the world—is common to and characteristic of all animals, including the human infant before and at birth. The second mode—action with others—is characteristic to some extent of all sexual species and is developed as a mode of adaptation among certain social species, such as insects and birds. It is characteristic also of the human infant from birth. The third mode—communicating with others—is also characteristic of all social species such as the social insects as well as birds and mammals that use signals of varying kinds to convey information. It is also characteristic of the human infant from birth through the reciprocal forms of cries and soothing. This general level of analysis tells us little or nothing uniquely human about development. However, with some elaboration of the scheme, we can see that human cognitive development is related to that of social animals in general but on a more complex level.

ACTION IN THE WORLD

Constructing representations of the experienced world is important to a complex individual creature's effective action in the world and thus to survival. Yet a critically important characteristic of action in the world for the human infant is that it is structured by adult caretakers in caretaking routines, family routines, and social games. These kinds of activities involve the child from birth. They are constituted of actions on and with the child as well as actions of the child. The child uses these activities as the basis for constructing individual conceptual knowledge of people, objects, and events and continues to use such activities, not just for the first 6 months, but for years. Indeed, all of us mentally model our activities as event representations that form the basis for anticipating our own and others' actions.

ACTIONS WITH OTHERS

When the child must take the other's role into account in gaining knowledge about event routines, such as the bath event, the initial focus is on what to expect in general and on knowledge of the event from the perspective of the self. This is presumably also the focus of social animals who engage in coordinated action with others. It is also the focus of the 2-year-old child in a new day care setting, as well as the infant in the crib. **But a different level of knowing comes into play when the role of the other is attended to and used as part of the knowledge base.** The mode of this level is **imitation**. Interestingly, Piaget (1962) placed imitation in the important role of internalization of action and thus of representation and symbolization. This aspect of his work has baffled American cognitive psychologists who are conditioned to discount imitation as a low-level, unproductive process.

The role of imitation in human development has been subjected to new analysis and given new theoretical significance in the theory of cultural learning (Tomasello et al 1993) as well as in Donald's evolutionary theory in the terms he designates as **mimesis**. Donald's use of the term *mimesis* refers to the broad human use of imitation and replication of action, as observed in the actions of others or in repetitive practice by oneself as a mode of learning and improving a skill. Tomasello et al and Donald both noted that fine-tuned imitation, taking into account the intention of the other's action and the means used by the other to achieve the intended goal, is rare among other primates. Meltzoff's and Moore's (1999) work on imitative recall also emphasizes its strong basis in human infancy and its incorporation of the intention of the other.

For Donald's evolutionary scheme, mimesis is the missing link between action and language in human evolution. This is probably his strongest and most controversial theoretical speculation. In mimesis, individuals attend to the actions of others, model the actions within their own motor capacities, and internalize the model such that it can be recalled and replayed later, both mentally and actively. This is a critical move: the partial copy of the other's model can be internalized even without an initial replaying by the imitator, thus making possible delayed imitation, via a mental representation that can be voluntarily recalled. Through mimesis, a range of motoric and cognitive achievements that were not initially in an individual's repertoire becomes possible, based on the actions of others. According to Donald, this is the basis of skill learning, skill practice of social games, dance, song, tool use, tool construction, and the acquisition of symbolic information through the exchange of imitated action. Mimesis takes a display of action and allows a mental representation of the display, but it does not explain anything beyond itself.

There is no implication in this idea of mimesis that the model will be incorporated precisely. To be useful, the imitator often will transform the original. In other cases, considerable practice will be necessary to acquire the skilled action that was in display. Mimesis is viewed as an important advance in conveying information, one that preceded language in human evolution and led to the establishment of many cultural forms. But like language, mimesis is generative and flexible; its forms can be recombined into new meanings. Moreover, like language, the acquisition of mimetic forms does not depend on direct teaching or rote imitation both kinds of representations are typically acquired through participation in the activities wherein they are used. Children's songs and games are examples of this kind of participatory mimetic process.

Early vocal forms are also acquired through such an imitative process, thus establishing a common form in use between people (in evolution as well as in development). These common forms have the potential to assume and convey stabilized information. Such stabilization through words was described earlier in relation to the bath event. Thus, mimesis carries the individual beyond self and other into the social group where group activity is engaged and cultural transmission takes place. It enables knowing the other's part as well as one's own. Having interiorized the other's part, the individual comes to appropriate shared knowledge, which individual action alone can never achieve.

COMMUNICATION

Is language different? Can we do it all by action? Language is different of course, both structurally and functionally. Conventional language goes far beyond what mimesis alone can offer. Although language can take many forms, both spoken and written, as well as signing, it begins for most children, and presumably also began in human evolution, as speech. Spoken language (like other forms) makes it feasible to talk about the possible and imagined, about the there and then, as well as the here and now. It enables the sharing of points of view, thus going beyond the perception and action sharing of mimesis, which takes place in the here and now, to thought sharing, which is timeless. Language shapes the concepts derived from individual event and mimetic representations into stable, conventional, culturally shared concepts or miniculturally shared forms, such as the word *Lardi*. Words then, provide for us a shared reality, a continuing reality, and a context—general reality, which goes beyond the particular context in which a word is learned and used. Words take the child into the larger cultural milieu where society and history are reflected in the very language forms that are used in everyday activities.

Each of these higher-order levels, mimesis and language, is rooted in the capacities that event knowledge provides. Event knowledge provides the framework for mimetic practices and for language learning and use. Knowledge grows outward from events; but from another perspective, event knowledge contains within it both mimetic and linguistic forms, and later still, the graphic and electronic modes of communicating and cognizing that we as adults use today. This is the nature of the mature hybrid mind. All representational levels may represent the same experience at the same time but in different ways.

FROM INDIVIDUALLY CONSTRUCTED EVENT MODELS TO CULTURALLY SHARED CONCEPTS

This is a developmental story, focused thus far on the early phases of development in infancy and the toddler language learning years. Whereas each individual must construct a mental model of one's own world, from experience that takes place within a social world where other people and their activities are most important, the move from there to conventional language is generally a smooth one because the child shares experiences with those of others, primarily the family members. Earlier, I provided examples of using words to refer to familiar events such as "bath" and to objects and people within those events such as "duck" and the idiosyncratic "Lardi." Learning to use words of this kind, in receptive and expressive forms, enables the extension of stability from one situation to the next and from one context to the next. We know that the preverbal child has action scripts based on active involvement in routines such as bathing, dressing, and feeding. These daily life events enable the child to anticipate moves and to signal needs and desires appropriately.

As previously stated, learning the words means achieving a shared reality, a continuing reality, and a reality that can be accessed in any context. Words enter into event representations and they also individuate the parts of the event represented. They establish parts of events as stable, individual **concepts** that also can be accessed outside of the event context. In these cases, the event representation serves as a basis for understanding and using the linguistic forms. In a sense, the event representation provides the conceptual potential, but the potential is only realized when the linguistic form gives it a stable, culturally shared existence. This is not a claim that one cannot have a concept without a word. But it is a claim that the shared linguistic form makes it possible to share that concept, whatever it is, with others who may or may not have shared the experience behind it.

SLOT-FILLER CATEGORIES

The process of forming shareable concepts can be seen on a different level in the guise of what I have called **slot-filler** (SF) categories. SF categories are posited to explain the process by which children come to construct general, hierarchically organized categories of objects. In brief, the claim is that children begin with functionally derived categories at the basic level, like ball, apple, and shoe. These categories are recombined into larger groups that enter into open slots in scripts for routine events and thereby form SF categories. Let me provide an example.

The food category may begin as different foods that occur in a lunch event. That is, the lunch event itself provides the slot, *eat X*. Experience with different lunch episodes indicates what Xs can fit that particular slot. The *eat X* slot becomes a category that constitutes lunch food slot fillers. SF categories are not true taxonomic hierarchical structures but form a basis in developmental experience for the formation of such conventional structures. Conventional structures are necessarily learned in collaboration with adult instruction and through experience with the categorical structure of the adult language. The point is that children do not build hierarchical structures from SF categories on their own; but, superordinate, basic level and subordinate terms are part of our language, and they are what children hear used by adults. The convergence of the child's SF categories with the language terms enables the construction of conventional categories to fit those of the language.

SYNTAGMATICS AND PARADIGMATICS

To comprehend the basis of the SF category, consider the syntagmatics and paradigmatics of event structures (Figure 6.1). This way of viewing event structure is an analogy to the syntagmatic-paradigmatic axes of structural linguistic theory, introduced by Saussure (1959, 1915), as one of the three major organizing principles of language. According to this analysis, language is structured first by **combinatorial** principles, formulated in terms of the allowable sequential combinations at a given level, for example, how words can be combined to make sentences. The second **substitutability** principle indicates what units (i.e., words) are alternatives in a particular combinatory position, or slot, to be filled. For example, in an ordinary English transitive sentence, a subject, a verb, and an object are obligatory. The words that can go into the verb slot are simply those that form a paradigmatic category of words that we call verbs. How these words

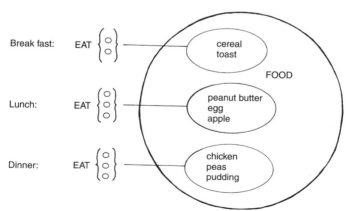

FIGURE 6.1 Syntagmatic and paradigmatic structure. Illustration of how events embed actions (eat) and associated objects (foods) that later become combined into larger paradigmatic categories. Reprinted from Nelson K. 1985. Figure 7.7, p. 204. *Making Sense: The Acquisition of Shared Meaning*. New York: Academic Press.

become defined as verbs, whether through their positions in sentences, through their semantic characteristics, or both, or by additional means, is not in question in this theory. However, Saussure did point out that paradigmatic structures are abstractions from experience, whereas syntagmatic structures are evident in experience itself. One hears the words, and their combinations, as the sentences go by. Thus perception may enable the extraction of the syntagmatic pattern. But no one hears the word classes of verbs and nouns; one can only encounter particular examples, in specific sentences, so that the construction of a class of nouns or verbs is an abstraction from experience. The two structural types are interdependent in that syntagmatic structures are defined in terms of the paradigmatic categories. Interdependently, syntagmatics are based on combinatory principles and paradigmatics on substitutive principles.

Analogously, the event structure consists of a sequence of actions, and as complements of those actions, there are alternative SFs. In the case of the lunch event, there is a more or less fixed sequence of actions and a less fixed set of alternative SFs of possible foods. For example, in the eating-lunch event, the child encounters a sequence of eating foods of types X, Y, and Z (e.g., sandwiches, fruits, and drinks). Yet in each experienced case only specific SFs for the foods can occur in X, Y, and Z slots (e.g., cheese sandwich, banana, and apple juice). Thus, basic level concept types of foods may be further categorized in terms of the meal events in which the particular foods appear, such as sandwiches at lunch. Hierarchical SF categories then may be formed by combining representations of food in different events under a single dominating term, the "slot header" term, *food*. This context-defined conception of SF categories contrasts with the logical conception of *food* as an abstract superordinate concept whose intention or definition is roughly "anything that can be eaten," and whose extension is all possible foods. This abstract taxonomic conception is a late achievement of categorical development by children, as classic research by Piaget, Vygotsky, and Bruner et al has shown. Our research indicates that it may be based to a very large extent in the earlier achievement of understanding SF hierarchies (Lucariello et al 1992; Nelson 1996).

Many familiar object categories can be derived from events as SF categories (i.e., items that can fill a particular slot in a particular type of event), for example, the foods that can be eaten at lunch. But objects and events also may be related in terms of contiguity, that is, what occurs in the same context. Often a contrast is made between the thematic and categorical with the assumption that the categorical is more advanced than the thematic. The event representation perspective indicates that they are both derived from the same underlying structure, the event, but that they have different relations, syntagmatic and paradigmatic, respectively, within that structure. Thus the relation between the individual, experientially based event knowledge and the construction of abstract category knowledge, is a dynamic constructive one that results in interacting planes of knowledge organization. Research has shown that under some circumstances, children will respond to a category task in thematic terms and under other conditions they will respond in categorical terms. Both relations are available, and it depends on what the task demand is as to which one is used. For example, in producing category items, children typically respond with SFs, while when judging what pictures go together they will rely on thematic relations (Lucariello et al 1992).

Similarity is another basic principle that has classically been invoked to explain association and concept formation. It is of considerable interest, however, that SF items need bear little similarity to one another. For example, bananas, cookies, and pudding may be alternative lunch dessert SFs for a child, but they are not similar in appearance, texture, or taste. Thus, the traditional bases for association—similarity and contiguity—do not explain the basis for SF categories. However, the paradigmatic relation of substitutability does provide an explanation. What is important to the story here is that the paradigmatic relation is displayed in real-life activities in which the child takes an active part. Moreover, it is defined in terms of the actions or functions of the items within the activity.

LANGUAGE AND CATEGORIES

In addition to the event structure basis for extracting SF categories, language plays an important role by relating the child's experientially based categories to conventional superordinate categories, which are more general and hierarchical. The contribution of language was documented in a study of the talk between 10 mothers and their 2-year-old children in everyday event contexts (Lucariello and Nelson 1986). In this study, we found, as other investigators have, that basic level terms like *dog, cat*, and *cup* were most common in the talk between mothers and their 2-year-old children. But there was also use of superordinate and subordinate terms by mothers as well as children. Superordinate terms such as *clothes* and *food* tended to be used most frequently in the context of familiar events such as eating lunch and getting dressed. Mothers provided clues to the use of the hierarchical terms, such as "what kind of a *drink* do you want" (using *drink* as a superordinate for milk, juice, and so on) and following up with alternative possibilities in the drink category. Another clue in mothers' speech was the use of basic-level items in the same syntactic frame as the higher-level category terms, such as "let's put on your *clothes*," followed by "put on your *shirt*" and "put on your *socks*," where "put on" provided a slot within which both the SFs and SF *header* or the superordinate term "clothes" could be inserted. Thus, language seems to provide a framework whereby the child can get a grip on the structure of the higher-level category. What is critical is that the higher-order term is not confined to a single event context but is "portable" to other contexts relevant to its use as well as to other nonexperiential, social, or cultural contexts.

In a study of a single child observed in a longitudinal study of pre-bed talk with her parents and by herself (Nelson 1989), the development over time of the construction of relations between events and object categories could be traced in the parent-child dialogue. In this study, the parents tape-recorded their conversations with Emily between the age of 21 and 36 months. Analysis of the pre-bed talk between parents (primarily father) and Emily revealed that much of that talk consisted of what was going to happen the next day. Some of the talk was about what would happen and what they would eat for breakfast. Consider the following example when Emily was not quite 2 years old.

> Emily: What we have on breakfast day? What we have?

> Father: What will we have for breakfast? You know, tomorrow morning you're going to have yogurt and bananas and wheat germ like mommy gave you this morning. Remember that? Instead of an egg tomorrow we're going to have yogurt and bananas and wheat germ . . .

Later, Emily enters into the dialogue more actively and she specifies what she wants.

> Father: We'll get up . . . and we'll go down and have breakfast. You can choose what type of egg you want.

> Emily: I want a boiled egg.

> Father: Okay, and you can choose what type of cereal you want, you can have either Shredded Wheat or Cheerios.

> Emily: Shredded Wheat!

A month and a half later, she's entering her own suggestion, no longer relying on Dad's scaffolding so much.

> Emily: And now, so tell me about today.

> Father: Well today you had a Tanta [the baby-sitter] day also.

> Emily: I want yogurt.

(I interpret this response as an indication that she did not mean today in the first utterance, she meant tomorrow morning for breakfast.)

> Father: And you want yogurt. I know, and I think I'll have some raspberries for you tomorrow.

> Emily: And I cereal.

> Father: Today you had strawberries, tomorrow I think you'll have raspberries.

> Emily: Cereal! Cereal!

> Father: You'll have cereal? Okay. Cereal and yogurt? You want bananas in yogurt, or raspberries in your cereal?

Emily: Yeah.

Father: Okay, that'll be good.

Emily: And strawberries in my cereal.

As can be seen in these discussions, Emily's breakfast food category was highly constrained to the particular situation and did not stray from the alternatives specified by this particular family, such as yogurt, cereal, fruit, and eggs. However, the talk is not constrained to the particular here and now, rather the breakfast food category is general, and language enables the discussion of what will happen in that regard the following day. But the category itself was constrained to breakfast and Emily's articulation of it did not wander into pizza, hamburgers, or other items appropriate for dinner. The point is that her category of alternatives for breakfast was specific to that situated event, constituting an increasingly elaborated SF category of breakfast foods.

These examples highlight the critical relation of language to the conceptualization of objects and events. Emily's monologues and dialogues reveal that her event representations are reflected in linguistic formulations and are subjected to re-representations through particular linguistic input from her parents. The conceptual system and the language system evolve together interdependently at 2 years old as well as later in life. But note that the language that simultaneously expresses and shapes the child's representations is not the language of abstract categories but the concrete language of experience. To be sure, her language includes category terms, but these are particularized to specific experience. The coordination of the child's language of categories with that of the adult takes place in everyday activities and the discourse that surrounds them. Children's mental event representations reflect the systematization of their own experience in the world. But this system is not the system that organizes the relevant cultural categories. The conventional cultural system is displayed to the child, not systematically as in a school text, but in bits and pieces through adult-child talk. The child acquires a partial system that is mediated by the adults' partial system and the child's conceptual system.

Figure 6.2 is an attempt to illustrate this process. At the top of the figure, I have symbolized what the language provides in terms, for example, of a superordinate tree structure, or (on the right) not a perfect superordinate tree-structure but something a little more complex. Language exhibits both hierarchical orders and also more complex organizations such as the cyclical ones typical of temporal systems of months and years (Nelson 1991). The adult has a representational system that probably is not a complete representation of what the language offers but some partial representation of that, as illustrated on the next line. What the adult presents in conversation with the child is then a further selection, such as what foods are going to be offered for breakfast, a selection from the total organization of food that the adult is capable of representing. What the child extracts from experience is something that is much less complexly organized, in terms of events or linked concepts, seen at the bottom of Figure 6.2. These extractions from experience must

Cultural System (Langue)

Adult Representational System

Adult Presentation (Parole)

Child Semantic Representation

Child Conceptual System

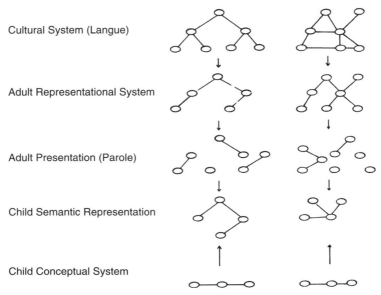

FIGURE 6.2 Levels of representation of categorical knowledge at the cultural level, the adult cognitive level, the display of categories in discourse, and the acquisition of the category structure from discourse by the child. Reprinted from Nelson K. 1985. Figure 8.1, p. 227. *Making Sense: The Acquisition of Shared Meaning*. New York: Academic Press.

come up to meet what the adult represents in the language. Children must somehow construct their own semantic representation so as to incorporate the structures that the adult (often unintentionally) displays in talk about experience in the world.

Achieving an abstract category language depends on the further development of a differentiated or abstracted level of semantic representation in which linguistic terms and their related concepts are not embedded in the experientially derived event representation system but constitutes a semantic system of abstract relations. That construction, carried out in collaboration with adult informants, is a major development of the preschool and early school years. This process was illustrated in a study of category production (Lucariello et al 1992). We asked 4- and 7-year-old children and adults to tell us all the things they could think of that belonged to categories of food, clothes, furniture, tools, and animals. We subjected the results to a cluster analysis and examined the clusters for content, specifically for whether they exhibited SF or conventional subcategory clusters. (Conventional subcategories of the food category would be meat, vegetables, fruit, and so on.) The furniture and tools categories were poorly structured and poorly clustered, by children as well as adults. They seem not to be organized in either a SF or taxonomic way, especially for the children, who included a large number of nonmembers in these categories. Furniture may be organized in some other way, such as situationally or by spatial context, as in living room furniture, bedroom furniture, and so on. In contrast, food, clothes, and animals, which were hypothesized to have a SF structure, were organized in clusters of single-event contexts for the 4-year-olds. The 7-year-olds produced multiple SF subcategories, such as lunch foods, dinner foods, and breakfast foods. Adults included conventional subcategories such as dairy foods and meat products, categories you find in your local grocery store, and SF categories, such as the foods that go together at breakfast. Thus, the conventional and the experiential remained visible in the category productions of the adults that we tested.

These results from our category studies illustrate the cognitive residue in the adult hybrid mind of different levels of representation modes. We found mixtures of different types and levels in their generations that were reminiscent of the earlier types found in children. Without understanding the developmentally earlier activity-based formation of categories, the explanation of these adult clusters would be *ad hoc*, and they would be considered anomalous in respect to most theories of category organization. The developmental history in conjunction with an experiential and language-dependent theory explains the adult cognitive structure better in terms of a hybrid system. The residue of SF categories reflects the basic event representation mode integrated into a linguistically generated and hierarchicalized system.

CONCLUSION

The full story, then, is one of integration and collaboration. The child begins with basic event knowledge followed late in the first year and into the second by coordinated action in mimetic schemes. The communicated perspectives and knowledge of others is a source through which the child elaborates and transforms prior experiential representations. At the same time, event knowledge provides the source of conceptual knowledge structures with the potential to take on new meanings implicated in the cultural community.

This feed forward and feed backward system is illustrated in Figure 6.3. This figure includes three levels. On the left, we have experientially based conceptual representation systems, which feed into the socially displayed systems represented in Figure 6.2. These are the kind of folk theories that are shared in the cultural community and are socially conveyed via folk language. Notice that folk language feeds back into the experientially based conceptual representations. Finally, the formally organized categories are what the child meets in school and what the adult meets daily in terms of formally organized knowledge systems. These are also fed into by the folk theories, and they feed back onto that level as well. Thus, all levels of the systems interact as they are developing. As is apparent, the representational potential for the preschool child is still incomplete. Ahead lie the formal systems of cultural knowledge that are taught in schools. Yet all the levels of the system are mutually interactive and influential, as in the examples produced by the hybrid adult mind.

Changes in Conceptual Representation Systems

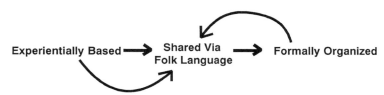

FIGURE 6.3 Changes in the child's representation of concepts and meanings, from the individual experiential to the shared, with social convention to formally organized structures, illustrating
feed-forward and feed-back influences. Reprinted from Nelson, K. 1996. *Language in Cognitive
Development: The Emergence of the Mediated Mind.* New York: Cambridge University Press.

This has been a complex story, but an important part of it is that action begins
the process. The process proceeds through event knowledge and then through
language and conceptual development. Action is linked to intelligent behavior at
all developmental phases throughout life. In particular, the effects of the shared
symbolic social system enables the integration of events and the derivation of
concepts that leads to conceptual development and thus to mature forms of intelligent activities that depend on cultural symbolic forms as well as on individual
action.

REFERENCES

Baillargeon, R. 1993. The object concept revisited: New directions in the investigation of infants'
physical knowledge. In Granrud, C.E. (Editor), *Visual Perception and Cognition in Infancy.*
Hillsdale, NJ: Lawrence Erlbaum Assoc.

Barrett, M.D. 1985. Early semantic representations and early word-usage. In Kuczaj, S.A., and
Barrett, M.D., (Editors), *The Development of Word Meaning: Progress in Cognitive Development
Research* (pp. 39–68). New York: Springer-Verlag.

Bauer, P.J., Hertsgaard, L.A., and Dow, G.A. 1994. After 8 months have passed: Long-term recall of
events by 1- to 2-year-old children. *Memory* 2:353–382.

Donald, M. 1991. *Origins of the Modern Mind.* Cambridge, MA: Harvard University Press.

Gibson, J.J. 1986. *The Ecological Approach to Visual Perception.* Hillsdale, NJ: Erlbaum.

Lucariello, J., Kyratzis, A., and Nelson, K. 1992. Taxonomic knowledge: What kind and when?
Child Dev 63:978–998.

Lucariello, J., and Nelson, K. 1986. Context effects on lexical specificity in maternal and child discourse. *Child Lang* 13:507–522.

Macnamara, J. 1982. *Names for Things.* Cambridge MA: MIT Press.

Mandler, J.M. 1992. How to build a baby II: Conceptual Primitives. *Psychol Rev* 99:587–604.

Meltzoff, A.N., and Moore, M.K. 1999. A new foundation for cognitive development in infancy: The
birth of the representational infant. In Scholnick, E.K., Nelson, K., Gelman, S.A., and Miller,
P.H., (Editors), *Conceptual Development: Piaget's Legacy* (pp. 53–78). Mahwah, NJ: Erlbaum.

Nelson, K. 1974. Concept, word, and sentence: Interrelations in acquisition and development. *Psychol Rev* 81:267–285.

Nelson, K. (Editor). 1989. *Narratives From the Crib.* Cambridge, MA: Harvard University Press.

Nelson, K. 1991. The Matter of time: Interdependencies between language and thought in development. In Gelman, S.A., and Byrnes, J.P. (Editors), *Perspectives on Language and Cognition: Interrelations in Development.* New York: Cambridge University Press.

Nelson, K. 1996. *Language in Cognitive Development: The Emergence of the Mediated Mind.* New York: Cambridge University Press.

Piaget, J. 1952. *The Origins of Intelligence in Children.* New York: Norton Library.

Piaget, J. 1962. *Play, Dreams, and Imitation in Childhood.* New York: Norton.

Rescorla, L.A. 1980. Overextension in early language development. *J Child Lang* 7:321–335.

Rosch, E. 1978. Principles of categorization. In Rosch, E. and Lloyd, B. (Editors), *Cognition and Categorization.* Hillsdale, NJ: Erlbaum.

Rothstein, L. 1991. Three-year-olds' symbolic representation of familiar events: Factors of decontextualization, Discrepant action and order. Unpublished doctoral dissertation, Cornell University.

Saussure, F.D. 1959, 1915. *Course in General Linguistics.* New York: The Philosophical Library, Inc.

Tomasello, M. 1992. *First Verbs: A Case Study of Early Grammatical Development.* New York: Cambridge University Press.

Tomasello, M., Kruger, A.C., and Ratner, H.H. 1993. Cultural learning. *Behav Brain Sci* 495–552.

Vygotsky, L. 1986. *Thought and Language.* Cambridge, MA: MIT Press.

7

THE INTEGRATION OF EXPRESSION INTO THE STREAM OF EVERYDAY ACTIVITY

LOIS BLOOM, PhD

How do young children acquire language in relation to the rest of their development in a dynamic world of action – a world of persons, objects, events, and relations? To answer that question, I have engaged in a program of research into children's emerging language, beginning before first words appear and continuing through the acquisition of a vocabulary of words and the emergence of simple sentences. The focus of this research is on how developments in language are coordinated with infants' emotional expressions, their mothers' speech in conversation, and their actions with objects in play activities.

The cognitive resources of the young language-learning child are fundamentally limited. Moreover, those resources need to be shared according to the competing demands of different actions and expressions in the course of everyday behavior. As a consequence, acquiring language is not easy; it requires effort. Language acquisition is the result of an essential tension between the **effort** that is required and a child's **engagement** in a world of persons and objects that provides the motivation for learning language (Bloom and Tinker 2001). The purpose of this chapter is to share results from longitudinal studies of language, emotional expression, conversational interaction, and object play that show the developmental effects of effort, engagement, and the essential tension between them in the coordination of these expressive actions.

The theory and research in this chapter are summarized from Bloom 1993 and Bloom and Tinker 2001. Also see Bloom and Tinker 2001 for a wider and more recent review of the relevant literature than is included here.

The theoretical perspective that guided this research departs from the prevailing contextualist and mechanistic world views (Pepper 1942) that have dominated theory and research in language acquisition for more than a quarter of a century. The contextualist metaphor, descended from Vygotsky (1962) and Bruner (1975), is that **language is a pragmatic tool** to influence other persons and get things done in the world. The emphasis is on the uses of language, the functions that language can serve, and the part that other persons play in a child's language acquisition. However, this instrumental, pragmatic view of language acquisition has to do with the **results** of language use. It ignores the origins of language in a young child's **intentionality**: the representations in mind that are interpreted from the actions of other persons and expressed by the actions of language, emotion, and object play. Thus, as explanation of how language is acquired and develops over time, instrumental, pragmatic theories are incomplete (Bloom 1993).

The **mechanistic** world view originated with and is epitomized by Chomsky's (1965) prescription for a "language acquisition device" in the brain. Again, the emphasis is on the end product: the adult grammar that the child acquires. Research begins with a theory of the adult grammar and asks how the linguistic theory (the end state or goal) is achieved (e.g., Wexler and Culicover, 1980). A language acquisition device is, by definition, constrained to explaining only the formal features of the language—its sounds, words, and procedures for sentences—independently of external events and internal states. Such a device also bypasses intentionality. Also, it ignores the essential agency of the child in the construction of the intentional states that language expresses and which are set up by interpreting the expressions of other people. The result is research and theory that focuses on **language as an object**. Words and sentences assume a life of their own, apart from the child who produced them and the situations in which they are learned. To be sure, no one denies that there is a child behind the words and sentences, but that child is forgotten, taken for granted, a "phantom child" in studies of the acquisition of language as an independent object (Bloom 2000a, 2000b; Bloom and Tinker 2001). In sum, instrumental and mechanistic theories are too narrow to adequately capture the acquisition of language.

When children acquire language, they learn a vocabulary of words and a grammar for combining them into well-formed sentences. They learn to use language to get other people to do things, to get things done in the world. But these things are possible only because acquiring a language means acquiring the **power of expression**: "What comes about through the development of language in the broadest sense is the coming to be of expressive power" (Taylor 1985, p. 238). In acts of expression, language embodies and makes manifest the representations of intentional states (e.g., Danto 1973; Taylor 1985). In acts of interpretation, language sets up representations with elements, roles, and relations in intentional states (Fauconnier 1985). Children express the representations they have in mind, and the child's contents of mind can be recreated in the mind of another person who interprets what the child says. Therefore, language influences what other people do only because interpreting the language changes what they have in mind.

THE INTENTIONALITY MODEL OF LANGUAGE ACQUISITION

The intentionality perspective that guided the research summarized in this chapter is the notion of intentionality in the larger, philosophical sense of the "aboutness" of mental states, that is, the representations in consciousness that are about objects, events, and relations in the world. The metaphor for this perspective is the **power of expression**, and it originates in an *organismic* world view. Language is only one aspect of a child's development and is connected to all its other aspects, including cognitive, emotional, and social developments, in particular. Language is acquired for expression and sharing the contents of mind with other persons, and language is only one form of expression.

The intentionality model (Figure 7.1) has two components, engagement and effort (Bloom 1993), and, as with development more generally, the acquisition of language is driven by an essential **tension** between them. (See Bloom and Tinker 2001 for a more extended discussion of the importance of tension for development.)

ENGAGEMENT

Language input to children is always part of a personal and interpersonal context. The concept of *engagement* in a theory of language acquisition embraces the part played by a child's social and emotional development. Social development is required because the reason for acquiring a language, in the first place, comes from the need to sustain intersubjectivity with other persons, that is, the need for togetherness, for being in touch. Connectedness between the child and other persons begins in earliest infancy, long before language. In the first year of life, intersubjectivity depends on the affective gestures and sounds of smiles, whines, grimaces, cries—the repertoire of affective emotional signals whereby caregivers attribute feelings and respond to the baby (see Bloom 1993).

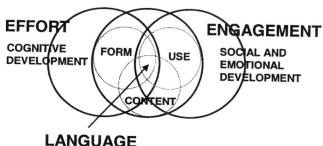

FIGURE 7.1   The intentionality model. From Bloom, L., and Tinker, E. 2001. The intentionality model and language acquisition: Engagement, effort, and the essential tension in development. *Monogr Soc Res Child Dev* 66:1–91.

By the end of the first year, the human infant is very adept at deploying these signals, and caregivers are very good at reading them. With developments in cognition, however, more elaborated forms of expression are required, motivating the child to acquire a language. Children learn to talk about the objects of their interest and engagement, those things that are **relevant** to them. Therefore, we cannot ignore childrens' affective investment in other persons and in the situations with which they experience language. Nevertheless, pragmatic and formal theories of acquisition tend to ignore affectivity, at best, or to discount it altogether.

EFFORT

The component of **effort** in the model brings in the child's cognition. Thinking is constructing the intentional states that are expressed by language and that are set up by interpreting the language of others. The cognition required for language also includes the timeless products of past thinking in memory that are the child's concepts, conceptual structure, and the child's knowledge more generally. The result of learning about persons, objects, events, and relations is that the contents of intentional states become increasingly elaborated, with more elements, more roles, and more relations between them. Language has to be learned because the affective, emotional signals that young infants depend on for expression cannot articulate these increasingly elaborated and complex representations in the mind of the 1- and 2-year-old child. Moreover, because these cognitive developments for language are intimately connected to a child's social interaction and emotionality, they have to compete for the essentially limited resources of the young language learning child. As a result, acquiring language is not easy; it takes work.

THE ESSENTIAL TENSION

Engagement provides the motivation for learning language, and effort propels the process forward. However, tension is inevitable between engagement in new encounters with the social and physical world and the effort to understand new input that does not match what the child already knows. New linguistic forms and functions are learned to resolve the tension that results when existing knowledge cannot accommodate new data. Development is about change that moves toward greater complexity and increased abstraction in making sense of new experiences. Thus, acquiring language is not simply accumulating linguistic experiences or adding language forms and functions to a repertoire of words and procedures. Neither linguistic input alone, neurological structure alone, nor both together can cause language acquisition. Language acquisition is caused by the child's agency in acts of interpretation and expression.

Three explanatory principles mediate between the components of engagement and effort for resolving the essential tension between them. They are the principles of relevance, discrepancy, and elaboration (Bloom 1993; Bloom and Tinker 2001). These principles are cognitive generalizations that explain the transactions between internal representations in intentional states and the external social and physical world. **Relevance** determines what a child finds interesting and engaging in new encounters for linguistic interaction and learning. The effort required to learn and use language is motivated by **discrepancy**. It is motivated by discrepancy between what the child already knows and new input as well as discrepancy between what the child and others have in mind that needs to be shared. Increasing *elaboration* of intentional states directs the child towards learning and using language that is increasingly more complex and abstract (Bloom and Tinker 2001).

According to the **principle of relevance**, development is enhanced when events in the context bear on and are pertinent to what the child has in mind, to what the child's feelings are about. "Relevance is the single property that makes information worth processing and determines the particular assumptions an individual is most likely to construct and process" (Sperber and Wilson 1986, p. 46). Things that are relevant to a child can, and often do, originate when other persons direct the child's attention to something new. But things that are relevant are just as often, if not more often, those things that a child is already attending to and cares about. In either event, the value of linguistic input for learning is determined by its relevance to what the child has in mind.

According to the **principle of discrepancy**, development is enhanced when the child acts to resolve a mismatch between the child's contents of mind and what others have in mind in the situation. As infants begin to remember past events and anticipate new events, they have beliefs, desires, and feelings about things that other persons cannot yet know. Language has to be acquired for their expression in order to share them. And discrepancy between what a child already knows and new encounters that resist understanding create tension in the mind of the child who is resolved by learning.

According to the **principle of elaboration**, children will have to learn more of the language to keep up with developments in other aspects of cognition that enrich the representations in intentional states. With developments in the symbolic capacity, intentional state representations become increasingly removed from the "here and now," as children come to anticipate new events and remember past events. Developments in concepts and conceptual structure make it possible to represent many more elements and the roles and relations between them in intentional states. Thus, the principle of elaboration presses the child to act in increasingly more detailed ways to express the increasingly elaborated intentional states that developments in cognition make possible (Bloom and Tinker 2001).

In sum, the principles of relevance, discrepancy, and elaboration that mediate between engagement and effort for language learning are responsive to developments in emotionality, social interaction, and cognition. According to the intentionality model, therefore, language is not separate from the rest of childrens' development more generally. The research program summarized in this chapter has been guided by the intentionality model. The studies described here have to do with children's emerging language in relation to other aspects of development in the course of language acquisition in the second year of life.

THE RESEARCH PROCEDURES AND RESULTS

Language begins around the first birthday, give or take a few months. Early progress is tentative and slow, and the first words are fragile and imprecise. At the same time, infants are very good at deploying signals of affect or emotion that express their internal states and feelings, such as crying, whining, whimpering, smiling, or laughing. The first question we asked in our research was how these two different systems of expression, emotion, which is already in place and language, which needs to be learned, come together in the period of early word learning in the second year. The second question was how developments in emotional development and language relate to other developments going on in the child's cognition, using children's play with objects as a window on their cognitive development.

COLLECTING THE DATA

Fourteen infants (seven girls and seven boys) and their mothers participated in our research, although the videotapes for two of the children could not be used for the lag sequential analyses described in this chapter. We first saw the children in our laboratory playroom at Teacher's College when they were 9 months old, followed by 1-hour visits every month until they were 2 years old. The children came from different ethnic and economic backgrounds in the New York metropolitan area, and their mothers were their primary caregivers at the time the study began. We also visited them at home every month until they were 15 months old and then every 3 months thereafter.

A group of core toys was on the floor when each mother and baby came into the playroom. Every 8 minutes, a research assistant brought in another group of toys according to a predetermined schedule. At the end of the first half hour, a snack was brought in instead of a new group of toys. The toys were counterbalanced so that the children had equal amounts of time to play with traditional girl toys (a doll, toy silverware, for example), boy toys (such as trucks), and gender-neutral toys with comparable appeal to both girls and boys (such as nesting cups). The selection of toys also provided the children with comparable time for playing with manipulative toys, like stacking blocks or nesting cups, and enactment toys, like little peg persons and toy cars.

These controls on the situation in the design of the study meant that the children experienced the same toys in the same sequence every month. The context in which we observed the children did not change from month to month and was, also, the same for all of them. Thus, changes over time in the children's behaviors and in their interactions with their mothers could be attributed to the children's development rather than to changes in the situation in which we observed them. At the same time, differences among the children and differences among the child-mother pairs in their interactions could be attributed to inherent differences among them rather than to differences in the context (which would have been the case had we visited them at home).

Because we were asking how developments in cognition, emotional expression, and social interaction relate to children's language acquisition, we controlled for level of language development and compared the children at the same levels. Three language milestones were used as reference points for examining developments in other behaviors that coincided with developments in language.

The first development in language was a time of emergence and transition, known as first words (FW). FW were defined as the first use of conventional meaningful words used at least two times in the playroom session. The acquisition of new vocabulary was tracked from one month to the next until there was a sharp increase in the slope of the number of new words after the child had already learned at least 20 words. This second achievement in language, a vocabulary spurt (VS), represented a **consolidation** in word learning. A summary of vocabulary growth showing the mean number of new words plotted relative to the mean number of total words in the children's vocabularies each month is presented in Figure 7.2, for the group of 14 children. As in virtually all other studies of early language, the children varied greatly in age of achievement and in the length of time that it took to progress from FW to VS, and this variability is indicated by the break in the *x* axis and the growth curve for new words in Figure 7.2.

A third development in language was also identified: the **transition** to simple sentences (SS) when mean length of utterance was 1.5 words. The mean ages

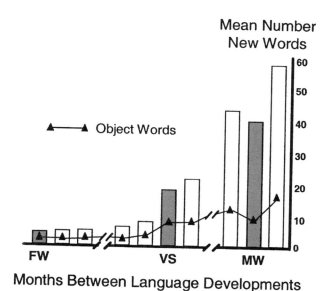

FIGURE 7.2   Mean total number of words and new words each month from first words (FW) to 1 month after the vocabulary spurt (VS), *n* = 14. Adapted from Bloom, L. 1993. *The Transition from Infancy to Language: Acquiring the Power of Expression.* Cambridge: Cambridge University Press.

AGE (months)

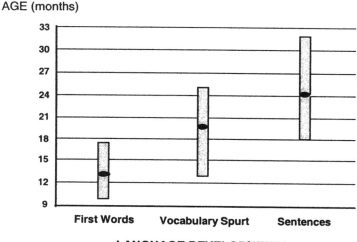

LANGUAGE DEVELOPMENTS

FIGURE 7.3   Mean age and variation in age at each of the language achievements, $n = 14$. Adapted from Bloom, L. 1993. *The Transition from Infancy to Language: Acquiring the Power of Expression*. Cambridge: Cambridge University Press.

and ranges in age among the children at the time of each of these three developments in language are shown in Figure 7.3.

Before showing how different actions and expressions are coordinated in the course of development in the second year, we examined developments in each of the behaviors separately. These results will be presented first before showing how they come together.

DEVELOPMENTS IN EXPRESSION

THE REFERENCE OF EARLY WORDS

Each word was examined in relation to its context for attributing what the word was about, that is, the aspects of its intentional state representations expressed by the word, at FW and VS (Bloom 1994; Bloom et al 1988). The representations expressed by certain words are already **evident** in the context. For example, when a child looks at the clock on the wall and says "tick-tock," or watches her mother pour juice and says "more," the content expressed is evident. However, when a word is said before the event that the word is about, the child is **anticipating** something that has not yet happened, for example, "juice" while holding out an empty cup.

Developmentally, children express more anticipated content at VS than at FW. They tend to talk more at VS about nonpresent objects and events that are imminent in the situation: things not yet present, or things they want to do, are about to do, or want their mothers to do. Consistent with the principle of discrepancy, then, the main development in word learning that accompanies the increase in vocabulary from FW to VS is an increase in **anticipated** content. What the child has in mind is discrepant from what the listener can attribute to the child's contents of mind based on the context. Saying the words makes the child's intentional state evident to other persons and resolves the discrepancy.

At the same time, words that express anticipated action events, such as saying "baby" when putting the doll in a dump truck and then pushing it, increase in relation to anticipated stative events, such as looking in a box for the doll or holding the doll out for mother to see. Anticipated actions have not yet happened; they are actions that children are about to do, are attempting to do, or want someone else to do. Thus, the second development in word learning coinciding with the VS is an increase in expression of **anticipated action** events at VS, and this result is shown in Figure 7.4. As children learn more words, they learn to express more elaborated meanings with more elements, more roles, and more relations between elements, consistent with the principle of elaboration. Changes in the meanings children express indicate developments in the symbolic capacity for intentional state representations and conceptual structure in the knowledge base. These developments in cognition anticipate subsequent developments in language, particularly learning verbs and the procedures for phrases and simple sentences.

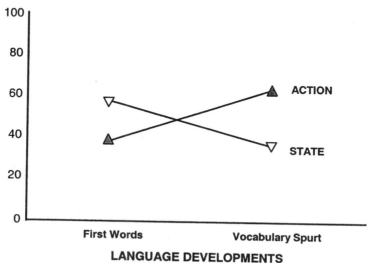

Mean % of Attributed Meanings

FIGURE 7.4   Percentage of attributions for words as expression of anticipated actions or states. Adapted from Bloom, L., Beckwith, R., Capatides, J., and Hafitz, J. 1988. Expression through affect and words in the transition from infancy to language. *Dev Behav*, 8:99–127.

OBJECT PLAY

Acting with objects in play is also the expression of contents of mind. Developments in object play provide evidence of developments in representation of plans and goals in intentional states and, therefore, evidence of developments in the **symbolic capacity**. Actions with toys and, in particular, constructing thematic relations between objects provides evidence of development in a child's **concepts** and **conceptual structure**.

We looked at what children do when they act on two objects in relation to one another, such as putting one block on top of another or a wooden peg person into a truck. The results of that study are represented in the hierarchy shown in Figure 7.5. The tree diagram in the figure captures the logical derivation of the categories of play and their developmental progression. In the period before language (9 to 11 months), children's primary actions are separations, as they take apart a thematic configuration. For example, they dump nested cups, take things out of containers, pull beads off a string, undress a doll, and so forth. Mothers, in turn, put objects back together again to create a thematic configuration, such as nesting the cups for their children to take apart again. Children learn about the thematic relations that are possible between objects by first learning to take them apart (Lifter and Bloom 1989).

When children begin to construct thematic relations with toys, their earliest constructions are recreations of the **given** relation in which the toys had been presented to them originally. In our study, for example, a series of cups were brought into the playroom with each one nested into the next larger one. When the children took one cup and put it into another cup, they were, therefore, recreating the same **given** relation, a configuration with nothing new. A child constructing a given relation only needs to recall how the two objects appeared when presented originally.

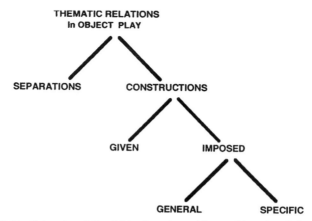

FIGURE 7.5 Categories of the children's actions with two objects in relation to each other. Adapted from Lifter, K., and Bloom, L. 1989. Object play and the emergence of language. *Infant Behav Dev* 12:395–423.

In contrast, an **imposed** construction creates a thematic relation between objects that differed from the way a child encounters the toys originally. For example, in our playroom the large wooden beads and a string were originally presented loosely in a box. When a child took a bead and put it on the string, or put a bead inside a cup, the child was imposing a new thematic relation on the objects. To create such relations, the child had to understand something about the bead and the string or the bead and the cup that differs from the way those objects originally appeared.

Given relations represent about half the relations children construct throughout the single-word period in the second year. Half the constructions create **imposed** relations, and these are of two kinds: general and specific. **General** relations depend only on perceiving the physical properties of objects, usually putting one object into another (containment) or putting one object on top of another (support). **Specific** thematic relations take into account something more than just the perceptual, physical properties of objects. When a child takes a wooden peg person that was originally seated in a see-saw, for example, and puts it into a truck as if it were a driver, the child is creating a relation that is specific to **both** the physical properties of the individual objects and also to the cultural or socially learned functions of the objects relative to one another. Mental plans for creating specific thematic relations, in particular, require knowledge of other possible roles and relations between objects than do plans for either recreating a given relation or simply constructing a new general relation of containment and support. Specific constructions draw on a child's sociocultural knowledge about how things go together (Lifter and Bloom 1989).

Given and imposed constructions do not change in relative frequency in the second year. Among imposed thematic relations, however, general relations decrease as specific relations increase. Thus, the first development that occurs in the single-word period is progress from separating to constructing activities. The second development is a shift from constructing general relations of containment and support to constructing more specific thematic relations between the objects. Moreover, achievement in constructing specific thematic relations in play coincides with the vocabulary spurt achievement in language. This result means that regardless of how old children are when they reach the VS, and how long it takes them to progress from FW to VS, achievements in language and object play are coextensive (Lifter and Bloom 1989).

AFFECT EXPRESSION

The **procedures** for coding affect expression used gradient information of valence and intensity. **Valence** was coded according to whether a child's expression was **neutral** or deviated from neutral in either a **positive** or **negative** direction for the expression of either positive or negative emotion. **Intensity** was coded on three levels according to the relative fullness of the display, from a minimal smile or frown to full laughter or crying. Affect expressions were coded continuously for all frames of the videotape. Every shift in valence or intensity was coded along with the time of the shift in minutes, seconds, and frames (with 30 frames of video to each lapsed second of time). See the rationale for and details of the affect coding procedures in Bloom and Capatides (1987).

The resulting affect code is a complete record of all a child's affect expressions, with times of onset and offset of each expression. The number of expressions could then simply be counted, or the number of video frames could be counted to determine the duration of each kind of expression or the total amount of time spent in expression. These measures of affect expression could then be compared over time to determine developments in emotional expression. Measures of affect expression could also be compared with measures of language and with actions in play, which was the primary goal of the program of research summarized in this chapter.

DEVELOPMENTS IN THE COORDINATION OF DIFFERENT EXPRESSIVE ACTIONS

To summarize so far, as language begins to emerge at the end of the first year, the behaviors that infants have available include emotional expression and actions with objects in play. In the course of the second year of life, the 1-year-old comes to deploy the emerging behaviors of language, emotional expressions, and actions in play to express intentional state representations. The basic question posed in the research summarized here has to do with the coordination of those expressive actions—how the 1- to 2-year-old child learns to coordinate speech, emotional expression, and actions with objects as expressions of their intentional state representations.

However, the resources of the young language-learning child are fundamentally limited and have to be shared among these different kinds of behaviors. In asking how different kinds of expression come together developmentally, therefore, we first consider three possible models of how cognitive and affective resources might be distributed for the integration of different behaviors in the course of development.

POSSIBLE RESOURCE MODELS

A Model of Independence

In an independence model, different behaviors within one domain, or behaviors from different domains, do not influence one another—either in their development over time, or in their relation to each other as they occur in real time. However, we already know that such a model of independence is not tenable within the domain of language, where different features of language can either compete with or complement one another because they evidently draw on a single resource pool. For example, in earlier research (Bloom 1970; Bloom et al 1975), I examined factors that make a difference in whether children produce sentences that are incomplete, like "more juice," or complete, like "mommy drink more juice." Incomplete, shorter sentences are more likely to occur with (1) demands from the discourse; (2) use of relatively new words, that is, words that a child does not know well; and (3) extra complexity like negation added to the sentence. Conversely, children produce longer, more complete sentences when they receive discourse support, such as repetition; when they used words they knew well, that is, words that are among their most frequent and earlier learned words; and when they do not add extra complexity to a sentence. There is, in effect, a dependence among the different features of language as discourse, lexicon, vocabulary, and syntax either compete with or complement each other. The evidence from the single dimension of language does not support an independence model but points, instead, to the need for a **model of dependency** between behaviors for deployment of cognitive resources.

Dependency Models

Different features of one kind of expression, like language, might depend on the same pool of resources, but different kinds of expression such as language, emotional expression, and actions in play might tap into correspondingly different resource pools. Different behaviors drawing on different resource pools should not compete with each other. Therefore, in a **multiple-resources model**, language, emotional expression, or actions in play do not influence each other because separate resources are available for the different kinds of behaviors.

However, in another dependency model, a **single-resource model**, different kinds of expressive action draw on the same pool of resources. If children's different behaviors tap into the same general pool, then we should see the effects of collaboration and competition for resources between different behaviors—in the course of development over time and in their relation to each other in real time. The research program described here set out to test which of these two dependency models, a single-resource model or a multiple-resource model, best explained the **processes** underlying children's early language acquisition from FW, to the VS, to the emergence of SS.

ENGAGEMENT AND EFFORT

The theory for the research built on the two hypotheses of effort and engagement. Distribution of **effort** is necessary when attending to more than one task at the same time: "Because the total quantity of effort which can be exerted at any one time is limited, concurrent activities which require attention tend to interfere with one another" (Kahneman 1973, p. 12). In our studies, expressing emotion, interpreting the speech of others, and constructing relations between objects in play should each have a cognitive cost. Moreover, the effort needed for each of these behaviors separately increases when different behaviors interact from moment-to-moment in real time. The effects of effort should appear in patterns of coordination between behaviors, as they unfold in real time and over developmental time.

Engagement "is characterized by approach, valuation, and feelings directed toward other persons and toward novelty in the physical world" (Bloom and Tinker 2001, p. 27). Engagement for language learning is closely tied to a child's investment in other persons, and the need to resolve discrepancy between what each has in mind in order to share contents of mind. Learning about the physical world also entails engagement to resolve discrepancy between what is already known and new encounters that resist understanding. Emotional expressions, as an index of arousal, provide evidence of a child's engagement in the social and physical worlds. In sum, engagement provides the motivation and directedness for development and, by inclusion, for language, while effort assures that the process goes forward.

Engagement and effort operate with an **essential tension** between them in the expression of a young child's intentionality. In the case of language, engagement meets resistance in the effort to overcome discrepancy between what the child already knows about language and linguistic input in new encounters. An essential tension also results when engagement in learning the language meets resistance in the effort to overcome competition for limited cognitive resources that must be shared. Resolving the essential tension between engagement and effort is the work of the young child's intentionality. Evidence of this essential tension and its resolution in the child's mind can be inferred from children's actions, particularly actions of expression and interpretation, in the stream of ordinary activities (Bloom and Tinker 2001).

Our playroom context provided a natural "experiment" for observing children's spontaneous everyday behaviors and examining the acquisition of language in relation to other aspects of development.

TIME SPENT TALKING AND EXPRESSING EMOTION

The first analysis described here is a simple comparison between the amount of time children spend expressing emotion and the time they spend in talking (measured as the mean percent of all video frames in the observations). The results are shown developmentally across time (Figure 7.6) for the three language developments, FW, VS, and SS.

Time spent talking increases over time, as expected with development from FW to SS. However, time spent expressing emotion does not change in this same period. The temporal stability of emotional expression as speech time increases means two things. First, the increase in language in the second year, from FW to SS, is not simply an overall increase in expressivity, in general. Otherwise, time spent expressing emotion would also increase along with the increase in speaking time. Second, the result shown in Figure 7.6 also means that **language does not replace emotional expression** – children are not saying words and then sentences instead of expressing emotion. Otherwise, emotional expression would decrease as speech increases. Thus, children continue to express emotion as they are learning the language to express what their emotions are about and what

Mean % of All Video Frames

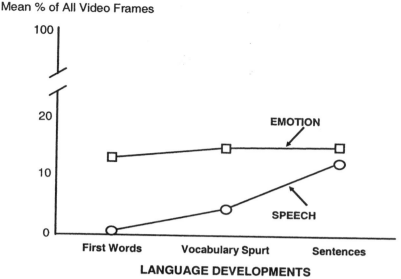

FIGURE 7.6   Amount of time the children spent expressing emotions and speaking at the three developments in language. From Bloom, L., and Tinker, E. 2001. The intentionality model and language acquisition: Engagement, effort, and the essential tension in development. *Monogr Soc Res Child Dev* 66:1–91.

might be done about the causes and circumstances of their emotional experiences. See, Bloom and Capatides (1987) for an earlier, comparable analysis and fuller interpretation.

TEMPORAL RELATIONS BETWEEN DIFFERENT EXPRESSIVE ACTIONS

How are different expressive actions (child and mother speech, child emotion, object constructions) coordinated in the stream of everyday activity? The remaining studies described in this chapter all used the same kind of analysis to examine the occurrence of one kind of expression (such as emotion), relative to its baseline rate, around a different kind of expression (such as saying a word) as the target event. The baseline rate of an expression is the overall probability of its occurring in any segment of the observation. Examining the observed incidence of one kind of expression relative to its baseline around a different, target expression, such as saying words, revealed whether and how the two different behaviors influenced each other. (See Bloom and Tinker 2001 for description of how baselines were determined.)

In these lag sequential analyses, every frame of video tape was scanned (each frame equal to 1/30 of a second), and instances of an expression (the lagged behavior) tallied in the 1-s intervals before, during, and after the target behavior. This observed incidence of the lagged behavior was then compared with its baseline rate. Deviations from the baseline revealed whether the target behavior influenced the occurrence of the lagged behavior in real time. On the one hand, if the observed incidence of emotional expression, for example, does not deviate from its baseline rate in the moments before, during, and after a child says words, then we can conclude that expressing emotion does not compete with saying words, and the two different kinds of expression recruit separate resources. On the other hand, if emotional expression does deviate significantly from its baseline rate around speech, then we can infer an effect of one on the other and conclude that speech and emotional expression recruit resources from the same general pool.

SAYING WORDS AND EXPRESSING EMOTION

The cognitive effort for saying words requires the following mental activities: At the very least, the child must construct an intentional state out of data from perception in relation to what is already known, in memory. The child has to recall linguistic units from memory and then enact the motor movements for the words to express the intentional state. Similarly, emotional expression, at the least, also requires an intentional state representation and an evaluation of circumstances in the situation in relation to that representation. The outcome of that evaluation results in a subjective feeling state, and the emotional display expresses it. Given these requirements for the two kinds of expression, we first asked whether saying words and expressing emotion influence each other in the course of activities at FW and the VS (in Bloom and Beckwith 1989).

Each analysis was performed for each child individually relative to that child's baseline rate, before the results were averaged for the summaries reported here. The pattern of results in Figure 7.7 shows the temporal relation between the two kinds of expression at FW and VS. The horizontal line represents the baseline scores for the group of 12 children at each time. The vertical line represents the target **interval**, from onset to offset, of the child's speech. The data points represent the mean standard deviation units from baseline in emotional expression in the five 1-s intervals before the word, during the speech interval, and in the five 1-s intervals after speech. Scores below baseline mean that children are less likely to be expressing emotion and, therefore, are more likely to be in **neutral** affect. Scores above baseline mean that they are likely to be expressing emotion more than expected given their baseline rates.

The transition to FW marks the **emergence of language**, and the VS represents an achievement or **consolidation** in early word learning. Emotional expression is below baseline levels immediately before the onset of a word at FW. This dip in emotional expression below baseline reflects the effort to construct an intentional state, access a word from memory for its expression, and articulate

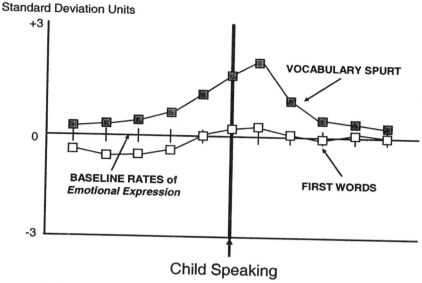

Child Speaking

FIGURE 7.7   Emotional expression in 1-s lag intervals before, during, and after speech, expressed as standard deviation units from the baseline rates of emotional expression at FW and VS. Adapted from Bloom, L., and Beckwith, R. 1989. Talking with feeling: Integrating affective and linguistic expression in early language development. *Cogn and Emot* 3:313–342.

the word. The effort entailed preempts the cognitive resources that would otherwise be available for expressing emotion at the same time. The peak in emotional expression comes immediately after saying the word, with release from the tension between effort and engagement.

At VS, the shape of the pattern of emotional expression around words is the same but differs in the direction and extent of deviations from baseline rates. Thus, once word learning is well underway and a child has achieved a basic working vocabulary, emotional expression is above baseline around speech, peaking to almost 2 standard deviations above baseline immediately after the word. In this period of language development framed by FW and VS, children are able to "get it together." The peak in emotional expression during and immediately after saying a word at VS is evidence of **engagement** in the relative absence of effort, with children evidently learning to talk about those things that are relevant to them.

Nevertheless, while saying words and expressing emotion are coordinated at VS, certain constraints continue to influence their coordination and indicate the **effort** that is still involved. The emotion expressed is significantly more likely to be positive than negative emotion. Most cognitive theories of emotion predict less cognitive work for a positive emotion than for a negative emotion. The children are also significantly more likely to express emotion with low rather than high levels of intensity in connection with saying words. Most importantly, the words they say at the same time they express emotion are the words that they know best. They are the words learned earlier and/or their most frequent words. Later learned, less frequent words require more cognitive work than earlier learned, more frequent words. In addition, the words said at the same time children express emotion at VS are words like "baby," "mama," "hi," "more," "no," etc., words that name the objects and circumstances of emotion or what their feelings are about. Children are not saying such names for the emotions themselves as "happy" or "mad," to tell people the particular emotion they are feeling (Bloom and Beckwith 1989).

EXPRESSING EMOTION AT THE TRANSITION
TO SENTENCES

However, the conclusion that children are now able to coordinate speech and emotional expression is challenged by the results of the same analyses repeated at the transition to saying phrases and simple sentences, about 6 months later on average (Bloom and Tinker 2001). This result is shown in Figure 7.8. All of the scores are below baseline before, during, and after child speech, which means children are expressing primarily neutral affect when speaking at the time of transition to sentences. The implication of this result is unmistakable. The same children who are able to express emotion in the moments around speaking at the time of the

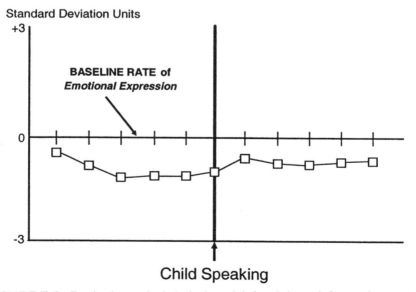

FIGURE 7.8 Emotional expression in 1-s lag intervals before, during, and after speech, expressed as standard deviation units from the baseline rates of emotional expression at the transition to sentences. From Bloom, L., and Tinker, E. 2001. The intentionality model and language acquisition: Engagement, effort, and the essential tension in development. *Monogr Soc Res Child Dev* 66:1–91.

achievement in word learning as represented by the VS, are not expressing emotion around their speech when making the transition to syntactic speech.

Because of the variation in their ages at the time of developments in language, the children were divided into later and earlier word learners depending on whether they were older or younger, respectively, than the mean age of the group at the time of developments in language. The amount of time the two groups express emotion and speak at development is shown in Figure 7.9. Later and earlier learners do not differ in the amount of time they spend talking, even though they differ greatly in age at each of the language landmarks (see the variation in the group as a whole in Figure 7.3). Thus, language development and not chronological age predicts how much talking children do. At the same time, however, the two groups do differ in the amount of time expressing emotion (Bloom and Tinker 2001). Children who spend more time expressing **neutral**, nonemotional affect, are earlier word learners. Children who express more emotion reach the developments in language somewhat later. This result using **time**, the number of video frames coded for either speech or emotional expression, echoes the same result reported earlier using the frequency of individual emotional expressions (Bloom and Capatides 1987).

The lag sequential analysis was then repeated separately for the subgroups of later and earlier learners, and this result is shown in Figure 7.10. Earlier and later

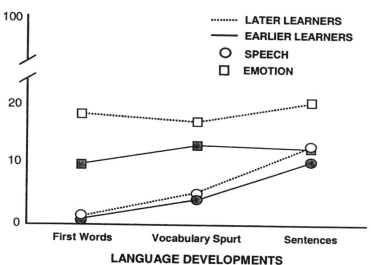

FIGURE 7.9   Amount of time the children spent in emotional expression and speech by later and earlier learners at the three developments in language. From Bloom, L., and Tinker, E. 2001. The intentionality model and language acquisition: Engagement, effort, and the essential tension in development. *Monogr Soc Res Child Dev* 66:1–91.

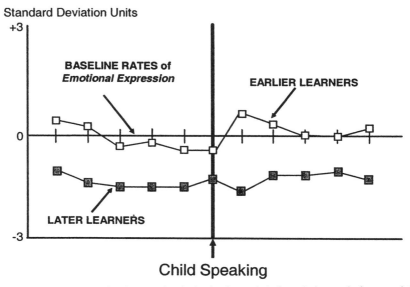

FIGURE 7.10 Emotional expression in 1-s lag intervals before, during, and after speech by later and earlier word learners, expressed as standard deviation units from the baseline rates of emotional expression at the transition to simple sentences. From Bloom, L., and Tinker, E. 2001. The intentionality model and language acquisition: Engagement, effort, and the essential tension in development. *Monogr Soc Res Child Dev* 66:1–91.

learners at the time of transition to simple sentences differed significantly in their expression of emotion around speech. Children who learn the procedures for phrases and simple sentences later are less likely to be expressing emotion around speaking than earlier learners, **even though later learners express more emotion overall**. The earlier learners, who are less likely to express emotion generally are, nevertheless, more likely than later learners to express emotion around speech. The effect of effort is clear: Later learners require more effort for speaking when learning procedures for sentence, while earlier (younger) learners make the transition to sentences more easily (Bloom and Tinker 2001).

To determine whether discourse context might influence the coordination of the two forms of expression at transition to sentences, the analyses were repeated to compare speech targets that were spontaneous, originating with the child, with targets that were imitated speech (repeating all or part of what someone else has just said). This result is reproduced in Figure 7.11. Significantly less emotion is expressed relative to baseline around spontaneous speech compared with imitated speech. Therefore, children are more likely to express neutral affect, indicating greater effort, when words are recruited from memory and do not have a model in the preceding discourse. In contrast, less effort is needed to recall words for expression when a child's speech is at least partially imitated from what someone else has just said (Bloom and Tinker 2001).

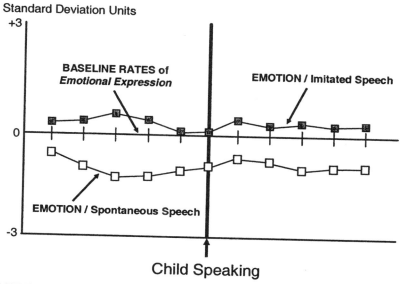

Child Speaking

FIGURE 7.11 Emotional expression and speech in 1-s lag intervals before, during, and after child speech that is either spontaneous or imitated, expressed as standard deviation units from the baseline rates of emotional expression at the transition to simple sentences. From Bloom, L., and Tinker, E. 2001. The intentionality model and language acquisition: Engagement, effort, and the essential tension in development. *Monogr Soc Res Child Dev* 66:1–91.

Taken together, these results show clearly that speaking at the time of the transition to sentences interferes with expressing emotion at the same time. More effort is required to coordinate speech and emotional expression at the transition to saying sentences than at the achievement in word learning represented by the vocabulary spurt. Learning procedures for sentences is not easy. The effort involved is mitigated, however, by support from the discourse context when children can include words they have just heard in their own speech. But more effort is evidently required by children who, for whatever reason, begin to learn sentence procedures somewhat later (although well within the accepted "norms") than children who are earlier language learners.

ACTIONS WITH OBJECTS, SAYING WORDS, AND EXPRESSING EMOTION

The analyses of emotional expression around speech in our playroom included **all** child speech and emotional expression regardless of what else was going on in the situation. However, a great deal was happening as the children and their mothers played with the objects provided in the playroom. Constructing thematic relations between objects in play also requires constructing an intentional state representation that is then expressed by the action. That intentional state, again, comes from the data of perception and memory and includes the child's goal as well as a plan for acting. The child also has to find the objects to use in constructing the relation and to perform the motor movements required to create the configuration. Thus, constructing relations between objects in play has a cognitive cost over and above the cognitive requirements for saying words and expressing emotion. Integrating these different expressive actions requires **effort**.

At the same time, the child's interest determines the level of **engagement** that the child brings to the task. Emotionality is an index of engagement in the context of children's other behaviors. Just as they are learning to talk at VS about things that are relevant, meaningful, and interesting to them; that is, things with which they are engaged as indexed by their emotional expression (Bloom and Beckwith 1989), they might be expected to also express emotion around their activities with the objects in play at VS. The next set of analyses explored the interaction between engagement and effort in the context of play with objects.

The lag sequential analysis was repeated, this time using as the target events the children's actions to construct thematic relations between the objects in play. Child speech and emotional expression were compared with their respective baseline rates of expression in the 1-s intervals **before** the onset of construction, **during** the act of constructing between its onset and offset, and in the 1-s intervals immediately **after** the construction. The result of this analysis is shown in Figure 7.12 for all constructions at FW and VS (from Bloom and Tinker 2001). Recall that the vertical line represents an **interval** of time encompassing the duration of constructing activity between onset and offset. The horizontal line represents the baseline rates of expression, here the baseline rates for emotional expression and speech at two different times in language acquisition. The data points represent the five 1-s intervals before onset and the five 1-s intervals after offset of the construction expressed in standard deviation units from the respective baseline rates for speech and emotion.

At FW, when children are just learning to construct thematic relations between objects, the incidence of speech around their constructing actions does not deviate from baseline rates for speaking. Thus, children say words in the context of actions with objects neither more nor less than predicted by their baseline rates of speaking. At the same time, however, emotional expression at FW is substantially below the baseline for emotional expression, which means that children express primarily neutral affect in the moments around constructing thematic relations between objects. Children are significantly more likely to say words than to express emotion around their constructing activities in play.

At VS, speech and emotional expression are below baseline levels, but with a tradeoff between the two **during** the actual interval of constructing activity. Up until 1 second before the onset of action, emotional expression and speech are about 1 standard deviation below their respective baseline rates. This deviation below baseline **before** the action presumably reflects the effort entailed in creating a goal and a plan for action in intentional states. However, during the construction activity, emotional expression decreases while speech increases and rises to baseline.

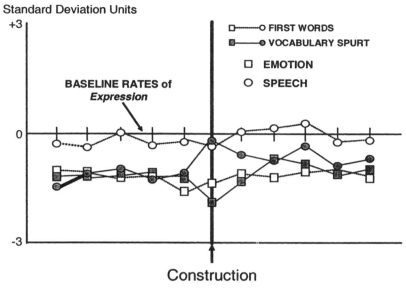

Construction

FIGURE 7.12 Emotional expression and speech in 1-s lag intervals before, during, and after constructions in play, expressed as standard deviation units from the respective baseline rates of speech and emotional expression at FW and VS. From Bloom, L., and Tinker, E. 2001. The intentionality model and language acquisition: Engagement, effort, and the essential tension in development. *Monogr Soc Res Child Dev* 66:1–91.

Immediately after the construction, speech decreases as emotion increases. This tradeoff occurs between speech and emotional expression when constructing thematic relations between objects despite the fact that emotional expression and speech, in general, are integrated at VS (compare with Figure 7.7). However, children are not likely to say words and express emotion at the same time they engage in constructing thematic relations between objects (Bloom and Tinker 2001).

Expression around Given and Specific Constructions

The two categories of thematic relations farthest apart in the hierarchy of object play (see Figure 7.5) are the given and specific relations. Constructing given relations consists of recreating the same configuration in which the toys were originally presented. Constructing a specific relation is creating a new relation with the toys that takes into account their perceptual properties along with the child's social-cultural knowledge about them. Moreover, the achievement of specific constructions is the major development in this early period of word learning and coincides with the vocabulary spurt (Lifter and Bloom 1989). The temporal relation between speech and emotional expression before, during, and after actions to construct these two mutually exclusive categories of thematic relations is shown in Figure 7.13, for VS. (See Bloom and Tinker 2001, for the earlier result at FW.)

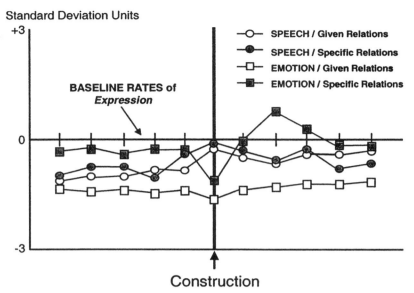

FIGURE 7.13 Emotional expression and speech in 1-s lag intervals before, during, and after constructing **given** and **specific** thematic relations at VS, expressed as standard deviation units from the respective baseline rates of speech and emotional expression at VS. From Bloom, L., and Tinker, E. 2001. The intentionality model and language acquisition: Engagement, effort, and the essential tension in development. *Monogr Soc Res Child Dev* 66:1–91.

Looking, then, at just the **given** relations, speech and emotional expression are substantially below their respective baseline levels before, during, and after the constructing activity. However, children are more likely to say words than to express emotion in the context of object play. Since the same given relations had been presented to the children in the playroom every month beginning at 9 months of age, they were familiar to them. We interpret the expression of neutral affect, with no change, as evidence of a relative lack of engagement in recreating the familiar thematic relations.

The result around the **specific** constructions presents a different picture. Both speech and emotional expression continue to be below baseline before the constructing activity. However, the same increase occurs in speech with a tradeoff between speech and emotional expression **during** constructing that was seen when all constructions were included in the analysis (see Figure 7.12). However, immediately after the constructing activity, emotional expression increases sharply and extends above baseline. This increase in emotional expression above baseline after specific constructions indicates children's **engagement** in the activities that represent an achievement for them at the VS, a finding consistent with the increase in emotional expression after speech at the time of achievement in word learning at VS (see Figure 7.7).

Word learning and specific constructions represent new achievements in learning at VS, and the increase in emotional expression immediately after these actions has ample precedence in the literature. Infants tend to be more engaged, with smiles of recognition and accomplishment with new learning and tend not to be engaged or interested in things that they already know about (such as the given relations). Nevertheless, with specific constructions, the tradeoff between saying words and expressing emotion indicates the **effort** required for the distribution of cognitive resources among these three different expressive actions: speech, emotional expression, and object play.

MOTHER SPEECH AND CHILD SPEECH AND EMOTIONAL EXPRESSION AROUND OBJECT PLAY

We also know that mothers talk to children in the context of their play activities, and children presumably make an effort to interpret what mothers say. At a minimum, to interpret mother's speech, a child has to be able to process the speech signal and construct a representation out of data from perception in relation to data from memory. The child also might formulate a response in the form of either a linguistic or emotional expression. Thus, interpreting and responding to mothers' speech add to the cognitive requirements already inherent in children's expressive actions.

Mother and Child Conversational Turn-taking Overall

To provide a background for the results from the study of mothers' speech in relation to children's speech and emotional expression around object play (Bloom and Tinker 2001), the results of an earlier study of the temporal relations between child and mother speech by Bloom et al (1996) is described first. The result for **all** the conversational interactions between the children and their mothers at VS, regardless of what else was happening in the playroom, is shown in Figure 7.14.

Although only the result at VS is shown here, the pattern at FW was the same, but with smaller deviations from baseline. Already at FW, then, speech interactions between children and their mothers are highly synchronized. When all child and mother speech is analyzed, without regard to what else is going on at the same time, children are most likely to take the lead in their conversations. Child speech is substantially above baseline levels before mothers' speech. Mothers, for their part, are most likely to be responsive, with speech substantially above baseline immediately after child speech. Children are most likely to talk before mothers' speech and far less likely to talk in response to mother speech relative to baseline. Mothers, in turn, are most likely to be talking immediately after child speech and far less likely to be talking before a child says something. Both mothers and children are least likely to talk at the same time the other is talking.

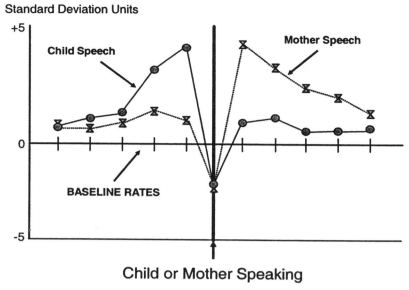

FIGURE 7.14   Child speech in 1-s lag intervals before, during, and after mother speech, and mother speech before, during, and after child speech at VS, expressed as standard deviation units from their baseline rates of speech and emotional expression at VS. Adapted from Bloom, L., Margulis, C., Tinker, E., and Fujita, N. 1996. Early conversations and word learning: Contributions from child and adult. *Child Dev* 67:3154–3175.

Mother Speech and Child Expression around Constructing Activity

Mothers also are most likely to be responsive to the children's actions with the objects, deviating above their baseline levels of talking **only after** the constructing activity (Bloom and Tinker 2001). This result is shown in Figure 7.15.

Mothers' speech increases above baseline 1 to 2 seconds after the completion of the activity. Mothers are least likely to be talking **during** the construction activity. Since mothers' speech does not deviate from baseline before the constructions, they are not, therefore, directing the children in their actions with the objects. Rather, mothers follow a child's lead more often than not by responding to what the child does with the toys and/or what the child says. They do not add to a child's cognitive load by presenting speech to process at the same time that the child is making the effort to construct an intentional state with a plan for creating thematic relations between objects.

CONCLUSIONS

"Actions depend on one's interest and engagement in an event as well as the attention and effort that they require. A balance is usually struck when we have to do two or more things either simultaneously or successively, and performance

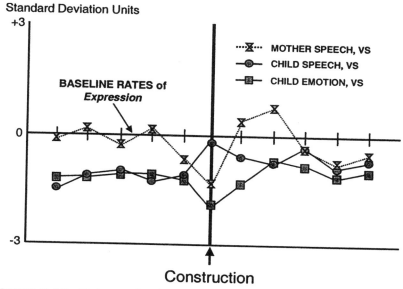

FIGURE 7.15   Mother speech and child speech and emotional expression speech before, during, and after constructions in play at VS, expressed as standard deviation units from their respective baseline rates of expression. Adapted from Bloom, L., Margulis, C., Tinker, E., and Fujita, N. 1996. Early conversations and word learning: Contributions from child and adult. *Child Dev* 67:3154–3175.

reflects accommodation to the effects of task difficulty. [The research summarized in this chapter] has only begun to tap the intricate and complex adjustments needed for the convergence of multiple behaviors in the stream of everyday activity—from moment-to-moment in immediate time, and over the course of the second year in developmental time" (Bloom and Tinker 2001, p. 73). Engagement, effort, and the essential tension between them are required for language acquisition just as they are required for development more generally.

One conclusion from the studies summarized here is that language is not separate from the rest of cognition, action, and emotion for the young child: "Every behavioral act, whether outward bodily movement or internalized cognitive operation gains its significance and status in terms of its role in the overall functioning of the organism" (Werner and Kaplan 1963, pp. 4–5). Development does not occur in separate domains of activity apart from each other (Bloom 1998).

The second conclusion is that language, emotional expression, and actions in play tap into the same general pool of resources. The resources of the young language learning child are fundamentally limited, and effort is required to coordinate different expressive actions and integrate them in the stream of everyday activity. The patterns of contingency between different kinds of behavior revealed in our research show the complementary effects of effort and engagement and the tension between them, requiring a model of development that integrates the two.

Aspects of the same intentional state representations are embodied—made manifest—by the child's different expressive actions: constructing relations between objects in play, saying words, expressing emotion, and interpreting what their mothers are saying to them. It is the child's intentionality, therefore, that provides the connecting link and mediates the coordination of different expressive actions. The Intentionality Model (Bloom 1993; Bloom and Tinker 2001) embraces a child's effort, engagement, and the essential tension between them for explaining language acquisition, in particular, and, ultimately, development more generally.

REFERENCES

Bloom, L. 1970. Language development: Form and function in emerging grammars. Cambridge, MA: The MIT Press. Original Ph.D. dissertation, Teachers College, Columbia University, 1968.

Bloom, L. 1993. *The Transition from Infancy to Language: Acquiring the Power of Expression*. Cambridge: Cambridge University Press.

Bloom, L. 1994. Meaning and expression. In Overton, W., and Palermo, D. (Editors), *The Ontogenesis of Meaning*. pp. 215–235. Hillsdale, NJ: Erlbaum.

Bloom, L. 1998. Language acquisition in its developmental context. In Kuhn, D., and Siegler, R. (Editors), *Cognition, Perception, and Language*, Vol. II, pp. 309–370. In Damon, W. (Series Editor), *Handbook of Child Psychology*. New York: John Wiley and Sons.

Bloom, L. 2000a. The intentionality model of word learning: How to learn a word, any word. In Golinkoff, R., Hirsh-Pasek, K., Akhtar, N., Bloom. L., Hollich, G., Smith, L., Tomasello, M., and Woodward, A. 2000. *Becoming a Word Learner: A Debate on Lexical Acquisition*, pp. 19–50. New York: Oxford University Press.

Bloom, L. 2000b. Intentionality and theories of intentionality in development. *Hum Dev* 43:178–185.

Bloom, L., and Beckwith, R. 1989. Talking with feeling: Integrating affective and linguistic expression in early language development. *Cogn Emo* 3:313–342. Reprinted in Izard, C. (Editor), *Development of Emotion-Cognition Relations*. pp. 313–342. Hillsdale, NJ: Erlbaum.

Bloom, L., Beckwith, R., Capatides, J., and Hafitz, J. 1988. Expression through affect and words in the transition from infancy to language. In Baltes, P., Featherman, D., and Lerner, R. (Editors), *Life-Span Development and Behavior*, Vol. 8, pp. 99–127. Hillsdale, NJ: Erlbaum.

Bloom, L., and Capatides, J. 1987. Expression of affect and the emergence of language. *Child Dev* 58:1513–1522.

Bloom, L., Margulis, C., Tinker, E., and Fujita, N. 1996. Early conversations and word learning: Contributions from child and adult. *Child Dev* 67:3154–3175.

Bloom, L., Miller, P., and Hood, L. 1975. Variation and reduction as aspects of competence in language development. In Pick, A. (Editor), *Minnesota Symposia on Child Psychology*, Vol. 9. pp. 3–55. Minneapolis MN: University of Minnesota Press. Reprinted in Bloom, L. 1991. *Language Development from Two to Three*, pp. 86–142. Cambridge, UK: Cambridge University Press.

Bloom, L., and Tinker, E. 2001. The intentionality model and language acquisition: Engagement, effort, and the essential tension in development. *Monogr Soc Res Child Dev* 66:1–91.

Bruner, J. 1975. From communication to language. *Cognition* 3:255–287.

Chomsky, N. 1965. *Aspects of the Theory of Syntax*. Cambridge, MA: The MIT Press.

Danto, A. 1973. *Analytical Philosophy of Action*. Cambridge, UK: Cambridge University Press.

Fauconnier, G. 1985. *Mental Spaces: Aspects of Meaning Construction in Natural Language*. Cambridge, MA: MIT Press.

Kahneman, D. 1973. *Attention and Effort*. Englewood-Cliffs, NJ: Prentice-Hall.

Lifter, K., and Bloom, L. 1989. Object play and the emergence of language. *Infant Behav Dev* 12: 395–423.

Pepper, S. 1942. *World Hypotheses: A Study in Evidence*. Berkeley and Los Angeles: University of California Press.

Sperber, D., and Wilson, D. 1986. *Relevance: Communication and Cognition*. Cambridge, MA: Harvard University Press.

Taylor, C. 1985. *Philosophical Papers: Vol. 1. Human Agency and Language*. Cambridge, UK: Cambridge University Press.

Vygotsky, L. 1962. *Thought and Language*. Cambridge, MA: The MIT Press.

Werner, H., and Kaplan, B. 1963. *Symbol Formation*. New York: John Wiley and Sons.

Wexler, K., and Culicover, P. 1980. *Formal Principles of Language Acquisition*. Cambridge, MA: The MIT Press.

8

FROM ACTION TO INTERACTION AS PRIMARY ROOT FOR DEVELOPMENT

FÉLICIE AFFOLTER, PHD

For many years we (a research/clinical team based in St. Gallen, Switzerland) did research and clinical work with children and adults. Our observations led us to conclude that nonverbal interaction experience in daily problem-solving events is the root of development. This chapter presents an overview of this theoretical perspective on development[1] and its broad implications for clinical practices.

The discussion of this chapter will follow the different stages of our research program. This research and clinical experience with children who were referred to our clinic as children with language disorders have revealed that they fail not only in verbal skills but also in more basic nonverbal skills, among them sensorimotor skills. Therefore, we refer to them in this chapter as children with pervasive developmental disorders (PDD).

At the beginning, we used the familiar notions of action as the *motor* part and perception as the *sensori* part of the concept of *sensorimotor* skills. As to the sensori part, perceptual skills are considered the most basic skills of sensorimotor performances. As to the motor part, we did not realize the importance of distinguishing between action and interaction. *Action* refers to moving or to the motor component of sensorimotor performances. *Interaction* refers to topological relationships and their changes in the sense of neighborhood relationship among objects/persons and the environment.

The first part of the chapter describes two types of studies that were done at the beginning of our research. The cross-sectional studies of perceptual development compared typically and atypically developing children on a variety of perceptual

---

[1] The text of this chapter is supported by clinical examples taken largely from Affolter and Stricker (1980) and Affolter and Bischofberger (2000). Also see these sources for a more detailed description of the theoretical framework described here.

tasks. The longitudinal study tracked children with PDD on a multitude of nonverbal skills. Taken together, these studies revealed perceptual deficits in children with PDD and mainly in their processing of tactual[2] information. This interpretation of the data led us to assume that tactual information is strongly related to acting in the environment. Acting in the environment could be described as interaction between actors and their environment, and that interaction could be crucial to development.

Hence, the second part of this chapter focuses on the concept of interaction and its theoretical and information aspects. The third section considers the evidence for the hypothesis that nonverbal interaction in daily life events shows the characteristics of problem solving. This leads to the discussion of interaction in daily-life events as a new source of learning and to the model of a root to account for our data. Finally, I address the implications of that model for assessing and treating atypical children and adults.

RESEARCH FINDINGS

PERCEPTUAL DEVELOPMENT

We did cross-sectional comparative studies of different groups of children ranging from 5 to 14 years of age. These groups included not only normal children and those with PDD but also children with just a hearing or visual impairment. The various clinical groups were compared with each other and with typically developing children of the same ages. They were compared on their recognition of the same nonverbal successive patterns and stereognostic forms on tasks that varied in stimulus complexity and the sensory modality of presentation (Affolter 1970; Affolter and Stricker 1980; Affolter and Bischofberger 2000).

The findings revealed progressive development of perceptual performances in children who were normal, deaf, or blind. Their correct responses increased with age on tasks with different levels of complexity and in the different sensory modalities (i.e., auditory, visual, tactual). However, the children who were deaf or blind had lower performances (deprivation effects) than normal children in their respective deprived sensory modality, as expected, as well as in their non-deprived sensory modality (Affolter 1970; Affolter and Stricker 1980; Affolter and Bischofberger 2000). This latter outcome suggested that the development of perceptual performances, which we had observed, could not be explained simply by maturation alone; one must consider that some kind of experience underlies the perceptual development. The data suggested further that such experience is not based on practicing modality-specific perceptual skills, such as visual recognition in the hearing-impaired or auditory recognition in blind children. Otherwise, blind children, who depend much on auditory cues, should have been

[2] Throughout this chapter, the term *tactual* is used broadly to refer to passive touch, which does not involve movement, and active touch, which refers to the combined input resulting from moving and touching, i.e., the tactile-kinesthetic senses.

better than normal children on the auditory recognition tasks. Conversely, deaf children, who depend much on visual cues, should have been better than normal children in visual recognition. But this was not the case. Therefore, it was inferred that modality-specific auditory or visual input is not the critical experience underlying the development of perceptual skills. In fact, the children with deafness or blindness eventually did reach ceiling perceptual performances like the normal children despite a delay. It seemed likely, therefore, that the critical experience underlying the development of perceptual performances includes tactual features. Tactual processes were intact for blind, deaf, and normal children.

This interpretation was justified given the observations of children with PDD. They presented no history of auditory or visual impairment. Yet despite their history of good hearing and seeing, they scored lower on the same perceptual tasks than did normal children and children with deafness or blindness, particularly on the complex tactual perceptual tasks. Furthermore, the children with PDD did not show a regular improvement in their performances on either the successive pattern or form recognition task as age increased, and they never reached ceiling level performances (at least up to the 14 years of age analyzed for our research). It was inferred that their failure to develop adequate perceptual skills might be caused by the lack of basic experience requiring tactual input, an inference corroborated by clinical observations of their poor performances on tactual tasks. With this conclusion, my colleagues and I turned to the longitudinal data to consider general development in PDD children compared with typical children.

GENERAL DEVELOPMENT

In addition to age cross-sectional studies of perceptual development, we did a longitudinal study of children with PDD. They were compared with normal children on a wide range of developmental skills. Children in the clinical group were assessed annually for 8 to 10 years. A profile of different skill deficits and competencies was established based on behavioral observation, formal test scores, and the analysis of videotaped behavior in informal, naturalistic settings. See summaries of this research in Affolter et al (1974) and Affolter and Bischofberger (2000). We observed that the clinical group progressed in some performances over the years. However, the group did not follow the same sequence of developmental levels as observed in normally developing children and those with just a hearing or visual impairment. Some skills (e.g., perspective drawing) that typically are acquired late in normal children were performed early by some PDD children. Conversely, some skills that are acquired early by normal children (e.g., direct imitation) were performed late by the clinical group. Still, many of the children in the clinical group did acquire some language despite the absence of direct imitation. It appeared, then, that the development of the clinical group was not simply delayed or slow; the developmental pattern was deviant.

These findings led to several questions. How can one explain the progress of the children in the clinical group when they fail in imitation? Traditional learning theory assumes that children imitate persons of their social group, parents, teachers, and other children. Is there a source of learning other than imitation that can account for the deviant skills and lack of progress in children with PDD and, at the same time, account for the regularity in the sequence of developmental levels in normal children and those with hearing or visual impairment?

Such a source of learning had to account for the observed similarities between the development of normal children and those with deafness or blindness. It also had to account for the deviant verbal and nonverbal development of children with PDD when compared with normal children and those with just deafness or blindness. This source also had to include tactual features to account for the failure in processing tactual information among children with PDD.

To establish a new hypothesis of learning, we began to reanalyze the available video-recorded data, which had been collected across the 10 years of longitudinal research. We concentrated on the spontaneous behaviors that could be observed in natural settings for normal children and for children with hearing or visual loss and those with PDD but no history of hearing or visual loss.

Our obsrvations revealed an impressive amount of spontaneous activity in normal children and in children with just a hearing loss. These activities always involved an environment. Neither group was content to walk demurely down the street or on a sidewalk. As soon as they saw a wall along the street, they tried to climb it and walk on it. Or they looked for something to jump over, like a small crack or break in the sidewalk. If they saw a small opening in a fence, they tried to squeeze through the opening. Both groups were delighted to throw stones into a creek or a pond. When adults tired of hiking and sat down to rest, these children usually maintained their level of activity.

In contrast to normal children and those with just a hearing or visual sensory loss, the behavior of children with PDD differed. When they chose similar kinds of activities such as walking along the street or on a wall, they would choose a low wall. Or, usually, they would just stay in one place and watch other children perform. Their differences were repeatedly corroborated in many video-recordings and confirmed by reported observations from professionals and family members. The data were collected during the years of the longitudinal study. We concluded that spontaneous activities of children were oriented towards the environment and problems to be solved and that PDD children failed in such activities. We began to consider acting in an environment in typically developing children and in children with PDD.

ACTING IN AN ENVIRONMENT

The question arises about what we mean by *environment*. The environment we refer to includes everything that is physical (i.e., not only objects but persons and living organisms). Horowitz (1987) mentioned the long history of discussing the role of the environment in development. He wrote that there is "no consensus on the questions of how critical, critical for what and when it is critical" (p. 128). Often in the psychological literature, the environment is restricted to social environment. The physical environment either is not considered at all or it is considered to be something very different, as Ulvund (1989) wrote:

> It may be argued that from a developmental perspective a distinction between the physical and the social environment is a highly arbitrary distinction, which hardly has any counterpart in nature. One argument against such a distinction is that the responses the individual makes to the social environment are probably based on similar processes of attention, perception, and learning as the responses the individual makes to the physical environment." (p. 63).

Most of the time, such responses are expressed by movement patterns that change whenever the environment is touched. Such changes allow for important interpretations, as is discussed next.

MOVEMENT PATTERNS AND TOUCHING

When a baby is born, the baby moves. Some psychologists have considered that even the very young babies do not move at random. Rather, very young babies' movements show patterns that indicate that the movements are already structured (Turkewitz and Kenny 1982). To illustrate, consider the behavior of T, a 2-month-old normal baby, in the following situations:

> In situation 1, T is lying on her back on the floor. Her legs move in free space. Repeatedly, one foot touches the other one; the little toes of one foot move along the other foot. In situation 2, her feet now can touch a wall. After touching it once, she stretches her legs and appears to search for that wall again. Whenever she succeeds, she keeps in contact with the wall for a short moment. At each contact, her toes move individually on the wall's surface. This kind of movement pattern (i.e., stretching her legs, staying in contact with the wall and moving her toes along it) can be observed repeatedly; her feet are not touching each other anymore. She never looks at the place on the wall where she touches. In situation 3, the mother lifts T. She jerks and gets tense. Then the mother sits on a chair and puts T on her lap. T snuggles her body along the body of her mother and becomes limp (Affolter and Bischofberger 2000, p. 60).

The first conclusion that can be drawn from these observations is that the baby's movement patterns change. The changes are observable whenever an actual situation changes. So the question arises about whether there is a relationship between the changes in movement patterns and the changes in situations. In the first situation, T was lying on her back on the floor. In the second situation, T's feet touched the wall. In the third situation, the mother lifted T up from the floor, then she sat down and put T on her lap. The differences among the three situations can be described as differences in spatial relationships between the baby and the environment. In the first situation, T was separated from the wall. In the second situation, T was together with the wall. In the third situation, T became separated from the wall and afterward was together with mother's lap. Such spatial relationships of being together or being separate are called topological relationships.

The notion of topology addresses spatial relationships that have to do with neighborhood, in the sense of how things/persons are connected in space. The most elementary topological relationship is being separate versus being together. Topological relationships become more complex when the relationship of being together includes situations like inside versus outside, around something, at something, and through something (Piaget and Inhelder 1948/1956; Piaget 1970). It can be considered that changing topological relationships affords not only actions but also requires information for judging the respective topological relationships. In our next section, we discuss this aspect of information provided when acting in an environment.

INFORMATION AND ACTING IN AN ENVIRONMENT

One has to ask what kind of information is critical when acting in an environment and changing topological relationships. Is the critical information visual, auditory, verbal, or something else?

Auditory and Visual Information

Consider visual information. I am standing on a balcony looking down at a city street. I watch the cars moving along and watch the people walking and the children playing. My eyes are busy getting all the visual information, and my brain is actively considering what all these people are doing. I am active. However, I do not change anything in this environment. I can stand on my balcony for hours, the world gets along whether I look at it or not. This is not acting in an environment as we have described it, as there are no changes in topological relationships.

The analysis of auditory information is similar. I can listen to all the noises in the street, but I do not change the environment. Again, I am active but not changing any topological relationships. Therefore, neither visual nor auditory information leads to changes in topological relationships. To act in an environment does not depend on visual information. This conclusion is supported by studies of blind children. Blind children engage in activities during which they change topological relationships that are similar to those of normal and hearing-impaired children, but they are active less often. This is expected because a lack of vision reduces the incentive to be active (Fraiberg 1977; Bischofberger 1989; Millar 1994).

Tactual Information

In our example of T, we described how that baby changed her movement patterns when she touched the environment. Touching the wall meant a change in topological relationship from being separate to being together with the wall. In other words, a change from being separate to being together always requires touching. For example, to sit down requires that I be together with the chair, so I have to touch the chair. To be together, topologically, with another person requires that I touch that person. Touching provides tactual information. This suggests that tactual information is necessary to get to know about topological relationships and their changes in the environment.

The example of T suggests that each change in topological relationship between the baby's body and the environment creates a new situation. For each new situation, the baby needs new information to know about the respective changes of the topological relationship between the body and the environment. On one hand, babies have to know where their body is and, on the other hand, where the environment is. While touching a wall, one can feel the resistance of the wall. That resistance may block the movements totally. We talk about a maximum change of resistance from no resistance when moving toward the wall to total resistance when touching the wall. The primary information is, thus, of a tactual kind. But this is not enough to explain the changes of T's movement patterns.

Searching for information requires an organism to determine where that information comes from, that is, where the source for a specific kind of information may be. To judge this, the organism has to determine which one of many sources at a given moment is related to a change in topological relationships. The organism has to differentiate that source from other sources of information. To find the wall again, T had to detect that there was a change in resistance between her foot and the environment. T's brain had to select the place or the source of the perceived change of resistance. The observation that T's foot stretched out toward the wall suggests that her selection was correct. For T, the important source of information changed from situation 1 to situation 2 and within situation 3. When foot touched foot, the source of information was between the two feet. When toes touched the wall, the source was between toes and wall. When the mother put T into her lap, the tactual source was between T's body and the mother's body. Through the mother's lap, the baby also could feel the stability of the chair and become oriented towards the tactual source of information between chair and body. The changes of movement patterns along with the changes of topological relationships suggest that with each change in topological relationship, T detected the corresponding new source of information.

Determining sources of information, then, is an active process, that is, one has to search for tactual information about changes of topological relationships between body and environment. To do that, a relevant source must be detected. The detection of such a source allows for a change in movement patterns: changing a topological relationship means moving, such as T is moved through the air. When the change is made and when a respective source is found, the moving stops; for example, T snuggles into the lap of her mother. When such a change occurs, one can infer that the person has detected an important source of information (Affolter 1987/1991; Affolter and Bischofberger 2000).

There is another important aspect in our example of T and the changes in movement patterns. These changes are related to the tactual information, and the tactual information is related to the physical condition or the stability of the environment. The degree of the stability of a physical environment is critical for eliciting changes of resistance and thus for judging the topological changes that result from acting on the environment. When T was moved through free space, the hands of the mother did not offer a stable environment, and T's body became rigid and body tone increased. Stability was offered when the mother sat down on the chair and took T into her lap. In this situation, the mother's body functioned like a "stick" (see stick phenomenon, as described by Gibson 1962), allowing T to feel the stability of the chair through the mother's body. She snuggled into the mother's lap. We concluded: changes in body tone seem to be related to the stability of the environment that is touched.

The differences among the three situations can be described further in terms of sources of information. When T is touching a stable environment, T can detect more easily the relevant source of information between body and environment where touching had occurred. The observed decrease in body tone can be related to detecting a tactual source, thanks to the stable environment. Touching an environment that moves, such as the mother's hands, made it difficult to find the exact place where the environment is touched. The rigidity of T's body when moved through free space is interpreted as a search for sources of tactual information, a search that was unsuccessful because of an unstable environment. This discussion points to the interrelationship among stability of the environment, changes of resistance, and detection of relevant sources of tactual information when changing topological relationships between body and environment.

Tactual Information in Atypical Development

Given the importance of tactual input, it is important to point out that there are disturbed babies, children, and adults who have difficulties detecting sources of tactual information. As a consequence of missing tactual information, acting in an environment becomes deviant. The following example illustrates such difficulties in S, a 6-month-old baby with brain damage, in the following situations:

Situation 1: He is lying on his back on the floor. His body is rigid. His legs are stiff and move rigidly in the air. Not once do his feet touch each other.

Situation 2: His legs touch the wall. His body becomes more rigid; he moves his legs faster and hits the wall, but they do not stay in contact with the wall; his toes do not move separately.

Situation 3: The mother lifts S and takes him on her arm. S's body becomes extremely rigid and his legs hard like sticks. This condition hardly changes even when his mother takes him on her lap (Affolter and Bischofberger 2000, p. 60).

Comparisons of the behavior of S to the behavior of the normal baby T reveal important differences. The observable change in S's movement patterns was a kind of hitting in the direction of the wall when the topological relationships changed from being separate to being together with the wall. The legs were stiff, and they were stiff before, during, and after the change of topological relation between the body and the wall. Thus, the stiffness did not change. S's movements became faster after touching the wall, and the rigidity increased. S seemed to have noticed that something had changed. But the feet were unable to stay with the wall to explore that source of tactual information. When the mother lifted the baby, the rigidity became extreme, the legs hard like sticks. This did not change when he was put into the mother's lap. These observations suggest that this baby could not differentiate sources of tactual information between his body and the environment, even when the environment was stable, in contrast to T.

The examples presented here are just a few of the many examples that support the importance of tactual information when acting in an environment. In view of its importance, the tactual system needs to be studied more. Yet few researchers have emphasized the importance of tactual information when acting in natural settings. Gibson (1962) described observations of "active touch." Lorenz (1964) analyzed animal behavior in natural situations. He inferred that animals react to emotional features of the environment, transmitted through tactual information and received even "at distance" by what Lorenz called a "sensorium-x." In general, however, studies of tactual processes refer to experiments removed from natural settings. Heller and Schiff (1991) pointed to this fact and stressed the importance of studying naturalistic touch:

> Aside from the early phenomenological descriptions of David Katz's classical observations there has really been no serious attempt to develop a natural history approach to the study of touching behaviors. Perhaps it is time for such an approach to emerge. (p. 334)

We conclude that changes in topological relationships create new sources of information. A tactual source of information is created at the place where parts of the body touch the environment. Feeling the stability of the environment allows for detecting changes of resistance. This seems to be a prerequisite for detecting, exploring, and organizing sources of tactual information relevant to the topological changes. Thus, the role of the environment becomes important for acting.

A change of topological relationships between body and environment always involves the body and the environment. When touching occurs, the body and the environment change. An action happens between (Latin: "inter") body and environment. If the actor is together with the environment, the environment is also together with the actor. This allows for a new concept, interaction. The next section elaborates this concept.

THE CONCEPT OF INTERACTION

Piaget (1947/1950) considered interaction between an actor and the environment to be an active process and to be fundamental to development and evolution. Coming from the field of biology, Piaget applied the notions of assimilation and accommodation used in biology to describe interaction. The organism takes out of the environment, that is, assimilates what it needs. Assimilating parts of the environment, such as light by the plant, food by us when eating, and so forth, induces changes in the environment.

ASSIMILATION AND ACCOMMODATION IN INTERACTION

When assimilating, the organism also has to change; it has to accommodate to certain conditions of the environment. Let us examine more closely the mutual dependency between changes of actor and changes of the environment when interacting. Consider K, a 5-month-old normal baby.

Situation 1: K is lying on her stomach on the floor. She is holding an orange on the floor with both of her hands and is sucking the orange intensely. Topologically, K is together with the orange on the floor. She is holding it with both hands. To do this, she must accommodate the grip of her hands to the roundness, the size, and the slipperiness of the orange. This requires her to get information from a relevant source of information, which is between her hands and the orange. She also sucks the orange with her lips and tongue. Thus, she is involved with another source of information, which is between the orange and her mouth. She explores this source; she assimilates the orange. By assimilating the orange, K changes the orange. The most obvious change is that the orange gets wet. There are also topological changes, which are elicited and create the next situation.

Situation 2: The orange rolls away from K, out of her hands, across the floor. K looks at the orange. At the same time she moves her legs and hands on the floor as if trying to locomote (which she is not yet able to do).

K appears to be distressed by that sudden change of topological relationship from being with the orange to being separate from it. When K grasps the orange again, she changes the topological relationship between herself and the orange. She sucks the orange and receives information about the orange, that is, K assimilates. In doing this, she changes the orange. While holding and sucking the orange, K changes the movement patterns of her hands, lips, and tongue accordingly, that is, she accommodates; not only the orange changes but K also changes. This means that K is not just acting on but is interacting with the environment. What is gained in knowledge from such interaction experience is taken up next.

INTERACTION AND KNOWLEDGE

Piaget (1947/1950; 1970) pointed out that interaction via the processes of accommodation and assimilation can be considered the source of evolution and also of knowledge. It also can be considered as the source of emotions (Lorenz 1964). Thus, interaction can be viewed as strongly related not only to perception but also to cognition. Reed (1993) referred to a strong relationship between cognitive behavior and perception, which leads to knowledge about the environment. Taking Gibson's (1979) viewpoint, Reed wrote, "Cognition is used to refer to any and all psychological processes that function to give an organism knowledge about its environments, and its situation within the environment. . . perception is cognitive because it yields knowledge" (p. 47). It is assumed, then, that interaction between persons and their environment leads to knowledge about themselves as individuals, knowledge about the social environment, and knowledge about the world in general. Thus, interaction becomes an important and complex kind of behavior and source of knowledge.

How can the knowledge arising from interaction be described? Observations of normal children and clinical populations suggest that at least two basic types of knowledge result from interacting. One kind of knowledge includes causes and effects that result from changing topological relationships between and among persons and objects in the environment. The second kind of knowledge has to do with the changes of topological relationships between the actor's body and the environment, which are necessary for getting to know about one's body position in space and at the same time about the environment.

Knowledge about Causes and Effects

The following example illustrates how knowledge about causes and effects involved in interaction can result from changing topological relationships among persons and objects.

> K is an 11-month-old baby. She is sitting for the first time in her life on a sandy riverbank. It is summertime, and she is barefoot. Her feet and toes dig into the soft sand; the feet enter the sand and the toes move individually. She touches the sand with her fingers and attempts to grasp it. K lifts her hands filled with sand and the sand flows away. She opens her fingers and looks at them. Her face shows surprise. Again she attempts to grasp the sand, and the feet dig deeper into it. After awhile she begins to pour sand over some small rocks, which are close by, and watches the sand gliding down the rocks. K continues her exploration (Affolter and Bischofberger 2000, p. 50).

To interpret: By observing K's behavior, one can analyze causal activities, some of which can be interpreted as assimilation and some as accommodation. These causal activities have different effects. She touches the sand and attempts to grasp it—the effect, sand flows away. It is inferred that K assimilates the softness and the flowing of the sand through her fingers. She applies what she has learned about interaction or changing topological relationships; she touches, moves, grasps, and tries to hold and to release the sand by displacing. She does it with her feet, toes, and fingers. She is continually involved in varying topological changes for getting different effects and thus gaining information about the sand. By searching for more information, she continues to change topological relationships between the sand and the environment and thus causing other effects, like the sand flowing away from the rocky support; the sand is not where it was a moment ago. One can also observe differences in causal activities that can be interpreted as accommodation: K changes the movements of her toes, feet, and fingers and hands according to the effects of the sand when grasping and holding it. She also increases the complexity of causes and effects: She explores first what happens between her body and that strange sandy support; later she includes parts of the environment, such as the relationship between the sand and the rocks. Her behavioral changes suggest that she is learning by interacting. In summary, interaction allows us to expand the knowledge about causes and effects when changing topological relationships between and among support/objects/persons.

Knowledge About Body, Body Position, and the Environment

The second basic kind of knowledge that can result from interaction has to do with topological relationships between the actor's body and the environment. We are put into an environment; we move continually in a physical space. To behave adequately, we have to get to know about our body and its spatial position in an actual environment. Basic concepts in the acquisition of such knowledge are the notions of stable support and stable sides.

A *support* refers to the surface that carries the body (from the Latin *portare*, to carry), a surface that offers resistance to the effect of gravity on the body, on objects, and on other persons. Such surfaces can be the floor, a chair, a street, a hillside, and so forth. A support connects our own body to objects, to other persons and living organisms around us, and to the inert matter of the world. In other words, through this support, people and objects are topologically related. This topological relationship of being together with a stable support is very important. If a support becomes suddenly unstable, as can happen in an earthquake, the effect is panic for any person.

The importance of a stable support offering resistance in interacting activities becomes observable. For example, when people become tired, they start to move their bodies while sitting on a chair. Or a speaker may rock back and forth on his legs when standing in front of an audience. We judge the person who demonstrates such behavior as "being nervous." In reality, these movements elicit changes of resistances between body and chair or between foot and floor. These changes of resistance allow a person to gain important information about the conditions of the support and at the same time about the position of the body in space.

Another important topological relationship exists between our body and those parts of the environment that are at our sides. For example, we all experience the help of a stable side when we are going down a steep stair (Affolter 1987/1991). In such situations, we realize that the world includes not only the support underneath our body but also what is next to us at our sides. One also feels secure as in a "niche" when touching stable sides and knowing where one's body is in relation to the environment. Niche behavior can be observed in children, adults, and even in animals. For example, children like to sit in a niche even when they have to crawl into it; adults in a restaurant may prefer to sit in a booth to eat instead of the open dining area (see also Affolter 1987/1991).

The sources of information created by touching the support and the sides are likely to be explored continually by the brain. We hardly notice this kind of search for information. Only in stressful situations can such a search be inferred. To emphasize this aspect, it is instructive to watch infants who are beginning to explore the environment. See descriptive observations of babies from this perspective in Affolter (1987/1991). Consider N, a 22-month-old typically developing child:

> N likes to climb on chairs so she can reach things on the tables. For a few days she is in a room she does not know well. There are two chairs in the room that she can use for climbing—one is a wooden chair and very stable, the other one is covered with a cozy warm sheepskin, which makes the surface of the chair rather unstable. After a few attempts at climbing on the less stable chair, she never chooses it again (Affolter and Bischofberger 2000, p. 66).

Touching a stable support and stable sides, then, allows for maximum changes of resistance and thus offers basic information for knowing where the environment is and also where the body is. Such knowledge is necessary to behave adequately in an actual situation and becomes important when considering daily life events.

INTERACTION IN DAILY LIFE EVENTS

Performing daily activities requires changes of topological relationships between a body and its environment and among objects/persons in the environment. For example, I want to make orange juice. To do this I need an orange. I have to grasp the orange from a basket on a shelf. To do this, I have to change the topological relationship between my body and its support, that is, I have to displace my body in the direction of the orange, a causative act. Furthermore, I have to change the topological relationships between and among orange/basket/table and the mutual support, that is, I have to grasp and lift the orange, a causative act. I have to get a knife and put the knife together with the orange to cut the orange. I have to manipulate the knife so the knife goes through the orange. Consequently, we can define an event as a sequence of changes of goal-oriented topological relationships between and among objects, body, and environment.

MAIN GOALS AND SUBGOALS OF DAILY
INTERACTION EVENTS

There is a network of interdependent goal-oriented events in daily life activities. For example, breakfast includes several short events, such as making a cup of tea or coffee and putting butter on a piece of bread. Each of these short events needs previous events like filling the cup with water, getting the coffee powder out of a package, and getting a knife for cutting and spreading the butter. Such short events are embedded into more extended events like preparing breakfast for a whole family. Where does the tea come from? When the tea box is empty I have to put tea on my shopping list and get it next time I do grocery shopping. Such analyses of daily life events reveal complex structures of embedded events that are hierarchically dependent on each other with optional actions or detours for required and nonrequired actions.

To reach specific goals creates problems—sometimes more, sometimes less. Most of them have to be solved. Daily life activities can, consequently, be regarded as interaction events involving problem-solving activities. We discuss this aspect in the following section.

DAILY INTERACTION AS PROBLEM-SOLVING EVENTS

Daily life interaction requires problems to be solved to meet the demands of particular goals. Such problems can be regarded as creating the possibility for elaborating existing knowledge. Therefore, problem solving can be viewed as an important aspect of cognition. To reach a goal, problems have to be solved. Kintsch (1977) wrote, "One talks about a problem whenever there is something that one wants to do or achieve, but it is not immediately clear how to go about doing it" (p. 426). For example, a child is going down the street and sees a wall. The child intends to climb on the wall and walk along the top. The goal is walking along the top of the wall. To reach that goal, the child has to solve several problems: How do I reach up? Where do I get a hold to lift my body, my hands, arms, and foot? How do I balance my body once on top of the wall? In the solving of one problem, another problem appears. Children are usually very skilled in predicting the extent of the problems. The wall they see has to offer some challenge; children will choose to climb a wall that is difficult to climb. This choice is skillfully made according to their possibilities and the situation: the height of the wall, their body height, their climbing skills, presence of familiar persons to help, and so forth.

Such spontaneous activities demand changes of topological relationships, between body and environment, that is, interaction. To do this always involves some kind of search for information. Whenever children are involved with such a search for information, that search is oriented toward solving the problems as in our previous examples of climbing a wall and going along on it. There is a relationship between perceptual skills and the ability to engage in or carry out such everyday goal-oriented interactions.

Considering these different aspects of daily interaction events, problem-solving activities seem to be important. We began to study them and find out about their development. However, data about the development of nonverbal problem-solving activities, the cognitive and information parts, were scarce and incomplete. Consequently, we designed the "seriation task" (Affolter and Bischofberger 2000) to study the development of nonverbal problem-solving activities in typically and in atypically developing children.

This task required the children to vertically arrange rectangular bars by physically placing them in order of increasing or decreasing lengths. The task was not chosen because we attributed the developmental disorders to just a seriation deficit. This task simply provided a context for observing the children's nonverbal physical behaviors on line, as they manually interacted with the test stimuli under a variety of task conditions that varied in stimulus complexity and sensory input modality. The Pitt and Brouwer-Janse's (1985) model of problem solving was adapted to describe the kind of nonverbal activities the children engaged in during the tasks. (See also Pitt 1985.)

The results of the seriation study revealed that normal children and those with hearing impairment showed a regular increase in the number of problem-solving activities with age in different task and modality conditions. But children with pervasive developmental disorders showed deviant profiles in problem-solving activities; they failed in information-seeking activities but were similar to normal children in more cognitive activities such as establishing hypotheses about cause-effect relationships or reaching conclusions. In all the children, the cognitive and information aspects were task dependent. Tasks with more complex stimuli (e.g., more bars to sequence) were performed less adequately than were those with simpler stimuli. (For more details see Affolter 1984; Affolter and Bischofberger 1991, 2000.)

Given the findings from the seriation study, we considered whether the problem-solving processes involved in daily interaction events could also be described in terms of their cognitive and informational components. This issue is considered next.

COGNITIVE AND INFORMATION COMPONENTS OF DAILY INTERACTION

The cognitive components include the activities of identifying the goal of interactions, establishing a hypothesis, and initiating the activities that reflect a mental plan of action. By closely observing and analyzing children's nonverbal interactive behavior in problem-solving events of daily life, we began to differentiate activities that reflect processes of establishing cause-effect relationships from those entailed in searching for information (Affolter 1984; Affolter and Bischofberger 1988). Establishing cause-effect relationships was presumably related not only to children's cognitive level at a given age but also to the amount and type of information they could extract from the environment in a given interactive situation. Both the cognitive and information aspects were expected to be related to the problem to be solved in the actual situation. The extent to which both aspects are connected can be demonstrated by an important aspect of the problem-solving process, namely, establishing hypotheses.

Cognitive Aspect: Establishing Hypotheses

An hypothesis is needed to begin an event or to initiate the first topological changes toward reaching a goal. If children want to climb the wall, they have to make hypotheses about which actions are needed and how to perform them. The way they grasp or lift their bodies will vary with a variety of factors in the situation, including its familiarity. To establish hypotheses, children will apply rules that have been learned from previous experiences (Holland et al 1987). Assuming that solving problems of daily activities requires a certain level of cognitive development, Holyoak (1990) wrote:

> All normal people do acquire considerable competence in solving at least some of the particular types of problems they habitually encounter in everyday life. We might therefore suspect that problem solving depends on general cognitive abilities that can potentially be applied to an essentially unlimited range of domains (p. 117).

Related to the cognitive aspect, making daily life hypotheses requires collecting information about different aspects. One must consider the many demands, which include one's own needs and the needs of the surrounding social group, the family, neighbors, co-workers, and so on. One also must consider the kind of events, as well as the actual situations. For a normal adult, such information typically involves all types of input that include the visual, auditory, and tactual modalities. But the question arises about the most basic kind of information needed to establish hypotheses about daily life events. The following sections discuss how critical the kind of information can be when interaction should happen in daily life.

The Information Aspect: The Tactual System

The Critical Role of Tactual Information

Besides leading to knowledge about topological relationships between body and environment, tactual information seems to be needed to establish hypotheses. Research data (Affolter and Bischofberger 2000) and clinical observations suggest that, to establish highly probable hypotheses about an event, the tactual sources of information may be very basic. Consider the following clinical case:

> Mr. P was in an accident and had suffered severe brain damage. In therapy, he is sitting on a chair. The therapist tries to make him change seats and sit on a stool at a table. The stool and the table are close to the patient. The therapist points with his hand to the stool and tells the patient

to sit on it. The patient does not move, even as he looks in the direction of the stool and table. The therapist puts the stool closer to Mr. P and guides the hands of Mr. P to touch the stool. Still the patient does not move. Now the therapist puts the stool so that it touches Mr. P's upper leg. After a short moment, Mr. P glides over to the stool and sits on it at the table (Affolter and Bischofberger 2000, p. 148).

What happened? First, Mr. P received visual and verbal-auditory information from the therapist. He did not move; we infer that he was unable to make the correct hypothesis. Then the therapist guided the hand of Mr. P to touch the stool. Mr. P did not move; we infer that Mr. P has still not reached a correct hypothesis. He could feel the object, the stool, but this was not sufficient. That feeling was not directly connected with the event. When the therapist pushed the stool so Mr. P could feel it touching his upper legs/hips, he moved over to sit on the stool. We interpreted: The change of resistance Mr. P felt the moment the stool touched his upper leg/hips comes from the same source that is critical when changing from the chair to the stool. In other words, the change of resistance that occurs at that source has to do with the first topological change required for moving from a chair over to the stool: to separate legs/hips from the chair and to put together legs/hips with the stool.

We interpreted: The therapist points to the stool and tells Mr. P to sit down. Understanding verbal commands or using visual input inherent in an actual situation requires that the corresponding events be retrieved from memory. Changes of topological relationships inherent in these events are first stored tactually. Verbal and visual information are added later on (Affolter 1987/1991). In small children and in persons with perceptual disorders, such retrieval is often impossible. This is the case when either there has been no storage of the event, or access to the stored content is not possible using verbal or visual information. Touching the stool with the hands provided tactual information about the object. But this was not the source of information about the event. To establish a correct hypothesis Mr. P needed tactual information about the beginning of the event, that is, the first topological change coming from the source between stool and legs/hips, which was needed for separating his body from the chair and bringing the body together with the stool.

In the next section, we discuss the importance of this interpretation of the role of tactual information provided by the first change of topological relationship of the event.

Tactual Information for Initiating the Event

All events have a beginning, a sequence of topological goal-oriented changes, and an end. To achieve an interaction goal, the sequence of interactions required may or may not require a hierarchically dependent set of topological changes leading to a goal. When I want to pour a drink out of a bottle into a glass, I have to first remove the cover from the bottle before I can pour the liquid into the glass. However, the sequences of getting the bottle and the glass out of the cupboard are interchangeable, I can begin with either one. Nevertheless, we should assume that the sequence of topological changes of an event reflect a mental plan of what to do to reach a goal. Initiating an action plan as well as the establishing of hypotheses are heavily dependent on the available information in the situation. The unequivocal situation to provide relevant tactual information for establishing a hypothesis about an event is provided by the first changes of topological relationships of the event. In other words, the basic tactual information has to do with the interaction part of the event and not simply with touching an object.

This requirement becomes particularly evident by observing children with PDD who often present tactual problems. Consider F, a 12-year-old boy with tactual problems who is described as someone who seems to know what to do but is poorly motivated.

> In a teaching situation, F is asked to prepare a banana milkshake. Seated at a table he slices the banana and opens the milk carton. Next he needs a bowl for mixing. The bowl is in a cupboard across the room from the table where F sits. F looks at the banana and the milk and says, "One needs a bowl," but he does not stand up and walk across the room to the cupboard. The therapist approaches F to help him move the chair so he could stand up. But still F does not move.

Is F not motivated? He knows what problem needs to be solved. He himself has formulated the problem; he needs a bowl.

> The therapist considers the situation. Then the therapist takes the milk carton, puts it into F's hands so F can feel it. He helps F to stand up, initiating the action. F continues the action, pushes the chair back, walks across the room with the milk carton in his hand and gets the bowl (Affolter and Bischofberger 2000, p. 35).

We interpret F's failure to initiate the event of getting a bowl out of the cupboard by standing up and walking across the room as a problem of information, not motivation. Once he got the tactual information about the first topological change of the event, then he was able to perform the event himself.

The next example illustrates how tactual information about the first topological change of the event seems to be important even for a normal child to establish a hypothesis about the event.

> B, a 2-year-old normal child, is being videotaped in a natural setting as part of a research project. She is putting on her slippers while sitting on the floor. One slipper is already on. The other foot is half in the other slipper; then difficulties begin. Her aunt D is close by and sees the rising difficulties. She sits behind B, taking both of B's hands and finishing the event by guiding B with no problem. B stands up—her foot slips out of the slipper. B sits on the floor between D's legs as she was before.

D takes B's hands and guides her to get the slipper, which is lying on the floor close by, to put it on again. The moment D touches B's arms, B shouts, wards off D's hands, and stands up, appearing to panic (Affolter and Bischofberger 2000, p. 181).

We analyzed the two videotaped situations carefully, the first one when D could guide B, and the second one when D could not guide B. We detected an important difference between the two situations.

In the first situation, B's foot was halfway in the slipper. The first important change of topological relationship of the event, putting on the slippers, had been performed; the foot was already together with the slipper. So the source of information was between foot and slipper. It was not yet inside the slipper. This was the next change of topological relationship to occur, and this was done by guiding. When guided, the tactual source of information was still between foot and slipper and connected with the event.

The second situation differed. Topologically, the foot was separate from the slipper. So the first change of topological relationship, foot separate–foot together with the slipper, was missing. There was no source of tactual information about the event; the foot did not touch the slipper. Aunt D took B's hands. The source of information was now between the hands of the aunt and the hands of B. There was tactual information, but not about the event. B had no tactual information to establish a hypothesis about putting on the slipper. This topological relationship, hand of D together with hand of B, had nothing to do with the event of putting the slipper together with the foot. Although this next step of putting the slipper together with the foot was apparent to D, it was not apparent to the child, B. So B refused to be touched to perform a topological relationship that was not required by the event.

To conclude, making hypotheses about daily events is strongly related to tactual information. Younger atypically developing children as well as patients with acquired brain damage may need relevant tactual information in an actual situation by experiencing the first topological change of the event. However, older children and adults may retrieve such information from memory when getting just visual and/or verbal information.

Problems of daily life are always solved in an actual situation. As discussed already, the actual situation has to offer the possibility to gain a critical amount of information so hypotheses can be established. When persons fail to make correct hypotheses, we do not know if this is because they fail in the cognitive part of problem solving or if they do not get enough information. To answer this question, one has to distinguish between competence and performance.

Information and the Distinction Between Competence and Performance

Making a distinction between competence and performance is especially important when one has to evaluate children or adults with behavioral disturbances and plan intervention programs for them (see Bischofberger and Affolter's

Chapter 9; Affolter and Bischofberger 2000). To discuss such a distinction, we have to consider that problems of daily interaction are always solved in an actual situation. This actual situation has to offer the possibility to gain a critical amount of information about the solving of a problem. When children are successful on a specific task in a certain situation, we can conclude that they have reached the cognitive level to deal with that task. However, they may fail to perform this task, if the situation changes. When this is the case, we may conclude that, in the changed situation, the children still have the cognitive prerequisites for doing the task in their competence, but they fail to perform the task because they are unable to extract enough information in the given situation.

K, a 6-year-old girl, likes to hike with us in the mountains. She can do it for several hours and is quite skilled at walking on stony, rough mountain trails. In this instance it is winter time, but there is not much snow on the roads. So we decide to take the mountain bus up beyond the village. We get off the bus. There is a very strong wind. The wind has piled up the small amount of snow so the road is hardly visible, and the depth of snow cannot be predicted. K refuses to step into the snow and walk on that kind of road (Affolter and Bischofberger 2000, p. 62).

The conclusion is that K's hiking skills are still in her competence, but K fails in performance because she cannot extract enough information in the changed situation. To perform, one has to consider the strong interrelationshipbetween cognitive skills and the information available in an actual situation. Thus, to make valid inferences about a child's cognitive level, we must differentiate between competence and performance (Chandler 1991). When children do a task successfully in a specific situation, they must have not only the cognitive prerequisites in their competence but they also have the task in their performance. In that specific situation, they are able to extract enough information from the environment to use their competence to solve the problem and perform the task. Therefore, when children fail to perform a task, it may be that they do not have the required cognitive prerequisites; that is, they are not competent to solve the task. It can also be the case that they do have the competence but cannot perform because the situation demands more information than they can search for (Affolter 1987/1991).

In daily life situations we encounter the relationship between cognitive and information aspects often, especially in situations when competence does not become performance. Riding on a city bus in my hometown may not require much new information. But doing this in a foreign country may create problems, which I have to solve. I apply rules I have acquired at home for riding the bus in the foreign country, but perhaps without success. If that is the case, I have failed to make correct hypotheses in this new situation. My competence has not become performance because of lack of information. To change rules and to establish new hypotheses, I need more information.

Children with PDD and interaction difficulties are often diagnosed with hyperactivity, poor memory, autistic-like behavior, and tactual defensiveness. Our observations raised questions about the correctness of such diagnoses. For example, a child reported as hyperactive in one situation can behave like a calm child in another. A child with poor memory in one situation can show adequate memory in another. A child who may jerk when touched in one situation may use tactual information adequately in another. The common cause in these examples seems to be the differences in information inherent in the respective situations. Disordered behavior occurs in the situation with inadequate information and more normal behavior in the situation with more adequate information. By applying the concepts of competence and performance to these examples, one may report that such children have calm behavior, or memory, or the use of tactual information in their competence. But their competence becomes performance only in situations that offer tactual information instead of just auditory-visual information (Affolter 1987/1991; Affolter and Bischofberger 2000).

The last question about cognitive and informational aspects of daily-life interaction deals with memory and retrieval. We underlined the importance of tactual information when interacting in actual situations. Does tactual information also play an important or even critical role in memory and retrieval?

Interaction Experiences Memorized and Retrieved

Children and adults do store their interaction experiences, and thus increase their basic experience. As we watch babies interacting in daily life picking up tactual and respective visual information, we can already observe behavior, which can be viewed as signs of memorizing and retrieving. An example follows:

> N, a 12-month-old boy, is videotaped as he is on top of a stair, which leads down to a porch. There are several objects on the floor of the porch. A red bowl is close to the last step. N looks at the bowl, then begins to climb down until he has reached the last step. Now he moves one leg towards the floor—and then that foot gets caught in the bowl. N looks at what has happened, tries to lift his leg, but the bowl moves with his foot. Unsuccessful, N sits down, his one foot still caught in the red bowl. He moves his hand to get the bowl off his foot, but still the bowl moves with his foot. N makes several attempts; topological relationships between foot-bowl-body-support change and keep changing. Finally, N is separated from the bowl; he crawls to other objects on the floor, interacting with them for about 10 minutes. Then, he is again at the top of the stairs. He turns and gets a glimpse of the red bowl still on the floor. He climbs down to the red bowl, lifts his one leg and tries to put his foot into the bowl (Affolter and Bischofberger 2000, pp. 187–188).

It is obvious that he tries to replicate the earlier interaction event. It appears that the resemblance of the actual interaction situation has helped the child to retrieve the stored interaction experience. In a general way, we may conclude that the similarity of an actual situation may facilitate retrieval of corresponding events. Clinical experience confirms this conclusion.

As in children, memorizing and retrieving in adults also are enhanced by information provided through daily interaction. The next example illustrates that it is mainly the tactual information inherent in the interaction situation, which is followed by the possibility of retrieval. Luria (1987), a famous neurologist, described the early stage of recovery of a lifelong acquaintance who had suffered brain damage after being shot in the head during World War II.

> Luria's patient was in the hospital, and Luria entered the patient's room. Later on the patient recalled that at that moment he did not know where he was. He heard voices and saw figures but was unable to relate them to himself. Only at the moment when Luria touched him, did he become aware that it was the physician who was talking to him. The patient's conclusion: Only when he was touched did he get to know where he was and where the world around him was (pp. 8–10).

Such examples suggest that when people are in a stressful situation as this patient was and cannot touch the environment, they may have difficulty organizing visual and auditory stimuli in that environment and retrieving the corresponding interaction experience from memory. As a consequence, the person will not know where the environment is and, at the same time, where his or her body is. It can be scary when retrieval is impossible and knowledge is missing.

It has been argued that daily life events include cognitive and informational aspects. These aspects are part of problem-solving processes and are related to the goal of events. Events of daily life consist of sequences of interrelated changes of topological relationships involving the actor and the environment. The beginning of this chapter referred to the conclusion from our longitudinal observation that imitation cannot account for developmental progress. To summarize, at the beginning of this chapter discussing data from our research we inferred the need for source of learning other than imitation. We observed how the spontaneous activities of children include the environment and the changing of topological relationships between themselves and the environment, thus manifesting all the characteristics of interaction. We analyzed the structure of events of daily life. It was concluded that they require interactions in sequences of interrelated changes of topological relationships, oriented toward a goal, involving an actor and the environment. I discussed how such daily life events include cognitive and informational aspects as part of problem-solving processes and how they depend on the tactual information inherent in an actual situation. We also discussed how processes of memory and retrieval are enhanced by the tactual information of an actual interaction situation.

The next section relates the discussion of daily events and interaction to the need for a new source of learning. I argue that daily life events meet the criteria for a new source of learning.

DAILY LIFE INTERACTION EVENTS AS A NEW SOURCE OF LEARNING

To account for the findings of our research studies, a source of learning needs to fulfill several criteria. This new source:

1. Must not require direct imitation skills.
2. Must be universal and function in any social environment.
3. Must be applicable to any group of children, typical or atypical.
4. Must account for the regularity in the sequence of developmental levels observed in normal, hearing-impaired, and blind children.
5. Must account for deprivation and missing compensation effects in children with blindness who grow up without the enhancing role of visual information.
6. Must require tactual information that can create specific difficulties for children with PDD and account for their deviant development.

To find such a source, we analyzed the spontaneous activities of the children in our longitudinal studies to find characteristics that could be generalized to all children. We were able to describe their daily activities in terms of tactual interaction and problem-solving events. We concluded that a **nonverbal daily interaction experience** meets all the criteria for functioning as a source of learning. It is observed in babies before they imitate. Children with PDD perform interaction events before they show imitative behavior. Nonverbal interaction is a universal function in any social environment and group of children. For example, it is observable in hearing-impaired and blind children. It includes tactual features and therefore can account for the normalcy of children with just blindness or deafness, and the deviancy of tactual problems in some children with PDD. This new source of learning then became the basis of our model of development.

THE MODEL OF A ROOT FOR LEARNING AND DEVELOPMENT

Because our research findings and clinical observations did not seem to fit existing models of development, we were faced with the problem of finding a new model of development. The root of a growing tree offered a good metaphorical representation of our findings. The growth of a tree depends on the growth of its root. When the root is small, as in a young tree, only a few branches are visible. As the root grows, the trunk gets stronger, and more and more branches appear. The stronger the root gets, the stronger the trunk becomes, and more branches will grow. When the root gets sick, the branches get sick as a consequence. The branches are not related directly to each other; rather, they are related to the root. So their relationship to each other is an indirect one.

The branches represent the levels of development. The growth of a branch represents the appearance of a given developmental level with its respective skills. Just as the branches are indirectly related, so are the levels of development. They are indirectly related to each other through the root (Affolter 1987/1991; Affolter and Bischofberger 2000). In other words, skills characterizing different levels of development, as noted in Piaget's work, for example, depend on a common source rather than a preceding skill or knowledge level (Affolter 1987/1991; Affolter and Bischofberger 2000).

The root symbolizes daily nonverbal interaction experience, which requires tactual information. The root is the source of the tree's growth. In human terms, the root stands for the basic physical, emotional, cognitive, and social experiences in the nonverbal problem-solving interactions of daily life events. Nonverbal interaction in daily life is defined as goal-oriented changes of topological relationships between actors and their environment, including not only objects but also persons and other living organisms. Just as the root needs soil, children need an environment in which to develop. But the root does not take nutrients directly out of the soil. The root assimilates; it takes out of the soil what it needs according to an actual level of need or of state. Similarly, children do not copy the environment in a direct way; they also assimilate the environment or take from it according to their actual level of development.

In their daily life activities, children accumulate interaction experiences. As they get older, they apply increasingly more complex changes of topological relationships and explore embedded cause-effect relationships within daily life events. As these nonverbal daily interaction experiences increase, the root grows and with root growth, the tree trunk expands, and the branches grow. As the size and strength of the root increase, perceptual organization and cognitive processes are expected to improve. Knowledge about the world (including social knowledge) will expand.

When using the model of a tree root, we can best illustrate that the range of deviant behaviors of children with pervasive developmental disorders can be traced to a common root, namely, an inadequate search for information while interacting to solve problems of daily life. We can refer to a sick root in such children because they fail in basic interaction experience. As a consequence, the growth of the branches, representing development, becomes deviant. The root of a growing tree can represent typical and deviant development. This model of a root for development is represented in Figure 8.1.

The circles in the model refer to the size of the root and to the growth of its trunk. Both are prerequisites for the appearance of specific branches. The dark

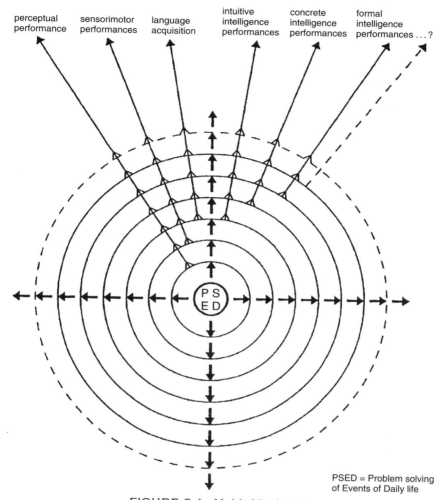

perceptual performance   sensorimotor performances   language acquisition   intuitive intelligence performances   concrete intelligence performances   formal intelligence performances ...?

PSED = Problem solving of Events of Daily life

FIGURE 8.1   Model of development.

arrows indicate the direction of growth in the root and the trunk. At each circle, arrows represent respective branches, which grow because of the size of the root. For example, when the child has experienced a critical amount of nonverbal problem-solving events of daily life (see second circle at the center of the figure), improvement of perceptual performances can be observed. The respective branches appear and will grow at least throughout childhood. As experiences in daily nonverbal interaction increase further, the trunk reaches another critical level of growth as represented by the third circle. Again new branches appear. These branches stand for sensorimotor performances such as rolling over, sitting, standing, crawling, and so on. Again, the further growth of these branches represents the growing of more complex sensorimotor performances such as signal acquisition and imitation. A further development involves the passage from the sensorimotor to the representation level, which is denoted by different branches. Again, this means that branches, as developmental levels, are not directly related. For example, the passage from the sensorimotor level to the intuitive level does not happen in a "direct" way but results from the growth of the tree root, that is, the growth in interactive experience. In this way development continues. Performances at higher levels will be observable as the tree grows and more and more branches appear.

One can also interpret the circles that represent the growth of the root and the trunk as signs of cybernetic processes in the form of dynamic equilibration systems. Brouwer-Janse (1983) described such equilibration systems of development. Thelen (1989) referred to a similar phenomenon in her theory of dynamic systems. Other authors pointed to self-regulatory processes (Fentress 1976; Edelman 1987). Piaget (1970) discussed self-regulatory processes involved in the equilibration systems. He wrote:

> The central problem of genetic epistemology concerns the mechanism of this construction of novelties, which creates the need for the explanatory factors, which we call reflexive abstraction and self-regulation. However, these factors have furnished only global explanations. A great deal of work remains to be done in order to clarify this fundamental process of intellectual creation, which is found at all the levels of cognition. (p. 78).

We argued earlier that the basic kind of nonverbal interaction experience, which is represented by the root, does not require vision or hearing as prerequisite but tactual information. Vision seems to enhance nonverbal interactive activity. Such a model of a root is considered valid for all people, irrespective of age or membership in a clinical or normal group. As the tree depends on the root throughout its life, so adult learning still depends on a healthy strong root. In old age the root may weaken, and afterwards this change will be observable in the branches. But still one can be aware of the root and try to keep it strong. The implication is that the root has to improve in order for development to occur and performance to improve.

To improve the root, therefore, clinicians and educators must provide the opportunity for children to experience interaction with the environment during the problem-solving events of daily life. All the educator can do is to offer children opportunities to interact in daily life, that is, create an environment and tasks for interaction that allow the child to pick up the tactual information needed; this is valid for emotional, cognitive, and social learning (Affolter and Bischofberger 2000). Such a model is also valid for learning language. Since the children with PDD were usually referred to our Center because of their language problems, the following section discusses the application of the model to language acquisition.

THE MODEL OF A ROOT AND LANGUAGE ACQUISITION

Language acquisition is not considered to be a separate entity or an independent skill. It is connected to the root of a growing tree, that is, with daily interaction experience. Research (Bloom 1996; Nelson 1995) suggests that children's language is connected to daily events. Piaget (1945/1962; 1963) described language as a semiotic performance, that is, language forms refer to events of the past or of the future. This description makes language different from signals (see also Bischofberger and Affolter's Chapter 9).

Signals also require forms, but they refer to events of actual situations. This differentiation captures the difference between human language and so-called "animal language." Animals use signals. A developing child will also first use signals. When a 15-month-old infant is asked to get daddy's shoes, the child searches for them immediately and brings them. The child shows signal behavior; the child refers the content of verbal forms to an event that happens immediately in the actual situation. At about 18 months of age, children begin to refer contents of verbal forms to past or future events. One can now tell a child in the morning that grandma is coming after lunch. The child will understand that this will not happen immediately but in the future.

Language is not the only semiotic performance. Piaget (1945/1962) described how children discover true language understanding (words refer to absent objects and events) at the same time they understand that pictures refer to past or future events. Children also will show deferred imitation, that is, a child will imitate the behavior of another child observed the day before. Referring to our model of a root, we can say: At around 18 months, children have acquired a wealth of interaction experiences, have stored them, and can retrieve them. Now they are able to take conventional forms, like speech sounds, to express stored events of the past or the future. Daily interaction events, then, seem to be the base of the content or semantic part of language acquisition (Affolter 1968; Affolter 1987/1991). Interaction experience is also basic to the acquisition of linguistic forms, for example, articulation skills. Babbling may not be a critical prerequisite for speech sound acquisition. We described K at 5 months, interacting with the orange (see p. 180 this Chapter). This interaction did not include just the hands but also the mouth, the lips, and the tongue, that is, oral structures. Babies show such mouthing all through the sensorimotor stage, and it is always connected with intensive interaction experience. Thus, mouthing is related to perceptual and cognitive processes, which are embedded in interaction activity, as described.

In summary, our research has shown that the deficits in language acquisition are not a separate problem but coexist with other nonverbal deficits (Affolter and Stricker 1980). Deviant language acquisition, together with deviant nonverbal development, as revealed by our research, can be traced to problems of nonverbal interaction as described in this chapter and elsewhere (see Affolter and Bischofberger 2000). Problems of interaction reflect problems with the growth of a tree root and thus are the primary problems. Such problems of the root are expressed as deficits in acquiring the semantics of a language, its grammatical and phonological forms as well as deficits in deferred imitation, and understanding the actions symbolized by pictures. For intervention, this means that one does not have to treat each one of these skills separately. Because all these separate deficits can be traced back to difficulties at the root, the root has to be treated. This requires one to provide better information in daily interaction experience for children with language and developmental disorders. As the root grows more adequately, the branches will get healthier. For language, this means that children will first develop signal understanding and performing. As the root gets stronger, language performances will appear (Affolter and Bischofberger 2000).

CONCLUSION

Our research data support the conclusion that it is neither action nor imitation per se but the interaction between a person and the environment that provides a source of learning and development. Interaction begins the moment an organism moves or is moved and touches the material world. Such interaction creates changes of resistance, probably the most basic information of human existence and the existence of other organisms (Lorenz 1977). The changes of resistance are elicited by changes of topological relationships that occur when one moves. Perceiving such basic information leads to learning causes and effects, that is, to cognitive processes including social aspects. In other words, interaction as we have defined it relates cognitive and informational processes.

We analyzed daily events and concluded that they require goal-oriented sequences of interaction. Such interaction embeds the structure of problem solving involving cognitive and information seeking processes. Tactual information seems to be critical for performing, memorizing, and retrieving daily events adequately.

It was argued that tactual interaction in daily life events meets all the criteria for a new source of learning and development. That source can be symbolized by the root of a tree. Development can be compared to the growth of a tree based on a healthy root. The root gets its nurture out of the soil, assimilating what it needs. Similarly, daily interaction needs an environment. The model of interaction as a root or source of development and learning is valid for all people, including children who are normal, children who are sensory deprived, and children with PDD and other handicaps. The model is also valid for adults who are healthy, brain damaged, or elderly.

It has been argued that the goal of clinical intervention must be improvement of the root, namely, experience with solving the problems of daily life events. To improve the root, intervention must be geared toward improving daily life interaction. Examples and discussion about how this intervention is realized are provided by Bischofberger and Affolter in Chapter 9. With increased interaction experiences with solving problems of daily life events, the root gets stronger and more growth of the branches can be expected. The branches stand for the skills or abilities that are learned and developed on different levels of development.

Since interaction always includes the environment, progress on the branches will be shown in different domains as in the cognitive, social, and linguistic ones.

Finally, the distinction made between action and interaction has to do with the importance to the environment. Living in a social group with other persons, children or adults, healthy or troubled, and being responsible for them, we always have to be conscious that we cannot change them directly. We can only change them indirectly by considering the environment. We have to create an environment for them in which they can interact. This environment has to be touchable, offer resistance, and allow for changes of topological relationships. This means we have to offer them the conditions to interact in daily life so that they perceive adequate tactual information. If we succeed in meeting this requirement, the roots of the people for whom we are responsible will stay healthy and grow.

REFERENCES

Affolter, F. 1968. Thinking and language. In the International research seminar on the vocational rehabilitation of deaf persons. pp. 116–123. Washington D.C.: Department of Health, Education and Welfare.

Affolter, F. 1970. Developmental aspects of auditory and visual perception: An experimental investigation of central mechanisms of auditory and visual processing. Unpublished doctoral dissertation, Pennsylvania State University.

Affolter, F. 1984. Development of perceptual processes and problem-solving activities in normal, hearing-impaired, and language-disturbed children: A comparison study based on Piaget's conceptual framework. In Martin, D.S. (Editor), *Cognition, Education, and Deafness.* pp. 44–46. Washington, D.C.: International Symposium on Cognition, Education, and Deafness.

Affolter, F. 1991. *Perception, Interaction and Language.* New York: Springer. Original work published in 1987.

Affolter, F., and Bischofberger, W. 1988. Perception and problem-solving activities. In Kalmar, M., Jackson, S., Donga, K., and Nagy, J., (Editors), *Abstracts of the Third European Conference on Developmental Psychology.* p. 298. Budapest: Hungarian Psychological Association.

Affolter, F., and Bischofberger, W. 1991. Nonverbal problem-solving activities in children. Poster presented at the XI Biennial Meetings of the International Society for the Study of Behavioural Development ISSBD, 3–7 July, Minneapolis, MN.

Affolter, F., and Bischofberger, W. 2000. *Nonverbal Perceptual and Cognitive Processes in Children with Language Disorders.* Mahwah, NJ: Lawrence Erlbaum Associates.

Affolter, F., Brubaker, R., and Bischofberger, W. 1974. Comparative studies between normal and language-disturbed children. *Acta Otolaryngologica* Suppl. 323.

Affolter, F., and Stricker, E., (Editors.), 1980. *Perceptual Processes as Prerequisites for Complex Human Behavior.* Bern: Huber.

Bischofberger, W. 1989. *Aspekte der Entwicklung taktil-kinaesthetischer Wahrnehmung [Aspects of development of tactual-kinesthetic perception].* Villingen/Schwenningen: Neckar-Verlag.

Bloom, L. 1996, The integration of expression into the stream of everyday activity. Lecture presented at Michigan State University's Symposium: Movement and Action: Links to Intelligent Behavior. East Lansing, MI.

Brouwer-Janse, M.D. 1983. The Concept of Equilibrium in Cognitive Development. Unpublished doctoral dissertation, University of Minnesota.

Chandler, M. 1991. Alternative readings of the competence-performance relation. In Chandler, M., and Chapman, M. (Editors), *Criteria for Competence: Controversies in the Conceptualization and Assessment of Children's Abilities*, pp. 5–18. Hillsdale, NJ: Erlbaum.

Edelman, G.M. 1987. Action and perception. In Edelman, G.M. (Editor), *Neural Darwinism: The Theory of Neuronal Group Selection*, pp. 209–239. New York: Basic Books.

Fentress, J.C. 1976. Dynamic boundaries of patterned behavior: Interaction and self-organization. In Bateson, P.P.B. and Hinde, R.A., (Editors), *Growing Points in Ethology*, pp. 135–169. Cambridge, MA: Cambridge University Press.

Fraiberg, S. 1977. *Insights From the Blind: Comparative Studies of Blind and Sighted Infants*. New York: Basic Books.

Gibson, J.J., 1962. Observations on active touch. *Psychol Rev* 69:477–491.

Gibson, J.J., 1979. *The Ecological Approach to Visual Perception*. Boston: Houghton Mifflin.

Heller, M.A., and Schiff, W. 1991. *Psychology of Touch*. Hillsdale, NJ: Erlbaum.

Holland, J.H., Holyoak, K.J., Nisbett, R.E., and Thagard P.R. 1987. *Induction: Processes of Inference, Learning, and Discovery*, ed. 2. Cambridge, MA: MIT Press.

Holyoak, K.J. 1990. Problem-solving. In Osherson, D.N., and Smith, E.E., (Editors), *Thinking: An Invitation to Cognitive Science*, pp. 117–147. Cambridge, MA: MIT Press.

Horowitz, F.D. 1987. *Exploring Developmental Theories: Toward a Structural/Behavioral Model of Development*. Hillsdale, NJ: Erlbaum.

Kintsch, W. 1977. *Memory and Cognition*. New York: Wiley.

Lorenz, K. 1964. *Er redete mit dem Vieh, den Vögeln und den Fischen He spoke to the cattle, the birds and the fish*. München, Germany: Deutscher Taschenbuch Verlag.

Lorenz, K. 1977. *Behind the Mirror: A Search for a Natural History of Human Knowledge*. London, England: Methuen.

Luria, A.R. 1987. *The Man with a Shattered World: The History of a Brain Wound*. Cambridge, MA: Harvard University Press.

Millar, S. 1994. *Understanding and Representing Space: Theory and Evidence from Studies with Blind and Sighted Children*. Oxford, England: Clarendon Press.

Nelson, K. 1995. Events as basic building blocks for concept development. A lecture presented at the Symposium on Movement and Action: Links to Intelligent Behavior, Michigan State University, E Lansing, MI.

Piaget, J. 1950. *The Psychology of Intelligence*. London: Routledge and Kegan Paul. Original work published in 1947.

Piaget, J. 1962. *Play, Dreams and Imitation in Childhood*. New York: Norton Library. Original work published in 1945.

Piaget, J. 1963. Le langage et les opérations intellectuelles (Language and intellectual operations). In Problèmes de psycholinguistique. Neuchâtel: Symposium de l'association de psychologie scientifique de langue française, (1962, pp. 51–61). Paris, France: Presses Universitaires de France.

Piaget, J. 1969. *Perceptual Mechanisms*. London: Routledge and Kegan Paul. Original work published in 1961.

Piaget, J. 1970. *Genetic Epistemology*. New York: Norton Library.

Piaget, J., and Inhelder, B., 1956. *The Child's Conception of Space*. London, England: Routledge and Kegan Paul. Original work published in 1948.

Pitt, R.B. 1985, April. Problem-solving heuristics in adolescence and early adulthood. Poster presented at the Society for Research in Child Development, Toronto.

Pitt, R.B., and Brouwer-Janse, M.D. 1985, April. Problem-solving heuristics in adolescence and early adulthood. Poster presented, Society for Research in Child Development, Toronto.

Reed, E.S. 1993. The intention to use a specific affordance: A conceptual framework for psychology. In Wozniak, R.H., and Fischer, K.W., (Editors), *Development in Context: Acting and Thinking in Specific Environments* pp. 45–77. Hillsdale, NJ: Erlbaum.

Thelen, E. 1989. Self-organization in developmental processes: Can systems approach work? In Gunnar, M.R., and Thelen, E. (Editors), *Systems and Development*, Vol. 22, pp. 77–119. The Minnesota Symposia on Child Psychology. Hillsdale, NJ: Erlbaum.

Tolman, E.C. 1949. *Purposive Behavior in Animals and Men.* Berkeley, CA: University of California Press.

Turkewitz, G., and Kenny, P.A. 1982. Limitations on input as a basis for neural organization and perceptual development: A preliminary theoretical statement. *Dev Psychobiol* 15:357–368.

Ulvund, S.E. 1989. *Cognitive Development in Infancy: A Study with Emphasis on Physical Environmental Parameters.* Atlantic Highlands, NJ: Humanities Press International.

II

CLINICAL APPLICATIONS: INTRODUCTORY COMMENTARY

IDA J. STOCKMAN, PHD

This second section of the book describes two clinical intervention approaches. These two approaches illustrate how principles of development, as described in Part I, can be broadly applied to clinical practice. I identify what some of these principles are. Then a brief overview of the three chapters follows.

BASIC LESSONS FROM PART I

I list some key concepts from earlier chapters that should be respected in creating clinical intervention frameworks for children with pervasive developmental disorders (PDD) in ways that meet the four criteria identified in Part I. They have something to say about what kind of experience motivates development. In particular, they focus on experiences with **ordinary** daily events and assign a significant role to the perceptual and cognitive consequences of acting and interacting in the process of learning from them. They also provide us with hypotheses about what can function as the homologous root of development.

- Action as perceptual-motor experience is not outside of perception and cognition, as once thought (Herbert L. Pick, Jr.). These relationships have had a historical presence in developmental psychology across more than a century of scholarly work.

- Purposeful actions and interactions occur in daily events. Perceptual-motor activity is among the fluid assembly of many factors that converge to perform a given task of daily life (Esther Thelen).

- The ordinary daily life events of eating, dressing, bathing, and so on are a rich enough source of information about the world to support the emergence and subsequent development of nonverbal and verbal cognition. Interactions with the physical and social world of daily events embed features of problem-solving activity (Félicie Affolter), logical relations (Jonas Langer) and event structure (Katherine Nelson) that are foundational for developing perception and cognition inclusive of social and linguistic knowledge.

- While children begin to learn a lot early on from their own physical interactions with the environment (Félicie Affolter and Jonas Langer), their participation in the socially mediated events of daily life provides access to the cultural habits of their group. A child's familiarity with repeated daily routines reduces information processing load for acting and interacting in events at the same time that their natural variability provides the opportunity to create and elaborate conceptual categories of nonverbal and verbal knowledge about the world around them. Event structure functions as the homologous root of all representational systems.

- The onset of children's physical knowledge about the world precedes the onset of their linguistic or verbal knowledge, but the later overlapping development of the nonverbal and verbal domains can inform one another in ways that enrich and accelerate the acquisition of intelligent behavior (Jonas Langer).

- Knowledge about the world is not fixed. Actions in and interactions with the environment contribute to the context dependency of the knowledge gained from learning in natural events (Esther Thelen). Behaving and learning in a given event is controlled by a dynamic self-organizing process that is attuned to the changing situational factors and stored experiences or memories for acting/interacting.

- The brain is biologically wired to accommodate contextual variability of experience across the primate life span by way of mechanisms of neuroplasticity (Jon H. Kaas), even though age constrains the type of neural reorganization possible after neurological insult.
- Although performance and learning can be influenced by a variety of conditions, the tactually embedded nonverbal interaction experiences in daily events is the **homologous** foundation for learning and developing across domains of function (Félicie Affolter).
- When learning language, a child's nonverbal actions/interactions in daily events are among the multiple factors that compete for the same limited pool of cognitive resources (Lois Bloom). So then language performances will be differentially influenced by what else is going on in the event as modulated by a child's own willingness or intentions to use language for connecting to other people and the effort required to do so (Lois Bloom).
- The process of learning requires engagement of the perceptual, cognitive and motor systems in solving problems of daily interactions with the physical and social environment, within biological constraints on the type and amount of information that can be handled at a given time. Therefore, the resulting knowledge is always provisional and subject to modification by new contexts of experience.

BROAD ISSUES IN CLINICAL APPLICATION[1]

The question here is, what might an intervention model look like if it embeds the kind of principles reflected in an embodiment constructivist view of mind as put forth in the earlier chapters of this book? The focus on everyday events in this book scales up the complexity of learning events by exposing their variable and multi-dimensional characteristics. So the challenge for clinicians is to

[1] The views of the contributing authors to Part I should not be taken as an endorsement of the clinical frameworks described in this book. Félicie Affolter's Chapter 8 does provide the framework for the clinical intervention model described in Chapter 9, but not Chapter 10.

figure how babies (young ones with pathology, in particular) can be expected to negotiate the complexity of daily life contexts for learning when it is already clear that they have not been able to do so on their own even when their brains were the most malleable. Therefore, one of two approaches can be taken to clinical work.

One approach is take the child out of the complexity and isolate very specific skills to teach in a therapeutic setting. This is the conventional approach, but it has always created some dilemma. The children still have to go back into their complex environments to apply the bits and pieces of what they have learned in isolation so that people can judge whether they make real progress in intervention. Clinicians may make learning events simple enough for children to negotiate within the artificial confines of an intervention session. However, the work of carrying over the new behavior to the natural environment is often left to the child and/or some mediating agent in that natural environment such as a school teacher or caregiver in the home. The task of applying the learned behavior in natural situations may be even more daunting because in teaching isolated skills, professionals may distort how they are actually experienced in natural situations.

The alternative approach is not to remove children from the complexity of the daily events in the world around but to give them direct help in negotiating that complexity. This latter alternative becomes a real challenge, however, if it is necessary to have the tactually anchored experience inherent in self-action/interaction experiences. How can we help children to experience the tactually anchored input that Affolter argues is so relevant to development and interacting? Given that clinicians cannot do the feeling for the child, are they relegated to presenting just the input that children can see or hear?

This section of the book describes two clinical intervention approaches that do not rely just on seen or heard input. One approach (Chapter 9) is guided interaction therapy (GIT), which was developed by Félicie Affolter in Switzerland (Affolter 1991; Affolter and Bischofberger 2000); see description also in Berglund-Bonfils 1996, 2001; Davies 1994, 2000). The other approach (Chapter 10) is prompts for restructuring oral muscular phonetic targets (PROMPT), which was developed by Deborah Hayden (Chumpelik Hayden 1984; Square 1999) and evolved in North America (Canada and the United States). While GIT and PROMPT have been evolving for more than a quarter of a century, they still are not described in the widely used clinical textbooks about children with PDD. Therefore, they can be included among the undercurrent of alternative clinical approaches referred to earlier in this book.

GIT, which is described in Chapter 9, facilitates nonverbal inter-action experience with problem solving in daily events. It aims to build the perceptual-cognitive foundation for nonverbal and verbal learning and behaving. As a nonverbal approach to developing cognition, the semantic or meaning base of language is in the foreground as opposed to its grammatical and phonological forms. In contrast, PROMPT therapy is described in Chapter 10 as an intervention for atypical speech production; but, it is framed to facilitate language learning more broadly than its phonological forms. These two clinical approaches were selected for presentation in this book for two reasons.

First, their treatment goals and strategies are guided by principles that are consistent with one or more of the four broad criteria for judging the adequacy of an intervention framework, as described earlier in this book. Like all behavior treatments must do, GIT and PROMPT assume that some kind of therapeutically guided experience is critical to learning and developing. They also are necessarily guided by assumptions about how learning happens to change performance. Both approaches differ from conventional interventions in their commitment to enhancing movement-embedded tactile-kinesthetic experience in order to change behavior. Both approaches have the built-in expectation that treatment outcomes will generalize across behavioral domains that have not been targeted directly in the intervention. So they have a homologous orientation to intervention, either directly (GIT) or indirectly (PROMPT).

The second reason to focus on GIT and PROMPT is that each approach represents a treatment system or model as opposed to an isolated treatment technique or strategy. A treatment system follows from particular assumptions about how learning happens either within or across the domains of performing and learning. These assumptions dictate how a clinical problem is diagnosed and treated, inclusive of the type of setting, stimuli, and sensory input to be used. In contrast, a clinical technique is viewed here as an isolated strategy for changing a particular "bit of behavior." A specific technique can sometimes arise accidentally and need not reflect theory-driven notions about how learning happens. For example, there are many little "recipes" or "tricks of the trade" for getting a child to produce a clear /r/ or /s/ sound, or getting a child potty-trained or eating with a fork, and so on. Because isolated techniques or recipes need not be based on any principles about why they should work with one or another child, they are replaced as easily as they are used. If one elicitation technique does not work in the given moment, a clinician simply chooses another one. While clinical techniques are more narrowly focused on changing some bit of behavior in the moment, a systems orientation to intervention is concerned with broad behavioral changes, as is the case for the GIT and PROMPT interventions.

Because GIT and PROMPT differ from more conventional therapy approaches, they are likely to be viewed with some skepticism, as any new approach often is. Therefore, Chapter 11 orients readers to broad issues in evaluating clinical efficacy. Chapter 12 considers some ways that clinical and research practices may be challenged by the theoretical and clinical orientation presented in this book. An overview of each of these three chapters follows.

CHAPTER 9: GUIDED INTERACTION THERAPY: PRINCIPLES OF INTERVENTION

In this chapter, **Bischofberger and Affolter** provide an example of an homologous approach to clinical intervention. This intervention approach was pioneered by Félicie Affolter and a clinical team based in St. Gallen, Switzerland. It has evolved from research and clinical observations of normal and abnormal populations that include children and adults, as described in Affolter's earlier chapter (see Chapter 8). Although this intervention has been evolving for more than a quarter of a century, it still is new to many audiences. In the United States, it is neither well known nor accepted clinical practice among those who now know a little something about it. Nevertheless, it was chosen for presentation in this book because it represents a therapy system or model as opposed to a technique, and its principles of treatment are consistent with developmental principles described in Part I of this book.

GIT aims to help children with PDD to pick up more adequate information from daily problem-solving events (Affolter and Bischofberger 2000). It does so by enabling a child to interact in the environment when physically guiding the body (hands, feet, torso) to solve problems in daily experiences. Children's nonverbal interactions with the environment also may be facilitated indirectly when practitioners or caregivers change or modify the environment in ways that allow them to solve problems on their own. For example, attention to a task may be increased by changing a child's chair so that feet touch the floor to get information about where the body is in space, as opposed to feet dangling in free space without such information. The assumption is that the nervous system stores tactile-kinesthetic-proprioceptive information from such interaction experiences regardless of whether patients move by themselves or their limbs are moved by another person to effect causative action. The rules of therapeutic guiding are structured to take into account issues of attention, task complexity, and available sensory input.

Consequently, acquiring skilled movement per se is not the intervention goal. The goal is **interaction** experience with solving problems of a daily event as this is assumed to be the root of development as Félicie Affolter argued in Chapter 8 of the book. Movement becomes relevant only as a means to the end of touching the environment to change the topological relationships between it and the body in ways that achieve problem-solving goals. Perceiving information from interaction is not assumed to depend on the ability to move independently or in conventional ways. Before normal babies can move independently, they presumably sense changes in topological relations between their bodies and the environments when caregivers handle them in routine diapering, nursing, and dressing routines, and so on. Similarly, children with physical/motor handicaps need not be deprived of such perceptual input either as long as there is some means to interact, that is, to experience the topological changes in the environment associated with reaching action goals in daily problem-solving events. Therapy events are structured to facilitate nonverbal and verbal skills even within the same intervention session.

Chapter 9 summarizes the guiding theoretical assumptions for GIT intervention. In addition, it offers a thumbnail sketch of the process entailed in changing behavior and evaluating treatment outcomes when using this intervention.

CHAPTER 10: PROMPT:
A TACTUALLY GROUNDED TREATMENT APPROACH
TO SPEECH PRODUCTION DISORDERS

Deborah Hayden focuses on intervention for speech production disorders. Given that speaking is one of the most complex skills acquired in development, it should not be surprising that unclear speech can be among the many deficits that children with PDD exhibit. Despite the relatively long history of treating speech production disorders (articulation errors, in particular), the question of how to remediate them is an issue for two reasons that are relevant to the themes in this book.

First, the clinical remediation of speech production disorders traditionally has entailed working on very specific articulation skills— skills that are as specific as the production of a single speech sound such as /s/ in the initial position of words like *s*oap, *s*ee, and so on. This kind of specific skill focus is at odds with the homologous developmental model proposed by Affolter in Chapter 8 and the GIT intervention described by Bischofberger and Affolter (Chapter 9). They argue that therapy should focus on the root of development, namely, increasing children's nonverbal interaction experiences with problem-solving events of daily life. Speech and other skills are expected to emerge once a critical level of underlying perceptual organization is reached. Metaphorically, this means that one works on the "tree" root (nonverbal interaction experience) to stimulate development and not on the tree branches (e.g., specific speech production skills) that presumably emerge from that root.

In applying such a homologous approach to therapy, the direct modification of specific speech sounds is not in the foreground. The expectation is that speech production (and other representational forms viewed as branches connected to the root) will emerge spontaneously once a critical level of root interaction experience is reached in a developing system. This may be a reasonable expectation when focused on the **emergence** of speech. There is evidence that speech can emerge even after 10 years of age in some persons with PDD (Windsor et al 1994) despite speech therapy along the way. It would seem to be a waste of intervention effort to try to get children to talk before they even express communicative intent in any form or have organized their sensorimotor resources well enough to produce speech.

Once intentional speech emerges, though, how clear or intelligible can we expect it to be among children with PDD? The clear echolalic speech of some children shows that they can produce phonemes, even if prosody is abnormal. Their problem is at least one of connecting clear speech forms with the semantic and pragmatic content of language. Many children, however, do not have clear speech. Their intelligibility can be so poor as to render speech unusable for most social interactions. Nonverbal interaction experience alone, which commits to no particular symbolic system of expression, may not be enough to render speech clear enough to use after it emerges from the "root." If not, how can or should speech therapy help them?

Consequently, a second reason to focus on speech production skills in this book is that conventional therapy for a speech production disorder is not always effective for children with PDD. One reason has to do with the narrow treatment of articulation errors as either a motor or linguistic problem. A linguistic approach stresses the mental representation of phonological rules and the contrastive function of speech sounds in a language. The contexts for practicing words are driven by linguistic units and not by sensorimotor ones. The sensorimotor requirements for producing speech are de-emphasized on the assumption that the problem is not a motor one. Sensorimotor approaches are reserved for those children who have difficulty with actually producing speech sounds.

Yet the global deficits of children with PDD mean that they can have difficulty with actually articulating speech sounds at expected ages (a motor problem) and difficulty with linguistic representation of sounds along with other language delays. A therapy approach that caters solely to either a sensorimotor or to a linguistic approach will not well serve children who may present deficits at both levels.

Even the conventional approaches to sensorimotor therapy may not be effective for some children. The reason has to do with the type of perceptual input emphasized in treatment. Children with PDD may be diagnosed with developmental apraxia of speech (DAS). Although this diagnosis has been a controversial one to give to children who present no frank neurological impairment, it has been viewed as a motor planning problem. The premise is that speech is disordered because the mental map or schema to guide articulatory movement is absent. Conventional strategies for creating motor plans require children to look at their own self-productions in mirrors (a source of enhanced visual input), or imitate clinician-modeled input (sources of enhanced visual and auditory inputs). Less often do clinicians enhance tactual input in mapping motor production targets. Earlier attempts to do so have had limited appeal. This may be because they have promoted tactual input in a general sense (McDonald 1964) or offered static tactual cues for a few phonemes (Stichfield and Younge 1938; Bashire et al 1984). Furthermore, modifying articulation patterns was done typically in isolation of what is required for speech production as a whole and for language and its use as a communication tool.

Hayden describes intervention using PROMPT as one solution to holistic speech production therapy. See also Square (1999). PROMPT is the acronym for prompts for restructuring oral muscular phonetic targets. Since the initial publication (Chumpelik Hayden 1984), this intervention paradigm has evolved to provide an increasingly more dynamic interface between speech production and the rest of development. This intervention is guided not only by speech production theory but also by learning principles governing the neurological, cognitive, linguistic, social, and emotional areas of function. This view is consistent with an expanding outlook that links the speech production process to cognition. (Kent, in press). The execution of an elaborate system of tactual cues for facilitating speech production is informed by general learning principles and speech production theory. Prompts enhance tactual input for producing not only discrete phonemes but also phrases and sentences along with the prosodic features associated with them. At the same time, PROMPT applies motor speech principles in ways that also can facilitate the development and use of language for functional social interactions. Chapter 10 gives an overview of the history of PROMPT and principal assumptions that guide assessment and treatment of children with speech production disorders.

CHAPTER 11: THE MULTIPLE FACES OF CLINICAL EFFICACY

Chapter 11 addresses the issue of how to determine whether an intervention is efficacious or not. This question is particularly relevant for an unknown intervention. The two interventions GIT and PROMPT, which are described in Chapters 9 and 10, are arguably not yet regarded as standard practice, even though they have been evolving for more than a quarter of a century.

Any new approach is naturally greeted with some suspicion and skepticism. This is the case even though some currently favored clinical practices have not been put to an efficacy test. When focused on a clinical population as severe as PDD, there also is the sense that a new therapy can take advantage of desperate families in their search for better solutions to a child's problem.

Skepticism is justified until a new approach has been tried out and judged efficacious. When judging the value of one or another approach, however, there is often a narrow sense of what constitutes the evidence for clinical efficacy. Claims that there is no evidence for one or another clinical approach can be motivated by the search for a particular form of evidence. A narrow view of efficacy can encourage the perception that the public trust is violated when this need not be the case. We must consider why professionals would devote untold hours to developing and implementing a clinical approach if there is no evidence whatsoever that it does not work or why caregivers may seek out a particular intervention, devote resources to it, and claim that it works. One should leave the chapter with the sense that efficacy is not a straightforward judgment. The effectiveness of an intervention can and should be judged by multiple sources of evidence, given that any one source has advantages and disadvantages in judging the truth about any given intervention.

REFERENCES

Affolter, F. 1991. *Perception, Interaction and Language.* New York: Springer. Translated from the original work published in 1987.

Affolter, F., and Bischofberger, W. 2000. *Nonverbal Perceptual and Cognitive Processes in Children with Language Disorders: Toward a New Framework for Clinical Intervention.* Mahwah, NJ: Erlbaum.

Bashir, A. Grahamjones, F., and Bostwick, R. 1984. A touch-cue method of therapy for developmental verbal apraxia. In Perkins, W.H., and Northern, J.L., (Editors), *Seminars in Speech and Language*, pp. 127–137. New York: Thieme-Stratton.

Berglund-Bonfils, K. 1996. The Affolter approach to treatment: A perceptual cognitive perspective of function. In Pedretti, L.W., (Editor), *Occupational Therapy: Practice Skills for Physical Dysfunction*, 4th, pp. 451–461. St. Louis: C.V. Mosby.

Berglund-Bonfils, K. 2001. Interactive guiding: The Affolter approach. In Millier-Kuhaneck, H., (Editor), *Autism: A Comprehensive Occupational Therapy Approach*, pp. 225–236. Bethesda, MD: AOTA.

Chumpelik Hayden, D. 1984. The PROMPT system of therapy: Theoretical framework and applications for developmental apraxia of speech. *Sem Speech Lang* 5:139–156.

Davies, P.M. 1994. *Starting Again: Early Rehabilitation after Traumatic Brain Injury or Other Severe Brain Lesion.* Berlin, Germany: Springer-Verlag.

Davies, P.M. 2000. *Steps to Follow: The Comprehensive Treatment of Patients with Hemiplegia.* New York: Springer-Verlag.

Kent, R.D. (in press). Models of speech motor control: Implications from recent developments in neurophysiological and neurobehavioral science. In Maasen, B., Hultsijn, W., Kent, R.D., Peters, H.F.M., and van Lieshout, P.H.M., (Editors), *Speech Motor Control in Normal and Disordered Speech.* London, England: Oxford Press.

McDonald, E. 1964. *Articulation Testing and Treatment: A Sensory-Motor Approach.* Pittsburgh: Stanwix House.

Square, P. A. 1999. Treatment of developmental apraxia of speech: Tactile-kinesthetic, rhythmic, and gestural approaches. In Caruso, A. and Strand, E., (Editors), *Clinical Management of Developmental Apraxia of Speech*, pp. 149–185. New York: Thieme Medical Publishers.

Stichfield, S., and Younge, E.H. 1938. *Children with Delayed and Defective Speech: Motor Kinesthetic Factors and Their Training*, pp. 95–163. Stanford, CA: Stanford University Press.

Windsor, J., Doyle, S. S., and Siegel, G. M. 1994. Language acquisition after Mutism: A longitudinal study of Autism. *J Speech Hear Res* 37:96–105.

9

GUIDED INTERACTION THERAPY: PRINCIPLES OF INTERVENTION

WALTER BISCHOFBERGER, PHD, AND
FÉLICIE AFFOLTER, PHD

Our research has revealed that children with language disorders[1] are not simply delayed in their development; they are deviant. We have hypothesized that their deviant development results from inadequate interaction experience due to abnormal perceptual processes (see Affolter Chapter 8; Affolter 1987, 1991; Affolter and Bischofberger 2000). This means that a person cannot wait and give the child more time to develop, expecting that the child will become normal. Instead, they need intervention beginning at an early age in the sense of working on the root of development, as proposed by Affolter (Chapter 8) and Affolter and Bischofberger (2000). The root represents nonverbal interaction experience in daily problem-solving events. The purpose of this chapter is to discuss broad clinical treatment principles that illustrate what is involved in "working on the root." Over the past 25 years, these principles have been the foundation of our therapy for children and adults in a variety of clinical settings, inclusive of schools, clinics, and hospitals. We discuss how the intervention approach follows from assumptions about the nature of the disorder. Specifically, we discuss (1) the clinical practices for assessing and modifying nonverbal and verbal behaviors, inclusive of the treatment goals, contexts, and perceptual inputs; and (2) some evidence that illustrates the efficacy of the treatment approach.

---

[1] We will call them in the following section "children with pervasive learning disorders" because they are not only disordered in language but also in nonverbal performances.

ASSUMPTIONS UNDERLYING CLINICAL
TREATMENT

Our clinical intervention is supported by several assumptions that differ from existing approaches. They have to do with what is assumed to be the basic nature of the disorder and what kind of sensory input will make a difference in changing behavior.

ASSUMPTION ABOUT THE NATURE OF DISORDERS

Practitioners working within traditional approaches often assume that children with pervasive learning disorders simply present immature or delayed development. They assume furthermore that intervention can enhance development by simply changing the amount of stimulation, and that all they have to do is to enrich the environment. So, often we are asked whether children with such disorders need more stimulation, that is, need an enriched environment. By enrichment, one usually means adding color, objects, or sounds to a child's environment (Hawkins 1983). These practitioners do not consider the deviancy of these children's development.

Other approaches assume a perceptual overload in children with nonverbal and verbal disorders (Niaz and Logie 1993; Crary 2000). These practitioners emphasize the importance of reducing the child's environmental stimuli such as colors or sounds; classrooms are painted in gray, and lights are dimmed. Some children are given ear protection to prevent distraction by acoustic stimuli; other children are put into acoustically treated rooms.

In contrast, Affolter (Chapter 8) discussed how the model of a tree root accounts for our research data on children with normal and disordered nonverbal and verbal behaviors. The tree root is a metaphor for nonverbal interaction experiences in daily problem-solving situation. Such interaction experiences were defined as changes of topological relationships between an actor and the environment oriented towards a goal. Thus, *interaction* does not refer here to social/pragmatic interaction but first and foremost to interaction as a physical event involving purposeful problem-solving behavior. Although some of these events are influenced by social and pragmatic rules of interaction, they need not be. Children with PDD are not simply immature or delayed, nor do they experience a perceptual overload. Their problem is, rather, a failure in getting adequate interaction experiences.

Failed interaction experiences result from the lack of information needed to interact successfully. The failure to perceive information to interact is not assumed to be a matter of auditory or visual perception. Some patients fail in interaction experiences because they do not pick up adequate tactile-kinesthetic information. Others may fail in interaction experiences because they are unable to integrate what they sense from touching and feeling with what they see, hear, and smell. Others may fail because they cannot serially organize such complex intermodal information in time and space (Affolter and Bischofberger, 2000). The children in all of these clinical subgroups may fail to interact because they cannot organize the stimuli present in an actual situation.

Therefore, it is the deviant underlying organization of the perceptual system involving tactual[2] input that leads to inadequate or failed interaction experiences or to a "sick root," which in turn gets expressed as **deviant development**. When a tree's root is sick, we can expect its branches and leaves to be unhealthy as well. Similarly, our model assumes that the numerous nonverbal and verbal deficits that can be observed among children with PDD reflect the adverse effects of a sick root or the failure in getting adequate input for interacting in daily life interaction situations. Enriching or reducing visual or auditory stimuli will not improve the "organization" of the stimuli or the picking up of adequate information from the input. Interaction experiences will still be inadequate, and the root's growth will still be deviant. What practitioners have to do, consequently, is to create an environment in which patients can interact, namely an environment that allows them to perform daily problem-solving events; and ensure that they pick up all the relevant information in events. In this way, learning from the environment is enhanced. This is called *working on the root*.

ASSUMPTIONS ABOUT THE TREATMENT FRAMEWORK

Treating Patients in Real Situations

A fundamental assumption of treatment is that children with PDD do have the ability to learn, and adults with acquired brain damage have the ability to relearn, but they need help in doing so. To help them, we must help them to organize their search for information in a better way, so that interaction improves, and the root can grow. Organizing the search for information requires detecting sources of information and separating relevant from irrelevant sources when interacting. To achieve this goal, patients need intervention in actual daily life situations, not in artificial environments.

Targeting Change in the Underlying System

We also do not embrace a symptom-by-symptom approach to treatment, that is, this therapy does not involve work on specific skills as isolated goals of therapy or as separate skills that are isolated from the interaction activity of solving problems in daily life. For example, if the child cannot eat properly or play properly, therapy does not focus on playing, eating, or putting on a shoe. The claim here is that all of these various skill deficits evolve from the same root and can be facilitated indirectly by applying the same principles, that is, enabling nonverbal interactions to occur by enabling the patient to pick up adequate information for

---

[2] Throughout this chapter, the term *tactual* is used broadly to refer to passive touch, which does not involve movement, and catice touch, which refers to the combined input resulting from moving and touching, i.e., the tactile-kinestetic senses.

interacting. The adequacy of the information is not presumed to be simply visual or auditory input but rather tactual perception. Tactual input is viewed as essential and primary.

When tactual information is missing, therapy must be designed to help patients pick up this information. However, the picking up of the information does not reside outside of the natural contexts for interacting in daily life. The amount and type of information available for interaction is considered to be highly context dependent; it varies with the situation demands from moment to moment and specifically with the information requirements for interacting. Thus, interaction activity is viewed in the context of a problem-solving event in all its aspects inclusive of creating, testing, and evaluating hypotheses in daily life (e.g., how can I get my shoe on, get my big package through a door, eat slippery spaghetti on my plate, retrieve my toy from the bathtub, and so on?). Whether or not a problem is solved will depend on the situation and the kind of information that can be accessed in that situation.

APPLYING THE SAME TREATMENT TO DIFFERENT CLINICAL POPULATIONS

Finally, our model assumes that all the deviant behaviors have the same root cause, namely, inadequate nonverbal interaction experience. This means that the same treatment should be applicable to all of the patients who come for treatment with various kinds of diagnoses. For example, children are referred to our center with different diagnostic labels. They are described as hyperactive, tactually defensive, emotionally disturbed, and autistic or having short-term memory and personality problems. The question arises as to whether the same principles can be used to facilitate or help patients with various clinical diagnoses and problems. To answer the question, we present several examples[3] of clinical cases with familiar diagnoses.

R, a 9-year-old boy, is in a normal children's classroom. He can hardly sit quietly on his chair; he twists his body wherever he is, has difficulty with concentrating, and speaks very rapidly. The psychologist describes him as **hyperactive**. The teacher brings R to see us. We advise the teacher to work with R on the floor, to sit behind R, and to guide him whenever difficult actions come up. The teacher tries this out, and R becomes calm and works on his task. No hyperactive behavior is observed.

T, a 15-year-old boy, was diagnosed as **having severe language and short-term memory problems**. His daily routine includes occupational therapy followed by language therapy. He goes from one place to

---

[3] The examples are taken from Affolter and Bischofberger (2000) if not mentioned otherwise.

the other through an extended hallway. When he arrives at the clinician's room, he is asked what he did in occupational therapy. Both therapists report that he never remembers. They say he has poor memory. Is this interpretation correct? In a teaching situation, our course participants worked with T. They asked him to prepare a sandwich. One of them guided his body and hands to perform the necessary actions. In this manner, he received tactual information about the event. Afterward, he returned to his school, had lunch, and then went to his language therapy. When asked what he did with us in the morning, he could tell the speech therapist what he had done. The speech therapist was amazed. Had she been wrong about T's poor memory?

F is a 14-year-old boy with a language-disorder. The therapist reports that F shows **autistic** kind of behavior; he refuses to be touched for guiding. When, for example, the therapist takes F's hands to guide him to get a tomato to cut for salad, F pushes away the therapist's hands. The therapist interprets this as tactual-defensive behavior. We work with F. We put a bedspread into his hands, and then start to guide him to put the fresh cover on his bed. We have his full attention on the task; not once does he push the guiding hands off.

Do all these children's behavioral disturbances reflect a primary kind of problem? Is hyperactivity R's main problem? Is T a child with poor memory, and is F a child who refuses to be touched? How can we explain these examples of contrasting behaviors in the same child? The referral reports had described these children as having a problem in an absolute and general way: the child is hyperactive, has poor memory, is autistic, and so forth. No one reported attempts to change the testing situation and explore whether a short attention span was always observable or to note if the child was always hyperactive, always had poor memory, always was autistic and refused to be touched, and so forth. Attention, memory, and allowing to be touched were considered to be primary skills and prerequisites for learning. In contrast, our clinical and teaching experiences suggested that what appeared to be hyperactive behavior, poor memory, autistic behavior, and refusal to be touched depended on the situation. Specifically, the type of information in each situation required nonverbal interaction in the actual situation. When tactual information was given, the behavior became more normal. When R, who had been called a hyperactive child, sat on the floor with the teacher behind him, he became quiet. In this position, the environment provided more tactual information than when he was seated on a chair. We inferred that hyperactivity was related to inadequate information. The lack of information appeared to be the primary cause, hyperactive behavior a secondary effect.

Reportedly, T usually did not remember what he did only a few moments ago and was viewed as having a problem with short-term memory. However, when he was provided with more adequate tactual information by being guided through a sandwich-making event, he could remember afterwards, even hours later after other intervening events had occurred. This observation suggested that T remembers an event when he receives adequate input about that event by being guided. Conversely, whenever he did not remember an event, it is likely that he had not received adequate information about the event and consequently could not store it. His problem appeared to be an input problem rather than a problem of subsequent memory processing. In other words, something that he did not perceive he could not store; something that he did not store could not be retrieved. T had, therefore, not a primary problem of memory, but a problem of information input, or perception.

When F was touched, he jerked. These movements were generally interpreted as signs of tactual defensiveness or avoidance. However, one can elicit similar reactions in normal people. Normal people also jerk when they are blindfolded, put in a dark room, or are touched unexpectedly. When a baby is touched during the first weeks of life, the baby makes jerking movements too. We can conclude: Whenever someone is touched by an unknown stimulus, he or she jerks. In an animal, jerking away from an unknown stimulus may mean saving its life. Jerking is, therefore, a normal reaction. What is not normal is the frequency with which jerking reactions were observed in children with language disorders, that is, the frequency with which they judge a stimulus received tactually to be unknown or unfamiliar. A baby normally gets familiar with tactual stimuli by tactual experiences. Perhaps tactual stimuli are more often judged as unknown to the disordered child because of difficulty with adequate processing of tactual information, which reduces tactual experience. When the therapist touched F's hands to begin guiding him, he might not have known why he was touched. However, when F touched the object that he needed to solve a problem, as in the bedspread example, F could be guided. He seemed not even to notice that he was guided. It suggested that through tactual information, he got to know about the goal and the event.

Touching the environment to gain such knowledge is also valid for adults, as in cases of acquired brain damage. Here are two examples from the same patient:

> We observed Mrs. R when we were teaching a course in a nursing home. She had suffered a severe head trauma some time before. She was judged to be a patient who could not be rehabilitated and was admitted to this nursing home. When we met her, she was being pushed in her wheelchair down the hallway toward the elevator. She moved her body back and forth in the wheelchair, arms in the air, body tense. She talked and talked, sometimes comprehensibly, sometimes in incomprehensible jargon. What I could understand was that she was afraid that she would be put into prison, that somebody would come and kill her, or poison her. . . She appeared to be in a panic. We were told that a few years ago she had come from Eastern Europe as a refugee and that she was severely disordered and agitated. Nurses and therapists were afraid to

care for her as she panicked when touched or moved. In the bathroom, she could not be alone even for a second because of her agitation.

Two of our student therapists were sent to observe Mrs. R's interactive behavior on the ward. They analyzed the situations when she was in the bathroom and in the dining room, when she was sleeping, when being dressed, and so forth. Two hours later the students reported: The nurse put Mrs. R on the toilet and said Mrs. R could not be left alone for one second because of her agitation. The situation: The commode was placed in the middle of the bathroom. The students changed the situation. They put Mrs. R into a corner of the room, so she could touch the wall when moving her arms. As soon as she was in the corner and touched the wall, she became calm. The nurse, very surprised, asked the students if they had other magic tricks. Lunchtime: Mrs. R is used to sitting in her wheelchair at a table in the middle of the room, very agitated. First, the students pushed the table to a wall, so that Mrs. R could sit in a corner. However, the armrests of the wheelchair were so high that they did not fit under the table. This meant that there was a gap between her body and the table, and she was not touching the table with her body. The students changed the wheelchair to one with lower armrests. Now Mrs. R could touch the table with her body, touch one wall with her right arm, the other with her back. She became calm immediately, so calm that the students could guide her to drink. Then Mrs. R looked around and said, "Today is a nice day."

Morning time: Usually the nurse dressed Mrs. R while she was on her bed. Only the head of the bed touched the wall while the sides of the bed were in free space. The students advised putting the bed into a corner, so the head of the bed as well as one side of the bed touched the wall, making sure that Mrs. R was positioned in the corner touching both the head of the bed and the wall when being dressed. The next day the nurse told them that Mrs. R got dressed in that changed environment, and she was calm. What had happened?

We inferred that the changes made in the environment allowed Mrs. R to pick up tactual information, to feel the resistance offered by the environment while she was interacting. The students observed that when Mrs. R was in the middle of the room, she was agitated. They inferred that in this position Mrs. R received only visual information about the world around her. The resulting agitation was a sign of panic because the visual information did not allow her to perceive the environment as existing and to know where she was (see also Affolter 1987/1991). The changes the students created allowed Mrs. R to touch the world around her, to elicit changes of resistance, thus providing her with tactual information. When Mrs. R perceived the world around her and her body at the same time, she became calm.

These examples emphasize the importance of providing tactual information when interacting in daily life. They illustrate the panic or other difficulties that result when the tactual information for interaction is missing. They also show how behavior can change when touching the environment helps to provide that information. This means one has to control and, when needed, change the environment so that the person interacting can touch the environment and, thus, extract important information from the touching, resulting in acquiring knowledge about body and environment, causes and effects.

Thus, our treatment model and its application to intervention, as discussed here, is valid for people with different kinds of disturbances/handicaps, including adults with acquired brain damage. It is also valid for normal children and adults who can learn throughout their life span (Ebner 2001).

TACTUAL INFORMATION AS PRIMARY INPUT FOR INTERACTION IN TREATMENT

The previous discussion makes it clear that tactual input is important in detecting the changes of topological relations that result when interacting. We assume that tactual input is stored as changes of resistances to movement. Movement happens when there is no force or resistance that opposes it. Movement stops when the body encounters something in the world around that resists or opposes it, that is, something that retards movement of the body keeps it from moving altogether at a given moment. When this happens, normal persons experience a sense of being in touch or in contact with something else in the world around them. This change from being separate to being together with another object can be described as a change of topological relations between a person's body and other objects in the world around them during nonverbal interaction events. They are sensed as changes of resistance to movement. For example, I want to get the knife on the table to peel an orange. I move my hand towards that knife until I feel the resistance of the knife on the table. Now I grasp the knife. It is this change from no resistance to resistance that allows me to judge that I am at the knife, or, more generally, that there is an object in the world around me and that my body touches that object. This suggests that changes in resistance are a basic source of information when touching the environment. Thus, touching goes along with a change in topological relationships: Before touching, my body is separate from the world/object around me; while touching, I am together with the world/object. Success in daily life interaction, then, depends on information about such changes of topological relationships. Affolter (1987/1991) described numerous examples to illustrate the need to search for information when topological relationships have to be changed and the failure of such a search even by adults with brain damage. Here is one example.

> Mrs. N has acquired brain damage. For six weeks, the therapist has tried to teach her how to peel apples and how to spread butter on bread, all without success. The therapist tells me about Mrs. N's problems. I think about these problems. How long can one continue to peel an

apple? The apple is round, and one can peel and peel until hardly anything is left in the hand. How long can one spread butter on bread? One can spread and spread for a long long time. How long can one go on drawing a circle? One can draw and draw. When peeling, spreading, and writing, one elicits only minimum or no changes of resistance. This, in addition to some visual information, provides enough information for a normal person to decide when the apple is peeled, the butter is spread, or a circle is drawn. However, the changes of resistance are too weak and do not give those who are perceptually disordered the information they need to reach such a decision. Perhaps this explains Mrs. N's difficulties and lack of learning. Could we change the situation? We tried. Instead of peeling the apple, we begin by cutting it on a cutting board. We divide the apple in half; then we cut each half in two to get fourths. We continue dividing until there are many little pieces of apple on the table. Only now, we begin to take the skin off with a chop of the knife – one piece of apple after the other. With the first piece, we cut once and the skin is off. With the next piece, we cut once and the skin is off. Mrs. N is beaming and exclaims, "I can do it." At the end, there are many pieces of apple, all peeled, on the table (Affolter 1987/1991, p. 142).

The critical information appeared to be related to the amount of change in resistance. When Mrs. N was able to elicit a maximum change of resistance, she could judge that she had performed the change in a topological relationship: separating the skin from the apple (Affolter and Bischofberger 2000, p. 161).

TREATMENT PRINCIPLES: WORKING AT A NONVERBAL LEVEL

A major assumption here is that behavioral changes are dependent on the interaction between the learner and the environment. This means that adaptive behavior is assumed to result from (1) the circumstances that involve the environment and the potential information it affords, and (2) the learner's ability to detect the information in ways that allow for interaction to occur. Therefore, therapists/teachers/caregivers must manipulate or be aware of both aspects when attempting to change behavior or to engage successful nonverbal interaction events. There are two important aspects to consider when "working on the root." The therapist/teacher/caregiver has to help a patient (1) to touch a stable environment when interacting, and (2) to receive relevant information by guiding while performing daily life events.

TOUCHING A STABLE ENVIRONMENT

A first step in intervention is to create a stable environment that can be touched when patients interact.

Touching a Stable Environment to Judge Where One's Body is in Relation to the Environment While Moving

To feel secure and to move around in an environment, we have to know where the environment is and where we are with our bodies. To gain that knowledge, we need a stable support and stable sides. Numerous observations of daily life behavior confirm this assumption. First we illustrate what the adaptive behavior of patients and typical learners may look like when searching for this kind of stable support.

> P is a 15-year-old boy who has problems picking up adequate tactual information. As soon as he is not actively involved in a task and has to wait, he rocks his body back and forth, lifting one foot and then the other. One day, I observe him when he was going down an unfamiliar stairs. He slides one foot along the support step until he reaches the edge of the step. He follows the edge with the heel of his foot downward until he reaches the support of the next step. There he puts his foot down. Then the other foot performs an identical sequence of movements. At the same time, he is holding onto the railing at the left side of the stairs with one hand, and touching the wall at the right with the other one. This is how he walks down the stairs, always in direct contact with the support, the steps, the wall, and the railing (Affolter 1987/1991, pp. 104–108).

We infer that when going down the stairs in this manner, the boy elicited changes of resistance. He felt no resistance when the foot was in the air. He felt a strong resistance behind the foot from the edge of a step when gliding down along the edge. Finally, he felt a change from no resistance to total resistance while touching the support of the next step when arriving there with his foot. In addition, he could elicit changes of resistance between his hand and the railing on one side and his hand and the wall on the other side.

> A few weeks later, I observed M, an 18-month-old normal infant who was also going down an unfamiliar set of stairs. At first, she behaves like P, the 12-year-old boy described in the preceding example. Then, during the next 3 days, she goes back to these stairs frequently. Already by the second day, she moves differently. She can now step down by lifting her foot into free space and placing it on the next step.

One can make similar observations of normal adults under certain circumstances. How does one walk down stairs in the dark? In addition, what about lecturers who are under stress in front of an audience? They begin to shift their body weight from the right leg to the left leg, from one side to the other. We infer that it is important for clinical cases and for normal children and adults to touch a stable environment when interacting. The stability of the environment allows them to detect relevant tactual sources of information and elicit changes of resistance between their bodies and the environment. With a successful search for information, important information can be extracted about the environment; a person gets to know where the environment is and where his or her own body is (see Affolter's Chapter 8). With this knowledge, a person can successfully move in the environment.

But what kind of behavior occurs when a person cannot get the necessary input to behave normally or adaptively in a situation? Can we intervene to change the behavior? Here is one example.

A is a 7-year-old child with language disorders and hemiplegia (paralysis of one side of the body caused by brain damage). The teacher reported that when A's hemiplegic arm becomes very tense, he raises it to a vertical position. A walks and moves around in this position, hardly ever lowering the arm. The doctor told the parents that they might have to consider surgery for A to control that problem of raising the arm. We observe A in the classroom. He arrives, takes off his jacket, and walks to his desk, not touching any environment at his sides, his arm always raised. Then he sits with the children around the teacher in the middle of the room.

We interpret the high tension in A's body as a sign of searching for information for knowing where he is exactly. A seems to be unsuccessful in detecting a tactual source. Consequently, he becomes very tense and his arm goes up. We analyze his environment. He performs his daily activities in the middle of the room. There he is unable to touch an environment at his sides. He does not get tactual information, and consequently he does not know where he is (where his arm is) and where the environment is. We change the situations.

Situation 1: We put a bench into a corner. Instead of removing or putting on his jacket standing in free space, we have A sit down in that corner. As soon as he sits down on the stable bench, he touches the wall behind and the wall on the side. His arm comes down. He puts on the jacket without raising his arm.

Situation 2: Instead of putting the children on chairs in a half circle around the teacher, in free space, we asked the teacher to line up the children and have them on the floor with their backs against the wall. In this position, they are in contact with the support, the floor, and with the wall behind. As soon as A changes his position and touches the wall, his arm comes down.

We interpret that in Situation 1, when A was sitting on the bench in the corner, he could touch a stable environment. This allowed him to turn toward tactual sources of information, one source of information was created between his hips/thighs and the bench, and the other source was created between his back and the wall. He got to know, through touching, where his body was and that he was sitting. At the same time, he became aware of his environment; he was sitting on a bench and a wall was next to him. His body tone decreased, and his arm came down. In Situation 2, sitting on the floor and touching the wall allowed A to turn toward tactual sources of information, one source between the floor and the body, and another one between the wall and the back of his body. The high tension of his body decreased, and the arm came down.

In summary, during the interaction events of daily life, we not only have to move, but we also change topological relationships between our body and the environment and among objects in the environment to learn from our experiences. The stability of the environment plays an important role in helping us to judge such changes.

The implication for clinical intervention is that we should make sure that patients can touch a stable environment from underneath and at the side. Even when sitting, patients should touch a stable environment. We cited examples of sitting on the floor instead of sitting on chairs to create a stable support for the body, including the legs. Patients also should not sit in the middle of a room; when sitting, they should be able to touch a wall at their backs or at their sides (e.g., for eating at a table). We may even create a niche where patients can touch a wall at their back and at their sides when sitting. School rooms/dining rooms should have several corners, perhaps cubicles or booths, where patients can sit to work or to eat. In the washroom, the sink should be close to a corner, so the patient can squeeze into a gap between the sink and corner and stand there for brushing the teeth, and so on. Such changes of the environment should allow patients to touch a stable environment when performing daily events. It can then be expected that hyperactive or agitated patients become calm.

Touching a Stable Environment to Gain Cause-Effect Knowledge

Touching a stable environment when interacting is important while moving around and detecting relevant sources of information about where the body is in relationship to its surroundings. It is critical in helping patients gain important fundamental knowledge about causes and effects of their own actions. The following examples illustrate this point.

Mrs. M is in a clinic for rehabilitation.

Situation 1: She is in her bedroom. She intends to clean a little table with wheels, next to her bed. The water bucket is on a chair also with wheels. Mrs. M is sitting in a wheelchair. As she starts cleaning, everything begins to move: the water bucket on the chair with wheels, the table with wheels, and her own body in the wheelchair. Mrs. M gets stiff, her face becomes very tense, she starts to panic, and, at the end, she bites into the cleaning towel.

Situation 2: After that incident, on the same day, her therapists prepare to eat lunch with her. They remember the panic Mrs. M showed a while ago when everything started to move. To avoid such a situation, they try to put her into a niche for lunch. There, Mrs. M is sitting on a chair. At her right, she touches the bed (which is stable). Behind her is the wall. Then, the therapists move the table close to Mrs. M, so that the table touches Mrs. M's body in front. Being able to touch the bed to her right, the wall behind her, and the table in front of her, Mrs. M sits in a niche. In that niche, she is very calm and a big smile appears on her face—a behavior one has not been able to observe since her arrival in the clinic a few weeks ago.

We interpret that in Situation 1, when Mrs. M starts to clean, the environment is unstable. The table moves, the chair with the bucket moves, and the wheelchair she is sitting on moves. Consequently, she has no stable reference and she cannot detect necessary tactual sources. Therefore, she cannot judge where her body is and where the environment is. She also cannot judge what is cause and what is effect when beginning to clean. The missing tactual information and the lack of knowledge leads to panic. In Situation 2, Mrs. M is sitting in a niche. The chair is stable, and the wall at her side and the table in front of her are stable. Now she has stable references to judge where her body is and where the environment is. Therefore, she feels secure.

Here is another example.

R, a head-trauma patient, is sitting in his wheelchair and tries to put a clean pillowcase on his pillow. To perform the activity, he puts the pillow on his knee. He has to handle the pillow and the pillowcase while doing this he also has to move his body. At the beginning, he is calm. However, the pillow, the pillowcase, and R's hands move. The knees also move. R's movements get faster and faster. His face and his whole body get tense.

In this situation, several objects move, including R's knees, as soon as he is acting. We interpret that he has no stable support as a reference point. He cannot judge what is moving, the pillow, or the pillowcase, or his knees. This situation is similar to the situation of the two trains (cf. Affolter's Chapter 8). Therefore, R cannot detect relevant tactual sources of information and is not receiving the information he needs to interact in this situation. The tension in R's body increases, and he reaches a state of panic.

A therapist nearby notices R's difficulties and changes the environment; he gets a table for R. Now, R can put the pillow on that table. He calmly continues his activities. We interpret that, when he holds the pillow on a stable table and not on his moving knees anymore, he can keep the pillow there. In this way, he feels a stable support, the table. This allows him to switch to the relevant tactual source between the table and pillowcase. The table becomes a reference for judging the moving of the pillowcase. Thus, he is able to finish the task.

Such clinical cases reinforce the need for treatment to provide stable reference points for patients to judge what is moving and what is not and thereby differentiate causal action from its effect. In clinical practice, we encounter many situations that are similar to R's case, as described. For example, a patient has to open a bottle or take something out of a box or a can. If this is the case, the therapist/educator has to make sure that the bottle or the box or the can is in a stable position so that only the cover moves or the "something" that has to be taken out of the box or the can is moving. When opening a door, we should try to touch the frame of the door with one hand as the stable reference, and move the door with the other hand. Similarly, when taking out an object from the cupboard, we try to touch the frame of the cupboard with one hand as the stable reference and move the object with the other hand. In this way, we apply in intervention what is meant by the "relativity of perception." See Affolter (Chapter 8) for definition and description.

Applying these different aspects of the interaction to a stable environment, we can help patients to detect important sources of tactual information, and thereby enhance the organization of input. This organization is needed to gain important knowledge about where the environment is and where a person's own body is and what is cause and what is effect in an event to be performed.

GUIDING AS A MEANS OF GETTING THE INFORMATION NEEDED TO INTERACT

This chapter, so far, discussed the importance of a stable environment for touching when interacting. Often, however, this is not enough for adequate intervention to occur. That is, simply putting disordered persons in a stable environment that they can touch does not mean they will be able to change their sources of information according to respective topological changes. The next condition for interacting is the search for information. Touching a stable environment is just the first condition for interaction to occur. The next condition for interacting is information. However, touching the environment adequately to get the information can be difficult for patients with perceptual disorders. The information cannot be handed over to them in a direct way. Patients must search for information. Such a search for information is connected to perception. Piaget (1961/1969) and Gibson (1966) stressed the importance of perception being structured or organized. Piaget referred to perceptual activity.

In our view, taking out of the environment that tactual information that is needed for interacting requires the organism to actively perceive. Furthermore, it requires that such active perception be organized. A fundamental kind of organization involves detecting critical sources of tactual information. This is a challenge because daily life situations change continually; so, we must continually search for information to deal with the changing situations. Children and adults without disorders may be hardly conscious of what they do to search for information until they are in unfamiliar surroundings. For example, I am staying overnight in an unfamiliar hotel; I have to find out where to park the car, if and where they serve breakfast, how the shower works, and so on. Success in solving problems in such situations requires adequate information. But children and adults with nonverbal and verbal disorders need help with adequately organizing their search for information. **Thus, improving the search for information becomes an important goal of intervention.**

Because we cannot hand information to patients in a direct way, we must help them to search for the information by providing them with adequate input. In some cases, this can be done by changing the environment, for example, providing a stable support in a way that enables patients to interact to solve a problem of daily life on their own. In other cases, we must be more direct. The best possibility is **guiding.** That is, we have to manually guide patients to actually experience the changes of topological relationships that occur when moving in or touching the environment in solving problems of daily life.

Guiding as "Doing With" the Patient and not "For" the Patient

Guiding allows us to intervene and enhance the selection of relevant sources of information available to the patient. To guide, practitioners/parents take the hands/body of patients and perform a daily event with them. We found that, through guiding, it is possible to transmit all the information needed to recognize an event (Affolter 1987/1991; Affolter and Bischofberger 2000). Guiding is assumed to elicit the same tactual information one receives when performing the movements for interaction by oneself. Thus, we can help them to pick up adequate information while changing topological relationships. Guiding can be used with children at all levels of development and with adult patients at all stages of progress.

How guiding is performed from a technical point of view is not the purpose of this chapter. Earlier literature (Affolter 1987/1991; Affolter and Bischofberger 1993, 1996) includes detailed descriptions of how to guide using guided interaction therapy (GIT). The aforementioned literature reviews the different kinds of guiding, including elementary guiding, intensive guiding, and guiding when nursing activities are performed. We refer interested persons (e.g., family members, therapists, and teachers) to these publications. Here we illustrate how guiding patients in daily life problem-solving events can help them.

It will not take much more time to do the activities with patients than for them. The next example of a brain-damaged patient illustrates this point. It shows that instead of opening the door for the patient, a person can open the door with the patient.

> After therapy, the speech therapist brings a patient back to his room. In the hallway, they arrive at a door. The speech therapist pushes the patient in the wheelchair close to the door, so that she can guide the

FIGURE 9.1 **A**, 9 years and perceptually disordered, prepares a filling for a lemon. **B**, She is being manually guided through the sequence of actions. She pours yogurt into a bowl. She is touching/feeling and watching! The filling is ready. She presses the filling into the lemon. She touches/feels and looks to what her hands are doing throughout the long event. Visual information becomes interrelated with tactile-kinesthetic information and both of them with the corresponding causes and effects of the event.

Reprinted with permission from Affolter, F. (1987/1991). *Perception, Interaction and Language: Interaction of Daily Living: The Root of Development.* New York: Springer–Verlag, p. 175.

patient's hand to open the door a little. The patient in the wheelchair can now squeeze through that opening (thus, touching the environment) and then push the door wide open so that it does not block the wheels of the wheelchair.

FIGURE 9.2 **A**, —CONT'D   Visual illustration of guiding while sitting in a daily life event. *I put my right hand on the right hand of the child and my left hand on the left one. I concentrate on the tactile-kinesthetic information I am receiving from the child's body and through it from the event. I do not need to see the child's face—the body tone indicates the amount of attention being paid to the event.*

Reprinted with permission from Affolter, F. (1987/1991). *Perception, Interaction and Language: Interaction of Daily Living: The Root of Development.* New York: Springer–Verlag, p. 179.

Opening a door by guiding patients in such a way helps the patient to perceive important tactual information about their self, about the environment, and about causes and effects involved in this event. Other examples illustrate the meaningfulness of such an approach.

We were teaching a course about GIT. The lecture hall for our course was on the second floor. Three children with severe cerebral palsy were supposed to come to our room for practical work. The three children came in wheelchairs, unable to walk. There was no elevator in the building. How do we bring them up? Do we carry them? The oldest was already 17 and too heavy to be carried. In addition, we were teaching the participants that they should not do an event for the patient but

FIGURE 9.2 **B** Visual illustration of guiding while standing in a daily life event. Even when a child stands, I guide from behind.

Reprinted with permission from Affolter, F. (1987/1991). *Perception, Interaction and Language: Interaction of Daily Living: The Root of Development*. New York: Springer–Verlag, p. 179.

with them. Therefore, we decided to guide these children to walk up the set of stairs. This we did, guiding them along the wall, step after step, higher and higher. I was standing at the top of the stairs on the second floor, when O, the first and oldest one, arrived. The therapists were almost exhausted from the guiding. But O looked at me with a big smile, and with his gruff speaking voice he pronounced, "That's the first time in my life I went up the stairs—I want to do it again." I will never forget this statement. How can it be that, in all his 17 years, no one ever realized that he was longing for this kind of interaction and not just being nursed? Later, I saw the three boys, on their way to lunch, having been guided to glide down the stairs and sit in their wheelchairs. This time I met the youngest, a 9-year-old boy. He also looked at me with a big smile and said with his gruff speaking voice, "I am content" (Affolter and Bischofberger 2000, p. 179).

Here is another example, which shows that caregivers, as partners in the intervention, also can be taught in the same way to guide their children in daily life events. We teach a GIT course for families. Two to four families, including father, mother, their handicapped children, and the nonhandicapped siblings live for 1week in rented apartments in the Swiss Mountains. In the apartments, they can perform their daily routines like cooking, eating, dressing, sleeping, taking a shower, and so on. One of the children is C, a 6-year-old child with cerebral palsy, a floppy (hypotonic) child.

C can hardly hold her head upright, and she cannot walk on her own. In addition, she is not speaking. The mother is preparing a snack for her. She is learning to do this together with C by guiding her, instead of doing it for her, which she did up until now. They walk from the table to the cupboard containing the refrigerator. When at the refrigerator, the mother guides C to touch it with the left side of her body, so the refrigerator can function as a stable reference for opening the door. Then she grasps the door with C's right hand and opens it. The yogurt for the snack is on the bottom shelf, so they have to kneel on the floor to get the yogurt. The mother guides C for this change of body position by moving her downward along the cupboard until she kneels on the floor. They take the yogurt out of the refrigerator and put it on top of the cupboard. Then comes the next change of body position: standing up. This is done by moving C's body up along the stable cupboard, until C stands in a secure position, the arms on the surface of the cupboard. Now, she is moved along the cupboard and the yogurt pushed along on top of the cupboard. The mother walks back with C along the wall to the table. At the table, the mother guides C to climb on the chair. Then the mother also sits down on the chair by squeezing herself between C and the chair until C sits on her lap at the table. Here they open the yogurt, and the mother guides C to eat the snack. During the whole event, C did not utter a sound whenever she touched a stable part of the environment, and she interacted in a meaningful way. She produced sounds whenever she was guided in free space while walking. The next day, the parents reported that C had a sound night's sleep, which was quite unusual for her.

We interpret then that the change of behavior, becoming quiet, suggests that in these situations C picked up important information and detected relevant tactual sources of information. This means that she is improving perceptual organization and that she is learning. Daily life nonverbal interaction requires information.

When to Guide

Guiding is possible only when the guided persons need information that they cannot pick up by themselves. Guiding can be used not only with disordered persons but also with normal children and adults, whenever they do not know about an event or they cannot perform daily activities. Guiding cannot be used when a person already knows about a task and can perform it (i.e, the task corresponds to the performance level of the person). In this case, the child or the adult will refuse to be guided.

Guiding should be applied in daily life events as often as possible. It always involves the whole body, as in the example of changing position or climbing. Climbing situations happen often in daily life. Children need to get a chair to wash dishes in the sink or to obtain an object from a high shelf of a closet. One may need to get a stool and climb on it to get the object. So, for intervention, we should profit from such situations not only in work with children but also in work with adults. Frequently, for example, patients in wheelchairs are transferred from the bed to the wheelchair, from the wheelchair to a chair, from a chair to a stool, back to the wheelchair, and from the wheelchair back to the bed. In intervention, we do not plan performance situations because they are not true learning situations. We mentioned that guiding cannot be used when a person already knows about a task and can perform it (i.e., the task corresponds to the performance level of the person). Instead, we have to focus on achieving the understanding and competence level of the persons.

Daily Life Events as the Intervention Context for Guiding

Daily life events involve sequences of interactions. Such sequences of interactions require changes of topological relationships between a person and the environment and within the environment. The sequences of changes of topological relationships of events are goal oriented and have a beginning and an end. Our observations (Affolter and Bischofberger 2000) have shown that guiding creates the possibility of transmitting enough tactual information to recognize an event. By guiding patients to perform daily life events, therapists/caregivers can provide the input that helps patients to work at a higher level than their existing performances (i.e., what they can do on their own without adequate tactual input). Guiding enables them to better match their performances to their capacity or competence to do a task with adequate information. In real events, guiding stimulates the changing sources of information that allow patients to enhance their interaction experiences and expand their knowledge of the world.

Therefore, to be helpful, we cannot teach persons with disorders to consider a tactual source of input in an absolute way without a goal. We insist on the importance of always changing the sources of information in connection with a meaningful interactive event. Often, patients will refuse to be guided when they do not connect it with a goal of an event, as the following example shows.

A, a 2½-year-old normal child, wants to do everything by himself. He wants to butter his slice of bread himself; he wants to cut his own bread. When his siblings or parents want to help him by guiding, he refuses and says, "No, myself." Later, I am in the kitchen preparing dinner. I need to pour some water into the grill pan in the oven. A wants to do it. A holds the pot to fill it with water. I stay behind A. I begin to guide his hands, which hold the pot. I guide him to fill the pot, to bring it to the oven, to pour the water into the grill pan. Then I let A's hands go. A brings the pot to the sink. A's older sister enters the kitchen, sees A, and says, "Oh, did you help F?" A responds, "No, I myself" (Affolter and Bischofberger 2000, p. 180).

This example illustrates that the first requirement to be able to guide a patient is that the information provided by guiding is event related. The event creates the goal. Reaching the goal requires changes of topological relationships. Changing topological relationships requires touching. This is an example of the interrelationship between perceptual activity and cognition. Consequently, guiding a person has to be goal oriented. This explains why A refused to be guided by his parents or siblings. Their guiding consisted of taking A's hands before the event had started, that is, before A. was touching the slice of bread to be buttered the knife to be used for cutting. His refusal can be related to the hypothetical processes and to the sources of information. We infer that when the siblings started to guide, the source of tactual information for A was between the hands of the person who touched him and his hands. This source of tactual information had nothing to do with the event. The sources were quite different when I started to guide A. (See previous reference: "A holds the pot to fill it with water.") At that moment, A's source of tactual information was already between the pot and his hands; this source provided tactual information needed for the event. In this situation, I could start guiding A to fill the pot with water. A's tactual source was still between the pot and his hands when filling the pot with water. This was the most important tactual source required for reaching the goal of filling that pot with water.

A's remark, "I myself," confirms our interpretation. Apparently, A did not notice that he was guided. This can be observed again and again when one guides a child through an event that the child cannot perform alone, but it is on the child's level of understanding or comprehension. Children with PDD who are guided often report similarly. It confirms that (1) being guided through an event and receiving tactual information about the topological changes included in the event allow one to perceive the same kind of information as when performing it oneself, and (2) the important kind of information is not elicited by the motor act per se (see Affolter's Chapter 8; Day and Singer 1964; Bischofberger 1989) but by the interaction. This means that the source of information is between the object (handled by the actor) and the environment. This source is the same if I am guided (or if I do it myself). We have discussed how the search for information is important and how one can help patients to pick up tactual information when interacting. Tactual information can transmit information about events. Whenever one performs daily events, problems will surface. Sometimes there are many, sometimes just a few. One has to solve those problems to complete the event, that is, meet the daily life goal. Thus we talk about nonverbal problem solving when performing daily events. Working with patients on their level of understanding elicits their attention.

Guiding to Gain Important Knowledge

Guiding to Elicit Causes and Effects

Each time the person who interacts has changed a topological relationship between objects/persons/support, that person must be able to judge the effect of the actions. For example, I want to write with a pen, the cap is on the pen. I take the cap off. Is it separate from the pen? I have finished writing; I put the cap back on the pen. Is the cap together with the pen? In other words, persons who interact need information to know what are the causes and what are the effects. Our earlier example of Mrs. N spreading butter on bread (p. 220) illustrated her need to elicit strong changes of resistance from changes of topological relationships. This aspect is important for guiding. One should not guide a person to perform actions where there are no changes of resistance. For example, one should not guide a patient to write, or peel, or spread. I may help the patient to write, but I am conscious that by doing this, the patient does not get the tactual information needed to change sources of information for improving interaction experience.

We illustrate here how guiding is done to maximize the search for information. It describes, in slow motion, the event of picking up a knife from the support to cut an orange. Let the person feel the resistance of the knife, which moves in contrast to the stable resistance of the support. Guide the patient's hands to press on the knife, and then move the fingers of the person along the resistance of the knife until the fingers are closed around it. Attempt to move the knife, to separate it from the support, and to lift it. By doing all these activities with the person, one enables the person to feel the different changes of resistances included in the event.

Having cut the orange, the patient has to release the knife. For the knife to be released, a similar sequence of interactive causes and effects has to occur. The sequence just described is now reversed in the following manner. The knife is put back on the support; the fingers of the patient holding the knife feel the stable resistance of the support. This information helps so that the fingers will loosen the grasp around the knife, thus permitting the release of the object on the support. These examples illustrate the way in which we can initiate changes of sources of information when guiding a person to interact to fulfill a primary goal of intervention, namely, to increase experiences in daily interaction by providing more adequate tactual information, thereby working on the root of development.

Guiding to Change Body Positions Involving the Whole Body

Guiding considers the hands and the whole body when interacting. For instance, a needed object has fallen onto the floor. To pick it up, a person has to change the position of his or her body. Alternatively, somebody wants to clean the bottom shelf in a closet. To do this, the person has to kneel on the floor. Each time a person changes his or her body position, he or she changes topological relationships between the body and the environment in a meaningful, goal-oriented way. At the same time, a person has to change the source of information. We assume that children and adults improve their organization of the search for information in a similar way. The following example illustrates such changes of body position associated with changes of topological relationships between the body and the environment and, therefore, with changes of sources of information.

> C is 16 years old and severely language disordered and behaviorally disturbed. She lives in a group home. C prepares tea for a social event. The pitcher is on top of a huge old-fashioned cupboard. The therapist who guides her tries to reach out with her to the top, but they do not make it. C is too short to get the pitcher when standing at the cupboard. What do we do now? C is guided to get a chair and to put the chair into a corner, against the cupboard and against the wall. The therapist guides her to climb on that chair to get the pitcher. When climbing, they touch the stable side of the wall. Standing on top of the chair, C still is too short to get the pitcher. They climb higher, from the chair to a projection of the cupboard. Standing now on this projection in an upright position and reaching for the pitcher, C suddenly touches the ceiling. She is puzzled by this touching and starts to explore the ceiling with her hands. First, her face expresses intense attention, and then a big smile shows on her face. "Ceiling," she says loudly. The therapist guides her to get the pitcher and then to climb down.

The climbing up to the top, the touching of the ceiling, and the descent—now with the pitcher in the hand—are tasks requiring changing topological relationships between the body and environment in a meaningful way. These changes demand changes of sources of information and thereby can enhance perceptual organization.

Tactual information also is needed to solve problems of daily life. We now discuss how it is needed for an important aspect of solving problems, **framing hypotheses**.

Guiding to Establish Hypotheses

There is a strong relationship between information-seeking processes and establishing hypotheses. The next example illustrates processes we go through each time we start a daily event. In an actual situation, there are many stimuli. Most of the stimuli are irrelevant to the event to be performed. Only a few are relevant to the task. A person has to order the surrounding stimuli. This requires that a person actively structures the situation by evaluating all the stimuli and judging which ones are irrelevant and which are relevant. Selecting the relevant stimuli for an event is strongly related to establishing hypotheses. The following example illustrates how guiding can be done to enable such structuring.

> J, a 14-year-old, has severe language disorders. She is guided to the refrigerator to take out cottage cheese to make sandwiches for a snack. The refrigerator is filled with many items. The therapist opens the door with J. They touch the milk, which is in front, and then they push the milk to the side. We observe that J touches the milk. We interpret: she evaluates this is milk. She establishes a hypothesis: we will use the milk. Pushing to the side leads to another hypothesis: it is not for use. They touch a package of meat, and then push it aside. We observe that J touches the meat. We interpret: she evaluates this is meat. She establishes a hypothesis: we will use the meat. Pushing the meat to the side leads to another hypothesis: it is not for use. In this manner they touch several items, each time pushing them to the side until finally, way in the back, they find the cottage cheese, which they touch, grasp, and take out. We observe that J touches the cottage cheese. We interpret: she evaluates this is cottage cheese. She establishes a hypothesis: we will use the cottage cheese. Touching, grasping, and taking out leads to the conclusion: yes, we will use the cottage cheese. The original hypothesis is confirmed.

This kind of organization, that is, structuring of the situation, is more difficult than one usually admits. Often, especially when a person performs events in a familiar setting, such as taking a shower in his or her own bathroom, he or she does not realize to what extent information is required. It is only when staying overnight in an unfamiliar place that one realizes what is entailed in finding out about how to manipulate an unfamiliar shower.

However, children and adults with nonverbal and verbal disorders often are not able to get adequate information when they are on their own. Consequently, they make incorrect hypotheses or they may even panic. Our interpretation is that these persons are not incompetent in establishing hypotheses, but they fail because they do not receive adequate information in the actual situation. To help them, people around usually talk to them and provide verbal-auditory stimulation, or they show them how to do a task by providing visual stimulation. Our research data (Affolter and Bischofberger 1993, 1996; Affolter et al 1996) suggest that verbal-auditory and visual stimulation does not help because it does not provide adequate information to them and, therefore, they are unable to make correct hypotheses. In an earlier example (Chapter 8) Mr. P was sitting on a chair. The therapist tried to make him change seats and sit on a stool at a table. Only when the stool touched Mr. P's upper leg did he glide over to the stool and sit on it at the table. A similar observation occurred with H, a 13-year-old with severe language disorders and diagnosis of autism.

H is stretched out on a long chair. The therapist tries to get him up and to put him to work to prepare tomato salad. The therapist shows him tomatoes enclosed in a plastic package and tells him to get up and cut the tomatoes. H does not move. Is he lazy? The therapist lets him touch the tomatoes in the plastic package. H still shows no reaction. Finally, the therapist puts the plastic package with the tomatoes against his chest and starts to remove the plastic foil. H looks at the tomatoes and brings his hands to the plastic package. Now, the therapist starts to guide him to finish opening the plastic package. Almost immediately, H stands up, takes the tomatoes with him, goes into the kitchen, and prepares the tomato salad. What had happened? First, H received visual and verbal-auditory information from the therapist. He did not move. We infer that he was unable to make the correct hypothesis. Then the therapist touched H's hand with the tomatoes. H did not move. We infer that H still has not reached a correct hypothesis. He could feel the object, the tomatoes, but this was not sufficient. That information was not directly connected with the event. Only when the therapist started the task by letting H feel the first change of topological relationships was he able to construct a hypothesis about the task. He now could be guided, and then he continued the event.

In sum, to establish a correct hypothesis, H needed tactual information about the beginning of the event, that is, the first topological change. At that moment, he could determine the source of tactual information between tomatoes and plastic wrap on his body, and he recognized the event.

We already discussed the importance of creating a stable environment so that children and patients can touch it when interacting. We referred to the possibility of helping patients to pick up more adequate tactual information by guiding them so they get to know where the environment is and where their own body is and also to know about causes and effects. In this section, we discussed that tactual information also provides knowledge about events that is needed to stimulate hypothetical processes. Enhancing hypothesis processing is important to helping patients to interact more independently in daily life. Thus, it is an important aspect of intervention and rehabilitation, but most of the time it is overlooked.

The implication for clinical intervention is that we should avoid verbal commands as the means of telling patients what to do. First, verbal commands are often not understood by our patients. Second, even if they are understood, the patients do not get the opportunity to experience "establishing of hypotheses." Instead of verbally telling patients what to do, the therapist should guide them to start an event. By guiding or helping patients to pick up relevant tactual information, they will be able to establish hypotheses on their own and thereby enhance experience with hypothetical processes. Once patients reach a correct hypothesis, they might continue the event by themselves.

TREATMENT: WORKING ON A LANGUAGE
LEVEL

According to Piaget (1947/1950), language is one of the many expressions of semiotic behavior. At length he described semiotic behavior as being more complex than sensorimotor behavior. He considered language as part of semiotic behavior, as opposed to the signal development that is observed at the sensorimotor stage. Semiotic behavior is shown when forms such as a sequence of speech sounds or gestures or graphic forms are used to represent a past or future event. Thus, language refers to past and future events (Piaget 1945/1962; De Saussure F.D. 1983). This criterion differentiates language from signal performance (Chapter 8; see also Affolter 1968; Affolter and Bischofberger 2000). By 18 months, a child is able to meet that criterion. By that age, a child has stored a wealth of interaction experiences and can retrieve them (see example of a 12- month-old infant with the red bowl, in Affolter Chapter 8), and language acquisition begins.

Linguists differentiate deep structure, that is, the semantic part of language, from surface structure containing conventional forms. They describe transformation rules, which relate deep structure to surface structure (Chomsky 1957; Fillmore 1968; Cook 1998). For intervention, we have to consider these three aspects of language and their relation to interaction.

NONVERBAL INTERACTION AND SEMANTICS

Experiences with nonverbal interaction events of daily life can be considered the fundamental basis of deep structure or the semantic part of language (Affolter 1968; Affolter 1987/1991; Affolter and Bischofberger 2000). The following example supports this point.

> J, 22 months old, looks at two pictures/photographs. On both pictures, J's daddy is sitting on a chair in front of the breakfast table. On the first picture, J sees daddy from behind, with just his head above the back of the chair. On the second one, daddy is taken from the side and his whole body is visible. J looks at the first picture and says, "daddy swimming." Then she looks at the second and says, "not swimming." How could J refer to swimming when looking at daddy sitting on a chair next to a table and having breakfast? I thought it over. Then I remembered. Now it is October. During summer daddy and J often went swimming. Then it always happened that daddy told J he will go to the pool and swim, watched him going to the pool, watched him disappearing into the water. Until J could only see his head (just like on picture 1). Later, he came out of the water. J could now see his whole body (just like on picture 2). Daddy was not swimming anymore (Affolter 1987/1991, pp. 277–278).

In such a way, children take conventional forms they hear in the environment (swimming) and use them during specific events to refer to their own experience from that event.

NONVERBAL INTERACTION AND SURFACE STRUCTURE

The surface structure of language consists of conventional forms transmitted by the specific linguistic group a child lives in; spoken forms, or the speech sounds for oral language; and graphic forms for written language.

Grammatical "Transformational" Rules

We will now illustrate work on transformation rules with an example. A is a 14-year-old autistic boy. He is in a school program for severely perceptually disturbed children. He had to clean the oven in the kitchen at the school. For that event, he was not told what to do. Instead, he was guided at the beginning of each step of the event to stimulate hypothesis processing. Whenever he reached a correct hypothesis, he was able to continue and to finish the respective step.

After he had finished cleaning, his teacher sat down at the table. A is next to her. The teacher writes, "A cleans the oven."

The teacher and A read the sentence.

"The oven is sticky." "A cleans the oven because the oven is sticky."	The teacher writes, She reads with A, emphasizing the word *because*. They repeat reading together. Then, A is quiet, thinking. Finally, he repeats alone, first slowly, hesitating, then all is correct. Later on they do more work with the text applying other transformation rules. For example, they change "A" to "I" (meaning the boy), they change present to past tense.

Speech Articulation Forms

Learning the speech sounds requires that children grow up in a speaking environment. It also requires that children hear. Deaf children do not learn to speak spontaneously because they do not hear the spoken language of their social group. Besides hearing, there is another requirement. A child has to master so-called "articulation skills." The production of speech sounds involves complex perceptual-motor processes of the oral structures. It takes a child up to age 6 or more years to produce all the speech sounds correctly.

Children with PDD also present articulation problems. Our research (Affolter and Stricker 1980; Affolter and Bischofberger 2000) revealed that the articulation problems of these language-disordered children are not of a primary kind and not a problem of an independent specific skill. They are a secondary problem. The perceptual problems are the more primary cause. The perceptual problems cause difficulties in early interaction, as described by Affolter (1987/1991) and Affolter and Bischofberger (2000). Also, they cause difficulties as one of the consequences, the articulation problems.

Affolter (Chapter 8) referred to "mouthing" as an elementary prerequisite to the functioning of oral structures. During the first year, babies normally engage in mouthing behavior. They put objects that they have grasped into the mouth to explore (see examples in Affolter's Chapter 8, K, at 5 months, exploring the orange). They also begin to babble during the first year. Both kinds of behavior are present in the babies before they develop speech sounds and are often considered prerequisites to speech acquisition. However, children with language disorders never babble like normal children. They mouth objects several years later than normal children. Yet, in spite of missing the babbling stage, children with language disorders can develop speech with a delay (Affolter et al 1978). In intervention, then, we do not require "babbling" nor train lip and tongue movements as specific skills, but we will include the mouth and the tongue of the patients in daily life interaction. An example here illustrates how the functioning of oral structures can be related to daily life events. It emphasizes that this approach also is valid for adult aphasia patients.

> Mrs. L is brain-damaged; she has severe aphasia. The language therapist tried very hard to get her to imitate lip and tongue movements as a prerequisite for training articulation skills without success. Now, Mrs. L is sitting at a table facing a mirror and a lipstick. The therapist guides her to open the lipstick and get it ready to apply it to her lips. Mrs. L looks in the mirror while she handles the lipstick. Suddenly, her lips and her tongue start to move, to change position, to adjust, and to get ready to apply the lipstick. Watching these events, we concluded: When asked to imitate lip and tongue movements, Mrs. L looked at the therapist and at the mirror but failed to perform.

When asked to perform lip and tongue movements within a daily life event, Mrs. L could do it. The difference between the two situations is the event and the goal orientation. In the first situation, the lip movements had to be produced without a goal, without an event, and without connection to interaction experience. Here, the production failed. In the second situation, producing lip movements was embedded into an event, that is, into interaction, and the lip movements were produced adequately. In other examples of patients, Affolter (1987/1991) describes how to involve the mouth, lips, and tongue in daily life interaction.

WHEN TO TALK TO PATIENTS

In GIT, we do not talk during the guided activity but before or after the guided activity or during a break in the guided activity.

Research on children's language acquisition (Bloom and Tinker 2001; and Bloom's Chapter 7) shows that a normal child at early stages will not talk while performing events but will talk after the event. When adults talk to the children during their interactions, children will stop or reduce their activities. The same can be observed when talking to children at the same time that they are guided. They may focus on the auditory input and not pay attention to the tactual input. They will be distracted. The same is true of the person guiding and talking. It is a capacity problem of our brain (see Affolter 1987/1991). In addition, since auditory-verbal information is not directly related to the respective topological changes, performance on the event may break down.

In not being able to talk during the event, we have to decide if we talk about the event before it happens or afterwards. This is a semantic problem. Spoken forms do not include a semantic content. They are only used to refer to a semantic content. The semantic content is created by interaction events. These events are perceived basically through tactual information. That information is stored independently of the forms as part of deep structure (Affolter 1968; Piaget 1945/1962, 1963). This means that one should add linguistic conventional forms to tactual nonverbal events after the event has been experienced. For intervention this means: Whatever a speech therapist has to teach to language-disordered children articulation skills, phonetic performance, syntactic features and so on, they should be done after the child has experienced a guided tactual event. This should not be done before the event or without connection to an event; otherwise, the semantic part is missing.

Similar advice should be given for presenting visual information when using graphic forms. Graphic forms are offered as examples by drawings, pictures, and written forms of letters or numerals. These graphic forms can be compared with the conventional forms of oral language. This means that before using such graphic forms for teaching reading and writing, one has to make sure that the child has already experienced respective tactual nonverbal events. This is valid not only for language but also for arithmetic. Forms used in arithmetic, such as numerals and signs used to express addition, subtraction, multiplication, and division, always refer to stored tactual nonverbal events. Thus, arithmetic, as well as reading and writing, should be taught in relation to and after having experienced tactual events (see Affolter 1987/1991).

JUDGING THE LEVEL OF LANGUAGE PERFORMANCE

For understanding the behavior of severely handicapped children, it is important to know whether they really have reached the level of semiotic behavior, that is, whether they have language. Signal behavior refers to actual events, and

Piaget (1947/1950, 1963) describes such behavior as less complex than semiotic behavior (see also Affolter's Chapter 8). Understanding a verbal expression only in an actual situation can also be observed in animals. Some children with language disorders in our research group did not perform on the semiotic level. They performed on a signal level. When they were told that they will go swimming tomorrow, they expected this event to happen right away. They went to get their swimsuit and coat to go out. For them, to be told, "swimming tomorrow," meant "swimming now"; the event had to happen at that moment. This does not meet the representation criterion for semiotic performance. These children recognized pictures of just objects, but not actions in pictures. They also did not understand fiction.

Traditional language therapy does not distinguish semiotic and signal behavior. Often, therapists try to teach children language by teaching signal performance: For example, children have to match pictures to objects, spoken words to pictures, usually an exhausting and frustrating kind of work for the teacher and the child. Years ago, we stopped doing such exercises and went back to *sensorimotor activities*, as we called them, during the first few years of our work. These were activities with real things. This stage of our thinking was followed by considering guiding children in activities of daily life.

By continuing such kind of intervention, the moment came when these children almost suddenly showed understanding of past or future events referred to by spoken forms. At the same time, these children began to speak and to understand actions in pictures. Vocabulary improved rapidly, which can also be observed in the normal children when they discover semiotic performances. And all this happened in our children with PDD without specific training of semiotic performances (see long-term effects discussed in Affolter's Chapter 8).

Our longitudinal observations counter theories that have asserted that children will never learn language if they have not done so by 6 years of age (Lenneberg 1967). In our longitudinal study, some children, who were not on the semiotic level at the beginning of the research, discovered language as late as 12 and 14 years of age (Affolter's 1987/1991).

MEASURING THE EFFECTS OF INTERVENTION

Our goal of intervention is to work on the root, that is, provide the patients with more adequate interaction experience. This requires improvement in the organization of the search for information. Such improvement cannot be observed directly. It has to do with input. The presence of input in another person can be observed only indirectly by observing certain changes in behavior. In this section, we discuss some patterns of behavior we expect to change and which we can interpret as a sign of improvement of the organization of input, that is, as a sign that the work on the root is adequate.

MEASURING INTERVENTION EFFECTS OF NONVERBAL INTERACTION EXPERIENCE: SHORT-TERM EFFECTS

The label *short-term effects* indicates that the behavioral patterns we are concerned with here are of short duration. They last as long as input lasts in the sense of getting adequate information at a given moment. We now describe several behavioral changes, which can be observed when GIT is performed.

Becoming Attentive

An important behavioral pattern of short-term effect is the one of **attention**. We all are more or less familiar with the behavioral pattern elicited when we pay attention. For example, students are described as attentive when they show a certain degree of tenseness in their body position and their facial expression, when they sit without much moving around, when they stop irrelevant activities, and so on. Children with language disorders are often described as being unable to concentrate, as being easily distracted. It is, therefore, impressive to observe how they can pay attention as soon as they touch the environment or are guided. This is illustrated in the next example.

> M, a 5-year-old language-disordered boy, is brought to our teaching program by a course participant. Reports of psychological diagnostic testing show an attention span of only a few seconds. We decide to use a real-life activity: making chocolate pudding. The session is videotaped for further discussion with the course participants. The therapist guides M's hands through the event for about 20 minutes, thus providing him with tactual information about the event. Throughout this time, the child's attention is focused fully on the event. When the therapist guides the child down from the chair to indicate the end of the event, M gets back on the chair, obviously wanting to continue. The guided event is continued for another 20 minutes, again with M fully attentive.

How can we explain this child's behavior, which contrasts with the referring person's observations? Is it true that M has a short attention span? We concluded from this example, and many similar ones, that short attention span was observable whenever a disordered child does not get enough information in daily life situations. It was assumed that in guided events, for example, making chocolate pudding, the child receives adequate tactual information about the event.

Becoming Silent

C, who was guided to get yogurt out of the refrigerator, revealed another behavioral change that can be related to attention. We mentioned that whenever she moved through free space, she was producing sounds. As soon as she touched the environment, she became silent. This short-term effect of becoming silent suggested that C now paid attention to tactual sources connected with the event. These two examples confirm that information is a prerequisite for sustained attention, as Broadbent's (1958) research on vigilance suggested. He observed that whenever human subjects are in deprived situations in which they have to wait a long time for a relevant stimulus, they have difficulty sustaining their attention over time.

Changing Body Tone

Another behavior pattern revealing short-term effects is body tone. Changes of body tone also can be related to changes of sources of information. We reported observations that children and adults get very tense (that is, body tone increases) when they appear to have difficulties in the search for information. We discussed the examples of R putting the pillowcase on the pillow and of Ms. M cleaning the table. Both showed a high increase of body tone when no stable reference was available. When they touched a stable environment, they relaxed, and the body tone decreased. We also described the tenseness of the hemiplegic boy with the raised arm when walking and working in free space. His body tone decreased and his arm came down when he touched a stable environment.

Becoming Calm

We described the hyperactive child R, who moved his body continually when sitting on his chair. He became calm when he was sitting on the floor. Similar observations were previously reported of the brain-damaged patient in the nursing home who changed her agitated behavior and became calm as soon as she could touch a stable environment. We concluded that the body tone tenseness and hyperactivity of disordered persons suggest that they are searching for information but have difficulty in organizing sources of information. Tenseness and/or hyperactivity are the effects of such difficulty. When touching a stable environment during the event, the child/patient gets less tense (body tone decreases) or the patient becomes more calm; we infer that the child/patient can now focus on tactual sources relevant to the event.

Retrieving from Memory

Another short-term effect has to do with memory retrieval, that is, a person takes out something from memory, or the access to memory is working. Affolter (1987/1991) describes similar examples, such as improvement in speaking and writing, when guiding aphasics through daily events. She also describes improvement in body movements connected with memory retrieval.

Mr. M, an adult with acquired brain damage and severely restricted in motor performances takes part in a course situation. The participants guide him to hang a bell over the entrance door so the bell can be rung when a course session begins. First, the hook has to be hammered into the wall. The patient's arm and hand, holding the hook, are guided up, farther up, until the right place is reached. The hook is drilled into the wall, still way up. Now, the patient's hands holding the bell are guided high up, higher, and higher until finally the hook is reached and the bell is fixed on the hook. That evening, I gave a colloquium at the medical center. To illustrate course content, I showed some videos that included the video taken from the guided event with Mr. M hanging the bell. It happened that Mr. M's physical therapist was in the audience. Watching how the patient's arm was guided higher and higher, she shouted from the audience, "Hundreds of times I tried to get that patient to lift his arm—he couldn't do it, and here, look at that," (Affolter 1987/1991, p. 172).

We concluded that when the patient is asked to imitate arm-lifting movements without an event, he reportedly fails. When arm lifting is embedded in a daily event, the patient is able to lift his arm as he used to do before his head injury. Such short-term effects may last for minutes or hours. When intervention continues, their duration gets longer, a sign that the root is growing. With the growth of the root, long-term effects will be observable. They were discussed in Affolter (Chapter 8).

Other clinical observations support the assumption that memory retrieval is activated by guiding patients when they interact in daily life events. One patient with acquired brain damage received guided tactual interaction intervention for 6 months. Neuropsychological tests at the beginning showed poor recall. Three times during the treatment period, the patient was evaluated on recall; he was videotaped when he performed events, matched on content under two conditions: (1) spontaneous performance and (2) guided performance. The findings supported the expectancies. The patient did not recall any of the actions of the spontaneously performed events but did recall the main steps of the guided event. Neuropsychological tests at the end of the period showed improvement of recall (Fischer and Peschke 1998).

Anticipating Effects

The question then arises whether they are learning. One of the behavioral changes allowing us to judge that learning occurs is **anticipation** (see Affolter 1987/1991). Anticipation is more than just input. Input is a prerequisite, but anticipation demands an elaboration of the input, even some kind of memory. An example illustrates this point.

A is an 8-year-old girl with severe cerebral palsy. She spends much time everyday attached to a device for standing. She can neither sit nor walk independently. She has never been guided for daily events. Everyday activities had been performed for her, not with her, except for attempts to walk with her. I was asked to counsel therapists on how to work on the root, that is, to provide interactions in daily events. I guided A to take an apple out of a drawer, to get a knife, and to sit on a chair at the table; the therapist sitting behind her guided her to cut the apple. While doing this, I was told that A does not eat apples. So I decided that A should give the piece of apple she had cut to the therapist next to her. Daily life events are not only directed towards our personal needs but also towards the needs of people around us, that is, the social group.

A then was guided to put the piece of apple into the therapist's mouth. This was done three times.

First time: It appears that A's eyes do not follow the movement of her arms, even when she is guided to put the piece of apple into the mouth of the therapist.

Second time: A's eyes follow the movement of her arms. When she puts the apple into the therapist's mouth, her face shows intense attention—and then a smile appears on A's face as she watches the therapist chew the apple.

Third time: As soon as A raises her arm, she looks at the therapist—and smiles. This smile happens **before** the apple reaches the mouth of the therapist.

We concluded that when A puts the apple into the therapist's mouth a third time, she shows anticipation. By seeing her smile **before** the apple touches the mouth of the therapist, we infer that A expects to put the piece of apple into the therapist's mouth and that the therapist will eat that piece of apple. This means that A has stored the first event tactually and the second event tactually and visually. Performing the third event, she retrieves what she has done before. She sees the therapist and feels her arm/hands touching the apple. Such tactual-visual information seems to help her to retrieve the event she has stored and to anticipate the next similar event. We conclude: A seems to be able to learn; she gets tactual and tactual-visual input; she demonstrates an ability to store and to retrieve. She also appears to comprehend what the person next to her will do, that is, eat the piece of apple. A shows social understanding. These observations suggest, that as we work on a competence level with guided daily events, A's root will be expanding and growing: A will progress.

MEASURING INTERVENTION EFFECTS OF NONVERBAL INTERACTION EXPERIENCE: LONG-TERM EFFECTS

Patients who receive GIT were expected to improve in understanding event goals, continue actions after having been guided, and perform events spontaneously. The following example illustrates observable long-term effects, which suggest improvement of the root, that is, improvement in understanding nonverbal daily interaction and on first branches of production of nonverbal interaction events. In a longitudinal study, two patients, X and Y, with acquired brain damage, received GIT for half a year, beginning at 6 months after their brain injury. Four times during this period they were videotaped and evaluated on different aspects of daily life interaction. They progressed from not understanding events in less familiar situations, to understanding events when they received tactual information (by being guided), to understanding events when visual or verbal information was provided. Spontaneous performance of events could not be observed during this period. However, at the end, they continued some actions when they had been guided through the beginning of the event (Trares and Stratthoff 1998). It appears then that there are observable long-term effects, which suggest growing of the root and of first branches of the tree when intervention focuses on daily life interaction.

As the root gets stronger, more branches will grow. Still, the work on the root continues. We do not work on the branches. But we expect the branches to grow, that is, children/patients will improve or progress in understanding and performances, characteristic first of lower levels of development, then of higher levels. It is expected that such progress shows regular features, so that one can predict what branches will improve, even when we continue to work on the root. We began to investigate long-term progress on "branches," and whether there is regularity in observable improvement in different children.

CASE STUDIES: CHANGES IN THE SAME PATIENT

Here is the case of T, a child with language disorders and autistic behavior. He did not speak at age 5 years. He never turned around to look at a sound source. Because of such a failure in localization, he was diagnosed as having severe hearing problems in addition to other perceptual and behavioral problems. He was fitted with two hearing aids when he was 3 years old. He did not imitate; he appeared not to be in social contact with other persons. At age 5 years, he was referred to the school for children with perceptual problems in our town. At school, his perceptual problems were diagnosed as being of an intermodal kind (see descriptions of subgroups in Affolter and Bischofberger 2000). This meant that his localization failure could be explained by his intermodal problems. Localization performance requires an integration of two sensory modalities: first, auditory processing for judging the direction of a sound source, and second, the integration of that auditory information with visual information for judging that what one hears is also something to look at. Perceptually, this placed T younger than 6 months of age, since a normal baby is expected to look at a sound source by the age of about 6 months.

At school, work on the root was applied in the sense of GIT (Affolter 1987/1991). It was expected that T's competence was far above that of a 6-month-old baby. T was guided through daily events, as they were relevant during the course of a day: getting undressed when arriving at school, emptying the school bag, preparing snacks, going to the store to purchase items, helping in the kitchen to get lunch ready, washing dishes, and so on. One could observe immediate effects (such as paying attention, showing understanding; see previous sections). Specific skills such as localizing a sound source were never practiced.

Six months later, T was making orange juice, working by himself at a table. He was videotaped for some staff discussions on that day. He was tending to his event when the door opened slowly, with average loudness, at his back, and a person looked into the room. At that moment, very clearly registered on the video, T turned his head in the direction of the door and looked at the door. An amazing performance, T localized. This meant he was not deaf. He had acquired, perceptually, the degree of intermodal integration necessary to turn his head in the direction of a sound source and look at it. For us, this was a sign that not only has the root grown but that new branches were appearing. From our example, we inferred that for T, progress was observable for a branch representing perceptual development.

In another case study, B, diagnosed with severe language disorders and autistic behavior, was referred to the school for children with perceptual disorders, when he was 6 years old. He did not relate to either adults or children. He did not speak or imitate. A normal baby begins to imitate movements and then sounds by the end of the first year. B's cognitive competence, however, was judged to be well beyond the age of such babies. So, he was guided through all kinds of daily events. This was work on the root. He was never trained to imitate or to speak. However, short-term effects, criteria for working on the root, such as paying attention, were observable. Time passed. When B was 8 years old, he spontaneously began to show the behavior of "doing with." For example, when other children stood up from their chairs to go to the other room to eat or to play, he would also stand now and do what they did. When other children put on their coats to leave for the bus, he would do the same thing. For people around B, this level or branch of social skills was important. It allowed staff to integrate B into a small group at school. At about the same time, B began to understand verbal commands as signals in a related situation; he could be told to get his swimming suit when preparing for swimming, or put his shoes away, or go and play. When he was 10 years old, he started to talk. He paid attention when one talked to him about a guided event of the past or when one drew pictures about such an event. Language began to evolve.

This example of B illustrates how branches higher up on the tree are growing; B started to show behavior of "doing with," to understand verbal commands, when he was 8 years old. When he was 10 years old, he started to talk and to understand past or future events when one talked to him about them. Thus, he began with the acquisition of true language. These different steps indicated that B first developed performances of lower levels of development represented by lower branches of the tree, later on more complex performances represented by higher branches of the tree. Thus, his progress showed a regularity, which corresponds to the regularity of normal development.

CASE STUDIES: COMPARISON OF DIFFERENT
INTERVENTION APPROACHES

For many years, we followed, longitudinally, children with language and behavioral problems and adult patients with acquired brain damage. There were those who were receiving GIT, and there were children who received different kinds of other therapeutic interventions in different settings. In the following section, we refer to some representative studies of comparing children and adults receiving different intervention programs over time.

The first study included two patients with the same kind and degree of brain injury. Patient H received only GIT; patient S changed therapy programs. They were periodically videotaped and evaluated on interaction performances. Patient H showed gradual improvement. He first understood events and then started to continue some actions of an event when tactual information was provided; he could not perform any event by himself. Later, he understood events when tactual or visual information was provided. After 10 months of treatment, he was able to solve daily events successfully step-by-step.

Patient S improved during the first period of GIT when tactual information was provided. He improved from understanding short, daily habitual events to understanding daily events of a more complex kind and continuing some actions on his own after guiding. He was dismissed at that time and received visual-auditory training for 41 months before he was referred back for GIT. He had regressed to his original level. After 6 months of GIT, he had recovered earlier gains. After 2 more months, he was functioning on a higher level. Daily activities in familiar situations were performed step-by-step when tactual or visual information was provided (Mohr and Nielsen 1998).

In a second study, two children with intermodal (autistic) perceptual problems were matched by diagnosis at age 5 years. Their performances reflected a similar low developmental level of interaction. Child A received GIT over 12 years, child B, another kind of treatment. At age 17 years, both were reevaluated. Child A was integrated in a working group, had developed some language, and was partially independent. Child B was found to function on the same low developmental level of interaction as at age 5 years, was totally dependent, and had no language (Bischofberger and Affolter 1998).

We revealed the longitudinal outcome of two children with severe learning disorder. Each child went through periods of different intervention programs; both were followed over 15 years and periodically evaluated and videotaped. At age 5 years, both children were evaluated; they were inactive, visually oriented, touched objects, but did not perform any goal-oriented sequence of topological changes as required in daily life events. A first period of 3 years of GIT followed. By the end of that period, they understood and performed familiar events in familiar surroundings with tactual or visual information, step-by-step. During a second period of about 6 years, they received educational programs based on visual-auditory/verbal training procedures. By the end of that period, both children showed severe behavioral disturbances and were dismissed from their programs because of psychiatric problems. A third period of 3 years followed. They again received GIT. By the end of that period, both were fully integrated in a group environment and showed adequate daily interaction (Affolter and Bischofberger 1998).

GROUPED DATA FROM CLINICAL TRIALS

Sweeney and Levine (1998) described the outcome of one study that included 10 children with a perceptual-motor deficits and significant language delays. GIT was applied three times a week for 8 months. The children were tested periodically in the course of that therapy. A comparison of pretest and posttest scores revealed significant gains in focused attention, language, and nonverbal cognition. The gains ranged from 1 to 23 months and were most evident for receptive language and basic concepts.

We conclude that the preliminary results of the research in progress support the validity of clinical work on the root, that is, working with the disordered children and adults on nonverbal daily events by trying to improve their search for information. Guiding seems to be an important tool for intervention with both children and adults in the efforts to improve daily interaction. These examples of long-term effects and comparison studies were selected from other studies to show that intervention based on the model of a root, meaning tactual interaction in daily life, is not only valid for disturbed children and normal children but also for adults with acquired brain damage or a growing group of geriatric patients.

CHANGING THE APPROACHES TO CLINICAL EVALUATION

Traditional approaches evaluate patients on numerous skills, and there are numerous deficits or disorders determined as a result (Hedge 1995). The following example illustrates such an approach.

> From an early age, T loved to meet other children. He would smile and run over to them, put his arms around their neck when greeting them, grasp their hair, and pull it. Doing this he would use too much force and the other children became afraid of him. T was always on the run, moving around. T's parents took him to see a psychologist when he was 3 years old. The psychologist diagnosed hyperactivity. T was put into a special preschool program. When T was 5 years, his speech was not at age level; he was diagnosed as having articulation problems and received speech therapy. After 2 years, his articulation had improved and he no longer received speech therapy. At 7 years, he entered regular school. When he was 8 years, his parents were told

that he was dyslexic, that is, he had difficulties in learning how to read and write. He received special help for his dyslexic problems. When he was a 10 years old, his parents were told that T had emotional problems because there were situations when T showed high temper. He received special counseling for that problem. In the course of such a history of T, the parents became very depressed and frustrated. They had to face the problem of having a boy with a multitude of disorders and receiving a multitude of therapies.

Nobody involved in evaluating T seemed to question the numerous deficits. Nobody seemed to consider the possibility that these different deficits might be secondary to a common primary and more basic problem.

We can argue that applying the model of a root of a growing tree changes the traditional approach to evaluation. Hyperactivity, articulation problems, and reading and writing problems can be related to different branches of the tree. These branches grow at different periods of life. Hyperactive behavior is represented by a sick branch that often appears before the sick branch representing the growth of articulation skills is observable. However, both branches become sick because the root is sick; nonverbal daily interaction is disturbed because of failures in the search for information.

THE AGE OF EVALUATING A CHILD

Evaluation should be done at a young age and, if the child presents perceptual problems, intervention should begin early. This means that in the presence of deviancies, one cannot simply wait for intervention. Waiting and letting years pass by means that a child with PDD will continue to present problems, as in T's case. This is similar to the tree with a sick root, which will continue to grow branches, but the branches will show deviancies as long as the root remains sick. Often, children with PDD are seen at the age of 3 or 4 years when it has become obvious that their language acquisition is inadequate. Parents of such children often report that their children already have had some difficulties when they were babies. Some parents illustrate their reports by bringing videotaped recordings they had made of their family at earlier times. They often mention that they were told by pediatricians and nurses just to wait, that their baby was immature, or a slow learner, and would catch up in time. Such reports and documentation support our hypothesis that children with severe developmental disorders could be identified during the first years of development, as early as the sensorimotor period. Research projects are in progress to test this hypothesis.

DIFFERENTIATING COMPETENCE AND PERFORMANCE

Evaluating the branches of a tree helps to identify a sick tree. The question is whether the branches indicate a normal, an immature, or a deviant tree. Similarly, one should ask whether the development of a child is normal, immature, or deviant.

Research data from children with PDD suggest deviant development (Affolter and Bischofberger 2000). Traditionally, a disordered child or adult is evaluated by a clinician that applies a variety of testing procedures. The judgment is based on success scores of the child in different skills. Among the different skills tested are those that are assumed to reflect intelligence. This is done, for example, with IQ testing to determine whether there is developmental delay (see Wingfield 1979a p. 382). Such testing requires the child to perform. Successful performance is interpreted as a sign of competence and serves to estimate a mental age. However, it is important to differentiate between competence and performance when applying our model. We argue that the judgment of developmental delay or mental age in the case of the children with PDD is a superficial interpretation and does not take into account the problem of information or the requirement to differentiate between competence and performance. In traditional evaluation procedures, hardly any time or effort is spent on analyzing situational features of testing situations (Bischofberger and Sonderegger 1974, 1976) or on varying situational features to distinguish between competence and performance. The next example illustrates this evaluation feature.

> D is an 8-year-old with severe developmental deficits. She is in a special school where educators have spent much time teaching her to sit quietly and work at a table. She finally can do it. However, when her parents take her to a restaurant she cannot sit still. She moves almost continually and they have much difficulty making her sit down. Is this a lack of motivation?

The example of D sitting quietly in the therapy room but moving around in the restaurant showed that, with respect to information, the two situations differed greatly. Situations in the therapy room do not change much and changes that do occur are predictable. This is not the case in a restaurant; there are many unpredictable changes. There is also the matter of familiar versus unfamiliar situations. D had difficulty differentiating relevant from irrelevant information and extracting adequate relevant information. The more complex the situation, the more pronounced this difficulty becomes. She was able to function in a familiar environment with few changes but not in a complex and changing environment where she needed to extract the relevant information and delete the irrelevant. In this complex environment, we infer that she reached the limit of her capacity for processing information; she became tense and stressed, may be near panic. Therefore, she moved around.

These examples, illustrating evaluating procedures, emphasized the importance of observing children's daily life activities (e.g., eating, dressing), differentiating between competence and performance (the above example of D), and considering situation-dependent information (example of the hemiplegic boy).

CLOSING REMARK

We hope this chapter brings new insights for clinical practitioners to evaluate and treat children with PDD more adequately.

REFERENCES

Affolter, F. 1968. Thinking and language. In Lloyd, G. (Editor), *International Research Seminar on Vocational Rehabilitation of Deaf Persons,* pp. 116–123. Washington. DC.: Department of Health, Education and Welfare.

Affolter, F. 1991. *Perception, Interaction and Language.* New York: Springer. Original work published in 1987.

Affolter, F., and Bischofberger, W. 1993. Die Organisation der Wahrnehmung, Aspekte der Entwicklung und des Abbaus [Organization of perception, aspects of development and regression]. In Affolter, F., and Bischofberger, W. (Editors), *Wenn die Organisation des ZNS zerfällt und es an gespürter Information mangelt.* pp. 24–55. Villingen/Schwenningen: Neckar-Verlag.

Affolter, F., and Bischofberger, W. 1996. Gespürte Interaktion im Alltag [Tactual interaction in daily life]. In Lipp, B., and Schlaegel, W. (Editors), *Wege von Anfang an* pp. 77–99. Villingen/Schwenningen: Neckar-Verlag.

Affolter, F., and Bischofberger, W. 1998. Outcome of daily life nonverbal interaction in two severely learning impaired children with different intervention programs: A longitudinal study. Poster session presented at the 15th annual meeting of the International Society for the Study of Behavioural Development ISSBD, Berne, Switzerland.

Affolter, F., and Bischofberger, W. 2000. *Nonverbal Perceptual and Cognitive Processes in Children with Language Disorders: Toward a New Framework for Clinical Intervention.* Mahwah, N.J.: Erlbaum.

Affolter, F., Bischofberger, W., and Calabretti-Erni, V. 1996. Nonverbal interaction in babies and brain-damaged patients. Poster presented at the symposium: The growing mind—La pensée en évolution, Geneva, Switzerland.

Affolter, F., Brubaker, R., and Franklin, W. 1978. Developmental features of speech sound production in language impaired children. *J Psycholing Res* 7:213–241.

Affolter, F., and Stricker, E. (Editors), 1980. *Perceptual Processes as Prerequisites for Complex Human Behavior.* Bern, Switzerland: Huber.

Bischofberger, W., 1989. Aspekte der Entwicklung taktil-kinaesthetischer Wahrnehmung [Aspects of development of tactual-kinesthetic perception]. Villingen/Schwenningen: Neckar-Verlag.

Bischofberger, W. and Affolter, F. 1998. Outcome of two different intervention programs, nonverbal tactual interaction in daily activities and visual-auditory training procedures in two autistic children: A longitudinal study. Poster session presented at the 15th annual meeting of the International Society for the Study of Behavioural Development ISSBD, Berne, Switzerland.

Bischofberger, W., and Sonderegger, H.U. 1974. *Ausfälle taktil-kinaesthetischer Leistungen* [Failure in tactual-kinesthetic performances]. In Schweizerischer Verband für Taubstummen- und Gehörlosenhilfe Hrsg. Wahrnehmungsstörungen—Elektroencephalographische und Elektrocochleographische Audiometrie. St. Gallen, Switzerland: Tschudy. 19–29.

Bischofberger, W., and Sonderegger, H.U. 1976. *Seriale Leistung-ein auditives Problem?* [Serial performances—an auditory problem?] In Bommer AG-Rexton Hrsg. Vorträge gehalten am III. Audio-Symposium, Zürich.

Bloom, L., and Tinker, E. 2001. The intentionality model and language acquisition: Engagement, effort and essential tension in development. Monographs of the Society for Research in Child Development, 66 4, Serial No. 267.

Broadbent, D.E. 1958. *Perception and Communication.* London: Pergamon.

Chomsky, N. 1957. *Syntactic Structures.* The Hague, Netherlands: Mouton.

Cook, W.A. 1998. Case grammar applied. Dallas: Summer Institute of Linguistics, University of Texas at Arlington.

Crary, J. 2000. *Suspensions of Perception: Attention, Spectacle, and Modern Culture.* Cambridge, MA: MIT Press.

de Saussure, F. 1983. *Course in General Linguistics.* London, England: Duckworth.

Day, R.H., and Singer, G. 1964. The relationship between the kinesthetic spatial after effect and variations in muscular involvement during stimulation. *Aus J Psychol* 16:200–208.

Ebner, F. 2001 April. Activity-Dependent Neural Plasticity and Experience-Dependent Recruitment of new Cortical Areas in the Neonatally Blind. In Rieser, J., Chair, Blindness, Plasticity, and the Development of Dynamic Perception and Motor Control. Paper symposium conducted at the SRCD biennial meeting, Minneapolis, MN.

Fillmore, C.J. 1968. The case for case. In Bach, E. and Harms, R.T. (Editors), *Universals in Linguistic Theory*, pp. 1–88. New York: Holt, Rinehart, and Winston.

Fischer, L., and Peschke, V. 1998, July. Recall in a brain-damaged adult: A of spontaneously performed events, b of "guided" events providing tactual input: A longitudinal study. Poster session presented at the XVth Biennial Meetings of the International Society for the Study of Behavioural ISSBD, Bern, Switzerland.

Gibson, J.J. 1966. *The Senses Considered as a Perceptual System*. Boston: Houghton-Mifflin.

Hawkins, R.P. 1983. *The School and Home Enrichment Program for Severely Handicapped Children*. Champaign, IL: Research Press.

Hedge, M.N. 1995. *Pocket Guide to Assessment Procedures in Speech-Language Pathology*. San Diego, CA: Singular Publisher Group.

Lenneberg, E.H. 1967. *Biological Foundations of Language*. New York: Wiley.

Mohr, S., and Nielsen, K. 1998, July. Outcome of two kinds of therapeutic intervention in two brain-damaged adults: a nonverbal guided tactual interaction in daily activities, visual-auditory training procedures: a longitudinal study. Poster session presented at the 15th annual meeting of the International Society for the Study of Behavioural Development ISSBD, Berne, Switzerland.

Niaz, M., and Logie, R.H. 1993. Working memory, mental capacity and science education: towards an understanding of the working memory hypothesis. Oxford Review of Education 194:511–525.

Piaget, J. 1950. *The Psychology of Intelligence*. London, England: Routledge and Kegan Paul. Original work published in 1947.

Piaget, J. 1962. Play, *Dreams and Imitation in Childhood*. New York: Norton Library. Original work published in 1945.

Piaget, J. 1963. Le langage et les opérations intellectuelles. (Language and intellectual operations.) In Problèmes de psycholinguistique. Neuchâtel: Symposium de l'association de psychologie scientifique de langue française, (1962, pp. 55–61). Paris, Fr: Presses Universitaires de France.

Piaget, J. 1969. *Perceptual Mechanisms*. London, England: Routledge and Kegan Paul. Original work published in 1961.

Sweeney, L.A., and Levine, M. 1998, July. Cognitive, language and behavioral outcomes following guided tactual interaction intervention. A poster session presented at the 15th biennial meeting of the International Society for the Study of Behavioural Development ISSBD, Berne Switzerland.

Trares, M., and Stratthoff, S. 1998, July. Improvement of nonverbal daily interaction in 2 brain-damaged adults following guided interaction intervention: a longitudinal study. Poster session presented at the 15th annual meeting of the International Society for the Study of Behavioural Development ISSBD, Berne, Switzerland.

Wingfield, A. 1979. *Human Learning and Memory*. New York: Harper and Row.

10

PROMPT: A TACTUALLY GROUNDED TREATMENT APPROACH TO SPEECH PRODUCTION DISORDERS

DEBORAH HAYDEN, MA, CCC-SLP

The purpose of this chapter is to describe the evolution and use of prompts for restructuring oral muscular phonetic targets (PROMPT), Chumpelik [Hayden] (1984), as an integrated, multisensory approach to the assessment and treatment of speech production disorders in a variety of clinical populations. A speech production disorder refers here to delayed and/or abnormal use of expressive speech for meaningful functional communication.

From its beginning, PROMPT has embraced "touch" as a primary sensory modality that can be used to: (1) develop or re-establish speech motor control; (2) provide a foundation for integrating sensory modalities (audition and vision) in developing concepts and expressive language; and (3) enhance social-emotional interaction and trust between clinician and child. As a tactually grounded treatment approach, PROMPT clinicians stimulate muscle activity and guide articulatory movement by touching and manually manipulating a child's external physical structures (torso, head, jaw, face, lips, and so on) that are used for speech production. Clinicians use their own hands to give postural support to a child's body and tactile-kinesthetic input about the place, manner, voicing, and sequential and temporal features of speech sounds in addition to auditory and visual input.

This chapter provides an overview of PROMPT's framework for assessing and treating speech production disorders. First, the history of PROMPT is described. Then PROMPT's conceptual framework and the clinical assessment and treatment principles that follow broadly from it are summarized. In the final section, a single clinical case is used to illustrate how PROMPT's clinical principles are applied.

THE HISTORY AND EVOLUTION OF PROMPT

THEORETICAL FOUNDATION

PROMPT has evolved over a period of 30 years. In the 1970s, the systematic manipulation of tactual-kinesthetic-proprioceptive input to oromotor structures for changing speech targets was begun with children who presented with severe motor impairment. These children did not respond to traditional treatment approaches that rely predominantly on auditory and visual input. The development of PROMPT treatment for them was grounded in theoretical and clinical perspectives that cross several disciplines concerned with physical, mental, and social development. Its focused use of tactile-kinesthetic input was influenced by the early work of scholars and practitioners who explored the tactile system in the neurological organization of normal and diseased brains (Head 1926; Jackson 1958; Mountcastle and Powell 1959; Mysak 1968) and embraced its use in the clinical treatment of motor disorders, including speech articulation (Stichfield and Younge 1938; Ayres 1974; Bobath 1971, 1980). As PROMPT evolved over time, it was influenced more broadly by scholarly work that included the neurobiological (Abbs 1988; Gracco 1990; Fletcher 1992; Kent 1981, 1992, 1997; Schmidt 1975; Kelso and Tuller, 1983), the cognitive-linguistic (Vygotsky 1978; Bruner 1977; Piaget 1954; Menn 1982; Nelson 1986; Thelen 1991; Strand 1992; Thelen 1995), and the social (Bates 1976; Gallagher 1991; Wetherby 1991) aspects.

Taken together, these multiple theoretical perspectives stimulated questions about how motor systems typically develop; how dynamic interaction and equilibrium among whole body systems affect speech, language, and social interaction; and how damage to the neuromotor pathways can unbalance the motor speech system and affect physical, mental, and social functioning either directly or indirectly. Answers to these questions have led to a much broader conceptualization of the speech production process than is described typically in the literature. PROMPT's multidimensional approach to speech production disorders has come to embrace not only the well-known physical-sensory aspects of motor performance but also its cognitive-linguistic and social-emotional aspects, as described later in this chapter.

EVOLUTION OF THE CLINICAL APPROACH: EMPIRICAL FOUNDATION

In the 1980s, the first empirical studies of PROMPT's treatment efficacy were done. The first study (Chumpelik Hayden and Sherman 1980) focused on an 8-year-old non-speaking child with autism and cognitive impairment. Using PROMPT, this child gained 30 functional words over a 4-month period. This study led to the development of the first manual describing the technique of prompting.

A later study (Chumpelik Hayden and Sherman 1983) was done with eight male patients (ages 6 to 11 years), four with normal cognitive and gross motor abilities and four with cognitive deficits and motor impairment. All participants had severely impaired speech and served as their own controls in a multiple baseline study design. They were randomly assigned to receive the traditional auditory-visual treatment condition or to the PROMPT treatment condition, which applied tactual in addition to auditory–verbal input. The results revealed that all the children significantly changed their productions of target words in the PROMPT treatment condition. Even the typically developing group changed more with the PROMPT than the traditional auditory-visual treatment condition. However, the motor impaired group changed only in the PROMPT treatment condition.

In 1984, the first publication describing PROMPT appeared (Chumpelik Hayden 1984). It described the technique and use of "surface" tactile prompts. They provide input about place of articulation, the amount and type of muscular contraction, movement transition, and timing needed to produce speech sounds. At the same time, the issue of how a three-dimensional "intraoral" target movement system might affect coarticulatory reality began to be explored. This exploration focused on how phonatory, mandibular, labial-facial, and lingual movements worked interactively in speech production and on how these subsystems could be rebalanced using tactile input to develop clear speech.

During the 1980s, collaborative research also began with Paula Square, whose research at the University of Toronto focused on acquired speech dyspraxia in adults (see Square-Storer and Hayden 1989). Two initial studies investigating PROMPT's treatment effectiveness were done. The first study in 1985 included a single participant (Square-Storer, Chumpelik Hayden, and Adams, unpublished) and the second study included three participants (Square et al 1986). The adult participants in both studies had been diagnosed with Broca's aphasia and symptoms of speech dyspraxia. Participants were at least 1 year poststroke and severely limited in functional speech. They had been discharged from other speech and language therapy programs because of lack of progress. A multiple baseline design with two treatment conditions (PROMPT and a traditional auditory-visual approach) were used. The results revealed significantly more changes in sound, word, and phrase productions in the PROMPT condition than in the auditory-visual condition. These studies led to formalizing the Motor Speech Hierarchy as a framework for assessing the motor speech system and organizing PROMPT treatment (Hayden 1986; Hayden and Square 1994), as described later in this chapter.

In the 1990s, standardized assessment protocols were developed, and PROMPT treatment was refined. The Verbal Motor Assessment for Children (VMPAC) (Hayden and Square 1999) was standardized on 1095 typically developing children from ages 2 to 12 years and 394 children with speech disorders, ages 3 to 12 years. This test assesses motor speech subsystem development in three main areas: (1) global motor control, (2) focal oromotor control, and (3) verbal and nonverbal sequencing of movements. Performance on the VMPAC showed that development of the speech subsystems (i.e., mandibular, labial-facial, and lingual control and sequencing) was consistent with the hierarchical, interactive model of the Motor Speech Hierarchy. Children with normal and disordered speech developed motor control, flexibility, and integration of the motor subsystems as age increased, although the disordered group was slower to develop than was the normal group.

Using the Motor Speech Hierarchy as a framework for intervention in a later study, Square et al (2000) measured PROMPT's effectiveness in treating children with oromotor deficits. The participants were six males (ages 4:2 to 4:6 years) with unintelligible speech who had made minimal progress in traditional therapy. They were seen in a 90-minute group session twice weekly for 15 weeks. Standardized tests of phonological, motor, language, and social skills were administered before and after treatment. The results revealed that PROMPT treatment resulted in perceptually improved speech even on untrained words. In support of PROMPT's effectiveness across multiple domains of functioning, it also was observed that the participants' overall behavior, social interactions, and language skills improved significantly as measured by the Speech and Language Assessment Scale (Hadley and Rice 1993), the Systematic Analysis of Language Transcripts, SALT (Miller and Chapman 1993), and the Social Skill Rating System (Graesham and Elloitt 1990).

In addition to the VMPAC, development began on another assessment tool, the Early Motor Control Scales (EMCS) (Hayden, Wetherby, Cleary, and Prizant, forthcoming). The EMCS, also based on the Motor Speech Hierarchy model, assesses infants at ages 12 to 24 months. Limb and oral development are assessed in relation to speech production.

With respect to PROMPT treatment in the 1990s, emphasis began to be placed on the concept of "planes of movement" (vertical, horizontal, anterior-posterior) used in coarticulated speech and on how these movement planes become coordinated in normal speech. Attention was given to how much motor control was needed to produce words (i.e., a lexicon) in either one or more movement planes. PROMPT treatment was refined with respect to selecting speech, language, and social interaction goals.

The empirical validation of PROMPT as a clinical approach continues into the current century. For example, a current project headed by Dr. Sally Rogers of the MIND Institute is an NIH-funded study comparing PROMPT (a holistic, multisensory, naturalistic approach), and the Denver Model (a developmentally, socially based, instructional approach) with nonverbal autistic children ages 24 to 50 months of age. The project is designed to gather data and develop research protocols that will allow for replication with a much larger subject group. The proposed replicated study will compare each model and a third integrated model of the two approaches. Currently, the results for PROMPT subjects are promising. In three subjects, with an average of 15 treatment sessions over a 6-month period, pre- and post-testing revealed an increase in expressive language from 9 months to 17 months. Other gains in visual reception and fine motor skills were also noted across subjects. They ranged from a 7-month gain to over 18 month's gain.

The rest of this chapter describes, in greater detail, PROMPT's conceptual model and its underlying clinical assessment and treatment principles, as they have been applied to the speech production disorders of children.

PROMPT'S CONCEPTUAL FRAMEWORK

A basic assumption of the PROMPT Conceptual Framework is that all behavioral outcomes, including speech production, result from the interaction of external and internal factors. As is shown in Figure 10.1, the factors external to the child include those that define the social and physical world in which speech production occurs. The internal factors include the physical, mental, and social-emotional resources that a child brings to all learning, including the acquisition of speech production skills.

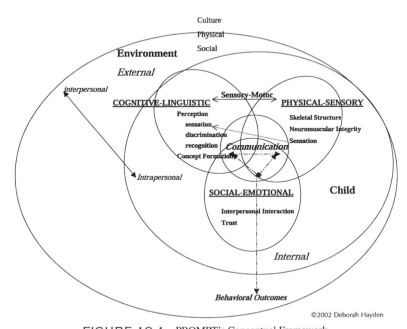

FIGURE 10.1   PROMPT's Conceptual Framework.

As a physical act, speech production requires peripheral and central (i.e., neurological) anatomical body structures inclusive of the skeletal structure that supports muscles, nerves, skin, and initial sensory information processes. As a mental act, speech production involves the cognitive-linguistic domain, namely the ability to perceive and interpret sensory input relative to stored experience, form concepts, reason, problem solve, represent, and express ideas in verbal and nonverbal forms. As a social-emotional act, speech production involves the use of socially acceptable rules for interacting with others in conversations and other forms of social discourse as well as one's affective attitude or feelings about self and others.

All three of these domains (namely, the physical, mental, and social-affective) are assumed to be interdependent in human functioning and to contribute to speech communication. Consequently, speech production may not be normal if any one of these global domains is disordered or delayed. All three domains should be considered when assessing and treating abnormal speech production. Consequently, PROMPT is about the holistic way that a client's speech production is viewed and treated from a developmental or acquired damage perspective. This broader viewpoint, along with an assessment of motor speech skills, drives decisions about when to use the tactile prompts and for what purpose.

Within PROMPT's philosophy, tactile information is viewed as the single most connecting and organizing factor in human development. Touch is "the variety of sensations evoked by stimulation of the skin by mechanical, thermal, chemical, or electrical events" (Cholewiak and Collins 1991, p. 23). In the PROMPT framework, however, touch involves more than passive surface skin deformations encountered from passive contact with another object. It also encompasses the sense of movement and body awareness perceived continually as we move, namely the kinesthetic senses generated by muscle, joint, and tendon receptors (Thelen's Chapter 3).

As an approach, PROMPT provides guidance about the type and depth of knowledge needed to assess speech production and how to conceptualize and organize the obtained information for intervention. As a technique, PROMPT prescribes the various technical or mechanical manipulations or operations (types of tactile cues among others) needed to actually change speech production performance.

As PROMPT has evolved, several interrelated ideas have become prominent:

1. Oral language is part of a dynamic system influenced by internal and external factors that interact to determine an individual's development over time. As Fogel and Thelen (1987) suggest, "There is no formal difference between endogenous and exogenous changes in components and their relationships. Emergent states can be created either by means of environmental support or as a result of changes of components within the individual" (p. 248).
2. It is necessary to evaluate external and internal factors that may affect a child's speech performance. The internal physical-sensory, mental, and

social-emotional domains in particular help us to understand what a child brings to the intervention and what a therapist needs to do to restructure or change speech production performance. In stressing the contribution and interaction of each of the three internal domains, PROMPT is consistent with the principles of dynamic systems theory which ". . . .views motor systems as belonging to a larger class of complex systems that produce patterned behavior" (Thelen 1991 p. 342).

3. Using tactile stimuli, the embedding of information within and across sensory and motor systems can be used to create motor schemas and associations for cognitive-linguistic retrieval.

CLINICAL ASSESSMENT

It is assumed here that all human communication (irrespective of its symbolic form as speech sounds, body gestures, and pictorial or graphemic images) results from the interaction of multiple domains of function, as has been described for PROMPT's conceptual model (see Figure 10.1). Consequently, the holistic understanding of a child's functioning needed to plan intervention requires that assessment focuses on more than the integrity of the motor speech system. It also must focus on the global internal and external factors that influence speech production, as considered next.

ASSESSMENT OF GLOBAL DOMAINS

PROMPT begins the minute your client walks through the door. This phrase underscores the importance of holistic assessment in PROMPT. An assessment can take advantage of everything that is immediately observable about the child with respect to the internal (i.e., its physical-sensory, cognitive-linguistic, social-emotional aspects) and the external domains of functioning. In the physical-sensory domain, for example, a clinician can observe a child's skeletal, cranial-facial structure and facial symmetry in addition to awareness of various forms of sensory stimulation. In the cognitive-linguistic domain, a clinician can observe a child's nonverbal behavior (e.g., visual tracking of objects) and verbal behavior (e.g., a child's understanding and use of some grammatical rules). In the social-emotional domain, a clinician can observe the child's behavior toward familiar and unfamiliar people and the kind of symbol system typically used to engage social interaction. In the external environment, a clinician can observe how caregivers respond verbally and nonverbally to a child's attempts at communication and social interaction in a given situation.

However, to systematically assess the global internal and external domains as shown in Figure 10.1, clinicians can use available assessment tools. They include the kind of norm-referenced and criterion-referenced tests frequently used to assess behavior and environmental conditions by a variety of professionals (e.g., psychologists, school teachers, social workers, physicians, speech-language therapists, physical and occupational therapists, and so on). The assessment procedures may also include the invasive and noninvasive diagnostic tests that physicians and other allied health professionals use to assess body structure integrity, including the brain and the larger central nervous system, as well as the peripheral and autonomic nervous systems.

The following discussion is structured around critical questions that guide a PROMPT assessment of the internal physical-sensory, cognitive-linguistic, and social-emotional domains. These questions take the assessment of function beyond the areas typically focused on in evaluating the motor speech system. In the physical-sensory domain, for example, the assessment goes beyond the cursory screening of the peripheral speech mechanism and auditory sensory system, which is typically done by speech-language therapists. Clinicians are required to consider the integrity of the tactile-kinesthetic sensory system in addition to neuromotor function generally. Assessing the cognitive-linguistic domain goes beyond a status check of general intelligence or language age. Clinicians must assess information processing constraints on the event contexts in which speech is produced as well as nonspeech communication efforts. In considering the social aspects, children's emotional or affective attitude toward people and events in the environment is as important as what can be assessed about their knowledge of the social world.

The questions for assessing each domain are identified below and discussed briefly in terms of their relevancy to describing and treating motor speech impairment using the PROMPT framework.

The Physical-Sensory Domain

Is Skeletal Facial Structure Development Normal for the Chronological Age and Symmetrically Aligned in the Vertical and Horizontal Planes?

Skeletal structure should be examined in terms of how adequately it can or cannot support speech production. Skeletal structure is the foundation on which the muscles and nerves are overlaid. Therefore, undeveloped or misaligned skeletal facial structures (e.g., a small mandible and protruding maxilla) may create problems with **if** or **how** certain muscles contract. When muscles cannot contract normally, their motor performance will be inhibited, thereby reducing the "flexible tradeoffs" (i.e., "degrees of freedom") in the muscle activity needed for coarticulated speech. Reaching movement "targets" is achieved by a motor system that dynamically regulates muscle parameters such as tissue mass, stiffness, and dampening. These parameters can be unbalanced and are not easily modified in the face of structural damage or muscle contraction biases. Therefore, they may be difficult to change. This is because misaligned skeletal structures can create or perpetuate abnormal or immature "attractor" states that are very stable. Very stable motor behavior reflects preferred response modes (i.e., "rigid attractor states") that make it difficult for a speech system to reorganize itself by changing from an existing attractor state to another more flexible or advanced state (Fogel and Thelen 1987). When the integrity of the physical system is compromised, a therapist may need to use other speech subsystems to compensate or bypass the muscular systems that are inflexible because of physical constraints. Clinicians should consider that compensations cost the speech system a loss of flexibility to reach target positions for sound production.

Is a Child's Body Tone Normal, and if Not, Is Either Hypertonus or Hypotonus Shown in the Whole Body, Trunk, or Face?

Tone is broadly defined here as the body's ability to hold itself up against gravity while maintaining the coordination and flexibility of muscle activity. Generally speaking, tone is mediated by neuronal activity in the reticular formation that exists throughout the brainstem and in portions of the diencephalons in the central nervous system (Guyton 1971). Upper motor neuron lesions can cause an abnormal increase in muscle tone. The resulting spasticity is marked by increased resistance to passive movement of the flexor muscles. In contrast, lower motor neuron lesions can cause an abnormal decrease in muscle tone. The resulting muscle weakness or flaccidity is marked by decreased resistance to passive movement of the flexor muscles (Love 1992).

In some instances, though, increased tone in specific speech muscles result from the muscle biases created when compensatory actions are used to control the movement of specific body structures. For example, increased lip retraction can help control the range of jaw movement. This type of increased tone, though often habituated, may not result from neurological damage. Instead, it can result from a disproportionate relationship in the development of articulatory structures.

The type and amount of abnormal tone, regardless of the cause, is a critical diagnostic indicator of whether neurological damage exists that can affect the motor speech system. When upper or lower motor neuron lesions exist as described, the musculature of the entire body is compromised with global effects on speech production. Such lesions will impair not only muscle tone, but they are also likely to compromise respiratory support, the base on which all the other speech subsystems develop. Depending on the amount of neurological damage, a child may not have enough motor control to maintain balance when sitting, standing, or ambulating, let alone to control the musculature in the graded and refined way needed for clear speech.

In PROMPT, clinicians should understand that abnormal tone can affect speech production, whether it exists in the entire body or the specific muscle groups that support speech production directly. Body movement is not normal when too much or too little tone compromises the contractility of muscles. Clinical assessment should determine whether and how body tone can be normalized. In PROMPT, this is done by identifying the "best possible" body postures in which to normalize tone and/or change the pattern of muscular biases so that more flexible, interactive relationships among the muscle groups can develop.

Is Neurological Damage Significant Enough to Prevent Higher Cortical Function from Inhibiting Lower Level Behavior, Such as Early Motor Reflexes?

Clinicians who use PROMPT must consider how neurological structures develop, and what happens to development as a result of brain injury. In children with global tone abnormality or uncontrolled muscle activity, simple lower-level patterns of behavior may predominate because they are unchecked by higher cortical control. This outcome is predicted by Jackson's (1958) theory (see also Mysak 1968; Ayres 1974); namely that development progresses from lower brain regions (e.g., the brain stem), which are well organized at birth and mediate simple automatic behavior, to higher brain centers (e.g., frontal cortex), which reorganize continually throughout life and mediate the most complex and least automatic behavior. The reverse of this ascending developmental course of "evolution" is dissolution, which happens in atypical development and diseased brains. The least organized and most complex aspects of function are reduced before the most organized and simple automatic aspects. But given that neuroplasticity is a **feature of all mammalian brains** (Kaas 1991), clinicians should be able to influence the development of neuromotor pathways with experience. Kaas (1996) points out that "increases in the relative activity of parts of the pathways in any sensory system [by manipulation or therapy that increases sensory input] can increase the sizes of the representations of those parts in cortical maps."

The clinical implication is that lower-level reflexes must be inhibited when clinicians try to modify an abnormal motor speech system. In PROMPT treatment, clinicians try to inhibit lower-level reflexive responses. This is done in PROMPT by (1) restructuring the environment to support more facilitating body postures, (2) enhancing development of sensory-motor pathways and cortical maps by using tactile in addition to auditory and visual inputs, and (3) linking sensory input for speech production with those required for conceptual development.

Does a Child Exhibit Difficulties Processing Tactile-Kinesthetic-Proprioceptive Input?

Only in movement (as opposed to static touch) does the organism fully experience tactile-kinesthetic-proprioceptive stimulation. This sensory information, which also includes the dynamic interaction of the articulators in coarticulated speech, can only be obtained when the organism is in movement or when the body structures touch something continually while moving through space and time. This sensory input is most directly associated with movement perception and is critical to the development of motor speech schemas as is discussed later in this chapter. In humans, the neural pathways connected to peripheral body structures, for example, the skin and muscles, send information to the somesthetic cortex where it can be detected and remembered. This cortex lies in the postcentral gyrus of the parietal lobe. Its relatively large representation of the face, lips, and tongue suggests that these structures, which are heavily involved in motor speech activity, are especially sensitive to tactile experience.

In PROMPT, clinicians must assess a child's sensitivity to tactile-kinesthetic input, and how much work must be done to prepare the sensory-motor system for the more complex, discrete input needed for speech. For example, clinicians can assess whether and how well a child's motor speech system responds when they use alternating light to moderate but firm pressure to grade the movements needed for adequate speech production.

The Cognitive-Linguistic Domain

How Does the Child Use and Coordinate Different Types of Sensory-Perceptual Information (Auditory, Visual, Tactile) for Learning Concepts and Producing Speech?

Answering this question focuses clinical observation on the information processing demands of learning. According to Thelen (1991), "an utterance of even a simple one-syllable word requires the coordination in time and space of over 70 muscles and 8 to 10 different body parts. . . . the achievement of human cognition, and motor coordination and control . . . is an essential component of this developmental landmark" (p. 339). Bloom (1996) also argued that the mental effort needed to produce words involves, at a minimum, "constructing an intentional state out of data from perception in relationship to what is already known in memory, the ability to recall linguistic units from memory and then to articulate or produce the motor movements from those words." She stated further that emotional expression, like speech, also has physical requirements that are dependent on the same limited pool of processing resources (see also Bloom's Chapter 7). Consequently, a child may sacrifice attention to some input or fail to translate input into its linguistic and/or motor equivalents depending on interest level in addition to task complexity and the efficiency of the neuromotor system for producing speech to get needs met.

Bates and MacWhinney (1987) proposed that, in the "competition" for limited processing resources, what gets attention and remembered may be determined by how important or relevant something is to the child. By knowing why a child is communicating and how processing factors impact task performance, a clinician can identify the variables that influence a child's attention and memories, and how a child may compensate for processing problems.

The clinical implication for PROMPT is that clinicians must focus on how and why a child approaches tasks in a particular way and not simply on the accuracy of performance. Furthermore, given a "limited resource" model of processing, clinicians should (1) restrict the input from competing sensory modalities for a given task at the same time (e.g., tactile and auditory input can be in the foreground as opposed to added visual input); (2) ensure that competing task demands for speech contexts are simple enough early on in the learning so that they do not interfere with the motor-speech planning and production requirements; and (3) increase the relevance of a task for the child socially and cognitively.

How are Perception and Action Schemas Used to Interact with the Environment?

Answering this question focuses the clinician's attention to how a child goes about learning and organizing information so it can be recalled with the least effort using limited resources. There is now a long history of regarding human actions as guided by some kind of stored mental plan or schema that is the residue of experience. Head, as early as 1926, proposed that a motor memory, or "schema," involves the process of extracting core elements from motor experiences. These elements reflect those rules that have led to success in reaching motor goals or performing a given action. A schema encompasses core properties of one's experience that can be tested continually and redefined by other experiences of a similar nature. These same features characterize successful speech schemas (Bellezza 1987). He proposed further that the rules underlying successful speech schemas are clarified through repetition. The larger the number and variety of experiences with a similar activity, the more effective a schema becomes. Variable but similar experiences across different situations allow schemas to become dynamic and usable. Patterns that require less effort and lead continually to more success are easiest to learn, particularly when they revolve around meaningful events involving real-world objects and routines (Nelson 1986; Fletcher 1992).

On a broader cognitive scale, Piaget (1954, 1964), like the contemporary scholars represented in Part I of this book (Thelen, Langer, Nelson, Bloom, and Affolter) proposed that children learn about the world from their physical and social interactions with the environment. Although social development was not emphasized in Piaget's framework, he did describe how in the first 2 years of life, a baby develops initial sensory-motor schemas (a well-defined sequence of physical or mental actions) into more organized and complex mental schemas. These action schemas almost always result from children's use of their own bodies to interact with the environment, behavior that naturally requires the use of touch for exploring and learning about the environment (see Affolter and Bischofberger 2000; Affolter's Chapter 8). Sensorimotor schemas increase in complexity as a child learns to experiment, predict, and control the outcomes from such interaction activity. For example, children progress from the ability to repeat one successful cycle of action during their physical interaction with the environment to being able to achieve new results by experimenting with the effects of the same or different actions on the environment (Piaget 1954). Such exploratory activity presumably provided the foundation for developing symbolic representation and more mature conceptual development.

The implication for PROMPT is that to develop speech schemas, or coordinative structures (patterns of movement that lead to meaningful expression), clinicians should use tactile-kinesthetic information within controlled but naturalistic conditions. It also implies that we be within the client's motor control ability, use repetition, employ variability, and use functional and motivational events, and that productions be made conscious.

How Tightly Structured Does the Event Context Need to be (i.e., Ranging from Highly Structured to Minimally Structured or Unstructured) for the Child to Maintain Successful Sensory Integration and Attention to Learning?

This question is motivated by the fact that behavior inclusive of speech production occurs in some kind of event context. Events are identified by their purpose, location, and the amount and type of human activity required to participate in them. Naturally, events vary all their information processing demands. The processing demands on all speech production events become important given the essentially limited cognitive resources for processing the multidimensional aspects of human activity. See Bloom (1996; Bloom and Tinker 2001; Bloom's Chapter 7 in this book). Nelson (Chapter 6) argued that ordinary daily events are well suited to the development of all representational systems because they are routinized and experienced often enough to free up mental resources for paying attention to the words used in them. This means that the more difficulty a child has in detecting the presence of a given sensory input, the fewer mental resources there will be for discriminating, recognizing, or storing information at other levels of perceptual organization. The more difficulty a child has in accessing and retrieving information from memory, the fewer the mental resources may be available for executing motor speech targets correctly without a high degree of prestructured and familiar event contexts.

Tightly structured events, which are familiar, can make less processing demand on participants because the activities and social roles are prescribed, even routinized, as are the words used. Once routinized event roles and sequences of activities are learned, one can participate in them without expending a lot of cognitive energy. More of the attentional resources can be given to other tasks at the same time as would be required for learning new speech production skills. In contrast, unstructured or low structured events make more mental demands on attention, planning, problem solving, and the creative use of words. When the event contexts for speaking create attentional demands, it will be more difficult to devote attentional resources to learning new motor speech skills at the same time.

The implication for PROMPT assessment is that clinicians must determine how much events need to be prestructured and simplified to support improved speech and what happens when such support or "scaffolding" is not given. This assessment can capitalize on the information gathered in response to earlier questions.

Why and How Does a Child Express His/Her Needs and Wants?

Because speech is the oral expression of a linguistic system, it is obviously important to determine whether a spoken language system has emerged for a given child. If so, then clinicians should determine its level of complexity and whether speech comprehension and production skills are present. The complexity and amount of spoken language used affect the available repertoire of words that a child can learn to say.

If speech has not emerged, then clinicians should determine what is being used to communicate. At a minimum, it should be determined whether any vocal sounds are produced to communicate needs or whether a combination of sound and other bodily expressions (e.g., eye gaze, gesture) is used. Wetherby (1991) has described a range of early behaviors that children use to express various communication functions, such as requesting, protesting, showing off, and directing another's attention to an object or event. Wetherby's categories of communicative behaviors can guide the clinical assessment of children with little or no speech production. If little or no sound is used for communication, then clinicians can try to elicit voicing whenever a child expresses communicative intent such as requesting an object or action. Alternatively, clinicians can identify situations in which a child already uses voice to express intent and explore in the assessment whether this vocal output can be shaped into more usable speech patterns by using tactile prompts.

The broader implication of this kind of PROMPT assessment is that treatment must be focused first at the level of a child's nonoral or oral expression before moving on to more complex motor speech production tasks.

SOCIAL-EMOTIONAL DOMAIN

How Does the Child Use Significant Others to Aid in Their Acquisition of Knowledge?

Proponents of social learning theory (Bruner 1977; Vygotsky 1978; Nelson 1986) assume that more sophisticated learning strategies and outcomes can occur when a more experienced adult participates in the learning event. Nelson (1986; Chapter 6) reminds us that "event knowledge" encompasses people, in addition to objects and actions. The assumption inspired by Vygotsky's (1978) social-cognitive learning theory is that the children can achieve higher levels of performance potential when guided or scaffolded by mature caregiver input than when not.

Bates (1976) reminds us that the point of adult "scaffolding" and use of events to solidify word forms and a knowledge base about the world, is to finally engage in peer relationships. Hartup (1983) says that "peer interaction is an essential component of the individual's development. Experience with peers is not a superficial luxury to be enjoyed by some children and not by others, but is a necessity in. . . . socialization" (p. 220). In PROMPT, the point of creating scaffolded events is to teach social interaction skills that require certain word forms. These words can be learned and used by a child to engage peers and caregivers in social interaction.

How Does a Child React Emotionally to Persons and Events in the Environment?

All behavior is likely to have an affective dimension. Affect reflects one's emotional state or attitude toward what is being experienced. Emotions can be described on a continuum that ranges from a negative to positive state (Bloom's Chapter 7). Like other behavioral domains, emotional or affective responses also require competing use of mental resources. A child in a negative emotional state, for any reason, may not have enough mental resources to produce accurate speech targets at the same time. So being tuned to how children feel about themselves and the ability to control situations and feel safe is essential for therapy. This understanding will set the tone of a therapy session, often leading clinicians to set boundaries on behaviors with consistent consequences. The need to provide a firm but gentle hand may be difficult for some clinicians to do. But it is essential for children whose inappropriate behaviors may reflect their way of coping with distrust and safety issues.

Behavior

In the PROMPT conceptual framework, behavior is viewed as the outward manifestation of a child's reactions to the internal and external environment. Behavior reflects what a child has learned about the world from sensing and organizing sensory input. Behavior also reflects a child's most intimate feelings about self and one's relationship to the world. In clinical assessment, clinicians must recognize that one child's behavioral expression may differ from another child's, and a given child's behavior can vary across different situations and communication partners. The implication is that clinical assessment procedures within the PROMPT framework must be adapted to the individual children and situations.

ASSESSMENT OF SPEECH PRODUCTION

This section focuses on what is entailed in assessing motor speech skills within the PROMPT framework. The importance of assessing skeletal and craniofacial structures has already been discussed. Therefore, a particular model of how the motor speech system functions in speech production guides the questions posed here for assessment. The Motor Speech Hierarchy (Hayden 1986; Hayden and Square 1994) was created specifically for PROMPT assessment and intervention and has been validated empirically using objective measures (Square et al 1999) and in part by kinematic data (Green et al 2000) (Figure 10.2).

The following questions posed for assessment relate primarily to each stage of the Motor Speech Hierarchy.

The Motor Speech Hierarchy as an Assessment Framework

The Motor Speech Hierarchy helps the clinician systematically evaluate a child's motor speech system and identify the level or stage where problems occur. The Hierarchy identifies seven stages of motor-speech development and control, as described later. These stages are assumed to be hierarchically dependent and interactive. To change speech production, the lowest levels need to be changed before change can be expected at higher levels (Hayden and Square 1994).

MOTOR-SPEECH HIERARCHY
(Hayden, 1986)

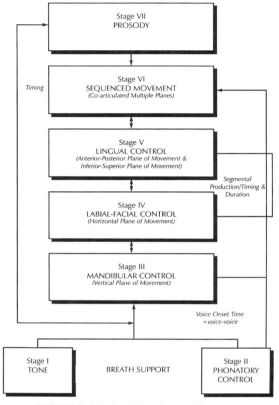

FIGURE 10.2   Motor Speech Hierarchy.

Stages 1 and 2

These two stages of the Hierarchy represent muscle tone, which is distributed throughout the body including the trunk, neck, and face (Stage 1), and the structures that support phonotory control (Stage 2), which depend on adequate tone and breath support. Motor speech functions at these two levels are assessed first because they provide the infrastructure for speech sound articulation at higher levels of the Hierarchy.

The following questions are relevant to Stage 1 (tone) assessment:

1. Are head, neck, and trunk stable and maintained in proper alignment at rest?
2. Are head and neck stable and maintained in proper alignment during trunk movement?

3. Are postural control and tone within normal range during ambulation?
4. Are head, neck, and trunk maintained in proper alignment during phonation?

(For discussion on tone, see p. 261 this chapter). Answers to the following questions will help the clinician understand the relationship between voicing and jaw movement at Stage 2 of the Hierarchy. When speaking, the laryngeal valving pressure needed for voicing must be sustained while the jaw is moving, and voicing needs to be maintained even when the jaw is closed.

1. Can the child only initiate voicing with the jaw open (i.e., full open to closed position)?
2. Can the child continue the voicing through jaw movement?
3. Can the child maintain voicing with the jaw closed (e.g., produce the /m/ sound)?

Stages 3, 4, and 5

The following questions relate to the more discrete functions of individual muscle groups that get coordinated in a single plane of movement. They are relevant to assessing motor functions at Stage 3 (mandibular control or the vertical movement plane), Stage 4 (labial-facial control or the horizontal plane), and Stage 5 (lingual control or the anterior to posterior movement plane) of the Hierarchy. In this model, developing mandibular control is essential to the lip and tongue movements needed for speech, and to normalizing the coordination of jaw, lip, and tongue movement. Answers to the following types of questions will help the clinician understand at what level of the Hierarchy a child needs tactual support, and the amount and type of prompting needed to further individuate speech subsystem movements.

1. Can the child maintain jaw stability and symmetry during speech production (i.e., there is no jaw sliding)?
2. Can the child open and close the jaw while voicing by smoothly grading the movement within a normal range?
3. Can the child move the lips independently of the jaw? To produce bilabials, for example, does the whole mandible move to the upper lip with little or no independent lip contraction, or can the lips move independently or with little or no muscle involvement from the mandible?
4. Can the child move the tongue body independently of the jaw (e.g., from front to back)?

Stage 6

This Stage of the Motor Speech Hierarchy represents the ability to sequence speech sounds across all movement planes (i.e., vertical, horizontal, and anterior to posterior planes). In other words, speech productions reflect the temporal and spatial mapping of movement sequences. However, before trying to sort out whether a child can sequence three planes of movement and maintain these trajectories across space and time, it is crucial to know about the level of control at earlier stages of the Motor Speech Hierarchy. If jaw control is poor, for example, then coarticulated movements across varying planes will be disrupted. The sequencing difficulty will be secondary to a more primary motor control problem. Essentially, the clinician can ask whether a child has difficulty maintaining a sound sequence across multiple planes of movement despite normal muscle tone and contraction.

It is important to separate underlying tone and muscle control/contraction difficulties within a single plane of movement from the ability to remember and produce action sequences across several planes over time. This information will guide clinical decisions about how to develop the lexicon to be practiced in therapy. The number of movement planes and manner of production constraints within each word need to be considered. For example, producing the word "mom" requires a single vertical plane, "daddy" a double plane (vertical/horizontal), and "pancake" multiple planes (vertical and anterior/posterior).

Stage 7

This final stage represents prosodic or suprasegmental sound patterns that include stress, duration, and so on. It is of note to remember that the development of some prosodic features begin much earlier—when motor control for phonation and jaw movement is achieved, or at Stage 3. It is hypothesized that this early prosody is created by a universal and underlying "movement generator" that is cyclic in nature and underpins all movement (Kelso and Tuller 1983). It also suggests that individual speech sounds are superimposed on this underlying prosodic rhythm. At the highest level, or Stage 7 of the Motor Speech Hierarchy, prosody can be described as related to the interaction and coordination of all the stages before it, thereby suggesting that the control of rate, stress, pitch, and pausing that lead to changes in semantic phrasing and meaning are controlled through motor and linguistic processes.

Overall Assessment

At each Stage of the Hierarchy, it is also important to determine whether speech production is differentially influenced by various sensory modalities (tactile, auditory, and visual) of input. Although all three sensory modality input sources are likely to be used in typical development, the children with speech production impairment may have more difficulty achieving accurate productions with some sensory modalities of input than with others. A PROMPT assessment is particularly geared to explore whether tactile information enhances the accuracy of speech production targets. The Motor Speech Hierarchy may also be used to look at how the development of movements at each Stage begin to create "phonemes" or "motor-phoneme links." Clinicians should also realize that refinement of movement is not developed all at once nor is complete independence of movement control needed for many motor-phonemes, syllables, or word productions. For example, the word "mom" may be produced using holistic jaw movement from closure, through voicing, to closure and requires minimal valving changes (Stage 3). Whereas, the word "scissors" requires a tightly controlled jaw, well-established valving, independent facial movements, and well-controlled, independent tongue movement (Stage 5).

The VMPAC; A Standardized Motor Speech Assessment Procedure

The Verbal Motor Production Assessment for Children

Hayden and Square (1999) offer a step-by-step protocol for assessing neuro-motor integrity of the speech production system at rest and when engaged in vegetative and volitional nonspeech and speech tasks. A unique aspect of this test is that it systematically probes which modality of sensory input changes motor-speech performance the most. If auditory and visual input does not change a targeted production, then a prompted, tactile-kinesthetic cue is offered. The information obtained from scoring these modality sources of input helps to determine what treatment approach may be useful for changing target behavior.

The VMPAC, normed on 1050 normal children and 350 speech-disordered children, ages 3 to 12 years, is designed to assess a range of skills that influence the development of speech motor control. Developed from the Motor Speech Hierarchy, it assesses three main areas: global motor control, focal oromotor control, and sequencing. Global motor control corresponds to Stages 1 and 2, which represent the infrastructure for speech, namely, respiration and phona-tion. Focal oromotor control corresponds to Stages 3, 4, and 5, which represent the control of muscle groups that support movements of the jaw, lips/face, and tongue. All test items are assessed at increasing levels of difficulty within a stage. Production precision is assessed first in the vertical plane of movement (e.g., a-m), then the horizontal (e.g., m-u), and anterior-posterior (e.g., t-k) movement planes. The sequencing subtest (Stage 6) assesses ability to sequence movements in more complex contexts over time, while maintaining precision and accuracy of coordinated movements. Production of words, in meaningful linguistic sequences of events, is also tested using pictures to depict the actions of cartoon-like characters in various activities. The VMPAC does not include specific items corresponding to Stage 7 of the Motor Speech Hierarchy. Performance in this area is assessed throughout the test, including the supple-mental ones.

Test observations can be plotted against normative data for children at ages 3 to 7 years for each subtest area. A child can be compared with typically develop-ing children of the same age at either the 5th, 50th, or 95th percentile. The study described at the end of this chapter illustrates how VMPAC outcomes are used.

PROMPT INTERVENTION

The goal here is not to provide a detailed description of the prompts used in treatment. This information is available in technical manuals (e.g., see Hayden 1985; 1999). Instead, the goal is to describe the general characteristics of the tactile prompts used in treatment and the principles and phases of treatment that support their use with children.

TREATMENT ASSUMPTIONS

To create speech production changes, the PROMPT clinician is expected to:

1. Match or slightly exceed a child's developmental level with respect to learning goals and tasks.
2. Consider the type and amount of physical, mental, and emotional resources available to a child when structuring treatment events and evaluating a child's response to them at any point in time.
3. Enhance attention to tasks by providing sensory input that includes tactile, kinesthetic, and proprioceptive experiences within structured learning events.
4. Provide speech production practice in functional activities that are relevant to social and physical interactions in the natural environment outside of therapy.
5. Take a child's interests into account when structuring treatment activities that can support meaningful vocalization and social interaction.

Most of these assumptions are not unique to PROMPT treatment. But one of the unique features of PROMPT treatment is its systematic use of tactile input to facilitate speech production in addition to the auditory and visual cues relied on so often in traditional treatment approaches. It is assumed that a child can build motor schema or maps for producing speech sounds more quickly and accurately when the coordinated sensory input includes the tactile modality than when it does not.

POSTURAL SUPPORT AND TACTILE PROMPTS

General Postural and Head/Neck Support

In general, prompting requires that postural control of the body-trunk; the neck and head are stable and supported. The clinician normally uses his or her nondominant hand to support the back of the head at the nape of the neck. This support provides head and neck stability and acts as a counter balance for pressure applied in prompts that are directed at the mylohyoid or the muscular tissue under the chin. See discussion of the importance of a stable environment for moving and interacting in Affolter (Chapter 8) and Bischofberger and Affolter (Chapter 9).

Tactile input is provided by four types of prompts: parameter, syllable, complex, and surface. These prompts are distinguished broadly by the amount and type of support to the skeletal and neuromuscular systems and the type and number of simultaneous tactile cues provided to create motor schemas or maps of sound targets, words, or phrases. Although each type of prompt is used for a different purpose, all provide the neuromotor system with tactile, kinesthetic, and proprioceptive input regarding the temporal-spatial aspects of speech movements. These aspects may involve the degree(s) of opening required by mandible or labial-facial musculature and/or the breadth, depth, and place of contraction in the lingual musculature. As prompting is dynamic input, it continually acts and reacts to shape and change the input to the child's neuromotor system. Therefore, the clinician will continually change the type and combination of prompts needed for the child to: (1) stabilize skeletal and muscular systems; (2) recognize the input; (3) organize the motor speech subsystems to produce the movement(s); (4) associate the movements to the acoustic or cognitive-linguistic concepts; and (5) transition the movements for words, phrases, and sentences. A brief definition of each PROMPT follows.

Parameter Prompts

Parameter prompts provide maximal support and stability to the mandible or facial muscles, setting either the degree of opening of the mandible or the broad action of rounding or retraction of the facial muscles. See example Figure 10.3. Parameter prompts function to stabilize facial structures or musculature so that other smaller structures or muscle actions (e.g., lips, tongue, and so on) can be freed up for more independent movement and become perceptually salient.

Syllable Prompts

Syllable prompts shape beginning CV or VC syllables. They set and support the mandible (degrees of opening) and actions of the facial muscles (rounding or retraction) (e.g., /pi/, /bi/, /mi/, /pu/, /bu/, /mu/). The shaping postures provided by syllable prompts always reflect the vowel shape, for example, rounded or retracted, they effectively reduce the motor load for the child and allow for early independent actions to be established (Figure 10.4).

Complex Prompts

Complex prompts provide information about how to produce a "static" neuromotor or single motor-phoneme "map." They provide input to the mandible about the degree of opening and specific information to labial or facial muscles for place, and if needed, the amount of rounding or retraction. They also give information about timing, degree, and breadth of lingual muscle contraction. The sensory input maps as many components of the sound as possible, so that a holistic motor schema for a phoneme can be constructed. Therefore, complex prompts are often given in isolation, and then re-embedded in the same or different word form (Figure 10.5).

Surface Prompts

Surface prompts provide the "most critical" but least information necessary for the neuromotor system to recognize or produce a phoneme and maintain its

A

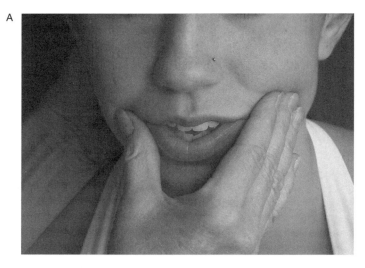

B

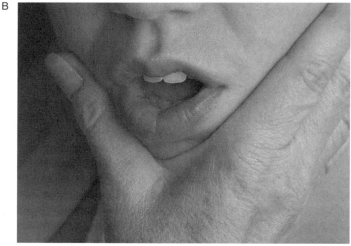

FIGURE 10.3   Visual display of a parameter prompt for /i/ and /a/. **A,** Parameter prompt for /i/. **B,** Parameter prompt for /a/.

essence throughout coarticulated movement transitions. When used in syllables, words, or phrases, surface prompts signal transition from one plane of movement to the next in addition to timing or place information. For example, in the word "mommy," surface prompts would be given for /m/, /a/, /m/ (in the vertical plane) and /i/ (in the horizontal plane). As the movements are sequenced, the timing, pressure, and stress provided by the clinician can be combined to give input about the transition from one sound to the other (Figure 10.6). In Figures 10.4 through

A

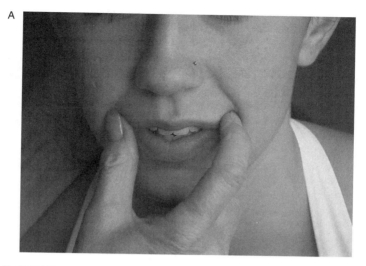

B

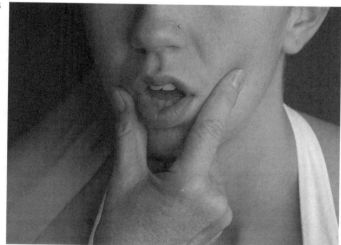

FIGURE 10.4   Visual display of a syllable prompt for /i/ and /a/. **A,** Syllable prompt for /i/.
B, Syllable prompt for /a/.

10.6, it is important to realize that although some finger placements may look the
same, they are not the same. One cannot see the differences between prompts in
amount of pressure and changes in timing that are applied depending on the context in which the motor-phoneme is placed.

Thus, the specific prompts used within each of four PROMPT categories are
distinguished by the particular tactile-kinesthetic cues needed to specify the
place and manner of production for individual speech sounds or motor phonemes

A

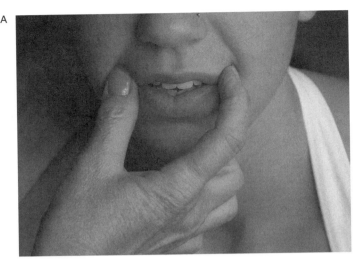

B

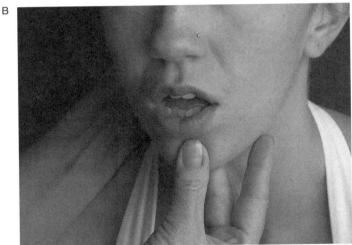

FIGURE 10.5   Visual display of a complex prompt for /i/ and /a/. **A,** Complex prompt for /i/.
B, Complex prompt for /a/.

in language. The use of any combination of parameter, syllable, complex, or surface prompts will vary depending on the nature of the speech production problem and the linguistic or corresponding coarticulatory contexts in which a motor-phoneme occurs. For example, the clinician's nondominant hand usually will support the back of the child's head to provide postural support. Then, saying, "let me help you" or "let me do it" or "my turn," a clinician may use the dominant hand to give a surface prompt (to provide cognitive-linguistic associations

A

B

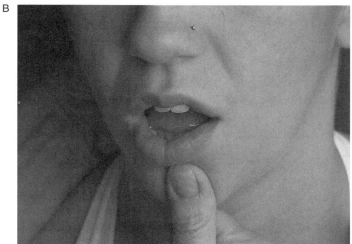

FIGURE 10.6 Visual display of a surface prompt for /i/ and /a/. **A**, Surface prompt for /i/. **B**, Surface prompt for /a/.

and temporal "mapping"). The clinician may ask the child to "do it with me" followed by a syllable prompt (to provide postural shaping for beginning linguistic use). If clinicians feel that a child is capable of a more intricate production than a simple CV shape, but still needs mandibular midline control or stability so that finer muscles can act, then they may say to the child "now you do it" and provide just a Parameter prompt. If a particular sound, within a syllable or word, does not have all aspects established, a Complex prompt (a static prompt that provides as much information as possible) may be given and the production honed to the neurological system's best effort. The sound then can be re-embedded in the CV and once more, the syllable or surface prompt can be given before the child produces it again. Normally in treatment, clinicians will use a combination of all prompt types.

Consequently, to do PROMPT intervention well, clinicians need to know the specific places where muscles insert and contract and how to apply deep pressure to soft tissue. They also must recognize that the length of time pressure sustained will affect how well the motor system learns to recognize when to set up and release muscle contractions, especially for movement transitions. As therapy progresses through the various phases, it becomes critical that a clinician has automatic skilled use of hand and finger placements.

PROMPT's tactile cueing system is now elaborate enough to create a motor map or schema for every consonant and vowel phoneme of general American English, and motor phonemes in other languages (e.g., French, German, Italian, Spanish, and Cantonese) have been created as well. Years of clinical experience now have revealed that the skilled use of PROMPT's evolving cueing system can help children learn to produce speech more accurately. Once they discover that prompt cues are helpful, it is not unusual for them to seek particular tactile input on their own when they have difficulty saying something. Children may bring the clinician's hand to their own faces or try to prompt themselves. They may also come to therapy sessions with a list of words to be prompted.

PROMPT TREATMENT PHASES

Prompt treatment typically consists of three phases presented in a structured progression. These phases are distinguished mainly by (1) the child's overall domain assessment and the chosen communication focus, (2) the complexity of the speech production movements required, and the (3) amount of clinician-dependent input needed to achieve good speech production. These broad criteria for distinguishing treatment phases are not unique to PROMPT therapy; but, PROMPT departs from traditional approaches with respect to how speech production complexity and clinician-dependent input are viewed. Speech production complexity is viewed in terms of the independence of the speech subsystems and the number of movement planes involved in producing a given speech output. For example, a word such as "mom" that requires just one plane of movement (a vertical plane) is developmentally easier to say than is a word involving two movement planes, such as "mommy" (vertical and horizontal planes). Complexity is also viewed in terms of the stages of the Motor Speech Hierarchy focused on in treatment (see Figure 10.2). Treatment, which focuses on just sustaining respiratory support and voicing for sound production at Stages 1 and 2 of the Hierarchy is at a more basic and simpler level than is treatment focused on coordinating respiratory support and voicing with the accurate production and sequencing of phonemes or prosody (Stages 2 through 7).

Clinician-dependent input can be described in terms of the amount of support needed to integrate tactile input with auditory and visual input when building motor-phoneme maps for speech production. For example, a treatment phase that requires fairly consistent tactile prompting to achieve good speech production is different than a phase in which little or no direct tactile prompting is needed; that is, a child can rely more on external auditory-visual cues that are already linked to an internalized motor map of the movement required. Clinician-dependent input is also measured by the degree to which communication events need to be prestructured or routinized for good speech production. For example, a child who produces good speech only in communicative events requiring highly prescribed ways of speaking and repeated word use is at a different treatment level than is one who flexibly uses new speech patterns in novel events with different levels of processing demands on attention. Treatment typically progresses from highly structured to unstructured events or activities.

A prior assessment determines the child's strengths and weaknesses across domains. Considering the affects of these disordered or misaligned domains, realistic expectations are developed and with caregivers input a "communication focus" is chosen. In other words, what phase of treatment a child may enter, and how quickly a child moves within a phase or from one phase to another, will depend on his or her physical, mental, and motor deficits or how much core prelinguistic conceptual information is already in place. Regardless of the treatment phase, every therapy session is expected to:

- Provide a short "warm-up" period of **mass** and **distributed** "motor phoneme" practice. Within the context of PROMPT, mass practice refers to repeated productions of the same motor phoneme or word while distributed practice refers to productions of that same stimulus now within altered coarticulated contexts and different but functional situations. In very young children or those without well-developed prelinguistic strategies, this step will be altered. Instead, voicing, sounds, or functional syllables will be targeted and used as frequently as possible within the context of appropriate activities or routines.
- Combine minimally two speech subsystems in a single plane of movement for production practice. For example, the jaw and lips are involved in producing the syllable, "up" in one plane of movement (the vertical plane).
- Promote a child's use of new motor patterns in functional, socially interactive, routines, games, or activities that require expression of communicative intent, turn taking, decision making, and so on.
- Prompt treatment rarely requires therapists to work inside the mouth. The use of specific oral-motor exercises, nonsense syllables, and mirrors is not typically recommended. These activities have not been shown empirically to normalize speech production for functional communication. When done incorrectly, they may even encourage abnormal or exaggerated movements during speech attempts.

Treatment Phase I

General Motor and Treatment Goal

The goal of Phase I treatment is to develop speech motor control in a single plane of movement (vertical or horizontal) for use in communication within tightly structured activities and routines. Children who must begin treatment in this phase may have minimal speech production skill.

Sensory Considerations

Some children who begin treatment in Phase I are not accustomed to being touched. Clinicians should touch the gross body structures (head, chest, or limbs) before touching the jaw and other facial structures. Touch should be natural and gentle, with sustained pressure through large joint areas such as the shoulders, head, and neck. The goal of the touch is to normalize the body's tone and readiness for movement, as well as increase conscious awareness of movement.

Occasionally, a child may show that he or she does not want to be touched. For example, he or she may jerk away from being touched or avoid contact. Such responses almost never have anything to do with the touch itself or with a neurological "tactile defensiveness," which may be seen by blanching, sweating, projectile vomiting, etc. However, such responses do indicate that the child is not ready or aware of the reason for being touched. Expectation and predictability of events will have a calming effect on the child. Touching, if natural and in context, will provide the stability and boundaries for cognitive and emotional learning. It is, therefore, important that children are approached and "touched" in an easy and natural way by the clinician and without preset clinician expectations of rejection. If therapy begins by naturally incorporating touch as part of helping children to produce some meaningful speech that they initiate themselves, then most of them quickly learn to use the help they get. Later on, some children will even bring a clinician's hand to their own mouths for additional help or attempt to prompt themselves and others.

Before asking a child to produce the targeted speech sounds, the PROMPT clinician identifies the motor phoneme targets to be produced. A child is asked to produce the targeted sounds following several trials of clinician-delivered tactile prompting coupled with the corresponding auditory and visual inputs about the targeted sound. This means that the child should be positioned in close enough proximity to the clinician to access such input. The visual input will be particularly enhanced if the child is positioned at eye level. Clinicians also may increase successful responses from children by slowing their speech rate and lengthening the response or production time required.

A child's independent production attempts may be preceded by a "doing with" production phase. That is, a given target word or phrase is spoken and prompted by the clinician at the same time that the child is attempting to produce it. The prompts are faded as soon as possible, and the child's independent productions are elicited in a variety of functional interaction routines.

THE MOTOR SPEECH HIERARCHY AND PROMPT
SUPPORT FOR SOUND PRODUCTION

Phase 1 relates to motor control at Stages 2 (phonation) and 3 (jaw movement) and 4 (facial retraction and rounding) of the Motor Speech Hierarchy. Stage 1 (Tone) is omitted for brevity's sake, as the purpose of this chapter is not to describe activities or postural positions that will enhance or "normalize" tone throughout the entire body. However, as has been stated many times throughout this chapter, if there are abnormal tone issues that exist throughout the whole body, they will greatly affect speech subsystem development. How tone affects the neuromotor system's integrity and its flexible use must be considered in all therapy plans (see Mysak 1968; Bobath 1980; Love 1992, for more information on this area).

At Stage 2 (phonation) several areas need to be considered. First, issues with tone that may be influencing vital capacity so that phonation is weak, strained, or produced through laryngeal tension need to be considered. If so, tactile support and compression can be given to the thoracic area to enhance and prolong breath stream and to normalize speech breathing. Second, phonation needs to be considered along with valving (pharyngeal and labial) and jaw gradation that help to maintain air stream control. To work at Stage 3, vowels and consonants are selected so that motor control can move from whole jaw movement to finer, graded jaw movement. Control of voicing (phonation) through graded jaw movement is essential for vowel production. So, the initial work is on vowel and consonant productions that require jaw movements ranging on a continuum from a fully open mouth position (e.g., /a/, /ae/) to an almost closed position (e.g., /o/, /i/, /u/). Production of the consonant /m/ requires moving the jaw to a fully closed mouth position. Then bilabial speech sounds (/b/, /p/), which require the coordination of jaw and lip movement can be added. Voiced sounds are targeted for production before voiceless ones because they require less motor speech control.

Stage 4 of the Motor Speech Hierarchy allows therapy to target coordinated lip rounding and retraction without changing jaw grading or plane of movement. Consonant-vowel (e.g., me, no) and vowel-consonant combinations (e.g., up, on) are created to make useful words for communication interaction. Thus, all movement is simplified in Phase 1 treatment. It is kept on either the horizontal plane (e.g., me and moo) or on a vertical plane, that changes from an open to a closed mouth position, (e.g., up, on) or a closed- to open-mouth position (e.g., ma). In this treatment phase, until motor control is established within one plane, it is not recommended to combine both planes of movement in the same word.

STRUCTURE AND CONTENT OF TREATMENT SESSIONS

Although all PROMPT treatment sessions are structured to engage participation in social interactions, the sessions in Phase one include highly motivating activities that have concrete beginnings and endings. The child also practices speech productions in simple visual-motor activities that require repetitive actions. Such activities may require putting blocks into a box, putting pegs into a peg board, putting large puzzle pieces into a form board, or hitting balls down a ramp to accomplish some goal of functional social interaction and play. In a game involving reciprocal social interaction, the child and the clinician take turns performing an action such as putting a block into the box after saying a target production. A repetitive action routine allows a child to easily comprehend the structure of the activity; the next step of the event sequence can be executed without a lot of mental effort. A child also can anticipate the boundaries of the event, for example, "I am done when all these blocks are in," and the interaction goal is reached.

When a child refuses to participate in activities or expresses either frustration or anger, these feelings are acknowledged, but therapy continues. With supportive boundaries, children typically begin to relax and trust that the clinician can help them.

Even the nonspeech like initial vocalizations attempts can be used to meet a child's immediate wants and needs as long as expression of communicative intent in some form (vocal or not) has emerged. A child with communicative intent but no usable speech can be taught a single vowel sound as a response class that can be used to get attention, ask questions, request actions, and so on. Single sounds may constitute an acceptable response for making requests or responding to them. For example, /m/ can be used to code "more," /a/ to code "yes," and /o/ to code "no." As the child begins to imitate or spontaneously initiate a vowel-like production for communication interactions, productions are shaped further, using tactile prompts.

During this initial intervention phase, a clinician begins to help the child to put simple syllables together from the isolated motor productions being practiced. If the child cannot yet produce such syllables or word forms, the clinician "maps" in the movements using surface prompts but expects only a production within the child's motor capacity. Mapping is used consistently in all phases of PROMPT treatment. It provides feed-forward information about motor plans and their variations and associations of motor movements to cognitive-linguistic information. Such syllable structures can include, for example, /ya/, /ba/, /bo/ or /ma/, and /mu/. Combining different vowels with initial and final consonants (e.g., /bo/ vs. /up/) allows the motor speech system to experience variable movement trajectories, transitions, durations, and degrees of muscle tensions that occur in ordinary functional speech. Therefore, clinicians should select linguistically meaningful sound sequences for production practice because they can be used immediately in social interactions. The closer the practiced sound combinations are to meaningful speech, the easier they will be learned.

Even at this early treatment phase, caregivers are expected to observe intervention sessions and spend the last 15 minutes in the session. They also are expected to participate in the intervention effort. The clinician guides caregivers to learn one activity in which the child has learned to use the turn-taking and the newly acquired sound and word forms. The caregiver is expected to play with the child using the activity to support and encourage the newly learned sounds or words minimally once a day in the home environment. The main goal of caregiver activities is to support "competence" and create successful social interactions. When a caregiver is asked to focus on successful interactions (supported by routines and functional word forms within the child's cognitive and motor levels), the dynamic of the relationship begins to change. The change occurs when caregivers can focus on what the child can do instead of what he or she cannot do.

Treatment Phase 2

General Motor and Treatment Goal

The goal of Phase 2 is to further refine and develop speech motor control by combining two planes of movement (i.e., the vertical and horizontal planes) in a speech sound sequence and embedding these new productions in short phrases for communicative interactions.

Sensory Considerations

When children reach this treatment phase, most of them recognize that touch helps them. They may even request tactile input when attempting a difficult production. The clinician moves among parameter, syllable, complex, and surface prompts to maximally support the child's production of more complex syllable structures and phrases.

THE MOTOR SPEECH HIERARCHY AND PROMPT
SUPPORT FOR SOUND PRODUCTION

Phase 2 includes treatment at three levels of the Motor Speech Hierarchy: Stage 3 (jaw movement), Stage 4 (labial-facial movement), and Stage 5 (lingual movement). The use of more refined jaw movements facilitates the independence of lip and facial movements and tongue and jaw separation. Lingua-alveolar stops and continuants (e.g., /t/, /d/, /n/, /s/) and the vowel /i/ are now incorporated into therapy. In addition, the clinician can now begin to "map in" the sensorimotor schema or pattern for midback tongue sounds such as /sh/ and /r/.

As PROMPT treatment refines the motor control at each stage, new roles emerge for all the speech subsystems. This evolutionary process shifts from developing anterior to midtongue control and continues with the development of midback and posterior tongue control. This refinement of movement develops from the child's changing motor speech systems interactions. It represents a type of evolutionary change in motor control that continues throughout the first 7 to 8 years of a child's life.

Structure and Content of Treatment Sessions

In this second treatment phase, the words and phrases added to the practice repertoire should require vertical and horizontal planes of movement. For example, in the word "happy," there is a change from the vertical plane in the first syllable (/hae/) to the horizontal plane in the second syllable (/pi/).

Another goal of Phase 2 treatment is to produce words with closed-syllable structure (e.g., boo versus boot) and combine words in short phrases (e.g., my boot; boot up). Producing such words within phrases or with more complex motor requirements can be simplified initially. This may be accomplished by embedding the newly practiced word in a motorically simplified carrier phrase. For example, "I want (vertical plane) *bee*" (horizontal plane). Once learned, such prestructured carrier phrases can help a child to reduce the motor and linguistic load of speaking when saying new words in longer utterances. Phrases such as "I want toy" or "I want ball" are perceived as more advanced productions and are functionally useful for social interactions.

At a still later stage, the words learned separately in either the vertical or horizontal planes of movement (e.g., "me, you, up go, more, hi, bye, yeah, ball") may be used to express a variety of communication functions and are flexibly combined in phrases and simple sentences to code early semantic-syntactic relations, such as agent action (e.g., ball go), agent-object (boy ball), and action-object (up ball) relations. Simple turn-taking games are appropriate activities in this phase of therapy as is the creation of "take home" activities or stories that include the words practiced in therapy. The practiced lexicon should include multiple classes or words and should not be restricted to just nouns.

Still more elaborate communication events can be identified with input from caregivers. As well as the activities carried over into the home, habitual daily life routines around food, games, or outings are good contexts for using new sounds and words outside of therapy. However, the motor complexity of each new word must be evaluated to determine whether it can be produced without clinician-supported input. If not, then it is replaced by another word with similar meaning and function but less complex motor production requirements. For example, a child may be able to say "me" in a turn-taking routine rather than "my turn."

Treatment Phase 3

General Motor and Treatment Goal

The general goals in this phase are to (1) further refine speech motor control by producing words and phrases involving three planes of movement (the vertical, horizontal, and anterior-posterior planes); (2) expand the complexity of the linguistic phrase structures produced; and (3) develop enough flexibility in motor speech skill so that the child has increasingly less need for concrete routines or structured clinician support to produce intelligible speech for functional communication.

Sensory Considerations

In Phase 3, direct tactile input and sustained control for motor execution begins to be reduced. Tactile input is faded by using "surface" and "air prompts." Surface prompts allow clinicians to give tactile input about transitions and main trajectory changes of coarticulated productions. In contrast, air prompts do not require the clinician to touch a child. Instead, a clinician may visually show the hand posture or movement for a tactile input. The visual cue should remind the child of how to produce the sound if it has been previously integrated with tactile-motor schema in previous learning events.

MOTOR SPEECH HIERARCHY AND PROMPT SUPPORT FOR SOUND PRODUCTION

Phase 3 focuses the treatment on Stages 5 (tongue control), 6 (sequenced movements), and 7 (prosody) of the Motor Speech Hierarchy. By the time this phase is reached, the child should already be able to control and combine speech movements (on two planes) requiring controlled valving changes, (e.g., phonation), jaw, independent labial-facial movements, and moderate anterior to posterior lingual contractions. For example, as in the words "got," "good," "take," and "can." To progress in Phase 3, the jaw must be stable or move with fine, graded control and have established independence of tongue from jaw. This type of jaw control is needed to produce such motor phonemes as /ʃ/and /r/ and vowels /I/ and /ɛ/. The therapy now focuses on continuing to refine lingual control in the anterior to posterior plane of movement. Broad to very specific narrow contractions are required as the speech subsystems move toward the complete individuation of movement needed by all physical structures involved in speaking. Individuated movement allows the lips to move independently of the jaw and one lip to move independently of the other one, as is required for producing /f/ and /v/. Intrinsic tongue muscles also are used to refine movement trajectories. Production practice can now include words that require narrow tongue contractions (e.g., /get/, /kick/) and those that require small, finely graded movements with good valving control and air pressure (e.g., consonant blends such as /sp/, /st/, /kl/).

Production practice also includes words and phrases that require the coordination of multiple planes of movement and changes in manner of production. A common characteristic of more complex productions is that all three planes of movement may be required plus several changes in manner of production. Consider the phrase, "I need scissors." Producing the word "I" involves primarily a vertical plane of movement, whereas the word "need" involves mostly horizontal plane movement. Producing the word "scissors" involves an anterior-to-back plane of movement. These types of productions require more flexible and refined motor control than do words and phrases produced in a one-movement plane or no more than two movement planes.

Structure and Content of Treatment Sessions

During Phase 3, the scope of a given treatment session expands. The changes include (1) increased variety and complexity of linguistic material to be practiced and (2) increased flexibility in the structure of treatment sessions so that speech production experience gets embedded within more complex social interaction routines and event sequences. As greater control is demonstrated over physical-motor, mental, and social-emotional domains of function, children assume more of the responsibility for changing their speech performance. The clinician now can become less directive.

In Phase 3 (and even as early as Phase 2), small group activities with other children can provide opportunities for peer practice, turn taking, and transfer of skills to more naturalistic environments. Motor and language goals are more often interrelated and codependent. Although often initiated in Phase 2, activities may now include grapheme-phoneme associations and the development of a lexicon for use in early literacy skills.

CONCLUDING COMMENTS ABOUT TREATMENT

The overall goal of PROMPT therapy is to move the child's speech motor system from a pre-existing "attractor state" (Thelen's Chapter 8) to a phase that allows new dynamic movement relationships to evolve. In Piagetian terms, this means that new schemas are developed (assimilated) as part of the child's response repertoire (accommodation). The information presented here for each treatment phase may apply more readily to some children than to others. Children come to therapy with unique learning profiles and varying levels of impairment in speech motor control and in other domains of function. For this reason, the rate of therapy progress varies from child to child. Progress is also dependent on how skilled the clinician is in bringing about the necessary changes.

By the second treatment phase, clinicians should be able to judge how much and how quickly a child's motor speech system has responded and developed. But not all children have the potential to achieve normal speech. For these children, the words that may be easily produced in a therapy environment may never be used outside of therapy without environmental-contextual support. If a child's motor or cognitive system is severely compromised, then it is crucial that clinicians develop a core lexicon from the motor movements possible and maximize their use in isolation or in short phrases for social communication.

However, years of clinical experience have revealed that the speech of many children (with adequate cognitive-linguistic and physical sensory domain strengths) can be normalized to a level typical for their ages within a year's time when given one or two sessions per week of approximately 30 to 50 minutes. The children who benefit from PROMPT treatment include those with various clinical diagnoses. They include children with delayed speech, developmental speech apraxia, cerebral palsy, and pervasive developmental delay inclusive of autism as well as those with hearing loss and fluency problems.

PROFILE OF A CLINICAL CASE

The following clinical case illustrates how all of the information presented throughout this chapter can be applied.

PRETREATMENT PROFILE

Jamie, a 2-year, 9-month-old male, was referred for PROMPT treatment with a diagnosis of developmental dyspraxia. Speech was profoundly unintelligible. Spontaneous productions consisted of isolated vowels and occasionally undefined stop consonant-like sounds. However, prelinguistic communicative intent was well established. Jamie used gestures (e.g, pointing) for most communication attempts. His birth history revealed full gestation with no complications and a birth weight of 7 lbs, 3oz. Hearing and vision were within normal limits. Before receiving PROMPT therapy, Jamie had been treated approximately twice a week for 40 1-hour sessions of speech therapy at school and a local university clinic. The clinical profile obtained after extensive diagnostic testing at age 2; 7 years or 31 months of age is described below.

The Physical Domain

Standardized Test Results

Jamie scored within normal limits for his chronological age on the Peabody Developmental Motor Scales (Folio and Fewell 1990). His age equivalency scores for gross and fine motor skills were 35 and 31 months, respectively. No neuromotor difficulties were reported.

The Verbal-Motor Production Assessment for Children (VMPAC) (Hayden and Square 1999) yielded the following scores as shown in Figure 10.4: global motor control, 85%; focal oral motor control, 32%; sequencing, 15%; connected speech and language, 22%; and speech characteristics, 57%. These scores ranked below the 5th percentile for Jamie's age group in all areas except global motor control. The modality scores, which indicate speech production accuracy under different sensory input conditions, revealed 17% speech production accuracy with only auditory input, 27% with added visual input, and 63% with added tactile input.

The Motor Speech Hierarchy

Figure 10.2 supports the following clinical profile: Stages 1 and 2: all functions achieved; Stage 3: poor stability and symmetry of jaw movement observed and overexcursion of the mandible with very poor grading and bilabial closure achieved with just the movement of mandible or jaw as opposed to lips; Stage 4: syllable and surface prompting needed to engage facial muscles for lip rounding and retraction; Stage 5: complex and surface prompting needed to achieve jaw-tongue separation, otherwise no independent lingual movement was seen; Stage 6: primary difficulty in the vertical plane of movement with breakdown in combining more than one movement plane; and Stage 7: minimal prosodic disturbances observed because of timing issues with jaw control. Modality testing revealed that Jamie needed tactile information to successfully modify speech motor patterns (Figure 10.7).

General Impressions

Overall, Jamie had normal tone and well-balanced skeletal relationships for gross and fine motor development. However, unbalanced and underdeveloped speech subsystems were observed with poor motor control and overexcursion of the mandible. Poor independent use of labial-facial movements and minimal to no independent lingual productions were observed throughout his test responses.

The Cognitive-Linguistic Domain

Standardized Test Results

On the Differential Ability Scales (DAS) (Elliott 1990), a test of intellectual abilities, Jamie scored 93 (PR = 32) on General Conceptual Abilities, which includes oral subtests. His Special Non-oral Composite score was 109 (PR = 73). The 16-point difference between these two subtests was statistically significant (p < .05).

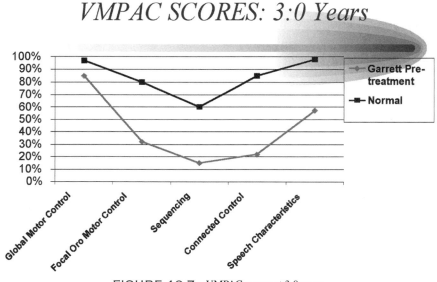

FIGURE 10.7　VMPAC scores at 3:0 years.

On the Vineland Social Maturity Scales (Doll 1947/1965), Jamie scored within the average range in all areas except communication. His standard score of 69 was ranked at the 2nd percentile for his age group. Motor skills were the strongest at the 88th percentile.

On the Preschool-Language Skills-3, PLS-3 (Zimmerman et al 1992), Jamie scored at the 3rd percentile rank. His age equivalency score corresponded to a 1-year delay in expressive language skills.

General Observations

At times Jamie appeared unorganized and immature and could become confused or hypersensitive with poor emotional modulation. Speech production was much improved with coordinated sensory input that included tactile input. He did participate in nonspeech events and routines at home and school to moderately support his overall learning and concept development. However, Jamie needed high structure to help him organize routines for learning.

The Social-Emotional Domain

Jamie indicated his wants and needs by using isolated vowel strings, eye gaze, pointing, and other gestures. He relied often on adult family members to anticipate his needs and required well-defined boundaries to control choice making.

Behavior

Jamie's responses to the Burks Behavior Rating Scale (Burks 1977) revealed excessive withdrawal, poor anger control, and lack of social conformity. Jamie was very withdrawn and fearful with peers and adults who were not his caregivers. His mother was his main communicator and facilitator. Failure and fear of failure were judged to be mitigating factors. Jamie's parents reported that he was "very aware" of his difficulty with speech production and that he has become less easily engaged in social interactions; he did not play with other children, and his temper tantrums had increased.

SUMMARY IMPRESSIONS

Given an overall evaluation of Jamie's performance within PROMPT's conceptual framework, Jamie's main problems appeared to result from an undeveloped and unbalanced speech motor system that reinforced a strong attractor state; that is, the jaw overrode a normal developmental progression towards independent movement of other oral structures.

The major domains focused on for treatment were the physical-sensory domain (the speech-motor subsystems only) and secondarily, the social-emotional domain. The communication focus was targeted at social-interactive routines and early academic behaviors.

TREATMENT GOALS AND PROCEDURES

Treatment Goals and Schedule

Given the aforementioned information from Jamie's assessment, the following motor speech treatment goals were identified for him:

1. Reduce jaw excursion.
2. Increase upper lip function for independent bilabial movement, rounding and retraction.
3. Close syllables using bilabials, and anterior lingual movement.
   a. Develop new motor schemas and motor-phoneme templates.
   b. Develop initial lexicon for use in routines and events.
4. Develop socially interactive routines that could be used with family and peers; namely, routines that require turn taking and use of phrases and sentences that embed the newly developed lexicon for speech production in structured events.

Jamie's therapy consisted of 22 individual sessions of approximately 55 minutes each over 1 year. Approximately 8 sessions were spent on Phase 1 treatment and 7 sessions each were spent on Phases 2 and 3 before discharge.

Treatment Phases and Activities

Given the chosen social-interaction focus, all phases of treatment were directed towards Jamie's need for understanding boundaries, developing competence, social interaction, emotional stability, and being able to use his speech to engage others. His strengths in overall physical-sensory systems and cognition meant that these domain areas could be used toward the development of social interactions and speech motor control. Sessions were developed to allow him to experience success in creating new motor schemas while engaging in activities he could use with his family and peers.

In treatment Phase 1, considerable time was spent in learning how to produce accurate target movements, which led to recognizable functional word forms. This included a brief warm-up of massed practice at Stages 3 and 4. These were targeted to control vertical and horizontal plane movements using different targeted motor-phonemes and syllables. Distributed practice included these targeted syllables in socially reinforcing games or activities, such as Mister Potato Head, Puppy Racers, simple concentration or matching games, or puzzles. A take-home book with the syllables/words used in each activity were specified and used by the family in such games or other appropriate situations. As well, all sessions were videotaped, and Jamie and his parents watched his session at least once during the interval between treatment sessions. Jamie's parents reported that he loved to watch the videos and would regularly go over his "book" with his parents and older brother.

As Jamie progressed to Phase 2, motor-phoneme practice "warm-up's" continued, but the emphasis was now placed on combining two planes of movement while increasing his comprehension and production of age-appropri-ate concepts and early grammatical forms. These forms were then used to encode and produce language in more complex routines and activities. For example, expectations of the carrier phrases used and numbers of pairs matched were expanded as in the pair's concentration game. Earlier productions, such as "bee" were now expanded to "I have bee, (they) match." Closing syllables, while increasing intelligibility, also provided more subsystems interaction (Stages 3, 4, and 5) and increased the available number of words that could be used in various combinations.

Social interactions in routines and game playing, book reading, and early academic material (numbers and letters) were instituted in Phase 3. At this point, only specific word forms or motor-phonemes still needing refinement were targeted for "warm-up" practice. Later in this phase, Jamie would ask for prompted "help" with certain words, or his parents would bring in words that had given him trouble within the context of phrases. If the expectations for these productions were too high, usually the word would be placed within an easier "phrase" form. For example, "I'm going skating tomorrow" (where skating was the "target") was changed to "I go skate tomorrow." When spe-cific word forms were not the issue, grammatical complexity became the focus. By this phase, Jamie understood routines, was able to select (from three or four) games he wanted to play, and could organize and complete tasks with less structure or "scaffolding." At discharge, Jamie was able to "monitor" and usually "self-correct" his own productions. He displayed good organizational and self-regulating behavior, could not wait to share what was significant for him, and would initiate conversations and social-play with neighbors and classmates.

POST-TREATMENT PROFILE OR OUTCOMES

Follow-up results from the VMPAC showed that Jamie's speech production improved with PROMPT treatment. When dismissed, he performed at age-appropriate levels in all areas except focal oral motor control, which was at 70% (or the 5th percentile, cf. Figures 10.4 and 10.5). Still, this score was higher than his pretreatment score at 32%. The scores also improved from 85% to 95% for global motor control; 15% to 78% for sequencing; 22% to 77% for connected speech and language control; and 57% to 85% for speech characteristics. Jamie's speech production accuracy after PROMPT treatment was still the best (84% accuracy) when enhanced by tactile input. However, production was accurate more than half the time even when just an auditory model was given (55%) or a visual model was given (63%) (Figure 10.8).

When dismissed at 3:11 years of age, Jamie performed within normal limits on formal and informal tests in receptive and expressive speech and language.

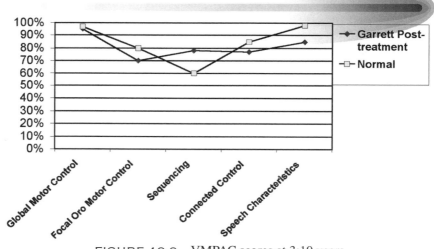

FIGURE 10.8   VMPAC scores at 3:10 years.

When asked to evaluate his progress and describe how PROMPT therapy had helped Jamie, his parents wrote,

"Jamie speaks better than he ever did, before receiving PROMPT therapy. Before we could barely understand him, now we understand 90% of his communication and he is constantly improving. This has led to greater harmony in our family. Frankly, we don't know what we would have done without it. Jamie now is less frustrated which has lead to better behavior. Before PROMPT therapy he would have temper tantrums that lasted on average about an hour each day. After PROMPT these tantrums have stopped and his behavior has improved remarkably. Jamie has also developed better socialization skills. Before PROMPT he was shy and withdrawn. After therapy he is much more outgoing. He is now a social butterfly with many friends. He has become much more independent."

FINAL REMARKS

Jamie's case illustrates how PROMPT's framework conceptualizes speech production within the context of multiple domains of function. It also stresses how motor speech subsystem development/rebalancing and touch can be used to enhance sensory input for achieving speech production accuracy and social interaction.

In a child with PDD, the framework of PROMPT is used similarly. However, the communication focus will directly alter the choice of words used and the environments in which the words may be used. Many children with PDD may have normal peripheral motor ability, but their sensory and integrative systems are disordered. In these children, the links between the sensory-motor and cognitive-linguistic areas are even more critical to establish. Ultimately helping them to develop more normal oral language is the goal and ensuring that all alternative communication approaches are used to support social interaction and communication with parents and caregivers are the goals. (See descriptions of ongoing research on page 7.)

As clinicians and researchers, we owe it to our clients to explore all sensory systems and their interactions when seeking to develop speech, language, and cognition. Recognition of the dynamic interconnectedness among these domains, especially those concerned with motor, language, and social development should not be underestimated. In short, it is time that we begin to develop methods of treatment for speech production disorders that merge the motor and language aspects. Such an integration is required to achieve our highest and most valued ability; namely, the ability to orally express ourselves and develop true human interconnectedness with others.

REFERENCES

Abbs, J.H. 1988. Neurophysiological processes of speech motor control. In Lass, N.J. (Editor), *Handbook of Speech-Language Pathology and Audiology*. pp. 154–170. Toronto: B.C. Decker.

Affolter, F., and Bischofberger, W. 2000. *Nonverbal Perceptual and Cognitive Processes in Children with Language Disorders*. Mahwah, NJ: Erlbaum.

Ayres, J. 1974. *The Development of Sensory Integrative Theory and Practice: A Collection of Works of A. Jean Ayers*. Rockville, MD: The American Occupational Therapy Association, Inc.

Bates, E. 1976. *Language, and Context*. New York: Academic Press.

Bates, E., and MacWhinney, B. 1987. Competition, variation, and language learning. In MacWhinney, B. (Editor), *Mechanisms of Language Acquisition*. pp. 157–194. Hillsdale, NJ: Lawrence Erlbaum.

Bellezza, J.K. 1987. Mnemonic devices and memory schemes. In McDaniel, M.A., and Pressley, M. (Editors), *Imagery and Related Mnemonic Processes*. pp. 34–55. Springer-Verlag: New York.

Bloom, L. 1996. *The Integration of Expression into the Stream of Everyday Activity*. A lecture presented in the Symposium on Movement and action: Links to intelligent behavior. Michigan State University.

Bloom, L., and Tinker, E. 2001. The intentionality model and language acquisition: Engagement, effort, and the essential tension in development. *Monographs of the Society for Research in Child Development*, 66, 1–91.

Bobath, B. 1971. *Abnormal Postural Reflex Activity Caused by Brain Lesions*. London: Heinman.

Bobath, K. 1980. *A Neurolophysiological Basis for the Treatment of Cerebral Palsy*, 2nd ed., Philadelphia: J.B. Lippincott.

Bobath, K., and Bobath, B. 1972. *Cerebral palsy*. In Pearson, P.H., and Williams, C.E., (Editors), *Physical Therapy Services in the Developmental Disabilities*. Springfield, IL: Charles C. Thomas.

Bruner, J. 1977. Early social interaction and language acquisition. In Schaffer, R. (Editor), *Studies in Mother-Infant Interaction*. pp. 271–289. New York: Academic Press.

Burks, H.F. 1977. *Behavior Rating Scale* 12th printing. Los Angeles, CA: Western Psychological Services.

Cholewiak, R., and Collins, A. 1991. Sensory and physiological bases of touch In Heller, M.A. and Schiff, W. (Editors), *The Psychology of Touch. pp. 23–60.* Mahwah, NJ: Erlbaum.

Chumpelik Hayden, D. 1984. The PROMPT system of therapy: Theoretical framework and applications for developmental apraxia of speech. *Semin Speech Lang* 5:139–156.

Chumpelik Hayden, D.A., and Sherman, J. 1980. Using a tactile approach in the acquisition of functional oral communication in a non-verbal, eight year old autistic child: A case study. Unpublished research.

Chumpelik Hayden, D.A., and Sherman, J. 1983. The efficacy of the PROMPT system in treatment of developmental apraxia. Unpublished research.

Doll, E.A. 1947/1965. *Vineland Social Maturity Scales.* Circle Pines, MN: American Guidance Service Incorporated.

Elliott, C.D. 1990. *Differential Ability Scales.* San Antonio, TX: Psychological Corporation.

Fletcher, S.G. 1992. *Sensorimotor Foundations for Speech Articulation: A Physiological Approach* pp. 17–54. San Diego, CA: Singular Publishing Group.

Fogel, A., and Thelen, E. 1987. Development of early expressive and communicative action: Reinterpreting the evidence from a dynamic systems perspective. *Devel Psychol* 23:647–761.

Folio, R., and Fewell, R.R. 1990. *Peabody Developmental Motor Scales* 2000. Austin, TX: Pro-Ed.

Gallagher, T. 1991. A retrospective look at clinical pragmatics. In Gallagher, T. (Editor), *Pragmatics of language: Clinical Practice Issues* pp. 1–10. San Diego, CA. : Singular Publishing Group.

Gracco, V.L. 1990. Characteristics of speech as a motor control system. In Hammond, G.E. (Editor), *Cerebral Control of Speech and Limb Movements.* pp. 3–28. North Holland: Elsevier.

Graesham , F.M., and Elliott, S.N. 1990. *Social Skills Rating System.* Circle Pines, MN: American Guidance Service.

Green, J.R., Moore, C., Higashikawa, M., and Steeve, R.W. 2000. The physiologic development of speech motor control: Lip and jaw coordination. *J Speech Lang Hearing Res* 431:239–256.

Guyton, A.C. 1971. *Textbook of Medical Physiology.* Philidelphia: W.B. Saunders Company.

Hadley, P.A., and Rice, M.L. 1993. Parental judgments of preschoolers' speech and language development: A resource for assessment and IEPplanning. *Sem Speech Lang* 14, 278–288.

Hartup, W. 1983. Peer interaction and the behavior development of the individual client. In Damon, W. (Editor), *Social Personality Development: Essays on the Growth of the Client.* New York: W.W. Norton.

Hayden, D. 1985. *Introduction to PROMPT: Technique Manual.* Santa Fe, NM: PROMPT Institute, Inc.

Hayden, D. 1986. Motor-speech, apraxia, phonological disorders: Diagnosis and Treatment. A paper presented at Overlook Hospital, Summit, New Jersey.

Hayden, D., and Square, P. 1994. Motor speech treatment hierarchy: A systems approach. In Square, P.A. (Editor) Developmental apraxia of speech: Intervention. *Clin Commun Disord* 43:162–174.

Hayden, D. 1999. *PROMPT Certification Manual.* Santa Fe, NM: PROMPT Institute, Inc.

Hayden, D., and Square, P. 1999. *VMPAC Manual,* San Antonio, TX: The Psychological Corporation.

Head, H. 1926. *Aphasia and Kindred Disorders of Speech,* vols. 1 and 11. London, England: Cambridge University Press.

Jackson, J.H. 1958. Evolution and dissolution of the nervous system. In Taylor, J. (Editor), *Selected Writings of John Hughlings Jackson* (vol. 2, pp. 45–75). London, England: Staples Press. (Original work published in 1884).

Kaas, J.H. 1991. Plasticity of sensory and motor maps in adult mammals. *Annu Rev Neurosci* 14:137–167.

Kaas, J. 1996. January. Functional Implications of Plasticity and Reorganization in the Somatosensory System of Developing and Adult Primates. An invited lecture presented in the Symposium on Movement and Action at Michigan State University, E. Lansing, MI.

Kelso, J., and Tuller, B. 1983. "Compensatory Articulation" under condition of reduced afferent information: A dynamic formulation. *J Speech Hear Res* 26:217–224.

Kent, R.D. 1981. Sensorimotor aspects of speech development. In Aslin, R., Alberts, J., and Peterson, M. (Editors), *Development of Perception*. pp. 161–189. New York: Academic Press.

Kent, R.D. 1992, The biology of phonological development. In Ferguson, C.A., Menn, L., and Stoel-Gammon, C. (Editors), *Phonological Development*. pp. 65–191. Baltimore, MD: York Press.

Kent, R.D. 1997. Gestural phonology: Basic concepts and applications in speech- language pathology. In Ball, M.J., and Kent, R.D. (Editors), *The New Phonologies: Development in Clinical Linguistics*. pp 247–268. San Diego: Singular Publishing Group.

Love, R.J. 1992. *Childhood Motor Speech Disability*. New York: Macmillian Publishing Company.

Menn, L. 1982. Development of articulatory, phonetic, and phonological capabilities. In Butterworth, B. (Editor), *Language Production*. Volume 2, pp. 3–50. NewYork: Academic Press.

Miller, J., and Chapman, R. 1993. *SALT: Systematic Analysis of Language Transcripts*. Madison, WI: Language Analysis Laboratory, Waisman Center, University of Wisconsin—Madison.

Mountcastle, V.B. and Powell, T.P.S. 1959. Neural Mechanisms subserving cutaneous sensibility with special reference to the role of afferent inhibition in sensory perception and discrimination. *Bulletin of the Johns Hopkins Hospital* 105:201–232.

Mysak, E.D., 1968. *Neuroevolutional Approach to Cerebral Palsy and Speech*. New York: Teachers College Press.

Nelson, K. 1986. *Event knowledge: Structure and Function in Development*, Hillsdale, NJ: Erlbaum.

Piaget, J. 1954. *The Construction of Reality in the Child*. New York: Basic Books original work published in 1937.

Piaget, J. 1964. Development and learning. In Ripple, R.E., and Rockcastle, V.N. (Editors), *Piaget Rediscovered*. pp. 7–20. Ithaca, NY: Cornell School of Education Press.

Schmidt, R.A. 1975. A schema theory of discrete motor skill learning. *Psychol Rev* 82:225–260.

Square, P.A., Chumpelik Hayden D., Morningstar, D., and Adams, S.G. 1986. Efficacy of the PROMPT system of therapy for the treatment of apraxia of speech: A follow-up investigation. In Brookshire, R.H. (Editor), *Clinical Aphasiology: Conference Proceedings*. pp. 221–226. Minneapolis, MN: BBK Publisher.

Square, P.A., Hayden, D.A., Ciolli, L. and Wilkins, C. 1999. Speech motor performances of children with moderate to severe articulation disorders. Paper presented at the American Speech-Language Conference, San Francisco, CA.

Square, P.A., Goshulak, D., Bose, A., and Hayden, D. 2000. The effects of articulatory subsystem treatment for developmental neuromotor speech disorders. Paper presented at the *Tenth Biennial conference on Motor Speech Disorders and Speech Motor Control*, San Antonio, TX.

Square-Storer, P. and Hayden, D. 1989. Prompt treatment. In Square-Storer, P. (Editor), *Acquired Apraxia of Speech in Aphasic Adults*. New York: Taylor and Francis.

Stichfield, S., and Younge, E.H. (1938). *Children with Delayed and Defective Speech: Motorkinesthetic Factors and Their Training*. pp. 95–163. Stanford, CA: Stanford University Press.

Strand, E.A. 1992. The integration of speech motor control and language formulation in process modules of acquisition. In Chapman, R.S. (Editor), *Processes in Language Acquisition and Disorders*. pp. 86–107. Philadelphia, PA: Mosby Yearbook.

Thelen, E. 1995. Motor development: A new synthesis. *Am Psychol* 50:79–95.

Thelen, E. 1991. Motor aspects of emergent speech: A dynamical systems approach. In Krasnegor, N.A., and Rumaugh, D. (Editors), *Biological and Behavioral Determinants of Language Development* pp. 339– 362. Hillsdale, N.J.: Erlbaum.

Vygotsky, L.S. 1978. *Mind in Society: the Development of Higher Psychological Processes*. Cambridge: Harvard University Press.

Wetherby, A. 1991. Profiling pragmatic abilities in the emerging language of young children. In Gallagher, T. (Editor), *Pragmatics of Language: Clinical Practice Issues*. pp. 249–281. San Diego, CA: Singular Publishing Group.

Zimmerman, I.L., Steiner, V.G., and Pond, R.E. 1992. *Preschool Language Scale – 3*. San Antonio, TX: Psychological Corporation.

11

THE MULTIPLE FACES OF CLINICAL EFFICACY

IDA J. STOCKMAN, PHD

Any intervention may help someone at some time under a given set of conditions. The task for scientists and clinicians alike is to figure out what works predictably across a broad range of patients in many contexts and holds up across time. This level of predictability cannot be reached without good science and theoretical models to figure out whether or how they work on a practical level. However, figuring out how they work may be less straightforward than we think. The goal of this chapter is to describe the various ways that the efficacy of clinical intervention can be demonstrated with an eye toward revealing the range of issues that can influence such outcomes.

WHAT IS CLINICAL EFFICACY?

Simply put, clinical efficacy is a judgment that an intervention does what it claims. In other words, it is a judgment about the validity or worth of an intervention. We should expect the efficacy outcomes to apply to a group of people and not just to a single person. When a physician prescribes us medicine for a stomach ache, we expect to get better. The physician is on better footing in predicting whether a given medicine will make us better if the medicine has helped patients with similar complaints in the past. Similarly, the more generalizable an intervention and its outcomes are to different people, the stronger the claim to efficacy can be. Simply put, measuring efficacy is how we **legitimize** a particular intervention.

WHY CARE ABOUT DEMONSTRATING CLINICAL EFFICACY?

There are at least three reasons to care about demonstrating the efficacy of any intervention approach: (1) funding of clinical programs, (2) gaining community respect, and (3) advancing scientific knowledge (Stockman 2001a). See also Craeghead (1999).

FUNDING OF CLINICAL PROGRAMS

Funding is a primary issue when children present with severe deficits requiring long-term intervention, as is the case for those with PDD. Clinical services can be expensive (Baum 1998; Hartley 1995a). One reason is that the children with PDD more often than not receive services in multiple areas that routinely include occupational therapy, physical therapy, speech therapy, and special education, in addition to any medical health related services. Who pays for all these services? In the United States, clinical services are very costly unless received in public schools. For private care, insurance companies can place stringent boundaries on how much intervention will be paid, if they pay at all. Insurance companies may not cover intervention services for PDD because of the need for sustained financial support and the difficulty of determining when someone is "cured." To reduce the costs of health care in the United States, clinicians are being required to get patients in and out of treatment quickly (Hartley 1995a). Fortunately, there is a 2 year moratorium on implementing the legislative mandate to allocate no more than $1590 per year for combined speech and physical therapy services to Medicare patients. Practitioners will be on much stronger footing if they can show that an intervention makes a child better (Baum 1998).

Resource needs pertain to more than the direct cost of therapy services. We also must consider the resources required for caregivers to take a child to therapy even when insurance pays for the services. There can be hidden costs in time and energy just to get a child to a service agency. This cost becomes all the more real when we consider the specialization of service delivery. A child may have to go to one place for occupational and physical therapy, a different place for speech therapy, a different place for medical care, and so on.

GAINING COMMUNITY RESPECT

Community respect is another reason to care about demonstrating efficacy. The various forms of media in contemporary society make information about new interventions abundantly available. Community respect is gained when the public trust is not violated by bogus claims about service outcomes. This amounts to professional accountability (O'Toole et al 1998) and ethics.

Community respect nets the professional reputation that can lead to more resources for doing clinical work. For instance, it translates into referrals from other professionals and any financial gain associated with that. If a field is associated with reputable outcomes, then families and professionals will seek out the intervention when there is need.

Community respect also translates into maintaining a supply of human resources to do the clinical services. It should be easier to recruit new professionals to a field that has proven the value of its services than to one that has not.

ADVANCING SCIENTIFIC KNOWLEDGE

Advancing scientific knowledge is yet another reason to be concerned with demonstrated clinical efficacy. Such research is viewed here as a tool of self-reflection in applied professional disciplines. Siegel (1975) observed that accountability is ". . .a call to self-evaluation and honest appraisal" (p. 796). Science can be a tool for evaluating and improving clinical services. This is because science embraces methods for testing ideas in rigorous and controlled ways. As a result, we should learn more about what we are doing so that services can be modified to improve the well-being of those whom we serve.

ISSUES IN DEMONSTRATING EFFICACY: TYPES OF OUTCOMES

We often discuss clinical efficacy as if it is a single truth about a given intervention. The issues surrounding demonstrated efficacy, however, are not simple ones. Numerous factors are relevant to judging whether a given approach is efficacious (Olswang et al 1990). These factors relate as much to the kind of outcomes expected as to the strength of evidence to support claims of efficacy. In the discussion that follows, I focus first on the selection of efficacy outcomes and then on sources of evidence for validating efficacy outcomes.

Intervention approaches can be chosen because of the particular types of outcomes (e.g., behavioral changes) they claim to offer as well as the type and/or amount of resources available to obtain desired outcomes. The choice of intervention outcomes reflects value biases. Such biases **implicitly** reflect cultural values and expectations. The possibility to develop behavior within the range of normal variability is one obvious reason to promote one or another intervention. But defining this goal is less straightforward than one might think. People with normal developmental histories can vary widely in their knowledge about the world and what they can do in it. What specifically is it about the wide range of normal behaviors that is to be valued? Is it a set of particular skills or behaviors (which vary among typically developing children even at the same age)? If so, which set? Is the learning of a specific set of skills or behaviors valued equally with learning something fast or flexibly or with learning something about the process of learning in the sense of learning how to learn? The broader question is on what basis can one particular set of behavioral outcomes be privileged over others?

ACHIEVING FUNCTIONAL OUTCOMES

Conventional interventions typically focus on the behaviors or skills that are missing or absent in a child's system. But this is not necessarily an easy solution when working with a clinical group that has so many deficits to be treated. Achieving normalcy is not a realistic goal for some of these children. Their learning potential may be too compromised by a flawed biological mechanism, brain plasticity not withstanding. In the context of communicative disorders, Goldstein (1990) argued that while achieving normalcy would provide a convincing outcome for the skeptical consumer or scientist, this expectation ". . .fails to consider the sometime profound differences among clients before intervention. . ." (p. 92). He stated further that clients and their caregivers should be satisfied with improved functioning even if the client falls short of normal functioning.

So short of expecting entirely normal behavior, however defined, we often settle for achieving functional outcomes. This means that an intervention must demonstrate not only some sort of learning gain, but the learning gains must be relevant to performing in the real world (Hartley 1995a, 1995b). In other words, the observed outcomes must have ecological value.

While functional outcomes have become valued in judging the worthiness of intervention for any clinical population, not just the PDD population (Enderby and Emerson 1995), we must consider that a continuum of possibilities defines what it means to be functional. The requirements for being functional at home are not likely to be the same as those for school and work, even when competence with daily life skills are used broadly as the outcome measure. For example, functionality can be judged by whether learned skills or behaviors are performed independently or with varying degrees of help or support. The following discussion considers other values that an intervention regimen could be held to but that are seldom discussed.

ACHIEVING GENERALIZABLE OUTCOMES

For persons with multiple deficits, a given intervention might be valued if it facilitates adaptive or flexible performance, for example, the ability to perform or act in a wide range of contexts as opposed to a restricted context. This latter sense of a valued outcome is closely allied with still another potential outcome value, namely whether an intervention teaches patients how to learn on their own and/or compensate for the deficits (Hartley 1995b). The latter outcome can be justified by the argument that no clinical intervention, however good it may be, will teach children everything they will ever need to know across a life span of living and learning. It also may not be realistic to expect a "cure," even if the availability of human and financial resources were not an issue. Therefore, teaching children with PDD how to bootstrap their way to continued learning after intervention could be a highly valued outcome in addition to their learning about how to predict and circumvent difficult situations.

ACHIEVING BREADTH IN OUTCOMES

Finally, value can be vested in the scope of intervention outcomes, that is, whether there is a single outcome as opposed to multiple ones. Conceivably, a given intervention can be highly efficacious for modifying one or two behaviors or teaching one or two skills. But this limited outcome may not be valued for working with a clinical population like PDD, which presents with so many deficit areas.

The scope of intervention also includes the number and types of clinical cases for whom it is effective, and whether the intervention is equally effective across the life span of the same person (children with PDD do grow up to become adults). This issue gets at the possibility that a single intervention approach may not be efficacious for everybody at every stage of life. For example, an intervention may be more effective for children than adults.

ACHIEVING MEASURABLE OUTCOMES

Finally, aside from focusing on which behavioral outcomes are desired, we must stay tuned to the fact that our observations of selected outcomes will be influenced by whether they can be adequately measured. For example, standardized test scores may underestimate expected outcomes. Nonstandardized measures also can be problematic. For example, the validity of the mean length of utterance (MLU) as an index of language growth has been used as a measure of grammatical achievement for a long time now. But its validity is being seriously questioned (Eisenberg et al 2001).

EASE OF IMPLEMENTATION AS AN OUTCOME VALUE

The reason to favor one intervention over another can be weighed in terms of the ease with which it can be used. Several factors influence the ease of implementation. One set of factors includes the amount and type of resources that are required to implement the intervention as well as patient and clinician access to them. For example, interventions involving intensive contact with patients (i.e., many hours of input from a lot of people) require considerable manpower resources. Such is the case for the Doman-Delacato Patterning Therapy (Delacato 1963) and for Applied Behavioral Analysis (Lovaas 1987). In one intervention study using applied behavioral analysis (Smith et al 1997), the 3;0 year old participants in the experimental group had a diagnosis of severe mental retardation and autistic features. They received 50 weeks of intervention for 2 years. Each week of intervention involved 30 hours with a professional team ". . . . consisting of 4 to 6 student therapists and a senior therapist" (p. 241). In addition, the children's parents were required to set aside 5 to 10 hours of time so that they could work along with the therapists.

Another factor influencing the ease of implementing a given intervention is whether it is consistent with a clinician and/or patient's own cultural practices and philosophical views about learning. Some professionals and parents can be discomforted by an intervention that requires children to be physically punished or requires the withdrawal of caregiver attention and privileges when children produce undesirable or maladaptive behavior. An intervention that requires children to be touched to stimulate learning can be uncomfortable as well.

Ease of implementation is influenced further by whether an intervention can be done within the scope of existing service delivery practices. A new intervention that requires existing service delivery practices to be stretched or changed a lot may not be viewed as favorably as one that does not require such accommodation. Making such a shift will be perceived more favorably, though, when it is clear that the intervention is effective in achieving desired outcomes than when it is not clear.

Finally, there is the issue of whether professionals have access to the education and training required to use an intervention. Access can be tempered by the cost of learning the therapy and the availability of personnel to teach the therapy. This is a particularly relevant issue for interventions that are not yet described in the standard textbooks for a clinical discipline.

OUTLOOK

Optimally, the most efficacious intervention is one that (1) modifies culturally valued behavior enough so that children can function adaptively in the real world; (2) modifies the behavior quickly with the least and most efficient use of human and other resources; and (3) leads to effects that hold up across time.

TYPES OF CLINICAL EFFICACY: SOURCES OF EVIDENCE

Selecting which efficacy outcomes are desired is a different issue than providing the evidence for whether an intervention actually results in the expected efficacious effects. Any new approach is viewed with some skepticism. People often ask, how do you know that the therapy works or should work? To answer this question in a way that leads to approval or affirmation, we rely on direct and indirect sources of evidence.

Direct evidence comes from systematic documentation of behavioral changes that occur in response to actually working with patients. There is powerful evidence for intervention efficacy when a child's behavior normalizes after a given intervention is applied in the moment. This kind of clinical evidence is even stronger if the intervention is theoretically motivated, and it can be corroborated by controlled clinical trials across many patients. Controlled observations in particular allow us to be more sure that an intervention effect is not due to extraneous bias, including our own wishful thinking or imagined success.

Indirect evidence is neither dispensable nor secondary to the kind of direct evidence so often appealed to (Stockman 2001b). In fact, even before trying out an intervention in the first place, there should be a sound reason to do so. That is, the intervention should make sense in terms of what is known about the way people learn and develop. Research that supports the theoretical assumptions of the therapy implies by logical argument that a clinical application is at least defensible. The evidence is considered indirect because it does not actually test intervention effects. That is, no direct evidence is provided for how well an implied clinical application actually works.

A major point to be made here is that direct and indirect sources of evidence should be valued. Simply put, there is more than one way to demonstrate efficacy, even though particular ones have been privileged, namely data from controlled clinical trial studies. A narrow view of how to demonstrate efficacy can lead to the judgment that a particular intervention must be fraudulent if it does not meet with a particular type of evidence. Siegel (1975) commented that,

> "there is an implication in the demand for *accountability* that what counts in clinical service is what is countable . . . What must be avoided, however, is the corollary implication that it is only those events that are countable that are important" (p. 797).

The major point made here is that multiple ways of demonstrating efficacy fit into the evolution of our coming to know how well a particular intervention works. All measures of efficacy have strengths and limitations. An intervention will be on stronger footing, though, when its use can be defended with **multiple types of evidence** for efficacy. I now consider four ways to demonstrate efficacy, which include (1) grounded efficacy, (2) theoretical efficacy, (3) empirical efficacy, and (4) ecological efficacy. These approaches are distinguished broadly by the type of evidence required to validate them.

GROUNDED OR SITUATIONAL EFFICACY

The word *grounded* is intended to focus attention on the behavioral changes that clinicians and families can actually witness when they intervene **in a given moment to help a child** to solve a problem in therapy or in daily life. Consider a child who is trying anxiously to put on a coat when preparing to go outside to play. The child becomes more and more agitated in attempts to accomplish this goal. The child calms down when someone intervenes in the moment by physically guiding the child through the interactions so that success follows. Or, in a therapy session, a child has difficulty saying a word even while watching and listening to a clinician's auditory or visual modeled production of it. The clinician intervenes by strategically touching the relevant oral structures so that more successful production follows. We can refer to grounded efficacy when an intervention immediately changes a child's performance in ways that were not observed in the moments just before the intervention.

It is easy to imagine that clinicians and caregivers alike have witnessed such effects of intervening in the moment using many different sources of input— inputs that can include not only enhanced tactual information but also enhanced visual or auditory information. So the grounded evidence for tactual input becomes particularly compelling when it achieves the desired behavioral outcomes after a child has failed to respond to auditory verbal or visual input in that moment. The tactual input need not be facilitated by touching a child directly. Facilitation of tactual input can be indirect as when a caregiver, teacher, or clinician alters the environment during an interaction event so that the child can get the tactual input to interact on his or her own. For example, just changing a chair so that a child's feet can touch the floor to feel the stability of the environment might make all the difference to altering attention and behavior in a given moment.

Grounded efficacy must always be viewed as important because the efficacy of any intervention must be demonstrable at the reality level of clinical use and observation. Such demonstrations give a face validity to intervention. It is likely to be such moments of grounded efficacy that motivate clinicians to say that they use one or another intervention because it works. This kind of testimony to efficacy can be made regardless of whether the application has been empirically validated or not. See Kamhi's (1999) discussion of one parent's testimony to the effectiveness of using holding therapy combined with applied behavioral analysis.

There are research models that allow us to empirically test what I refer to here as "grounded efficacy." The synchronic model of demonstrating therapy effectiveness aims to explain "what treatment does at the moment of delivery. . ." (Griffer 1999, p. 397). See also the notion of "immediate outcomes" (Olswang 1990). The latter type of research focuses on what makes a good therapy session in exploring the intervention process.

As powerful as the evidence for "grounded" intervention can be, it alone is not enough to demonstrate clinical efficacy. This is especially the case when intervention outcomes are documented only in the clinical archives of video and/or written reports of clinical sessions. Such archival evidence for clinical efficacy, although not simply anecdotal or hearsay, is still limited, even when they are based on numerous clinician-patient interactions. Clinical logs of therapy sessions are not accessible to the public. The evidence for behavioral change also must be based on a clinician's uncorroborated judgment that an effect has occurred in a given session. More importantly, given a dynamic systems theoretical perspective, we can expect a given therapy session or situation to represent the confluence of many variables that could differentially influence performance besides what a clinician does to change behavior in a given moment. Such factors can include seemingly irrelevant but definitely uncontrolled variables like the time of day for the therapy, the temperature of the therapy room, the child's hunger state, and so on. So when a particular intervention works in the moment, we may not know whether the changed behavior was due only to the use of a particular intervention in the session. If we do not know why an intervention worked in the moment, then we may not be able to elicit the same effects reliably in different situations for the same child or for different children. Not knowing why can reduce intervention to trying out a variety of strategies in the moment just to see whatever will work.

Nevertheless, grounded evidence for clinical efficacy is on much better footing when (1) the same professionals and different professionals can repeatedly elicit behavioral changes using a given intervention in the moment for the same child in different situations and for different children; (2) the altered behavior reflects a sustainable learning effect over time; and (3) the use of a particular intervention in the first place is theoretically motivated. That is, clinicians can defend why a given intervention works or is likely to work in the moment. The latter basis for efficacy is discussed next.

THEORETICAL EFFICACY

Theoretical efficacy refers to the fit between clinical observations and the body of empirically derived knowledge about how people learn and develop. While no theoretical or empirical evidence for clinical efficacy is usable unless it can be translated into observable moments of changed behavior within and outside of therapy, theoretical efficacy allows us **to explain** why a particular intervention is expected to yield a certain behavioral effect. Siegel (1987) proposed that the most important question to ask of a therapy is not whether it works but whether it makes sense, given the underlying assumptions. Theoretical efficacy then provides the construct validity for an intervention. It takes the form of indirect and direct evidence for clinical efficacy.

Indirect Theoretical Support or Evidence

Indirect evidence is vested in the consistency of an intervention with the principles of human learning and developing (Stockman 2001b). For example, if action/interaction experiences are relevant to understanding human learning, then an intervention that does not allow for such experiences should have questionable theoretical efficacy. Just how critical this kind of efficacy is depends on how good a fit the theoretical model is to the reality of how people learn and develop. The two intervention frameworks (guided intervention therapy [GIT] and prompts for restructuring oral muscular phonetic targets [PROMPT]) described in this book were selected because they are guided by assumptions that fit embodied constructivist views of developing and learning, as described in Part I of this book. Fortunately, the empirical evidence for the significant role that action experiences play in development is continuing to surface. See studies of infant cognition (e.g., Booth 1998; Sommerville and Woodward 2002), children's language and cognition (Slackman 1985), and more recent studies, (Glenberg 1997; Glenberg and Robertson 2000; Glenberg and Kaschak 2002).

Direct Theoretical Support

Direct theoretical support contrasts with indirect sources of evidence. Indirect theoretical support is not guided by a particular clinical population or intervention in mind. But direct theoretical support for clinical efficacy is vested in testing one or more theoretical assumptions about a particular intervention in a controlled way. A good intervention approach should stand up to rigorous empirical testing of its basic tenets or assumptions.

Demonstrating the validity of intervention assumptions obviously is important, particularly when the use of an intervention procedure is controversial, as is the case for tactually guided input in GIT and PROMPT. In as much as tactually guided input is a unique aspect of the GIT and PROMPT intervention approaches, an important question to ask and answer is what do children learn from added tactual-kinesthetic input as opposed to just looking and listening when learning something new? This is an important issue because the tactual-kinesthetic system is often viewed as having marginal value to perceptual-cognitive development, as pointed out already in this book. The broader question is what kind of perceptual input matters to what kind of performance outcomes in experimental task manipulations?

My students and I have been investigating this issue with typical and atypical groups of children. For example, one study Mitchell-Futrell (1992) showed that children who learned novel words and nonverbal tasks in a blindfolded condition did as well as those who were sighted. They did even better than sighted children on the visual recognition task!

In another study (Stockman and Latham 2002), the typically developing 4- and 5-year-old children were not blindfolded. One group was exposed to a novel nonverbal task and to novel words after being guided through the task using all the senses that ordinarily are available (the "hands-on" condition). Another group was exposed to the same verbal and nonverbal tasks but was not allowed to touch or handle the material (observation condition). This group got visual and auditory input about what to do from a videotape of the same actions. It turns out that the "hands-on group" obtained statistically higher scores than did the observation group on the verbal and nonverbal tasks. This group difference was even stronger when the same investigative methods were applied to children with developmental difficulties. Some of the children in the latter group were in a self-contained classroom for autistically impaired children (Latham and Stockman 2002). As a group, the children with special needs who got just the auditory-visual input performed the poorest of all participants.

More recently, Carrie Luce (2003) observed 14 typically developing preschoolers. They were randomly assigned to an experimental condition involving participation in a novel "hands-on" juice-making task or in a corresponding simulated or pretend juice-making task. Participants in the real event earned better verbal and nonverbal scores than did those in the simulated condition.

Janelle Rowe (2003) showed that the performances of even normal adults on a novel task is differentially influenced by the sensory modality of input. Twenty-one male college students received instructions for doing a novel oragami task in one of three randomly assigned input conditons: (1) auditory-verbal only, (2) auditory-verbal + visual demonstration, and (3) auditory-verbal + visual-demonstration + hands on performing of the task. The latter group that received hands-on input in addition to auditory-verbal and visual input fared the best on some verbal tasks. Both groups that received additional hands-on or visual information fared significantly better than the group that got just auditory-verbal input.

In addition to behavioral evidence, Beretta (1999) showed that changes in brain activity as a result of tactual input can be inferred from using a particular evoked potential measure of brain activity. At issue in this study was the notion of passive movement or action. GIT and PROMPT intervention approaches involve guided tactual input. There is the assumption that such input is passive, and by implication, not helpful to learning. The latter assumption suggests that the brain is not stimulated in response to passive input. A counter view is that such input is helpful if the recipient is cognitively tuned to the movement goal and the recipient needs this input to achieve the goal.

In Beretta's study, three children (6 to 8 years old) with a PDD/autism diagnosis were observed in a research laboratory using an EEG measure of brain activity known as *contingent negative variation* (CNV). CNV responses have been correlated with attention in learning. The children were exposed to simple novel and non-novel tasks in manually guided and unguided conditions. A strong CNV response, which matched the response criteria used in the study, was elicited in the most severe participant in the guided condition for novel and non-novel responses. Other participants showed a CNV response to at least one of the conditions, and electrical activity was greater for novel than the non-novel tasks. One conclusion from this study is that the brain does respond to manually guided input.

Such studies, although pilot in nature, are useful for developing rigorous empirical studies of action performances in development. Nevertheless, theoretical support for efficacy, rigorous or not, can go only so far. One reason is that the empirical validation or manipulation of an isolated intervention principle in a laboratory context is not like the dynamics of clinical intervention in real situations. The reality of applying any intervention in real-world terms is that factors other than the particular ones manipulated in a laboratory experiment become relevant to whether a child improves or not. These extraneous factors include the uncontrollable and even unknown ones that can differentially influence an outcome, for example, how much ambient noise or other distractions may exist in the intervention environment, and the fact that children go home and back to their classrooms between experimental manipulations. So it is understandable why the empirical evidence from clinical trials becomes so important.

EXPERIMENTAL CLINICAL TRIALS

Clinical trials refer to the actual implementation of an intervention in a real-world context They provide the kind of evidence that often is regarded as the *sine que non* or gold standard for empirically judging clinical efficacy. This is the case even though no intervention should be applied without grounded evidence of behavioral changes in the actual moments of intervening. Nor should an intervention lack theoretical backing, either direct or indirect, for applying a particular intervention in the moment.

Why do we need clinical trials? We need clinical trials because they test the force or effectiveness of all the factors coming together in a real-world application of an intervention approach in a more or less controlled way. So they are a better fit to the reality of how therapy gets done in the real world than are the isolated experimental manipulations of a particular intervention principle in a laboratory study. Clinical trials can empirically validate in a more or less controlled way whether an intervention actually induces change when it is applied and whether one intervention is better than another.

Nonetheless, clinical trial studies are not uniform in the type of evidence they yield. The evidence can vary depending on the scope of the intervention and the type of research designs used to obtain evidence (Fey 1990).

Scope of Intervention

Intervention studies can test the efficacy of either a specific intervention strategy or a whole intervention program or package. The former approach seems to be used more often, probably because the research is easier to do. But Fey (1990) pointed out that a focus on a single procedure or "procedural complex" can yield limited evidence for efficacy. Such an isolated experimental manipulation does not reflect holistically the scope of intervention procedures used by most clinicians to treat even a single child. Therefore, efficacy outcomes may be more artificial than real when studied in isolation of what else goes on in an intervention program.

Other research studies focus on the efficacy of using particular intervention programs or packages. Such a field study also can have limitations. Fey (1990) pointed out that the outcomes of such programs can be compromised so much by methodological weaknesses in controlling variables (e.g., subject selection and implementation procedures) that it can be difficult to sort out ". . .which aspects of the approach were essential to obtaining the effect." (p. 36).

Type of Research Design Used

Irrespective of whether a single intervention procedure or program is investigated, the empirical evidence can be obtained by doing either group or single subject comparisons, each approach offering different types of evidence for an intervention effect (Siegel and Young 1987; Baum 1998).

Independent Group Comparisons

When this experimental design is used, one group gets the focal intervention of interest, and another "control" group gets a different intervention or none at all. Before intervention begins, the comparison groups ideally should be matched on performance variables that can differentially influence the outcomes and then should be randomly assigned to an intervention group. After the intervention, the groups should be compared again on the same or equivalent measures used before the intervention. When the pre-intervention and post-intervention performances are compared on whatever behavioral outcomes are tested, the investigator hopes that the focal intervention group has made significant gains between the pre-test and post-test measurement phases, and that these gains are larger than those observed for the "no intervention" and/or alternative comparison groups.

This approach is classic and well respected even though it too has limitations. One has to make sure that the groups are identical on extraneous control variables that could differentially affect intervention outcome like the experimental or manipulated intervention is expected to do. But group equivalence can be hard to achieve with severely disordered children who present variable patterns of deficits and strengths as well as clinical intervention histories.

Furthermore, when intervention is extended across different sessions, we must consider that children do go home at night. They can have learning experiences outside of the therapy sessions that could impact intervention outcomes in a study. The researcher cannot know or control all such extraneous factors. Not unsurprisingly, then, there can be more within group variability on the targeted outcome measures than is desired. Thus, even when a significant intervention effect is obtained in the desired direction, one still must be cautious when arguing that the effect was due just to the particular intervention offered in the few minutes of a child's day. One group may be better than another because of uncontrolled (maybe unidentified) variables that were not under investigative control.

Single Subject Comparisons

This approach is appealing not only because it comes even closer to how therapy is implemented, but it also aims to neutralize the confounding effect of individual variability on an intervention outcome. It does so by using each participant as his or her own control. The investigator compares the pre-intervention and post-intervention scores for an individual participant, as opposed to a group of participants. In multiple baseline designs, a single participant performs at comparably low levels on multiple skills, for example, skills 1, 2, 3, 4, and 5a before intervention. Then intervention focuses on just one skill at a time. After a period of intervention with that skill, the postintervention trials ideally should show changed effects for just that skill worked on in therapy. In the same time period, the other low skills, which were not treated, should remain at the same low baseline level, as they were not targeted in the intervention. At Time 2, a new skill (still at baseline performance) is targeted while the first treated skill is expected to remain at or near its postintervention levels. Therefore it can be claimed more definitively that an outcome is due to the intervention as opposed to extraneous factors that would have been constant for the same participant (Ingham 1990). An especially strong case can be made for an intervention effect if a control group shows no learning effect as well.

So what is limiting about an approach that seems as optimal in its control features as the single subject design of clinical trial studies? By focusing on the learning of a single prespecified skill in the intervention, we might not observe the emergence of other skills or, worse, claim that no effect was observed, if the particular isolated skill focused on remained unchanged. The strength of a homologous intervention approach like GIT is that multiple skills are expected to emerge for the same child by working at the "root" of development. PROMPT intervention is also expected to yield outcomes that were not targeted directly in the intervention. It is reasonable to expect the same brain to generalize a new skill to other skills not targeted in the intervention. So issues of treatment interference or carryover effects from one skill to the next are among the reasons why single-subject designs are not well suited to determining whether one intervention is better than another (Ingham 1990). Differential intervention effects observed for different interventions given to the same child must be tempered by the difficulty of equating the different behaviors to be taught using each type of intervention. Therefore, the observation that one intervention is or is not better than another one must be cautiously viewed when the data are based on single-subject designs. For example, see Dodd and Bradford's (2000) comparison of PROMPT intervention with the Phonological Process and Core Word approaches using three participants in a single-subject design.

When all is said and done, the measurable gains that do occur using either a single subject or group comparative approach need not make consumers feel good about an intervention. This will be the case if the reported gains with intervention cannot be translated into perceivable changes in real-world behavior (ecological effects). Consumer satisfaction is too often omitted from discussions of efficacy. Yet, it is important in judging whether a particular intervention is viable or not, as discussed next.

ECOLOGICAL EFFICACY

Controlled empirical studies of efficacy are likely to be most valued when the effects of an intervention translate into what ordinary people can notice and respect about behavioral changes. Clinical efficacy in this context refers to consumer satisfaction or to what others refer to as social validity (Goldstein 1990). Goldstein, quoting Hayes and Haas (1998), stated that social evaluation is "a humble, straightforward measure based on the common-sense view that important changes can be seen" (p. 90). Such evaluations include the subjective impressions or ratings of community observers (caregivers, relatives, peers, other professionals, and so on) whose observations may be neither informed nor confounded by formal training in a clinical profession field (Enderby and Emerson 1995). In the end, though, one must decide which consumers or bystanders are to be privileged in judging the validity of an intervention, especially if conflicting outcomes are observed.

Social validity assessments have become commonplace in some professional journals. Evaluation of intervention effects are based on feedback from people other than the investigators or clinicians involved. Such assessments are especially helpful when one can actually trace the source of consumer disapproval or dissatisfaction. Consumers may be asked to list what they judge to be the most important aspects of intervention. However, Goldstein (1990) pointed out that consumers are likely to rate behavior as improved when they believe that performance **will** improve with training and not whether it actually has done so.

Other factors also can influence such ratings. Wetherby et al (2001) stated that "outcome measures need to go beyond child outcomes to include family oriented outcomes. Family characteristics (e.g., socioeconomic conditions, stress, supports available) and the parent involvement in the child's development are strong predictors of a child's outcome" (p. 133).

For example, an intervention may be judged positively if it minimizes a caregiver's sense of helplessness when dealing with a child who has special needs. GIT might be favorably viewed by caregivers for just this reason. Manual guidance or prompting can lead to an immediately observable outcome when neither visual nor auditory verbal input is effective. An intervention that rids caregivers of a sense of helplessness is very powerful.

Consumer ratings are also likely to be influenced by whether a child can participate in the routines of family life. Can significant others engage interaction with the child, or provoke a child to smile or show displeasure? Perhaps this kind of efficacy is undervalued because consumer judgments can be influenced by factors other than the actual behavioral changes created by the intervention. For example, caregiver satisfaction with intervention outcomes will be influenced by their own goals for a child, realistic or not, and colored by the disappointment or pain felt when realizing that life had given them the challenge of caring for a child with special needs.

Caregivers' judgments also are likely to be influenced by resource needs and availability (both human and financial) for dealing with a child's care. Judgments about how efficacious an intervention is can have as much to do with a family's resourcefulness and expectations as it does with how well practitioners effect observable behavioral change, especially when the changes come in little steps and do not make a child suddenly normal.

Still, we cannot afford to disregard consumer satisfaction in any discussion of clinical efficacy, however subjective or biased it may be. Ideally, professionals hope that the families seek out one or another intervention because they believe and bear witness to the possibility that a particular intervention empowers them and their loved one to function more normally in their environments.

CONCLUSION

This chapter has attempted to reveal the complexity of the issues in determining the efficacy of intervention approaches. The challenge is not restricted to the usual focus on the type of evidence for efficacy. It is necessary to consider first what kinds of outcomes are possible or even desired from interventions.[1] See discussion of this point in Amiot's (1998) and Gallagher et al's (1998) studies. The conclusion here that all approaches to establishing efficacy have some limitation should be humbling. It should make us careful about dismissing an intervention out of hand just because a particular kind of efficacy has not yet been demonstrated. Even the evidence from controlled clinical research must be provisional as it reflects the particular participants and observation conditions for a given study. But the limitations of doing empirical research should lead neither to the judgment that science is to be distrusted nor to the judgment that empirical justification is unnecessary. To the contrary, efficacy must be demonstrated empirically (Apel 1999) along with all the other ways to demonstrate efficacy. To echo Jacobson et al's (1995) discussion of facilitated communication,

> "scientists-practitioners and others who prepare, train, and supervise therapists, especially, have an obligation to balance exploratory use of experimental or unproven but promising interventions with skilled application of treatment methods that conform to accepted community standards and responsible interpretation of evaluation findings . . ." (p. 762).

So it may be unrealistic to expect one or two studies to provide sufficient evidence that an intervention works or does not work. It is likely that an intervention will become most valued and accepted when its efficacy is supported by multiple sources of evidence, which more often than not must be gathered over time. Practitioners and scientists alike share responsibility for demonstrating the worthiness of intervention procedures and communicating the outcomes to the public.

REFERENCES

Amiot, A. 1998. Policy, politics, and the power of information: The critical need for outcomes and clinical trials data in policy-making in the schools. *Language, Speech, and Hearing Services in Schools* 29:245–249.

Apel, K. 1999. Checks and balances: Keeping science in our profession. *Language, Speech, and Hearing Services in Schools* 30:99–108.

Baum, H.M. 1998. Overview, definitions, and goals for ASHA's treatment outcomes and clinical trials activities (What difference do outcome data make to you?). *Language, Speech, and Hearing Services in Schools* 29:246–249.

[1] The American Speech-Language-Hearing Association has developed a national outcomes database. Clinicians from the field are encouraged to share their stories and data.

Beretta, C. 1999. Contingent negative variation (CNV) in autistic children. Michigan State University. Unpublished master's thesis.

Booth, A.E. 1998. The role of functional information in the development of concepts of objects in infancy. Unpublished doctoral dissertation, Pittsburgh: University of Pittsburgh.

Creaghead, N. 1999. Evaluating language intervention approaches: Contrasting perspectives: Prologue. *Language, Speech, and Hearing Services in Schools* 30:335–338.

Delacato, C.H. 1963. *The Diagnosis and Treatment of Speech and Reading Problems.* Springfield, IL: Charles C. Thomas.

Dodd, B., and Bradford, A. 2000. A comparison of three therapy methods for chidren with different types of developmental phonological disorder. *International Journal of Language and Communication* 35:189–209.

Eisenberg, S.L., Fersko, T.M., and Lundgren, C. 2001. The use of MLU for identifying language impairment in preschool children: A review. *Am J Speech-Lang Pathol* 10:323–342.

Enderby, P., and Emerson, J. 1995. *"Does Speech and Language Therapy Work"?: A review of the literature.* San Diego, CA: Singular Publishing Group.

Fey, M. 1990. Understanding and narrowing the gap between treatment research and clinical practice with language impaired children. In Shewan, C. (Editor). *The "Future of Science and Services" Seminar ASHA Reports* 20:31–40. Rockville, MD: American Speech-Language-Hearing Association.

Gallagher, T., Swigert, N., and Baum, H.M. 1998. Collecting outcomes data in schools: Needs and challenges. *Language, Speech, and Hearing Services in Schools* 29:250–256.

Glenberg, A.M. 1997. What memory is for? *Behav Brain Sci* 20:1–55.

Glenberg, A.M., and Robertson, D.A. 2000. Symbol grounding and meaning: A comparison of high-dimensional and embodied theories of meaning. *Journal of Memory and Language* 42:379–401.

Glenberg, A.M., and Kaschak, M.P. 2002. Grounding language in action. *Psychon Bull Rev* 9:558–565.

Goldstein, H. 1990. Assessing clinical significance. In Olswang, L.B., Thompson, C.K., Warren, S.F., and Mingheti, N.J. (Editors), *Treatment Efficacy Research in Communication Disorders.* pp. 91–103. Rockville, MD: American speech-Language-Hearing Foundation.

Griffer, M.R. 1999. Is sensory integration effective for children with language-learning disorders? A critical review of the evidence. *Language, Speech and Hearing Services in Schools* 30:393–400.

Hartley, L.L. 1995a. Developing a functional perspective. In *Cognitive – Communicative Abilities Following Brain Injury: A Functional Approach.* pp. 1–20. San Diego, CA: Singular Publishing Group.

Hartley, L.L. 1995b. Functional approaches to cognitive-communicative treatment: Laying the groundwork. In *Cognitive–Communicative Abilities Following Brain Injury: A Functional Approach.* pp.115–140. San Diego, CA: Singular Publishing Group, Inc.

Hayes, S., and Hass, J. 1988. A re-evaluation of the concept of clinical significance: Goals, methods and methodology. *Behavioral Assessment*, 10, 189–196.

Ingham, J.C. 1990. Issues of treatment efficacy: Design and experimental control. In Olswang, L.B., Thompson, C.K., Warren, S.F., and Mingheti, N.J. (Editors), *Treatment Efficacy Research in Communication Disorders.* (pp. 51–62). Rockville, MD: American Speech-Language-Hearing Foundation.

Jacobson, J.W. Mulick, J.A., and Schwartz, A.A. 1995. A history of facilitated communication: Science, pseudoscience, and antiscience. *Am Psychol* 50:750–765.

Kamhi, A.G. 1999. To use or not to use: Factors that influence the selection of new treatment approaches. *Language, Speech and Hearing Services in Schools* 30:92–98.

Latham, S., and Stockman, I. 2002, July. Novel verbal and nonverbal learning by children with special needs in embodied and non-embodied contexts. A paper presented at the *Joint Conference of the International Congress for the Study of Child Language and the Symposium on Research in Child Language Disorders*, Madison, WI.

Lovaas, O.I. 1987. "Behavioral treatment and normal educational and intellectual functioning in young autistic children." *J Consult Psychol* 35:3–9.

Luce, C.W. 2003. The effects of representational and real event contexts on verbal and nonverbal learning. A master's thesis in progress, Michigan State University.

Mauer, D.M. 1999. Issues and applications of sensory integration theory and treatment with children with language disorders, *Language, Speech and Hearing Services in Schools* 30:383–392.

Mitchell-Futrell, K. 1992. *Action verb learning in observation and manipulation contexts.* Unpublished master's thesis, Michigan State University.

Mostert, M.P. 2001. Facilitated communication since 1995: A review of published studies. *J Autism Dev Disord* 31:287–313.

Olswang, L.B. 1990. Treatment efficacy: The breadth of research. In Olswang, L.B., Thompson, C.K., Warren, S.F., and Minghetti, N.J. (Editors), *Treatment Efficacy Research in Communication Disorders.* pp. 99–103. Rockville, MD: American Speech-Language-Hearing Foundation.

Olswang, L.B., Thompson, C.K., Warren, S.F., and Minghetti, N.J. *Treatment Efficacy Research in Communication Disorders* 1990. Rockville, MD: American Speech-Language-Hearing Foundation.

O'Toole, T., Logemann, J.A., and Baum, H.M. 1998. Conducting clinical trials in the public schools. *Language, Speech and Hearing Services in Schools* 29:257–262.

Rowe, J. 2003. *Completing a novel task under different sensory imput modality conditions.* Unpublished master's thesis, Michigan State Universiy.

Siegel, G.M. 1975. The high cost of accountability. *ASHA* 17:796–797.

Siegel, G.M. 1987. The limits of science in communication disorders. *J Speech Hear Disord* 52:306–312.

Siegel, G.M., and young, M.A. 1987. Group designs in clinical research. *Speech Hear Disord* 52:194–199.

Shonkoff, J., Hauser-Cram, P., Krauss, M., and Upshur, C. 1988. Early intervention efficacy research: What have we learned and where do we go from here? *Topics in early childhood special education* 8:81–93.

Slackman, E. 1985. The effect of event structure on young children's ability to learn an unfamiliar event. Unpublished doctoral dissertation, City University of New York.

Smith, T., Eikeseth, S., Klevstrand, M., and Lovaas, O.I. 1997. Intensive behavioral treatment for preschoolers with severe mental retardation and pervasive developmental disorder. *American Journal of Mental Retardation* 102:238–249.

Sommerville, J., and Woodward, A. 2002. Learning through doing: Performing and understanding goal-directed action in infancy. A paper presented in Symposium Session 9: Hands on learning: An examination of how different embodied representations influence concept learning. *The 32nd Annual Meeting of the Jean Piaget Society: The Embodied mind and consciousness: Developmental perspectives,* Philadelphia, PA.

Stockman, I. 2001a, september. The four faces of clinical efficacy: Implications for the Affolter concept. An invited paper presented at the *Jubilaum Conference in Celebration of the 25th Anniversary of the Founding of the School and Clinic for Perceptual Disorders in St. Gallen, Switzerland.*

Stockman, I 2001b. Theoretische verbindungen zum Affolter-Behandlungskonzept in den USA. APW-Informationsblatt 6:1–48.

Stockman, I., and Latham, S. 2002, July. Novel verbal and nonverbal learning by normal children in embodied and non-embodied contexts. A paper presented at the *Joint Conference of the International Congress for the Study of Child Language and the Symposium on Research in Child Language Disorders,* Madison, WI.

Wetherby, A.M. Prizant, B.M., and Schuler, A.L. 2001. Understanding the nature of communication and language impairments. In Wetherby, A.M., and Prizant, B.M. (Editors), *Autism Spectrum Disorders: A Transactional Developmental Perspective.* Baltimore, MD: Paul Brookes.

THE EPILOGUE

12

POTENTIAL CHALLENGES TO CLINICAL PRACTICES AND RESEARCH

IDA J. STOCKMAN, PHD

In the introduction to this book, I proposed that the clinical intervention for children with pervasive developmental disorder (PDD) should be guided by a framework of learning and developing that embraces (1) daily life experience; (2) cognition as a learning process in addition to cognition as stored knowledge representations; (3) collaborative sensory input that includes tactile-kinesthetic[1] information embedded in movement and action/interaction experience; and (4) homologous modeling of skill acquisition. Part I of the book focused on how these criteria are met by theoretical perspectives broadly attuned to the principles of an embodied constructivist view of the mind.

Part II of the book described two clinical interventions (guided interaction therapy [GIT] and prompts for restructuring oral muscular phonetic targets [PROMPT]) whose principles illustrate how such a theoretical view may translate into clinical practices. GIT and PROMPT have grounded efficacy. Years of clinical work bear witness to the immediate behavioral changes that can occur in patients with tactually enhanced input when auditory and/or visual input alone are ineffective. They also have theoretical face validity given their consistency with principles of learning described in Part I of this book. Their ecological value is attested by the growing numbers of parents as well as professionals in schools, clinics, and hospitals who have sought out one or both of these approaches for intervening with "hard to treat" children in more than a half dozen countries. Although more controlled clinical trials data are needed

---

[1] Throughout Chapter 12, the term *tactile-kinesthetic* is used synonymously with the word *tactual* to refer to dynamic or active touch, which combines the tactile sense with the sense of moving (Affolter and Bischofberger 2000, p. 7).

and are planned to validate their claims empirically, both interventions can potentially challenge some conventional intervention practices.

This chapter has three goals. First, I identify how GIT and PROMPT are alike and different. Second, I discuss how they may challenge conventional clinical practices with PDD. Finally, I single out issues that can inform research on PDD and its clinical management.

COMPARISON OF GIT AND PROMPT INTERVENTIONS

GIT AND PROMPT IN PARALLEL

GIT and PROMPT are necessarily like all behavioral therapy approaches in their commitment to guided expert experience for changing abnormal behavior and to some learning process that achieves behavioral change.

GIT is a perceptual-cognitive approach to intervention. Mere movement is not its goal. Knowledge about self and the world around us is its goal. Movement is the conduit for getting the tactile-kinesthetic input into the multisensory experience that leads to knowledge of causes and effects, which is gained from nonverbal problem-solving experience. GIT differs radically from interventions that disregard tactile-kinesthetic input for learning. It also differs from movement-focused interventions that respect tactile-kinesthetic input but that are not conceptually framed to deal with cognition and language or that isolate treatment from the natural contexts of daily experience.

PROMPT is a systemic intervention for speech production disorders. It differs from interventions that de-emphasize tactual input in modifying speech behavior. It also differs from those interventions that are not conceptually framed to link motor speech learning to other domains of function, inclusive of language, concept formation, and affect.

Consequently, GIT and PROMPT differ from conventional practices in respect to what kind of learning process and sensory experience matter to achieving desired intervention outcomes. Conventional clinical practices emphasize enhanced auditory and visual experiences. In contrast, GIT and PROMPT view enhanced tactual input as primary in the multisensory experience needed to develop. Both interventions insist on connecting treatment experiences to the functional "real-world" contexts of acting and interacting that cross the verbal and nonverbal domains. Homologous modeling of skill acquisition is embraced directly (GIT) or indirectly (PROMPT).

GIT AND PROMPT IN CONTRAST

GIT and PROMPT differ in their focus and scope of intervention. GIT aims to build the perceptual-cognitive foundation for nonverbal and verbal development. Using its "tree" metaphor, GIT creates and strengthens the "root and stump" support for all behavioral domains. Its facilitation of experiences with nonverbal interaction in daily problem-solving events is not dependent on any particular system of symbolic representation. Practitioners can focus on any symbolic medium (e.g., pictures, signs, spoken or written forms) to represent events. The comprehension of symbol/event mappings is facilitated by respecting what has been just experienced in the nonverbal interaction event within the same lesson. Comprehension or understanding the meaning of symbols is in the foreground and not their production. Practitioners can rely on conventional strategies for honing grammatical skills (see Nelson 1998; Paul 2001). However, those therapies that emphasize holistic language learning (e.g., Constable 1986; Norris and Damico 1990; Kaiser and Hester 1994; Nelson 1998) and strategies for teaching verb relations (e.g., Watkins 1994) are likely to be the most compatible with GIT (Stockman 2000b).

In contrast, PROMPT expands and prunes a major tree branch (e.g., speech production) once emerged from the root. Speech production was chosen as the symbolic system of focus in this book because it is the most common form of human communication, yet one of the most complex human skills acquired. Speech production engages not only the sensorimotor system, but also the perceptual, cognitive, social, and emotional systems. To profit from PROMPT therapy, children must have already reached some minimal level of sensorimotor and perceptual-cognitive development. They modify speech in response to a therapist's simultaneous delivery of tactual, auditory, and visual input. To do so, a child must be able to integrate sensory input across modalities at some level. Other abilities (i.e., communicative intent, some concepts, and words) also must be in the repertoire at a minimal level to change speech so that it is perceptually clear and, at the same time, linguistically meaningful and useful for social communication. However, PROMPT aims to expand the linguistic repertoire for expressive social communication given the constraints of the motor speech system. To enhance functional speech, production targets are strategically selected to change the underlying organization of movement patterns. So PROMPT, like GIT, is process driven.

GIT and PROMPT can be viewed as complementary rather than adversarial interventions. The perceptual-cognitive organization of nonverbal experience and the **comprehension** of the meaning of symbols that refer to such experiences are in the foreground for GIT. In contrast, the meaningful *production* of spoken language as a particular medium of expression is in the foreground for PROMPT. The relationship among speech forms, meaning, and daily events is depicted in Figure 12.1.

Intervention using PROMPT does not replace the need to engage a child in nonverbal problem-solving interaction activity of daily life, despite its holistic approach to speech production. Its focal concern is with the causative oral movements that create the symbols to code events. Its focal goal is not to

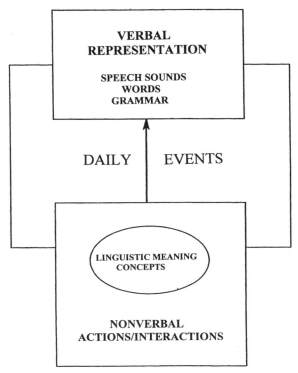

FIGURE 12.1   Relationships among verbal and nonverbal actions/interactions and daily events. (Adapted from Stockman, I. 1996. Wo sind die Worte? –Wie kommen wir zu unseren Sprachlichen Begriffen? In Lipp, B., and Schlaegel, W., [Editors], *Wege von Anfang an Fruhrehabilitation schwerst hirngeschadigter Patienten.* pp. 244–259. Bern: Springer).

teach the causative nonverbal events in which speech is used. If the child cannot do the event in which a speech act is to be embedded, then another one is chosen that optimizes such participation. PROMPT therapists are not required to teach the functional sequence of nonverbal actions/interactions for the event in which speech sound symbols are used. However, therapists must consider the complexity of such events when choosing suitable therapy activity. GIT, on the other hand, is concerned with events—teaching about the causes and effects of the events. The whole body, including the oral structures as connected to causative events, is in its venue.

Taken together, the GIT and PROMPT intervention approaches can challenge our thinking about several clinical and research issues. In the discussion to follow, I focus first on their implications for clinical practice and then for research.

CHALLENGES TO CLINICAL PRACTICES

The following discussion is structured around the four guidelines for framing an intervention framework as identified on the first page of this chapter and in earlier chapters of this book.

The view of conventional clinical practices presented here may not apply to all clinical approaches. We have become increasingly more knowledgeable about PDD over time. Yet, there is more variability in clinical practices than we would like to admit. It should not be surprising that some of them are challenged by the type of interventions described in this book.

IMPLICATIONS FOR CLINICAL PRACTICE: FOCUSING ON DAILY LIFE EXPERIENCE

This book has called attention to the value of learning from the ordinary daily routines of dressing, eating, toileting, bathing, going to the store, and so on. This view, which is advocated by GIT, has direct implications for choosing intervention contexts. Daily events as contexts for therapy are aligned with the notion of functional treatment in conventional practices. However, functional treatment need not translate into the routines of eating, dressing, toileting, and so on. An interactive play activity that is not a routine daily experience may be viewed as functional, if its features are analogous to what is actually experienced in real life. For example, a speech-language therapist may regard a context as "functional" so long as interactive social communication is required in the therapy activity as opposed to drill routines done by the child.

Reasons to De-emphasize Daily Routines

There are a couple of reasons why practitioners may be reluctant to frame intervention contexts around the ordinary daily living events of eating, toileting, and so on. One reason is that children with PDD may be mainstreamed into conventional school programs, which are not set up to stimulate learning in such situations even though some of them (e.g., eating and toileting) do occur at school. School programs are set up to meet academic learning goals (e.g., literacy, arithmetic and so on), and often in ways that do not relate to daily living skills. For example, eating is a routine daily event whether at home or school. At school, the meals are prepared for children and eaten in a cafeteria. In some U.S. schools, refrigerators and microwave ovens may be prohibited in classrooms for liability reasons. So the opportunity for children to participate in preparing their own snacks as a daily routine is minimized.

There is a second reason to de-emphasize daily living skills even for preschoolers who get therapy at home. Practitioners may think that a child with PDD needs some kind of special intervention. After all, their global learning deficits make it clear that they have not negotiated daily experiences well enough to develop normally. There is the sense that to be helpful, therapy must offer special experiences, which enhance or simplify the learning context. This often means that formal and direct teaching of missing skills is done in isolation of real events. Caregivers too may have the bias that nothing much is happening in therapy when it focuses on what are regarded as the ordinary events of daily living that also occur at home.

Such views encourage the creation of special intervention environments that are likely to contrast with the natural contexts of daily living. For example, occupational and physical therapists may work with a child's motor skills using special equipment that is removed from daily experience. Clinical and educational specialists, who work on nonverbal skills, may assume that they are teaching concepts in a real way so long as the child is allowed to handle objects used in play and games. For example, teaching the concept of "in" and "out" is sufficient if the child makes a doll go in or out of another object. But such symbolic play activity is not the same as having the child's own body move in and out of a container.

At the same time, the room for language therapy can be filled with pictures, puzzles, and games. In isolated therapy rooms, children map words onto symbolic representations of events (e.g., pictures, toys) and not necessarily onto real events that are experienced right there in the therapy room or before hand. If the concepts or events are not already in the child's repertoire, then it is someone else's job to teach them. The speech-language therapist's job is to teach the words for events, and typically just the spoken ones at that.

What emerges then is a fragmented picture in which verbal and nonverbal behaviors can be isolated from one another in intervention. Daily events, which converge verbal and nonverbal events, are viewed as either too mundane or too simplistic for developing abstract conceptual categories or language. To the contrary, GIT's emphasis on daily events is supported by Katherine Nelson's theory of event knowledge (Nelson 1986 and Chapter 6). She has argued that the development of meaningful action and language are rooted in the early representation of daily event structure. Routine daily events provide an integrative structure for experience. They embed information about more than objects and their static visual properties, for example, shape and color. They also embed information about actions and interactions, the social roles and relationships of persons, along with the verbal scripts for talking about them. Because daily life events reoccur, they provide familiar contexts within which old and new objects can be conceptually related; events can be recognized, anticipated, and information processing load thereby can be reduced!

Reconciling Different Views of Functional Contexts

It is recognized that as children get older, their daily events do change in any culture, as does their expected participation in them. Particular games can be among the frequently experienced contexts of social interactions for older children at home, at school, or on the playground. If such play routines are a natural part of what people do in the child's world, it seems reasonable to help a child to participate to the extent possible. But a steady diet of just this kind of experience with social games will not maximize the development of children with PDD from GIT's perspective. This will be the case if such games demand rules of social engagement and symbolic representation at too high a level, and/or do not require the kind of "grounded" problem-solving experience in interaction events that feeds perceptual-cognitive development at a basic level. The more severe the developmental deficits are, the more likely will this be the case.

One lesson then to be learned from the focus on daily events in this book is that event experiences are likely to promote learning when practitioners emphasize repeatable event routines for whatever settings are culturally relevant to a child's life experiences. Development will be especially enhanced in such event routines if (1) a child's attention is engaged by introducing novelty into the routines, and (2) a child is required to participate by doing something to change the topological spatial relationships between the body and the environment to solve some problem in the actual situation. This latter criterion means that practitioners should be concerned with more than just looking, listening, and speaking acts during events. They should be concerned with bodily participation in events that are consequential for learning about how the world works in terms of causes and effects, and they should be concerned with **comprehending** the symbols for representing such events in some shared communicative form. To this end, mainstreamed school environments need not be ideal for children with PDD if they are too removed from the kind of "hands on" experiences that problem solving in nonverbal physical interaction requires. See Kaufman and Hallahan (1995) for a critique of mainstreaming practices in special education for schools in the United States.

IMPLICATIONS FOR CLINICAL PRACTICE: A FOCUS ON LEARNING PROCESS

Knowing something about the learning process is important to framing intervention in ways that can effect broad scale developmental changes. Yet assessments and interventions are more often competence than process driven. This means that conventional therapy focuses on expanding the repertoire of specific skills in a direct way. If a child does not know how to use a spoon, therapy targets spoon use. If the child does not know how to throw a ball or know colors, particular grammatical forms, or words, those specific skills are taught. How long should therapy have to last to teach all the many skills that a child with PDD may not have?

In contrast, a focus on learning process aims to achieve a more general outcome. Skills are strategically targeted to facilitate change in some underlying process or mechanism responsible for the multiple specific skills observed. In dynamical systems terms, this means that a practitioner facilitates learning by choosing some kind of experience that can serve as a catalyst for systemic reorganization so that new skills emerge on their own. It is likely to be just this kind of scenario that explains how a child seems to suddenly improve in several areas after learning one or two new things. Development may work like this even for typically developing people.

How does process-driven intervention work then? What does one do in the therapy if not work on specific skills? The therapy must be driven by some model of what is entailed in learning.

Git

In the GIT intervention, the focus is on the procedures governing problem-solving activity in nonverbal interaction events. Learning is stimulated by giving a child **new** problems to solve in daily interaction event—problems that the child cannot solve alone: How do I get this toy from the shelf, put on my shoe, get some water to drink, and so on? Therapy also facilitates the learning by enhancing the tactile-kinesthetic input that a child gets while eliciting the causes and effects required to solve the problem in an event, that is, activities that require hypothesis generation, testing, and so on.

Practitioners working within GIT's framework can use their conventional assessments to evaluate how well children progress overall in developing the expected skills for their ages. They also are required to make observations beyond those usually made in conventional practices. GIT's focus on the problem-solving process encourages practitioners to ask and answer questions that many are not accustomed to asking and answering. For example, how much perceptual support (i.e., physical guiding) is needed to solve a problem? Do all the objects needed to achieve a goal have to be in sight before a hypothesis is generated about the actions needed to solve the problem? Can detours be handled when executing an action plan, that is, does a child become upset or frustrated when confronted with unexpected change in the situation that requires a different action sequence than was planned or initiated? For example, the object being handled in the event falls to the floor and is broken. Is the goal achieved with alternative actions? How many steps in a sequence of actions can be handled alone?

Prompt

The PROMPT intervention is guided by its model of the motor speech hierarchy for solving problems with speech production. This model is used to pinpoint where the motor speech system breaks down. The same model is used to solve the problem by supplying tactual information to the system—tactual prompts that have been developed to correspond with the motor speech hierarchy. Refer to Deborah Hayden's description of the PROMPT framework in Chapter 10. This process-driven therapy does not focus just on whether a /p/ or /k/ can be produced but rather on the underlying organization of the motor speech system that can yield more than /p/ or /k/ productions.

The PROMPT framework also requires therapists to expand their observations beyond those traditionally required to assess speech articulation and language. Observations are also expected to reflect the underlying processes that support speech production and also oral language as a whole. For example, the assessment of oral movement planes yields a far more dynamic picture of articulatory function than a traditional test of the speech sound repertoire offers.

IMPLICATIONS FOR CLINICAL PRACTICE: A FOCUS ON TACTILE-KINESTHETIC SOURCES OF INPUT FOR LEARNING

The emphasis on the movement and action/interaction experience in this book has strong implications for the kind of perceptual input that should be emphasized in clinical work. I consider first its implication for diagnosis and then for treatment.

Tactile-Kinesthetic Perception and Clinical Assessment

Git

With respect to diagnostic subgroups, conventional hypotheses about learning disability have been framed most often in terms of auditory or visual processing difficulties. For example, a central auditory processing disorder is now a commonly known clinical diagnosis. Less often is the tactual system included in identifying diagnostic categories. The sensory integration diagnosis promoted by occupational therapist Jean Ayres (1972) is one exception.

One reason the tactual system may have been ignored is that some children with PDD do not appear to have tactual problems. Those with classic autism symptoms in particular can move quickly. Their rapid stereotypical handling of and repetitive twirling of objects, for example, require good manual dexterity as well. Clear echolalic speech suggests no oral sensorimotor problems either. Affolter and Bischofberger (2000) proposed that these children with classic autistic symptoms have an intermodal perceptual problem. They do not connect the information input across different sensory domains. Since most complex skills depend on the cross-modal integration of experience, children without it can appear profoundly abnormal in contrast to other clinical groups, those with PDD-NOS, in particular. Their heavily canalized sensory-perceptual systems (Waterhouse et al 1996) can produce fearless climbers and movers who disregard potential hazards in sight.

Affolter and Bischofberger (2000) also described two additional clinical subgroups with less severe forms of PDD. One subgroup presents a primary deficit in processing tactile-kinesthetic information, and another one presents a primary temporal processing deficit. This latter group is the least severe group; many of these children with a primary temporal processing deficit can follow regular school programs with some help. Their performances become less adequate in any modality as soon as the sequential processing demands exceed some critical limit for a given child's perceptual system. They are likely to reach this critical limit more often when performing verbal than nonverbal skills given the greater demand for sequential processing in the former than the latter domain. So such children can appear to be more impaired in their verbal than nonverbal skills.

While there is robust evidence for temporal processing deficits in children, particularly those along the SLI-LD continuum (Leonard 2000), the children with tactual processing difficulties are less easily identified This is because their strange grasping and postural and locomotive patterns often are attributed to a motor deficit and not to a perceptual one. As Herbert Pick allows us to infer from Chapter 2, motor behavior, viewed simply as the outward display of learning, was historically separated from perception and cognition. When delivering clinical services, this kind of dualistic thinking has been reinforced by domain-specific professional roles that carve up the body and its function in different ways. Physical and occupational therapists deal with motor skills but not necessarily in ways that connect movement acts to cognitive development, including language. Speech-language therapists focus on verbal skills, spoken ones in particular. An assortment of other professionals, including psychologists and different types of special educators, focus on nonverbal and verbal skills that have to do with academic, social, literacy, and vocational development.

To defend the claim that aberrant movement patterns have anything to do with perception and cognition, a narrow view of motor behavior must be abandoned, as is done in dynamic systems theory. Esther Thelen (Chapter 3) argues that a motor act is input (sensory) and output (motor) driven and selectively tuned to internal cognitive and external context factors. Also see Thelen (1995). The multisensory system involved in movement dynamics includes the tactile-kinesthetic modalities in coordination with vision and audition. In this view, aberrant movement patterns need not be caused by a motor-output problem. They could also result from a sensory-input problem.

The children with tactual dysfunction present challenges to current clinical service delivery systems because they have systemic deficits; yet, they have no clear diagnostic tag. They may be included in that undefined category of children with the diagnosis of PDD-NOS. They also fit the profile of some children with sensory integrative dysfunction (Ayres 1972; Fisher et al 1991), multisystem disorders (MDD) (Zero to Three/National Center for Clinical Infants Programs 1994), and those with the nonverbal syndrome described by Rourke (1989). They may even look like the subgroup of children with specific language disorders and pragmatic/semantic disorders referred to in Bishop (1989), Leonard (2000), and Rapin and Allen (1983).

If severe enough, children with a primary tactile-kinesthetic deficit are simply included in the group diagnosed with autism. For educational placement decisions, the diagnostic label of autism can be applied practically to any child who is too severe to function in a regular classroom, and the problem cannot be blamed on frank mental retardation or obvious physical or emotional impairment. No distinction is necessarily made between children with PDD who present with classic autistic symptoms and those who do not. In my clinical experience, it is the children without classic autistic symptoms (PDD-NOS) whose educational placement is the most contentious for parents because there is often no clear diagnostic label for them. Even a PDD-NOS diagnosis is not a meaningful distinction to make because it is not yet associated with a signature clinical profile.

The three diagnostic subgroups (intermodal, tactual, and serial) I have just singled out are worthy of further study, as discussed later. They may allow us to account for some of the heterogeneity among children with PDD. A child with PDD (one with PDD and intermodal processing deficit in the GIT framework) may not be afraid to jump into a swimming pool once it is seen, even though the feel of the body cannot be coordinated with the visual and auditory information well enough to swim. Another child with PDD and tactual difficulty may be afraid to get into the water because of gravitational insecurity. But once supported in the water, this child is likely to integrate that sensory input with visual and auditory patterns well enough to organize movement patterns for swimming. Children with PDD and serial processing deficits will not have difficulty learning how to swim as long as the sequential processing demands for any modality do not exceed their level of perceptual development. They may be able to swim simply, that is, deploy simple repetitive strokes as opposed to sequentially complex ones.

Prompt

The children with PDD, particularly those with oral tactual deficits, may present speech production deficits typical of developmental apraxia of speech (DAS). In conventional clinical practice, DAS typically is applied to any difficult to treat child with unclear speech who does not respond to conventional treatment practices despite the absence of frank neuromotor damage. It is assumed that a motor (not a perceptual) problem exists in the absence of known cause. While such children commonly are lumped into a single diagnostic category, DAS, clinical observations reveal variability in the level of speech motor control that children exhibit, PDD or not.

Deborah Hayden (Chapter 10) distinguishes two clinical subgroups based on a hierarchical model of speech motor control. DAS is applied only to the subgroup with specific difficulty in sequencing oral speech movements. This group has no difficulty creating the motor phoneme maps for discrete speech sound production. In contrast, children with difficulty at the lower level of the motor speech hierarchy have difficulty creating the motor phoneme maps for producing clear speech sounds within and across planes of movement. The hierarchical nature of Hayden's speech production predicts that they will have difficulty with sequencing movements as a secondary deficit. These children with the more severe intelligibility issues are diagnosed with developmental dysarthria of speech, DDS as opposed to DAS. Both types of subgroups respond to intervention with enhanced tactual input.

Tactile-Kinesthetic Perception and Clinical Intervention

Perceivable input is all that practitioners ultimately can control in trying to change behavior. They cannot learn for the child. In conventional practices, clinician-controlled input may be influenced more often by the choice of therapy materials and activities than by the sensory systems to be stimulated in the learning.

The two interventions described in this book offer tactually guided ways to stimulate learning. When using GIT, manual guiding during nonverbal inter-action events provides a tool for stimulating learning directly. One should not get the impression that the goal of manual guiding is to create a specific or rigid way of doing a task. The input is dynamic. The particular actions/interactions involved in doing even the same task are expected to vary with the requirements for achieving goals in a given situation at the moment. When a child is manu-ally guided to do a particular functional task, it is assumed that the perceptual input will vary naturally depending on the actual situation, even though some aspects may remain the same for routinely repeated events. Therefore, enhanced tactual input for doing a functional task occurs across multiple episodes of experiencing the same event in different ways. Given increased experience with multimodal sensory input, children should become able to organize their perceptual activity well enough to extract and store critical perceptual-cognitive information. Such information can be recruited to do not only a particular task on their own in a given situation, but also to do tasks gen-erally in different situations.

In contrast to GIT, managing difficult to treat children in conventional practices can involve advising caregivers and professionals how to talk to a child or provide a stimulating environment of color and sound to elicit attention. How-ever, Affolter and Stricker (1980) asked, how does one establish interaction with patients in a new problem-solving event when they do not follow verbal instruc-tions or reproduce what the therapist shows or tells?

> If patients need therapy because they fail in language, one cannot expect such complex means to effectively transmit information. One also cannot force them to look at therapy material. Neither can one take the ears and make them listen. But there is one modality that can be manipulated directly, namely, the tactile-kinesthetic system. By taking the hands of the patient and guiding them, helping them to explore the presented stimuli, one may be sure of some input. (Affolter and Stricker 1980, p. 114).

Similarly in speech production therapy, children with severe deficits can be confused by a clinician's auditory—verbal explanations of how and where to position body organs for speech sound production. That is, it can be difficult for them to translate a therapist's externally delivered visual and auditory demon-strations into their own self-produced sensorimotor patterns. Such performances require complex cross-modal integration of sensory input. Direct tactual cueing as offered by PROMPT can help children to create perceptual-motor maps for speech production. In Vygotskian terms, manual guiding as a general intervention strategy reveals what children can do with support. However, the oral tactual prompts are not used with the presumption that rigid motor speech production targets can or ought to be created. A child is expected to extract perceptual motor maps from dynamic input. Speech production outcomes are expected to vary dynamically with the situations for speaking. Real speaking events involve not only the speech production system but also all the physical, mental, and emotional systems that are involved in learning and participating in linguistic and nonlinguistic events as a whole.

The emphasis on tactually enhanced input as an intervention strategy is likely to be contentious for traditional practices. Physical guiding as a procedure for enhancing tactual input will be foreign to practitioners who erroneously view it as having a motor rather than a perceptual-cognitive goal, and therefore in the domain of just the occupational or physical therapist when this is not the case. Practitioners are likely to be most comfortable with using auditory or visual input. The distance senses favor the "expert model" of service delivery. It requires practitioners to control learning events by showing (visually) or telling (auditory-verbal) children what to do, especially in fields other than occupational or physical therapy. Practitioners may cling even more to the familiar auditory-visual sensory inputs if it is assumed that manual guiding is passive input and ineffective in getting the attention of the nervous system and/or tactual input, guided or not, plays just a secondary role in developing perception and cognition. It is particularly problematic for practitioners to assume that nonverbal tactually guided interaction experience is foundational for developing language, even if they believe that it can be helpful to remediating nonverbal behavior. The professional education and clinical practices of speech-language therapists have not historically required them to emphasize the nonverbal aspects of learning. The nonverbal context is viewed as the means to the end of facilitating the acquisition of grammatical/phonological forms and/or their semantic-pragmatic uses.

A Skeptical View of the Verbal and Nonverbal Relationship

Skepticism about a critical relationship between language and any kind of nonverbal performances, tactually enhanced or not, is fueled by a variety of observations (Stockman 2000b). For one thing, the notion of physical nonverbal interaction experience as the root of development is at odds with the notion that the verbal and nonverbal domains are entirely separate learning domains. To support this view, one can point to the lack of congruity between nonverbal and verbal development in some clinical populations. Language skills can be better or worse than nonverbal cognition. The research even on typically developing children has not shown a general dependency of linguistic knowledge on the prior emergence of some nonverbal concepts (e.g., object permanence), which presumably were rooted in prior nonverbal sensorimotor activity, as described by Piaget

(Bates et al 1979). The relationship of verbal to nonverbal conceptual perform-ance is very complex, as revealed recently in Bowerman and Levinson (2002).

Furthermore, the fact that some children with physical and motor handicaps achieve a more mature stage of nonverbal cognition (e.g., Decarie 1969, Fourcin 1975; Bishop 1990) and language understanding (Bishop 1993) than is expected, suggests that development does not solely depend on sensorimotor experience, which Piaget's theory was thought to predict. However, see Lourenco and Machado's (1996) response to common criticisms of Piaget's theory.

The movement-oriented therapies created by physical and occupational therap-ists have not given a reason to change this view. They have failed to yield impressive treatment gains in linguistic and academic achievement despite theor-etical claims to do so, for example, see critiques of sensory integration therapy (Daems 1994; Hoehn and Baumeister 1994). In sum, conventional views of language development and learning do not encourage one to take seriously a theor-etical framework that links language learning to nonverbal physical interaction processes as put forth by Affolter (Chapter 8), Bischofberger and Affolter (Chapter 9); and Affolter and Bischofberger (2000). Mogford and Bishop (1993) concluded that ". . . the normal ability to perform actions on the world and note their sensory consequence is not necessary for linguistic development" (p. 249).

Defending the Relevance of Nonverbal Development to Language Learning

The relevance of nonverbal interaction experiences to language learning has been argued in this book and elsewhere (Stockman 2000b). One issue concerns the relevance of nonverbal experiences to constructing the conceptual content that words refer to. Another issue concerns the relevance of nonverbal experi-ences to the process of actually mapping that content onto the words of a language or the issue of acquiring semantic reference. On both counts, action/interaction experiences in nonverbal events are likely to contribute to language learning. With respect to the mapping process, it is intuitively obvious that people do not experience words in isolation of what else goes on in daily life, including their participation in nonverbal action/interaction events. At a minimum, nonverbal events complicate the language learning process when they compete for the same cognitive and attentional resources as Lois Bloom (Chapter 7) has discussed. At the same time, nonverbal action/interaction events are part of the raw material that feeds the conceptual knowledge for construct-ing the meaning of words Nelson's Chapter 6; Huttenlocher et al 1983; (Bloom 1994; Nelson 1986; Tomasello and Merriman 1995). Languages have a sen-tence grammar because people do not talk just about single objects; they talk more often about events involving object relationships and their causes and effects in physical and social action/interaction experiences.

Although the indirect relationship between conceptual knowledge and language requires a process of figuring out word meanings that includes multiple factors (e.g., social and attentional), a person's knowledge about action/interaction relation-ships also is relevant. Woodward et al (1994) showed that the timing of the children's own manipulation of an object with the presentation of a novel word was successful in cueing their attention to the desired word/object mappings. Hollich et al (2000) were not so successful when just the experimenter's object manipulation was used as a social cue. Such contrastive experimental outcomes suggest that children's own intentional states and actions may reduce their range of hypotheses about the event to word mappings possible, as Lois Bloom's intentionality model of language learning would predict (Chapter 7). These self-action/interaction events may turn out to be even more critical to learning the meaning of action verbs and other relational words than nouns. People in general refer to what they have done, are doing, or are about to do. Typically developing children do so early and frequently (Bloom 1991), and they talk about their own actions before they talk about the observed actions/interactions of other people (Huttenlocher et al 1983).

CHALLENGES TO LANGUAGE INTERVENTION PRACTICES: THE SEMANTIC MAPPING ISSUE

Theories of language learning that emphasize the acquisition of meaning are expected to be particularly helpful for intervening with PDD. This is because their global developmental deficits more often than not result in disordered semantic and pragmatic systems. The premise of GIT is that with increased non-verbal daily interaction experiences, perceptual organization will become increasingly more adequate for learning about the world. Children can reach a point in development when they become able to recruit their own strategies for establishing language form-meaning relations from among those typically available to children across age, as summarized in Hollich et al (2000).

Nevertheless, the language comprehension deficits in some children with PDD make clear that they do have difficulty figuring out the meaning of words and sentences on their own. This is not surprising, given the indirect relationship between a person's conceptual knowledge and linguistic representation. Intervention must help them with semantic mapping issues. The issue is how to do it.

Just having the goal of establishing the meaning of words/sentences challenges some conventional therapy practices, nevermind how it is done. This is because practitioners can be less focused on facilitating the acquisition of semantic knowledge than the acquisition of the more easily observed grammatical and pronunciation forms or their social-pragmatic uses. A child with nonverbal perceptual-cognitive issues is referred to other professionals (e.g., psychologists, special education teachers, and so on). The role of speech-language therapists can be narrowly relegated to linking communicative forms, spoken words in particular, with already stored experiences.

When semantic mapping is singled out as a therapy goal, another challenge to conventional practices is created by GIT's insistence on linking words to real events actually experienced in the therapy as opposed to what could be or may have been experienced. This is the case when words are not mapped onto real events, as already pointed out. Instead, therapists use pictures or toys, which are themselves symbolic representations of reality, as referents for words. Such approaches may work well enough for those children who have already reached a certain level of semiotic development so that such symbols can be used to retrieve their stored experiences for learning the meaning of new words and sentences. But what about children who do not recognize pictures, play with toys, or operate a computer adequately?

When using GIT, professionals also are not supposed to talk at the same time that a child is guided to do an event. The words are given **after** the event. This intervention principle is contentious probably because it seems to violate natural intuitions about teaching someone to relate two things to one another, as the semantic mapping of words onto events requires. Intuitively, a child ought to be able to make the best connection between words and events when they are simultaneously experienced in time and space, that is, experienced at the very same time. But the talking and doing at the same time presumably create competing sources of information that can tax a child's limited attentional resources. Children with PDD and perceptual disorders reach a breakdown even sooner than normal because they have to work harder to get information.

Lois Bloom (Chapter 7) provided good reason to believe that human performance is sensitive to the amount of information to be processed at one time. She called attention to the multiple types of stimuli that compete for attention in the natural contexts of learning language. It turns out that despite our intuitive notions about the mapping of words onto events, the caregivers of even typically developing children do not ordinarily talk at the same time as their children are constructing an object relationship in play (e.g., placing one object onto another). Tomasello and Kruger (1992) also appealed to attention in explaining why the mothers of typically developing children in their study talked to their children more often before or after an action event than during it.

While the use of tactual prompts to map speech production targets requires the simultaneous processing of tactual, auditory, and visual input, PROMPT therapists must reduce complexity by regulating the type of nonverbal and verbal event used. At the beginning of therapy when motor phoneme maps are first being built, simple repetitive nonverbal events, which require minimal competing use of cognitive resources, are selected. As speech improves, the complexity of the nonverbal contexts is increased, as are the language skill demands. Language and other skill domains are expected to improve as a result of freed up attentional capacity that used to be devoted to producing speech.

What should emerge from this discussion is an image of intervention in which nonverbal and verbal experiences should be combined around the same event. This holistic view of intervention sessions is likely to be less typical of conventional therapy than one might think. Admittedly, it can be difficult to create real nonverbal functional events for guided interaction in most isolated therapy rooms. Some language interventions, for example, whole language (Kaiser and Hester 1994) and Milieu therapy (Norris and Damico 1990), come closer to holistic intervention contexts than do others. See also Constable (1986) for the use of verbal scripts and Watkins (1994) for the use of verbs in event-oriented interventions with language impaired children. These approaches to language therapy reflect the shift toward broader and more interactionist views of language learning and impairment than before (Chapman 2000).

IMPLICATIONS FOR CLINICAL PRACTICE: HOMOLOGOUS MODELING OF SKILL ACQUISITION

Advocating a homologous model of service delivery impacts conventional practices in at least two ways that challenge conventional clinical practices. First, it challenges a specific skill focus in intervention. Second, it challenges service delivery practices and practitioner preparation for working with PDD.

Targeting Specific Skills in Intervention

Conventional intervention is geared toward teaching particular skills, as stated already. What should be the skill learning goals of therapy when so many deficits exist, as is the case for children with PDD? How do clinicians select particular ones to focus on? In conventional practices, the selection of target skills is driven by a deficit view of competency. Intervention targets skills that are not already in the repertoire but should be given a child's age. The intervention goals typically are framed as specific skills that may be worked on one after the other and in isolation of one another. The goals can be as specific as a child will learn three colors or will learn to say a specific speech sound or will learn to eat with a spoon.

Isolating specific skills to be taught one after the other is at odds with homologous modeling of development. In typical human development, skills normally are not learned one at a time or in isolation of one another. Parallel learning occurs in multiple domains. In fact, the overlapping development of multiple skill domains benefits learning, given Jonas Langer's (Chapter 5) comparative research on the heterochronicity of human and nonhuman primate development. He attributes the accelerated developmental rate and level of intelligence achieved in humans to greater temporal overlapping of experiences in different domains of knowledge acquisition. The implication is that nonverbal human learning can inform verbal learning, and the converse also is true. It is instructive here to review what is entailed in working at a nonverbal and verbal level using GIT and PROMPT.

GIT

GIT does not isolate specific skills to target. Its homologous treatment model focuses therapy at what is presumed to be the foundation or root of development, namely, nonverbal problem-solving experience in daily interaction events. This model predicts that whatever skills do emerge as a result will reflect changes in the underlying perceptual-cognitive organization of experience at a given developmental level, that is, how well a child can process and store tactually anchored multimodal information from nonverbal interaction experiences in daily problem-solving events. To determine whether the repertoire of skills changes over time, practitioners can do assessments that make use of the same types of informal and formal observations that they are accustomed to. The expectation is that many more skills may emerge than happen to be experienced directly in the therapy. For example, it is commonly observed that speech production and other motor skills do improve right after a GIT session, even when they have not been worked on in the therapy. This should not be surprising because the sensory input experienced from an effective tactually guided experience should affect the whole brain.

Practitioners are likely to be concerned, though, about how to attribute newly observed skills directly to the intervention if they are not targeted for therapy before hand. In other words, how can we make an intervention directly accountable for a child's progress when the intervention does not prespecify the specific skills to be taught or enabled? This is a kind of contentious issue that can be resolved by doing clinical efficacy research, as discussed later in this chapter.

PROMPT

In contrast to GIT, PROMPT is specific skill oriented in changing motor speech performance. However, the skills are not specified in terms of particular speech sounds or patterns to be remedied, as conventional practices require. Instead, the skill goals are framed in terms of what needs to be done to change the underlying movement patterns—a process orientation. For example, a goal of therapy might be to "increase upper lip function," reduce "jaw excursion," expand speech productions in the vertical plane of movement, and so on. Some examples are given in the clinical case profile in chapter 10 in this book. More often than not, multiple speech sounds could be used to target the underlying movement pattern. Therefore, PROMPT is homologous in its expectation that principled goals of speech production will lead to many more changes in the motor-speech system and other areas of function than a clinician works on directly.

As motor speech patterns normalize and become habituated, cognitive resources are freed up so that attention can be given to other skills, for example, grammar and social interaction. Improved speech also can have cascading effects on a self-organizing system with tightly coupled domains of function, as predicted by dynamic systems theory. Improved speech should expand socialization experience directly with concomitant effects on other areas such as emotional affect, interpersonal trust, and the self-confidence to communicate with and learn from others. However, in conventional clinical practices, we are not accustomed to expecting or measuring such broad effects of speech production therapy. More typically, progress is described in terms of very specific speech sounds or phonological patterns that were the pre-targeted goals of therapy because they were absent in a system before hand.

Service Delivery Systems and Professional Training

A homologous view of development challenges modular service delivery systems and practitioner preparation for doing clinical work. A modular service delivery system follows from the balkanization of professional training. It can require a child to get services from at least three to four different experts, typically occupational, physical, and speech-language therapists along with other services that may include a resource room specialist for school-age children, psychological counselor, and social worker.

Although multidisciplinary team approaches to intervention have come to be valued, clinical teams can exist with nonoverlapping professional roles. In the worst case, the various professional experts all work with a child at the same time, but their respective interventions are not driven by the same goals or philosophical approach. The intervention experience is fragmented. It is the child who must integrate all the bits and pieces from them. In contrast, GIT is used by all the practitioners, that is the therapists and teachers in addition to home caregivers. Evaluation of outcomes, however, takes advantage of the specific expertise and role of the various contributors to the intervention.

Another solution has been to involve professionals in co-treatment across disiciplines. In the most progressive therapy centers and school districts, a speech-language therapist may team with an occupational and/or physical therapist to deliver a session of intervention to the same child. While such co-treatment effort is to be applauded, it often demands too many resources in time and money to be used on a wide basis, even for the same child. Such co-treatment efforts exist largely because neither professional is adequately trained to deal with multiple areas of deficits in the same child. There is a great deal of specialization in educational preparation and service delivery. Speech-language therapists may know little about the body beyond the body organs that support speaking; occupational and physical therapists may know little about speech, language, or cognition. The larger questions are: What kind of training is needed? What discipline is qualified to deal with pervasive developmental deficits that cross traditionally defined areas of service delivery? What seems to be needed for efficiently servicing children with PDD is professional education and clinical praxis that combine the competencies of speech, occupational, and physical therapies in the same practitioner. If so, then we ultimately may need to appeal to a new disciplinary focus and professional training model—one that combines the clinical praxis training across multiple areas.

In addition to the four criteria for creating intervention frameworks, the ideas presented in this book also challenge other conventional practices. The following discussion calls attention to the timing of intervention experiences.

TIMING OF INTERVENTION EXPERIENCES

The ideas presented in this book can challenge our notions about the timing of intervention experiences, specifically when to initiate professional intervention and for how long.

How Early to Begin Intervention

With respect to starting intervention, best clinical practices have always promoted early intervention. In the United States, there is even a government mandate to provide services beginning at birth, if needed. Jon H. Kaas's study (Chapter 4) of the neuroplasticity of the nervous system reaffirms this value of early diagnosis. He pointed out the possibility of reversing or offsetting some of the biological error induced by neurological insult when starting early enough. But how early is early, given that many children with PDD can look normal, see, hear, and move the body at will early on—even at birth? Fortunately, when daily events are the contexts for intervention, practitioners can start early because such natural contexts are the only ones that babies experience.

However, intervention is likely to be recommended early on for just those children whose behavioral abnormality is obvious. This is the case for children with classic autistic symptoms who fail to bond even with caregivers. In other cases, though (e.g., children diagnosed with PDD-NOS), behavior may not appear abnormal from superficial observation. By the time many of these children with PDD are diagnosed at 3 or 4 years old, there has been a lot of abnormal experience with the routines of daily life.

Waiting so late to intervene is likely to happen for more than one reason. For one thing, practitioners respect the normal variability in human development. Waiting so late to intervene also may reflect a lack of knowledge about what to look for as early signs of deviant development or how to intervene when sure that intervention is needed.

Early diagnosis can be informed by some of the work described in this book. Affolter (Chapter 8) suggests that a lot can be learned by observing differences in a baby's adaptation to daily situations when there is a change of topological relationship between the body and the environment.

Moreover, much may be learned from observing babies' nonverbal problem-solving activity in spontaneous situations. Affolter et al (1996) identified an age-graded sequence of sensorimotor performance (birth to 24 months) that reflects the level of problem-solving activity reached in development. Hayden, Wetherby, Cleary, and Prizant (forthcoming) are developing the Early Motor Control Scales, a norm-referenced test for evaluating the integrity of early sensorimotor skills in a variety of domains, including speech production. Affolter (Chapter 8) and Hayden (Chapter 10) would advocate comparing how a baby's actions change when the sources of sensory input are deliberately modified to include the tactile-kinesthetic sources of input relative to when they are not.

I am also intrigued by Jonas Langer's (Chapter 5) proposal that a child's ability to perform second and third order operations on objects in play with a standard set of objects may be early prerequisites for developing language. This conclusion was reached after observing differences between human babies and nonhuman primates.

Katherine Nelson's (Chapter 6) notion of event structure offers yet another possibility for framing observations about how well a child negotiates daily events. For example, there is evidence that children are attuned to the structure of repetitive daily routines when they spontaneously anticipate or initiate the next steps in a sequence of actions within a daily event or show other behaviors that reflect familiarity with the structure of repeated daily events.

The Temporal Course of Intervention

In conventional practices, the termination of intervention is guided by many factors, practical ones included. Neuroplasticity becomes relevant, though, whenever children are dismissed from intervention with the presumption that no further learning can take place. Such a stance is at odds with the plasticity research described by Jon H. Kaas (Chapter 4). If neuroplasticity exists throughout the life span, then a child's dismissal from treatment should never be grounded in the argument that no further change is likely. Yet, if neural organization of an abnormal brain cannot be reversed as Kaas suggests is possible when damage occurs after a certain age, then practitioners should not view any intervention as a lifetime "cure." A dynamic systems perspective, as described by Esther Thelen (Chapter 3), encourages a different approach to intervention goals when working with PDD. Practitioners should approach intervention with the notion that a child needs help in getting "unstuck" at a given point in the developmental cycle.

Dynamic systems modeling of learning and developing views competence as context dependent and always emergent. This means that the critical factors needed to effect change are expected to vary over a child's life experiences because of the changing contexts of experience. In Western societies, for example, going to school, learning to drive a car, mating , working, and so on present changing contexts for solving daily problems across the life span. Sometimes, children with special needs can negotiate these later learning contexts without special intervention if there is a supportive environment. In other cases, special intervention services are warranted. The intervention goal is to move a child to another developmental level, that is, "getting unstuck" for the contexts of doing and learning at a given time in the life history. Across the life span there might be multiple episodes of intervention, each requiring attention to different parameters to facilitate developmental progress.

This outlook is different than what we are accustomed to in clinical work. Too often, practitioners expect their interventions to have a direct lifetime impact on a child. When children with PDD need intervention again in a new context, they may be given a different diagnostic label. For example, a child diagnosed with PDD early in childhood (e.g., before age 3 years) may be diagnosed later (e.g., around nursery school age) as simply language impaired once the nonverbal performances have been normalized enough to pass some diagnostic criterion. That same child may be diagnosed as learning disabled still later once school aged and faced with the task of learning to read and write. The assumption seems to be that a new disability exists as opposed to the changing contextual face of an existing one. Such lifelong learning issues may be inevitable though, if the brain, though capable of change, is nevertheless a brain that is forever organized differently relative to the typically developing brain.

CHALLENGES TO RESEARCH

This book addresses issues that are relevant to not only clinical practices but also to research. The challenges exist because of historical biases in research practices and/or the adequacy of methodological procedures for making sound empirical observation. In the discussion to follow, I identify some of these issues for each of the proposed guidelines to framing intervention frameworks, namely, the focus on (1) daily life experiences, (2) the learning process in addition to stored knowledge representation, (3) multisensory information that includes the tactile-kinesthetic senses, and (4) homologous modeling of skill acquisition. This discussion is meant to be illustrative rather than comprehensive. See Stockman (2000b) for a more detailed discussion.

THE CHALLENGE OF STUDYING BEHAVIOR IN DAILY EVENTS

Researchable Issues

Future research on children with PDD should be expanded to include descriptions of behaviors that occur in natural problem-solving situations. This expansion would be informative for two reasons. First, some children with PDD can be so severely impaired that they cannot give reliable responses to laboratory controlled tasks or standardized tests. Second, observation of behavior in a natural environment should be grounding for framing and verifying testable experimental hypotheses about the nature of PDD. They also should be informed by careful documentation of what these children with PDD actually do in natural situations. We should want to know what they do all day long at home, for example. How do they approach the problem of trying to put on a shoe, opening a door, or retrieving a distant or hidden toy? Under what conditions are they likely to pay attention to words? Is there a hierarchy of attentional constraints on good motor speech production in the natural spontaneous events of everyday talk? We cannot answer these types of questions, or perhaps we do so less well than we should. This is because their answers require descriptive and often qualitative observations of behavior in natural spontaneous events. Such observations are under valued in research practices.

Countering Bias in Research Practices

To do naturalistic descriptions of behavior in everyday events, we must redress biases in research practices. One type of bias has to do with what kind of research counts as valuable to do. Stockman (1997) pointed out that there is a deeply rooted preference for experimental and quantitative research over observational and qualitative research—the kind of research that would be required to describe behavioral patterns in everyday contexts. The investigation of naturally occurring behaviors in daily events is outside of the tradition of conducting controlled experimental research on learning and behaving. Experimental research favors the controlled study of one or so variables at a time. This is the case even though both experimental and qualitative descriptions of behavior have necessarily played complementary roles in the evolution of scientific knowledge. Experimental research plays a critical role in justifying theoretical interpretations. It is not appropriate as the first step for studying unknown phenomena because researchers must know a lot beforehand about what is being studied to design controlled observation conditions.

In contrast, the less valued observational, qualitative research plays an important role in discovering new knowledge by revealing firsthand descriptions of phenomena, often in their untampered naturalistic states. In other words, qualitative research is concerned with theory generation rather than theory testing. Henwood and Pidgeon (1993) referred to qualitative research as the basis for "grounded theory" that arises from close inspection and analysis of data within some broader understanding of what constitutes "legitimate and warrantable knowledge" (p. 14). This view contrasts with the view of qualitative research as nonnumeric, local descriptions anchored by participant observations of single cases that have no relationship to theory.

Qualitative descriptive research may provide relevant clues to how children manage or fail to manage all the information that arises in natural situations in which input is available from verbal and nonverbal interaction events. In this respect, Mulder and Geurts (1991) expressed concern about the simplicity of the laboratory contexts for studying human movement. Such contexts severely limit the ". . .degrees of freedom with which one is allowed to operate" (p. 565). In the natural contexts of daily events, movements are connected to events in which people participate. How one produces speech sounds, walks, runs, or hops can vary with whether an object is in the hand, or one is talking at the same time, and of course why one is doing the action in the first place.

Nevertheless, the research paradigms described in Part I of this book suggest that we are further along than before in coming up with ways to describe and even quantify spontaneous daily behaviors. The theoretical hypotheses generated by Nelson (Chapter 6) and Affolter (Chapter 8), in particular, have been derived from observations in natural daily events. The observations described in other chapters of this book have been based on spontaneous behaviors generated in stimulus-controlled laboratory settings. For example, these useful methodologies include ways to study childrens' attentional resources by analyzing the temporal relations among their action play with objects, their spoken words, and affective expression (Bloom's Chapter 7). They also include ways to study the spontaneous manipulative actions of children using standard stimuli (Affolter's Chapter 8; Langer's Chapter 5; and Thelen's Chapter 3). Except for the research described by Langer and Affolter, it seems that these methods have been used most often to study typically developing children; but, they could be adapted for use with atypical clinical groups that include children with PDD.

THE CHALLENGE OF INVESTIGATING
PROCESS-FOCUSED INTERVENTIONS

It has been argued that a process view of intervention can be anchored by the problem-solving process. Existing nonverbal problem research has been limited in a couple of ways (Stockman 2000a). First, it has focused on the product or outcome of a problem-solving event as opposed to the process of solving a problem; and second, it has focused on problem solving in a fragmented way. That is, a study has typically emphasized just one or so aspects of problem solving in isolation of other aspects. For example, it has focused on either hypothesis testing or on planning, or memory or rule induction, and so on. Each component has been treated as a separate, isolated skill. Thus, problem solving is not studied online as the holistic process that fits with the reality of real experience—a reality that is likely to involve interrelated activities.

Lederman and Klatzky (1987) suggested that haptic tasks provide a window into the way the mind works. Such tasks allow one's manual activity to be observed in the attempts to match what is heard with what is seen or felt. While haptic tasks have been used to study abnormal language learners (Kamhi 1981; Montgomery 1993), their actual manual exploratory activity during tasks is not described. The focus has been on success scores or the end goal of solving a problem under one or another task condition. The focus has not been on the process that leads to the end goal. As a result, little is known about disordered childrens' exploratory patterns even in the laboratory, not to mention natural situations.

Fortunately, the research on problem solving, which supports the GIT framework for intervention, is more holistic. (See Bishofberger and Affolter's Chapter 9). The adaptation of the Pitt and Brouwer's model of problem-solving (Affolter and Bischofberger 2000) offers an alternative way to analyze and quantify problem-solving activities on-line, that is, while a child interacts to solve a problem. This procedure has been used to study typically developing babies and brain-injured adults.

In their recent work on the nonverbal interactions of babies, Affolter et al (1996) elaborated the notion of an "interaction unit" as a metric of observation. If an interaction unit can be equated with a single goal-directed change of topological relationship between the body and the environment, then it may be possible to quantify task complexity in terms of the number, type, and ordering of interaction units involved in daily problem-solving events. Consider how many changes of topological relationships involving touching, grasping, displacing, and releasing of objects are involved in the nonverbal interaction event of washing the hands as opposed to washing a dish or a window. This approach to nonverbal problem-solving performance may be a more sensitive and sensible index of problem solving in real events than is the visual discrimination experimental paradigm used in many problem-solving studies. Its replication in other studies is needed.

At the same time, neural and kinematic measures of sensorimoter activity during various types of speech production events are likely to be helpful in verifying the model of the motor speech hierarchy that guides the PROMPT intervention developed by Hayden (Chapter 10).

THE CHALLENGE OF INVESTIGATING THE
MOVEMENT SENSES

The perceptual-cognitive aspects of moving and interacting in the environment are important to clinical frameworks for children with PDD. Movement and interaction have perceptual (input) and motor (output) roles in effecting causative action in a problem-solving event. While intelligent behavior is presumably built on sensory collaboration, that is the multisensory storage of experience, the tactile-kinesthetic senses, which guide physical movement and interaction with the environment, have been undeniably emphasized in this book's discussions of intervention. The ultimate value of emphasizing tactual input in interventions like GIT and PROMPT will hinge on how well we come to understand the tactual system and its role in development.

Investigating the Tactual System

This sensory-perceptual system has been under studied and underused in contemporary research and clinical practices. There are at least two reasons for this investigative bias. One reason is that the tactual system, particularly active touch that combines moving and touching, is difficult to study in a controlled way. It is usually the investigator who does the moving, not the child under study. For example, in a study of how children learn word meaning, Hollich et al (2000) reported that their initial plan was to have the children handle the play objects as a possible variable in what they pay attention to in their word-to-object mappings. This plan was abandoned because of the variability in how the children handled the novel objects. The investigators settled for the experimenter's handling of the object as a social cue, a cue that turned out not be effective for establishing the word/referent relationship. Unfortunately, much of the experimental research on developing semantic reference has been restricted to just the acquisition of noun words. One should wonder if a child's own actions would be even more relevant to learning the meaning of verbs, which refer to movement and action events.

There is a second reason why the tactual system is less often studied than are vision and audition. It has to do with the bias that tactual perception does not contribute much to higher-order perceptual-cognitive representations. We know enough already to predict that tactile-kinesthetic input is likely to add to the amount and complexity of information processed in skill acquisition. It seems to add information that may be difficult to process relative to the focal sensory inputs of audition and vision. The tactile-kinesthetic system, which detects the changing topological relations between the body and environment, is extremely complex. It is far more complex than is the passive tactile experience that is measured by the skin's sensitivity to static touch (e.g., two-point discrimination). Tactile-kinesthetic input also includes force perception and the intermodal integration of multiple sources of information arising from skin, joints, and muscles, as pointed out already in earlier chapters. The input from the skin, which covers the entire body as the largest receptive field of all, is made even more complex because the just noticeable difference (JND) thresholds are higher at some body sites than others (Stuart 1996). Given that one or more body parts are always in contact with at least one support surface in the environment, the brain must continually register and integrate input from multiple body sites, and it must do so across different thresholds of sensitivity. It should not be surprising that tactual input reportedly is processed more slowly (Streri and Pecheux 1986; Heller and Schiff 1991) than are inputs from other modalities. Such complexity no doubt contributes to why even typically developing children perform the lowest in the tactual modality (Montgomery 1993; Affolter and Bichofberger 2000).

Unfortunately, lower performances also lead to the impression that the tactual system is inherently inferior to the vision and audition for processing information about the world. In the extreme, it would not be surprising that vision is viewed as comparable and even superior to the tactual system. Indeed, the burgeoning cognitive research on infants shows just how smart babies can be in controlled laboratory studies that rely on their looking and listening responses before they manipulate objects, crawl, or walk. This does not mean that these early representations are good enough to sustain the kind of perceptual-cognitive development that occurs after experiencing the world in other ways later on.

To demonstrate the relevancy of nonverbal interaction experience to development, we need better and easier ways to measure tactual function for research and clinical purposes. Studies are needed that focus on more than the psychophysical sensitivity to static sources of tactile perception (e.g., two-point and dichhaptic discrimination). They should focus on the dynamic interface between sensory and motor processes in purposeful activity, that is, haptics. When haptic studies have been done, though, with atypically developing children, they have not stressed the nature of the exploratory activity itself as a performance indicator. For example, Montgomery (1993) proposed that poor haptic performance in children with specific language inpairment (SLI) was caused by the inability to scan and maintain a mental image as opposed to generating one. He did not discuss the possibility that memory stability and scanning are linked to the exploratory activity required to extract tactual input in the first place. Some of the investigative issues that are relevant to exploring the infant's manipulatory actions in studies of perception are reviewed in Rolfe-Zikman (1987).

Haptic research can take advantage of the nearly two decades of research done by Lederman and Klatzky (1987). Some of this work has been motivated by the practical issues of building functional devices for the blind. Their methodological procedures, which have been used with adults, may be adapted to studying children with PDD. Besides that, it would be interesting to find out whether the outcomes from such studies would reveal differences between the tactual systems of children who can see and those who cannot.

Implications of Tactual Deficits for Differential Diagnosis

Clinical nosology is another researchable issue. Bishop (1989) reviewed issues related to differentiating autism from Asperger's syndrome and from semantic-pragmatic disorders in children diagnosed with SLI. The proposed distinctions among these three diagnostic categories does not include tactile-kinesthetic dysfunction as a signature feature. Yet there is ample evidence to support the coexistence of PDD with tactual deficits, although the boundaries of this relationship are unknown. Some children with PDD may not exhibit obvious tactual deficits. The question is whether particular subgroups of them do so. If so, then how stable is the relationship across age and task complexity? In this respect, it is worth considering whether Affolter and Bischofberger's (2000) three broad categories of tactual, intermodal, and serial perceptual deficits can help us to make sense of the behavioral differences observed within and across the subgroups of children with PDD. These diagnostic categories may be particularly useful because subgroup differences are based on proposed areas of underlying perceptual deficits. In contrast, most taxonomies for classifying clinical subgroups are geared toward describing the particular type of behaviors exhibited and not the reason for the deficits, at least as specified in perceptual terms.

Affolter and Bischofberger's (2000) taxonomy is useful too because it offers a perceptual explanation that goes beyond auditory processing hypotheses, (for example, fast forward, central auditory processing and auditory reintegration, and so on) for describing children with developmental disability. An expanded perceptual hypothesis may be especially needed to specify the clinical profile of those children who present with PDD-NOS. Stockman (2000b) suggested that this clinical group may exhibit the characteristics of a primary tactual processing impairment. More descriptive studies are needed of those children who end up with the PDD-NOS diagnosis to figure out what they may or may not have in common. The outcomes of such work could have major ramifications for educational placement and the intervention provided.

The diagnosis of children with PDD-NOS will be clarified by research that compares them with more established diagnostic categories in cross-sectional and longitudinal research. Unfortunately, children along the autism spectrum have continued to be studied in isolation of other clinical groups, for example, those along the SLI-learning disability (LD) spectrum, in particular. More comparative studies of children with PDD and those along the SLI-LD spectrum could be helpful. For some time now, the question of whether SLI is indeed a language-specific deficit has been debatable, as evidence continues to grow that at least some of these children have pervasive perceptual-cognitive deficits (Johnston 1994). Studies that compare children along the SLI-LD spectrum to those with frank mental retardation (e.g., Down's syndrome) or neuromotor impairment (e.g., cerebral palsy) would be helpful. Research on the language and perceptual-cognitive performances of physically handicapped children provide a critical testing ground for the relevance of perceptual-motor processes to language and cognitive development. But studies of these populations do not seem to have been designed to rigorously assess the functional effects of the physical handicap on nonverbal interaction experience in daily events.

Longitudinal studies also would be helpful because the clinical expression of PDD seems to change over the course of a lifetime. The question is whether these children look more like one or another different diagnostic group with increasing age, as Bishop (1989) also pointed out.

Validation of Tactually Based Interventions

An important question to address in further research is whether tactually based interventions work. The efficacy of using the GIT and PROMPT interventions should continue to be pursued. At the same time, the credibility of tactually based interventions will be enhanced by studies designed to test the validity of their assumptions in a controlled way. One assumption of GIT is that bodily activity or participation is necessary to experience interaction. Looking or listening is not enough. A second assumption is that a person who is unable to interact alone to solve nonverbal problems of daily living can be physically guided by someone else to experience the same kind of input received when a person interacts alone. Similarly, PROMPT assumes that a child who cannot produce speech sounds can get enough information from coordinating tactually delivered prompts with heard and seen sound effects to create perceptual-motor maps for producing speech sounds. At the core of these assumptions is the importance of self-action and the tactually anchored, integrated sensory input it provides for learning.

It would be instructive to systematically document the frequency and conditions under which behavioral changes occur in real events when using tactual input after auditory-verbal or visual inputs fail. In addition, it should be possible to do controlled observations in learning experiments that focus on the role of spontaneous self-action/interaction in learning and/or the role of manual guiding for learning. My students and I have explored one or both types of input in at least a half dozen studies with some promising nonverbal and verbal outcomes. (See earlier descriptions in Chapter 11.) These pilot efforts need replication with larger numbers of children and more tightly controlled observation conditions. The increasing access to neuroimaging techniques makes it easier to study brain activity. Using EEG and other measures of neural activity, it should be possible to compare brain activity under manually guided and unguided conditions in the same child under different problem-solving conditions. The validity of manual "guiding" as an instructional procedure would be supported by evidence that the patterns of brain activity, which correlate with attention and memory, are generated in guided and unguided conditions.

With respect to speech production, it is surprising that the tactual system has not been exploited in speech production therapy more often, given that speaking is obviously a perceptual-motor act. But the types of paradigms for exploring the oral tactile system need to differ from the ones used in earlier studies. These studies in the 1970s and early 1980s focused on oral stereognosis (exploration of abstract forms by mouth and static psychophysical measures of oral function), for example, two-point discrimination. See brief reviews of this work in Bernthal and Bankson (1988). The participants in these studies also were not necessarily discriminated in terms of tactual processing difficulty. They presented with articulation errors, which need not be a consequence of a tactual deficit. Yet many of these earlier studies did yield differences between children with and those without articulation difficulties in sensitivity to tactual information. Future research could take advantage of instrumental procedures for measuring the actual movement produced on-line during speaking activity. Such measures may include cinefluroscopic and kinematic measurements. They can be taken before, during, and after the speech system is perturbed with tactually guided input. One question is, how do oral movement patterns change in response to tactual prompts as opposed to visual and auditory prompts in learning new sounds? Self-produced speech may not be needed to get the auditory form of a speech code well enough to recognize it for some comprehension tasks, but total reliance on auditory and/or visual input could slow down the rate at which these patterns get laid down. This should be a testable experimental hypothesis.

THE CHALLENGE OF INVESTIGATING HOMOLOGOUS INTERVENTION MODELS

Homologous models of development become especially relevant to validating the multiple outcomes expected from process-driven interventions like GIT and PROMPT. Such interventions create a difficult challenge to meet using conventional approaches to studying clinical efficacy. Particular outcomes are expected to follow from the intervention. The targeting of specific skills as evidence of treatment outcomes is at odds with the cross-domain intervention effects expected from applying a homologous intervention model. The appeal of intervention approaches like GIT and PROMPT is that multiple skills are expected to result from intervention even when they have not been targeted directly. For example, PROMPT was shown to be associated with increased receptive and expressive language as a result of paying attention to the motor speech system. In GIT, multiple nonverbal and verbal skills reportedly emerge in response to nonverbal interaction experiences with solving the problems of daily living. How can we account for the emergence of skills that were not treated directly in therapy?

The expected effects of the therapy are complicated further by the expectation that multiple skills will emerge at the same time, even when therapists do not work on them directly. But there seems to be no way to predict which ones might be observed in a given child at a given time. If not, then it is impossible to get baseline or pre-therapy data on all the skills that could turn up as therapeutic effects but that cannot be detected in the absence of knowing whether they were there all along in some performance context.

In contrast, immediate therapeutic effects, which can be observed within a single session, may be more easily documented and attributed directly to the treatment. These changes include verbal comprehension and expression before and after the guided event, in addition to changes in attention, body tonus, event recognition, and planning. But, before such clinical impressions of grounded efficacy are widely respected, it will be necessary to reliably document what happens in these actual moments of intervention and to do so using different observers who do not have a vested interest in whether the child does well or not in the therapy. The efficacious use of homologous intervention models will be supported further by tracking a child's performance over time to verify whether the new behaviors observed as evidence of grounded efficacy actually do stabilize and transfer to other behavioral contexts and are cross-verified from other sources of observation, for example, the observations of behavioral changes made by caregivers, school personnel, and on formal tests.

Of course, whether or not a particular outcome is observed will depend on more than just the possible intervention effect; it also will depend on how the outcomes are measured. The expectation that language outcomes will be related to the kind of nonverbal interaction experiences proposed by the GIT framework is likely to be controversial for reasons already pointed out. Similarly for PROMPT, the assumption that sensorimotor-based interventions for speech production disorders can effect change in the phonological representation will be doubted, irrespective of whether the claimed effect is direct or indirect.

GIT assumes that the effect of enhanced tactual experience in nonverbal interaction experience will show up in the meaning base of language as opposed to its grammatical and pronunciation forms. Of course, meaning is harder to measure than are the grammatical and pronunciation forms of language. It is not overt, nor are its boundaries finite. Researchers, like practitioners, rely frequently on rather simplistic measures of meaning, lexical meaning or vocabulary, as measured by picture naming or identification tasks such as those on the Peabody Picture Vocabulary Test III (PPVT III) (Dunn and Dunn 1997). It is fortunate that the latest version of the PPVT-III has expanded its lexical items to include action verbs in addition to the nouns that are more often assessed (Stockman 2000c). Still, the assessment of isolated word meanings, action, or object words do not assess directly the sentence meanings about events, which have to do with the relationships of objects and actions in events. Research related to the semantics of propositional meaning will inform efforts to measure intervention outcomes that cater to movement and action/interaction events.

The little bit of experimental work done already on the differential effects of sensory input on learning has yielded conflicting outcomes. Whereas Stockman and Latham (2002) and Latham and Stockman (2002) obtained outcomes for typically and atypically developing children that favored "hands on" input over visual input for learning new words, other research outcomes have been mixed. Olswang et al (1983) reported that two of their four subjects with language disorders learned nouns and verbs better in an "object-manipulation" than in a picture-identification condition. One child learned best with picture identification while another one learned as well under either condition. Clearly the role of self-action in the learning process deserves further study. It is possible that the depth of semantic knowledge could be more readily revealed by integrating observations of word and sentence (Stockman and Vaughn-Cooke 1992). Clearly, more work is needed here.

CONCLUDING REMARKS

This chapter has called attention to intervention and research issues that are relevant to working with PDD. Although these issues can stimulate our thinking about intervention practices on multiple fronts, they bring to the fore the relevancy of tactual input to learning and developing in particular. Many practitioners may say that they already use a "hands-on" approach to intervention, but they are likely to mean that children are given a chance to practice whatever gets stored from prior auditory-verbal and/or visual input, and the corrections are made to that practiced output by the practitioner once it is observed. "Hands on" learning typically does not refer to the practitioner giving tactually guided input to lay down the map of what actions to do in the first place. The two interventions reviewed in this book, however, have developed ways to enhance tactual input on-line in order to help children map actions-interactions onto real-world experience with nonverbal events and their spoken representations.

Advances in clinical work ought to be particularly helpful when they are driven by research observations. To this end, the present book encourages the use of new and more complex research methodologies than have been used typically to study children with PDD. The many potential areas of research singled out suggest that more than one or two studies are needed. We need a program of research dedicated to examining children with PDD, using fresh methodologies and procedures for making observations. Interestingly, the National Institutes of Health, the multibillion dollar arm of the U.S. government devoted to biomedical research, does not have a visibly named program for supporting research on the tactual system. But it does have visible institutes dedicated to vision, audition, balance, taste, and smell among its 27 programs and centers. Therefore, pursuing funded research may present yet another challenge to conducting research that explores the tactual system of children with PDD.

REFERENCES

Affolter, A., and Bischofberger, W. 2000. *Nonverbal Perceptual and Cognitive Processes in Children with Language Disorders: Toward a New Framework for Clinical Intervention*. Mahwah, NJ: Erlbaum.

Affolter, F., and Stricker, E. 1980. *Perceptual Processes as Prerequisites for Complex Human Behavior*. Bern, Switzerland: Huber.

Affolter, F., Bischofberger, W., and Calabretti-Erni, V. 1996. Nonverbal interaction in babies and brain-damaged patients. Poster presented at the Symposium: *The Growing Mind*, Geneva Switzerland.

American Psychiatric Association 1994. *Diagnostic and Statistical Manual of Mental Disorders*, 4th ed. Washington, DC: Author.

Ayres, J. 1972. Types of sensory integrative dysfunction among disabled learners. *Am J Occup Ther* 26:13–18.

Bates, E., Benigni, L., Betherton, I., Camaioni, L., and Volterra, V. 1979. *The Emergence of Symbols: Cognition and Communication in Infancy.* New York: Academic Press.

Bernthal, J., and Bankson, N. 1988. Factors related to phonological disorders In *Articulation and Phonological Disorders*, 2nd ed. pp. 145–199. Englewood Cliffs, NJ: Prentice-Hall.

Bishop, D.V.M. 1989. Autism, Asperger's syndrome and semantic-pragmatic disorder: Where are the boundaries? *Br J Disord Commun* 24:107–121.

Bishop, D.V.M. 1990. The relationship between phoneme discrimination, speech production and language comprehension in cerebral palsied individuals. *J Speech Hear Res*, 33:210–219.

Bishop, D.V.M. 1993. Language development in children with abnormal structure or function of the speech apparatus. In D. Bishop and K. Mogford (Editors), *Language Development in Exceptional Circumstances.* pp. 220–238. Hillsdale, NJ: Erlbaum.

Bloom, L. 1991. *Language Development From Two to Three.* New York: Cambridge University Press.

Bloom, L. 1994. Meaning and expression. In Overton, W.F., and Palermo, D.S. (Editors), *The Nature and Ontogenesis of Meaning.* pp. 215–236. Hillsdale, NJ: Erlbaum.

Bowerman, M. and Levinson, S.C. 2001. *Language Acquisition and Conceptual Development.* Cambridge, UK: Cambridge University Press.

Chapman, R. 2000. Children's language learning: An interactionist perspective. *J Child Psychol Psychiatr* 41:33–54.

Constable, C.M. 1986. The application of scripts in the organization of language intervention contexts. In Nelson, K. (Editor), *Event Knowledge: Structure and Function in Development.* pp. 205–231. Hillsdale, NJ: Erlbaum.

Daems, J., 1994. *Reviews of Research in Sensory Integration.* Torrence, CA: Sensory Integration International.

Decarie, T.G. 1969. A study of the mental and emotional development of the Thalidomide child. In B.M. Foss (Editor), *Determinants of Infant Behavior*, Vol. 4. pp. 167–187. London, England: Methuen.

Dunn, L.M., and Dunn, L.M. 1997. *The Peabody Picture Vocabulary-III.* Circle Pines, MN: American Guidance Service.

Fisher, A., Murray, E., and Bundy, A. 1991. *Sensory Integration: Theory and Practice.* Philadelphia: F.A. Davis.

Fourcin, A.J. 1975. Language development in the absence of expressive speech. In Lenneberg, E., and Lenneberg, E. (Editors), *Foundations of Language Development*, Vol. 2. pp. 263–268. New York: Academic Press.

Heller, M.A., and Schiff, W. 1991. *Psychology of Touch.* Hillsdale, NJ: Erlbaum.

Henwood, K., and Pidgeon, N. 1993. Qualitative research and psychological theorizing. In Hammersley, M. (Editor), *Social Research: Philosophy, Politics and Practice.* pp. 14–32. London, England: Sage Publications.

Hoehn, T.P., and Baumeister, A.A. 1994. A critique of application of sensory integration therapy to children with learning disabilities. *J Learn Disabil* 27:338–350.

Hollich, G.J., Hirsh-Pasek, K., and Golinkoff, R.M. 2000. Breaking the language barrier: An emergentist coalition model for the origins of word learning. *Monogr Soc Res Child Dev* 65:1–123.

Huttenlocher, J., Smiley, P., and Charney, R. 1983. Emergence of action categories in the child: Evidence from verb meanings. *Psychol Rev* 90:72–93.

Johnston, J. 1994. Cognitive abilities of children with language impairment. In Watkins, R., and Rice, M. (Editors), *Specific Language Impairments in Children.* pp. 107–122. Baltimore: Brookes.

Kamhi, A. 1981. Nonlinguistic symbolic and conceptual abilities of language-impaired and normally developing children. *J Speech Hear Res* 24:446–453.

Kauffman, J.M., and Hallahan, D.P. 1995 . *The Illusion of Full Inclusion: A Comprehensive Critique of a Current Special Education Bandwagon.* Austin, TX: Pro-ed.

Kaiser, A., and Hester, P. 1994. Generalized effects of enhanced milieu teaching. *J Speech Hear Res* 37:1320–1340.

Latham, S., and Stockman, I. 2002. July Novel verbal and nonverbal learning by children with special needs in embodied and non-embodied contexts. A paper presented at the *Joint Conference of* the *International Congress for the Study of Child Language and the Symposium on Research in Child Language Disorders,* Madison, WI.

Lederman, S., and Klatzky, R.L. 1987. Hand movements: A window into haptic object recognition. *Cognit Psychol* 19:342–368.

Leonard, L. 2000. *Specific Language Impairment.* Cambridge, MA: MIT Press.

Lourenco, O., and Machado, A. 1996. In defense of Piaget's theory: A reply to 10 common criticisms. *Psychol Rev,* 103(1): 143–164.

Mogford, K., Bishop, D. 1993. *Language Development in Exceptional Circumstances.* Hillsdale, NJ: Erlbaum.

Montgomery, J. 1993. Haptic recognition of children with specific language impairment: Effects of response modality. *J Speech Hear Res* 36:98–104.

Mulder, T., and Geurts, S. 1991. The assessment of motor dysfunctions: Preliminaries to a disability-oriented approach. *Hum Mov Sci* 10:565–574.

Nelson, K. 1986. *Event Knowledge: Structure and Function of Development.* Hillsdale, NJ: Erlbaum.

Nelson, N. 1998. Childhood Language Disorders in Contexts: Infancy Through Adolescence. Columbus, OH: Merrill.

Norris, J.A., and Damico, J.S. 1990. Whole language in theory and practice: Implications for language intervention. *Language, Speech, and Hearing Services in Schools* 21:212–220.

Olswang, L., Bain, B., Dunn, C., and Cooper, J. 1983. The effects of stimulus variation on lexical learning. *J Speech Hear Disord* 48:192–201.

Paul, R. 2001. *Language Disorders from Infancy Through Adolescence: Assessment and Intervention* (2nd Edition). St. Louis: Mosby.

Rapin, I., and Allen, D. 1983. Developmental language learning disorders: Nosology considerations. In Kirk, U. (Editor), *Neuropsychology of Language, Reading and Spelling.* pp. 155–184. Orlando, FL: Academic Press.

Rolfe-Zikman, S. 1987. Visual and haptic bimodal perception in infancy. In McKenzie, B. E., and Day, R.H., (Editors), *Perceptual Development in Early Infancy: Problems and Issues.* pp. 199–218. Hillsdale, NJ: Erlbaum.

Rourke, B. P. 1989. *Nonverbal Learning Disabilities: The Syndrome and the Model.* New York: Guilford Press.

Stockman, I. 1997. The social-political construction of science: Evidence from the language research on African American children. W.E.B. Du Bois Distinguished Visiting Lecturer Series. The Graduate School and University Center: The City University of New York.

Stockman, I. 1996. Wo sind die Worte? –Wie kommen wir zu unseren Sprachlichen Begriffen? In Lipp, B., and Schlaegel, W., (Editors). *Wege von Anfang an Fruhrehabilitation schwerst hirngeschadigter Patienten.* pp. 244–259. Bern, Switzerland: Springer.

Stockman, I. 2000a. From product to process in investigating problem solving in children with language disorders. In Affolter, F., and Bischofberger, W. *Nonverbal Perceptual and Cognitive Processes in Children with Language Disorders: Toward a New Framework for Clinical Intervention.* pp. xi–xxv. Mahwah, NJ: Erlbaum.

Stockman, I. 2000b. Epilogue: Language learning and nonverbal interaction in daily events. In Affolter, F., and Bischofberger, W. *Nonverbal Perceptual and Cognitive Processes in Children with Language Disorders: Toward a New Framework for Clinical Intervention.* pp. 197–246. Mahwah, NJ: Erlbaum.

Stockman, I. 2000c. The new Peabody Picture Vocabulary Test-III: An illusion of unbiased assessment. *Language, Speech, Hearing Services in Schools* 31:336–349.

Stockman, I., and Latham, S. 2002. Novel verbal and nonverbal learning by normal children in embodied and non-embodied contexts. A paper presented at the *Joint Conference of the International Congress for the Study of Child Language and the Symposium on Research in Child Language Disorders,* Madison, WI.

Stockman, I., and Vaughn-Cooke, F. 1992. Lexical elaboration of children's locative action expressions. *Child Dev* 63:1104–1125.

Streri, A., and Pecheux, M.G. 1986. Tactual habituation and discrimination form in infancy: A comparison with vision. *Child Dev* 57:100–104.

Stuart, R. 1996. *The Design of Virtual Environments.* New York: McGraw-Hill.

Thelen, E. 1995. Motor development: A new synthesis. *Am Psychol* 50: 79–95.

Tomasello, M., and Kruger, A.C. 1992. Joint attention on actions: Acquiring verbs in ostensive and non-ostensive contexts. *J Child Lang* 19:1–23.

Tomasello, M., and Merriman, E. 1995. *Beyond the Names for Things: Young Children's Acquisition of Verbs*. Hillsdale, NJ: Erlbaum.

Waterhouse, L., Fein, D., and Modahl, C. 1996. Neurofunctional mechanisms in autism. *Psychol Rev* 103:457–489.

Watkins, R. 1994. Grammatical challenges for children with specific language impairment. In Watkins, R., and Rice, M. (Editors), *Specific Language Impairments in Children* pp. 53–68. Baltimore: Brookes.

Woodward, A.L., Markman, E., and Fitzsimmons, C.M. 1994. Rapid word learning in 13- and 18-month-olds. *Dev Psychol* 30:553–556.

Zero to Three/National Center for Clinical Infants Programs 1994. *Disorders of relating and communication*. pp. 40–45. Arlington, Va.

FINAL REMARKS

IDA J. STOCKMAN, PHD

This book has been about movement action/interaction in learning and development within a broader set of proposed guidelines for modeling intervention with pervasive developmental disorders (PDD). It is not one chapter but the collective set of chapters in this book that tells the story of purposeful movement acts as dynamic physical, perceptual, and cognitive activity. According to Thelen (1989),

> Movement is the "final common pathway" for many subsystems working together to accomplish a task or goal. For a child, perception, motivation, plans, physiological status, and affect must all interact with a mechanical system that is composed of muscles, bones, and joints. Although we may not choose to study all these contributing elements at the same time, it is conceptually impossible (and empirically foolish) to encapsulate movement outcome from the motives that inspired it, the information that guided it, and the body parts that produced it" (p. 947).

These movement experiences are undoubtedly part of what the brain must sift through in creating memories and representations of the world. However, any claim that movement acts are critical to development should raise the question of how to explain development in children with atypical movement histories (Bebco et al 1992). Such children include those with congenital neuromotor impairment or anatomical abnormality. At the same time, one can question how we account for the learning that infants can do before they crawl, walk, or manipulate objects.

CHILDREN WITH ATYPICAL MOVEMENT
HISTORIES

INTERACTION AS DETERMINANT OF DEVELOPMENT

The critical determinant of development is not simply whether a person can move but rather whether there is a means for him or her to interact; that is, experience the causes and effects that arise from changing topological relations between the body and the environment in solving daily problems. For guided interaction therapy (GIT), the physical interactions that feed perceptual-cognitive development are not dependent on the ability to move *independently* or in *conventional* ways. Presumably, the brain gets the same information when severely impaired children are moved by others in the course of solving problems of daily living. If so, then children with motor handicaps should still develop, given an intact brain and sensorium that register the tactually anchored multisensory experiences. Nevertheless, it is rare that physically handicapped children have no means to interact on their own, even if they move in conventional ways (Lewis 1987). For example, the mouth or feet may substitute for the hands. In Decarie's (1969) study of congenital anomalies caused by thalidomide exposure in utero, most of the children could bring their limb stumps to midline, and one or more digits were attached to the stumps. Of the 30 children studied, 27 exhibited normal cognition as measured by object permanence and social understanding.

In the case of cerebral palsy, spasticity (reduced movement) is associated with more developmental risk than is athetosis (excessive uncontrollable movement). More risk is associated with four than with fewer impaired limbs. Even with four impaired limbs, the head may be movable as an instrument of causative action. Enough movement can be available in one limb or eye to operate a switch as an instrument of causative action to reach a goal or solve a problem of daily life. See literature citations in Stockman (2000). Lewis (1987) reminds us that the quality of the interaction experience is likely to be a better predictor of development than is the severity of the physical handicap.

However, many children with congenital quadriplegia do not develop normally or they may achieve cognitive milestones more slowly than normal children (Eagle 1985).

THE RELATIVE FUNCTIONAL EFFECTS OF EXPERIENCE

We still must be cautious about assuming that a brain that functions without a missing source of experience is the same brain that functions with such a source, neuroplasticity notwithstanding. The brain is arguably not an entirely equipotential organ (Bates et al 2000). This means that brain organization based on reduced tactual-kinesthetic experience is not likely to be the same as when such experience is included. But the consequences for functioning may be task or situation dependent. In Bishop's (1990) study of older children with cerebral palsy and good hearing, the children with anarthria (absent speech production) performed like their physically handicapped controls with normal speech on some tasks but not others. They were like the control group on tasks requiring auditory discrimination of real words and sentence understanding. But they were less successful than controls on auditory discrimination of nonsense words (the equivalent of unfamiliar words), and they also had poorer receptive vocabularies. Whether or not the less adequate performances will count against them will depend on the value of these performances to functioning in their social groups.

Thus, what is abnormal and/or functionally handicapping is relative to the contexts of function. In many modern societies, the demands for reflective intelligence, literacy, and multi-tasking scale up the complexity of daily living in ways that do not exist in all cultures. In cultures that do not depend on print literacy and formal schooling to function, children with PDD will not be disadvantaged by their difficulty with learning to read and write. Similarly, the functional consequences of not learning to drive a car or to swim will be relative to the value attached to these skills in a culture. Typically though, children with PDD are easily judged as abnormal and handicapped because there are functional consequences for so many of the basic skills that fall outside the range of normal variability in any culture.

EARLY PERCEPTUAL-COGNITIVE LEARNING

In the mix of what makes babies intelligent early on, we should not dismiss the relevance of the movement senses. This kind of input is used to learn about the world before babies can manipulate objects, crawl, or walk. During gestation, movement may propel the development of the mammalian nervous system (Edelman 1987). From birth on, babies experience the material world by way of touch. They come to know that something else exists besides their own bodies when movement of their own bodies meets with resistance from other persons who pick them up and hold them, or their own idle spontaneous movements encounter inanimate objects (e.g., the crib railing). By the time typically developing babies are participants in research experiments at 3 to 4 months of age, they have had many moments of correlated experiences with moving, feeling, touching, looking, and listening – enough to understand that a seen object is separate from a background visual field. The visual representation of an object includes knowledge about what actions are possible with it even in adulthood (Tucker and Ellis 1998). Renee Baillargeon (2001) acknowledged though that it is not easy to train babies to do some experimental tasks in laboratory situations.

The baby's early correlated experiences with moving, touching, looking, hearing, and so on can be sufficient for them to establish superficial hypotheses about causes and effects based on the temporal and spatial contiguity of objects and persons, for example, they smile and there is an effect, someone smiles back; they cry and there is an effect, a caregiver appears in sight. The question is whether this kind of associative learning is the same kind of knowledge that results from actually touching or manipulating the environment to effect causative action later on. If it is, then we must ask why babies, who can make such early associations, still need more time to experience the world before they typically get language or learn how to do many other things that identify intelligent behavior.

A THORNY ISSUE: CASTING TOO BROAD A NET

Anybody who reads the clinical intervention literature can come to the conclusion that just about any kind of intervention has reportedly helped some children. Richer and Coates (2001) included caregiver descriptions of what was effective with their children. What seemed to work included approaches as different as holding therapy and applied behavioral analysis. One also can find reports that a given intervention did not help a child. There is counter evidence (e.g., Smith et al 1997) for the effectiveness of even those behavior therapies, which are so tightly specified that it has been comparatively easier to document the kind of discrete changes that research empiricists respect and look for. So practitioners, caregivers, and researchers are kept busy searching for the single intervention that really works.

One reason for the fragile courtship with any single intervention is the expectation that a single one will be the solution across the life span for all persons regardless of developmental level or context for learning. But in dynamic systems theory (Thelen and Smith 1994), everything counts in learning and developing. This theory not only legitimizes the relevance of physical actions/interactions and their corresponding movement senses to development; but it legitimizes everything else too. Performance in a given situation is argued to result from a self-organizing system of heterogeneous forces – physical, mental, and emotional forces that reflect a person's whole history of experience in addition to the situation at hand for performing. If the premise that "everything counts" is valid, then it is possible that any intervention might have helped someone at a given point in time. Conceivably, an intervention that results in the acquisition of just one specific skill could be effective if it happens to be a catalyst for moving the development forward on other behaviors or skills that are not worked on directly in the intervention. This interpretation suggests that the dynamic systems theory of development legitimizes eclectic clinical practices. This is worrisome because electicism has been historically viewed as an undesirable attribute of clinical work. It is presumed to exist when we do not know enough to make discriminating judgments about what to do in intervention.

Some flexibility in clinical procedures must be allowed to accommodate the varied contexts of human experience even for the same person across the life span. What may be needed to stimulate development could differ for the same person at different points in development. Indeed, most interventions do allow for variation in the strategies applied. Generally, less direct support is given in the learning event as a child matures and progresses; for example, cue fading is a strategy that comes out of a behaviorist learning tradition. GIT and prompts for restructuring oral muscular phonetic targets (PROMPT) have the same expectation.

GIT should not conjure up images of hovering hands on bodies in intensive guiding experiences for every learning event possible. The more severe the child is, the more likely that kind of intensive therapeutic guiding is required. As children mature, more of the tactual input can be indirect as when a caregiver or practitioner just alters the environment so that independent nonverbal physical interaction is possible, or only part of an event is guided when a child gets stuck and does not know the next action step to take. The tactual input replaces visual imitation or repeated auditory – verbal instructions with raised voices. Similarly, PROMPT intervention for speech production disorders provides for graduated decline in the use of oral tactual cuing as speakers become more proficient (cf. the use of surface and complex prompts).

Therefore, the broader issue is whether different philosophical approaches to intervention are coequal stimulants for learning across all contexts and developmental levels. Clearly, this is an issue for further reflection and research. But are not the movement senses foundational, and therefore play special roles in development? This is a powerful claim. It implies that clinical intervention will forfeit critical aspects of developing by focusing just on visual and auditory information. This is an important issue because practitioners are taught to gear their interventions to a child's sensory modality strengths as if the same kind of functional outcomes can be achieved. If not, then we should find ways to enhance tactual-kinesthetic information regardless of what intervention is used.

GIT and PROMPT interventions may indeed tap something very fundamental about learning, given their use with different types of clinical populations. GIT is used as often to treat adult patients with acquired stroke and traumatic brain injury as it is used to intervene with PDD in children. It is also used with persons in a coma (Lipp and Schlaegel 1996). PROMPT is used to intervene with children and adults with neuromotor, hearing, fluency disorders; in fact, it is used with any kind of speech production disorder.

Tactual input could be especially critical for changing deeply entrenched maladaptive behaviors in ways that stimulate reorganization of a perceptual-cognitive system. This requires a perceptual-cognitive system organized chiefly around auditory and visual input to be replaced by one that is organized around a more integrated perception that includes the movement senses.

BOLD REFLECTIONS

The ideas presented in this book have the potential to reorient our thinking about tough clinical problems in a fresh way. It is likely that the experienced, reflective practitioner or caregiver has already happened on the value of giving children the opportunity for tactile-kinesthetic experiences that come from purposeful moving, acting, and interacting. This book aims to make it a choice that is informed by theory and tested clinical practice. The challenge is for future research and careful observations of applied practices across multiple disciplines to help professionals predict the conditions under which touch and movement experience is most favorable to stimulating nonverbal and verbal development in its typical and atypical forms.

REFERENCES

Baillargeon, R. 2001. A lecture presented in the Distinguished Speaker Cognitive Science Forum. Michigan State University, East Lansing, MI.

Bates, E., Vicari, S., and Trauner, D. 2000. Neural mediation of language development: Perspectives from lesion studies of infants and children. In Tager-Flusberg, H. (Editor), *Neurodevelopmental Disorders*. pp. 533–582. Cambridge, MA: M.I.T. Press.

Bebco, J.M., Burke, L., Craven, J., and Sarlo, N. 1992. The importance of motor activity in sensorimotor development: A perspective from children with physical handicaps. *Hum Dev* 35:226–240.

Bishop, D.V.M. 1990. The relationship between phoneme discrimination, speech production and language comprehension in cerebral palsied individuals. *J Speech Hear Res*, 33:210–219.

Decarie, T.G. 1969. A study of the mental and emotional development of the Thalidomide child. In Foss, B.M. (Editor), *Determinants of Infant Behavior*. Vol, IV, pp. 167–187. London, England: Methuen.

Eagle, R.S. 1985. Deprivation of early sensorimotor experience and cognition in the severely involved cerebral-palsied child. *J Autism Dev Disord* 15:269–283.

Edelman, G.M. 1987. Action and perception. In Edelman, G.M. (Editor), *Neural Darwinism: The Theory of Neuronal Group Selection*. pp. 209–239. New York: Basic Books.

Lewis, V. 1987. How do children with motor handicaps develop? In Lewis, V. (Editor), *Development and Handicap*. pp. 82–103. New York: Blackwell.

Lipp, B., and Schlaegel, W. 1996. *Wege von Anfang an (Paths to Follow: 5 Years of Clinical experience)*. Villingen/Schwenningen: Neckar-Verlag.

Richer, J., and Coates, S. 2001. *Autism: The Search for Coherence*. Philadelphia: Jessica Kingsley Publishers.

Smith, T., Eikeseth, S., Klevstrand, M., and Lovaas, O.I. 1997. Intensive behavioral treatment for preschoolers with severe mental retardation and pervasive developmental disorder. *Am J Ment Retard* 102:238–249.

Stockman, I. 2000. Epilogue: Language learning and nonverbal interaction in daily events. In Affolter, F., and Bischofberger, W., *Nonverbal Perceptual and Cognitive Processes in Children with Language Disorders: Toward a New Framework for Clinical Intervention*. pp. 197–246. Mahwah, NJ: Erlbaum.

Thelen, E. 1989. The rediscovery of motor development: Learning new things from an old field. *Dev Psychol* 25:946–949.

Thelen, E. and Smith, L. 1994. *Dynamic Systems Approach to the Development of Cognition and Action*. Cambridge, MA: MIT Press.

Tucker, M., and Ellis, R. 1998. On the relations between seen objects and components of potential actions. *J Exp Psychol Hum Percept Perform* 24:830–846.

SUBJECT INDEX

AUTHOR INDEX